PSYCHOANALYTIC CULTURE

For
Adam and Ben Beechey
&
Jean and Hugh Ledigo

PSYCHOANALYTIC CULTURE

Psychoanalytic Discourse in Western Society

Ian Parker

SAGE Publications
London · Thousand Oaks · New Delhi

First published 1997

SAGE Publications Ltd
6 Bonhill Street
London EC2A 4PU

SAGE Publications Inc
2455 Teller Road
Thousand Oaks, California 91320

SAGE Publications India Pvt Ltd
32, M-Block Market
Greater Kailash - I
New Delhi 110 048

British Library Cataloguing in Publication data

A catalogue record for this book is
available from the British Library.

ISBN 0 7619 5642 5
ISBN 0 7619 5643 3 (pbk)

Library of Congress catalog card number 97-067536

Typeset by Typestudy, Scarborough
Printed in Great Britain by Redwood Books, Trowbridge, Wiltshire

Contents

Preface

This book traces the contradictory ways in which psychoanalysis circulates and functions in contemporary culture. The central argument of the book is that psychoanalysis can be used to illuminate cultural phenomena, but that this is because psychoanalytic discourse already *structures* those phenomena. If we read texts carefully we will often find traces of psychoanalytic reasoning and psychoanalytic prescriptions for how we should understand ourselves. So, in each chapter I review different psychoanalytic theories in some detail and then go on to show how those versions of psychoanalytic discourse are already present around us in a particular cultural phenomenon. I use the methodological device of the 'discursive complex' to explore social representations of self and society, and to draw attention to psychoanalytic notions sedimented in the texts of everyday life.

There must be something here to displease everybody. Some readers will feel that it is too hostile to psychoanalysis, and I certainly have reservations about it. It is often homophobic, misogynistic and racist (and I may have been a little unfair in pouring my spite into attacks on Jung in the book as if he was the only one at fault on this count). It often pathologizes the victims of oppression for wanting what they get, and it then makes us feel individually responsible for what we want when we are incited to confess. It warrants a kind of clinical practice which mystifies the patient, and it draws its devotees into the delusion that it can account for everything and to the reactionary conclusion it is just too difficult to change society because of the way people are deep down.

Some readers will object that the book is too friendly to psychoanalysis though, and I guess I am still advertising it here at the same time as I argue that it is socially constructed. The fact that something is socially constructed does not then mean that it is possible to wish it away or to simply construct something else from scratch. Psychoanalysis is a cultural resource, and it helps us to reveal some of the symbolic forces that bear upon our lives and the ways in which we often collude in patterns of action that are oppressive and self-defeating. Psychoanalytic psychotherapy can be a practice in which we may make our distress public and puzzle with an other as to how that distress works. It is, if nothing else, a mode of sustained self-reflection which encourages us to trace the sources of things we do to ourselves and others.

I must admit that I cannot make up my mind whether psychoanalytic accounts are 'true' or not. I am ambivalent. But even at those moments when I am most certain that psychoanalysis is wrong, I look around and find a culture that is saturated with references to childhood memories, repression and the unconscious, and so I would still argue that we must take it seriously as a representation of how we are at least some of the time. Some readers will object to the theoretical framework that I use to stain out the psychoanalytic structures that are now sedimented in much of our self-talk and practices of identity and community. When I use the term 'psychoanalytic discourse' I know it strikes a certain chord with analysts of discourse inside and outside psychology, and even they may not buy the device of the 'discursive complex', but I could just as easily have written about 'social representations' of the self, and told a story about the circulation of science in the everyday world. If you have another favourite framework to understand the circulation of accounts through culture and the way they story us into being, then I hope you read my account through that filter without too much trouble.

Most readers will want to challenge the specific analyses I present of different texts. There are extracts from books, newspaper advertisements, committee documents, scenes from films, bits of pamphlets and news-letters, letters and descriptions of organizational processes, and so more than enough to draw the reader into my account and to provoke them to read something else there. But these are not definitive analyses, and there is much more to be said about these bits of text. What I want to do is to lead you through them and along a certain kind of narrative about the implantation of psychoanalysis in culture. Even if the overall analysis seems to work, it will strike you that my choice of phenomena is some-what arbitrary. You may be aware of other phenomena where the psycho-analytic subtext is even more striking, but I have tried to thread what could be a repetitive and tedious argument through some interesting cul-tural material, and I hope that at the very least you will enjoy what you read.

Acknowledgements

Many thanks to those who have either read portions of this manuscript or earlier versions of the arguments in different chapters or posed constructive objections and difficult questions to my account in various forums where I discussed these ideas. I am indebted to these people, and hope they will not be too disappointed with what appears here. In addition to the many others who helped along the way, best wishes and good reading to: Dick Blackwell, Rufus Bulbring, Erica Burman, John Churcher, Jaime Cortez, John Cromby, Miriam Dembo, Eugenie Georgaca, Brenda Goldberg, Angel Gordo-López, Grahame Hayes, Bob Hinshelwood, Sean Homer, Dan Heggs, Helene Hurme, Bernardo Jiménez-Domínguez, Gordana Jovanovič, John Kaye, Deborah Marks, Terence McLaughlin, Joan Pujol, Steve Reicher, Eero Riikonen, Andrew Samuels, Francesc Tirado and Bob Young.

Arguments in some of the chapters have been rehearsed as journal articles, and I am grateful to the editors and publishers of these for permission to rework them for my narrative in this book. Some of the material used in Chapter 1 first appeared in my paper 'Staff–student relationships in Universities: boundary disasters and "Minus K" ', *Group Analysis* (1996) 29: 99–111. © The Group-Analytic Society (London). Some material also appeared in 'Group identity and individuality in times of crisis: psychoanalytic reflections on social psychological knowledge' published in *Human Relations* (1977). I developed the main lines of argument and illustrations for Chapter 3 in 'Communion and invasion: outer space and inner space' which appeared in *Free Associations* (1995) 5 (3): 357–376. The basic structure of the analysis extended in Chapter 4 was used in 'Reflexive research and the grounding of analysis: social psychology and the psy-complex', *Journal of Community and Applied Social Psychology* (1994) 4 (4): 43–66. That basic structure was also employed in 'El retorno de lo reprimido: complejos discursivos y el complejo-psi' in *Revista de Psicologia Social Aplicada* (1995), 5 (1/2): 147–164, and the paper was included in A. Gordo-López and J. Linaza-Iglesias (eds) (1996) *Psicologias, Discursos y Poder* (Madrid: Visor). The analysis and discussion of the bit of Bly text in Chapter 5 was published first in 'Masculinity and cultural change: wild men' which appeared in *Culture and Psychology* (1995), 1 (4): 455–475. A version of the analysis of the scene from *Total Recall* in Chapter 7 first appeared in 'Psychology, science fiction and postmodern space' in the *South African Journal of Psychology* (1996) 26 (3): 143–149. Material in Chapter 9 first appeared as 'Postmodernism and its discontents:

therapeutic discourse' in the *British Journal of Psychotherapy* (1996) 12 (4): 447–460. I would also like to thank the King George's Fund for Sailors, the Royal National Lifeboat Institution, and The Mental Health Foundation for permission to reproduce their advertisements as Figures 1, 2 and 3 respectively in Chapter 2.

Introduction: Psychoanalysis and Discourse

Where id was, there ego shall be. It is the work of culture – not unlike the draining of the Zuider Zee.

Sigmund Freud (1933a: 112) *New Introductory Lectures in Psychoanalysis*

It's up to us. All some of them need is a break. With a little understanding and guidance maybe we can salvage some of this waste.

William Holden (1948) In R. Maté, dir., *The Dark Past*. New York: Columbia Pictures.

Psychoanalysis is barely a century old, yet it appears to stretch back to human pre-history at the same time as it extends into the deepest interior of the self in contemporary culture. For many people psychoanalytic and associated therapeutic concepts structure how they understand themselves and social relationships. Yet we need to ask why psychoanalysis has taken root in the West, how it has spread through culture in the West and beyond, and how we can best study this peculiar and pervasive phenomenon. This volume explores these issues through a consideration of a variety of different cultural preoccupations and versions of psychoanalytic theory. The central argument that runs through my analysis of the myriad of cultural practices we will encounter in the following chapters is that psychoanalytic discourse can be found there in those practices and that it *structures* those practices and the subjectivity of those who participate in them. First, however, we need to review some general theoretical and methodological points that underpin the ways in which these questions about the modern mind will be addressed through the body of the book.

Most conventional accounts of the development of psychoanalysis trace it back, of course, to the writings, and then to formative influences and experiences in the life, of Sigmund Freud. The cultural climate in the Austro–Hungarian empire toward the end of the nineteenth century when he started writing is often portrayed as playing a powerful role, but that climate usually forms but the backdrop to descriptions of the innovations in Freud's work. The economic conditions which structured key cultural motifs in psychoanalysis are occasionally cited, but the predominant image, and one deliberately fostered by Freud himself, is of one man alone struggling to bring forth the truth. One would imagine from these accounts that we have now been blessed in the twentieth century, just in

time it would seem, with insights of a singular genius into enduring problems of the human condition, and that only now do we have the language
to understand what drives individuals to love and work. We need a different account.

Why is there psychoanalysis?

A sustained examination of psychoanalytic phenomena needs to comprehend the ways in which specific notions of selfhood, sensuality and
emotion have been constructed in Western culture, the ways in which
those specific notions have been governed by particular apparatuses of
self-knowledge, and the ways in which Western representations of the self
and prescriptions for psychological health are located in networks of
power, and power in a global context.

The construction of self

It is worth emphasizing that while Western forms of psychological theory,
including psychoanalysis, often pretend to explain how the human mind
operates in each and every culture back to the dawn of time, actual
'indigenous psychologies' seem to be as varied as the places they inhabit
(Heelas and Lock, 1981; Stigler et al., 1990). Different indigenous psychologies define different selves for people to inhabit, suffer or enjoy. The
'self' is difficult to catch and define, and the contours of the self are
ambiguous and changeable. Its contours have changed over time along
with the ways in which people are invited to elaborate a theory of what it
is to possess a self (Harré, 1983). Everyday theories of the self operate as
forms of 'commonsense'. They are constructed, but they have to be maintained and verified as theories so that they can be felt to be natural, good
and true.

Many Christians, for example, want their abhorrence of homosexuality
to be sanctified by the church and so they believe that the holy union of
marriage reflects a natural order of companionship. Those who are lonely
can then only hope to 'complete' themselves by finding an other who is
also necessarily of the other sex. But first, what is the 'other' sex? Laqueur
(1990) describes the way in which a 'one-sex/one-flesh' model of male and
female was split and transformed at the end of the seventeenth century
into a 'two-sex' model of gender that has covered over and re-written the
way the Western world once imagined bodies to be. From Renaissance
images of a Christ with breasts, and dissection plates which revealed the
male genital organs as the female's turned inside out – representations of
an essential similarity and symmetry between the genders – we have
moved to a condition in which we define our gender by our genitals, bits
of flesh which now look so *different* to us. And then, second, this fixing of
difference in the body is sedimented in religious bonding rituals which

forget a past in which the Catholic and Orthodox churches did once ratify same-gender, same-sex relationships. Both these churches had rites for recognizing and blessing what we would now call 'gay marriage', with reports of men and women taking part in such ceremonies in South-Eastern Europe until the late eighteenth century (Boswell, 1994).

The sensual pleasures that may be obtained from touching a part of one's own or another's body also feel so direct and immediate that it is difficult to imagine how it could be otherwise. Kissing, for example, as the rubbing of mouths together, assumes a delight that must, we feel, be normal and universal. Kissing begins for many of us as part of the greeting ritual and then may lead, as if naturally, to full sexual arousal and sense of release. But not all cultures kiss when they meet, and the kiss, according to some accounts, may have a quite different history; it is said that men in ancient Rome who wanted to detect whether their wives had been drinking, a capital offence for women at the time, could do no better than to taste deep the inside of her mouth (Toussaint-Samat, 1992). It is as if the move beyond the oral stage may also be a rather unpleasant historical accomplishment rather than simply being a necessary step for each human child to enter culture.

Emotions feel as if they are so deep within us that they could not possibly be constructed out of culturally available resources, yet experimental studies in social psychology indicate that simple adrenaline arousal can be interpreted as either anger or euphoria depending on the social context (Schachter and Singer, 1962). There are many descriptive studies which show that relationships and self-talk in different cultures produce entirely different emotions from those currently experienced in the West (Harré, 1986). So, emotions in medieval England, such as 'accidie', a feeling of despondency at not having done one's duty to God, have disappeared (Harré, 1983), and new emotional states have welled up as if they were always there. A history of tears in France, for example, traced the way weeping was but one ploy in the arts of seduction in the eighteenth century, but from the nineteenth century was felt to be a dammed up sobbing which then must find release (Vincent-Buffault, 1991).

The 'psy-complex'

The development of capitalism in Europe and North America provided fertile ground for 'depth psychological' experiences and explanations. Psychoanalysis provided a vocabulary for the experience of self that was provoked by an economic system that operates much of the time out of people's control, cloaked and encouraged by a cultural climate of commodification and individualization, but this psychoanalytic vocabulary also developed in the context of other equally powerful but more thoroughly institutionalized models of mind.

There is now an intricate network of theories and practices in place which govern how far we may make and remake mind and behaviour and the ways in which emotional 'deviance' should be comprehended and cured. This network is most dense in the urban interior of the modern West where it informs day-time television discussions and 'step' programmes for self-improvement, and as it sprawls throughout the world it carries with it prescriptions for how the modern self should be investigated and treated. This network is the 'psy-complex', and it includes academic and professional psychology and all the varieties of psychoanalysis sedi-mented in the clinic and diffused through the wider community. Pro-fessionals in the different sectors of the psy-complex define what abnormal emotional and correct mental functioning looks and feels like (Ingleby, 1985; Rose, 1985), and how child-care and family processes should be described and relayed to mothers and fathers (Donzelot, 1977; Riley, 1983).

The development of the psy-complex in various apparatuses of surveil-lance and regulation furnishes the context for the uptake of psychoanalytic ideas about the unconscious and the ego in Western culture. It also pro-vides a machinery for the implementation of certain theories of the mind in the West and then for the enforcement of these theories in the rest of the world as ways of accounting for cultural differences and ensuring that other cultures develop ways of thinking that are as 'civilized' as ours. A complete critical history of psychoanalysis would need to locate cultural representations of the self which appeal to notions of the unconscious and childhood fantasy in the context of clinical *practice*. There may be aspects of that practice that are indeed helpful to selves schooled to speak and think about their interior and past in psychoanalytic terms. That critical history of the institution of psychoanalysis and its participation in the psy-complex is beyond the scope of this book, but we will return to notions of therapy in culture in the final chapter.

Cultural imperialism

There have been a number of attempts to capture the way in which psycho-analytic notions have 'taken' in Western culture. Psychoanalysis has been described as the 'triumph of the therapeutic', and as an integral part of the modern struggle with questions of identity and morality when religious anchors have been cut away (Rieff, 1973). An even more sardonic argument from philosophy and social anthropology portrays psychoanalysis as an elaborate and efficient scam played by a new Freudian clerisy on a public looking for someone to offer pastoral support (Gellner, 1985). Sociological accounts have explored the 'cultural affinity' between psychoanalytic con-ceptions of selfhood and North American society (Berger, 1965), and these accounts have been used to describe the wider canvas of twentieth-century English-speaking culture (Bocock, 1976). Within social psychology Moscovici (1976) studied the 'social representations' of psychoanalytic ideas in the press of different political and religious organizations in France at the end of the 1950s, and showed how scientific modes of representation were translated into everyday talk about 'complexes' and unconscious 'slips' of the tongue and what they may mean.

The civilizing imperative of psychology and psychoanalysis can be seen in various descriptions of mental development in colonial 'cross-cultural' work from the beginning of the century. Stages of cognitive and moral development described by Piaget were used in Africa to grade levels of cultural development (Bulhan, 1981), and similar assessments of 'backward' cultures were made by Vygotsky across the Soviet Union (Kozulin, 1994). Freud's (1930) use of anthropology bought the now discredited idea from that discipline, that a detailed description of other existing present-day cultures that had not industrialized could be taken to be equivalent to uncovering 'primitive' life forms that were the deep dark past of the West. The priority which is accorded to the mentalities of the industrialized 'first world' in regimes of psychological testing and comparison is also reproduced in the way that academic and professional institutions legislate how research and training might be carried out from the centre and to the 'second' and 'third' worlds.

This priority is also reflected in the conceptual and organizational division of the world by the International Psychoanalytical Association (IPA) into three parts: North America, where the American Psychoanalytic Association (APA) oversees all training and so effectively governs that 'third' of the world independently of the IPA; Latin America, which includes Mexico and the countries of South America (with hardly any representation from groupings in Central America); and the rest of the world, which in effect means the countries of Europe, Africa and Asia dominated organizationally by the UK.

This mapping of institutional frameworks upon the 'real' world has had repercussions for the way training in the provinces is handled (in, for example, the monthly visits by South African trainee analysts to London, to the centre), and on the way that opposition trends have been dealt with (for example, in the way that UK analysts played a key role in the expulsion of Lacanians from the IPA in the 1950s). From the vantage point of a French analyst reviewing the state of the movement after the Second World War, the psychoanalytic 'empire' seemed to be tightly controlled and closed to dissent: 'the two world wars had the effect of ensuring the triumph of the West over the East and of recentering control of the empire's affairs onto an increasingly Anglophonic scene, which was itself more and more an American-dominated fiefdom' (Roudinesco, 1990: 171).

It is then difficult for 'indigenous' psychoanalysis that might respect the cultural particularities of, say, Indian or Japanese society to develop without drawing upon Western frameworks (Kakar, 1985; Doi, 1990). The repeated attempts to do this, sometimes at the risk of expulsion from the IPA, are testimony to the way in which psychoanalysis has had to compete with other models of the self, emotions and distress. Any critical appraisal of psychoanalysis, however sympathetic, must acknowledge that *all* varieties of psychology are shot through with cultural material, material which has a history and geographical location, and a position in networks of power.

Everyday psychologies are suffused with psychoanalytic notions, then, but these notions are *constructed* rather than being natural and universal. Contemporary constructions of the self are now indebted to the work of Freud and the psychoanalytic movement, but they are also maintained by institutions which define how the mind and behaviour should be described and experienced. Freudian theory 'works' not because it is true but because it is structured into Western culture. A focus on the social construction of psychology in different contexts helps us to strike a critical distance from psychoanalysis as a type of 'truth', and we can take that further with the development of analytic tools which locate it in language. This book takes us through various cultural phenomena which carry psychoanalytic notions of subjectivity, and analysis of these phenomena will also serve to illustrate how we may 'read' culture with a psychoanalytic eye and with an eye to how psychoanalysis operates in culture. To do that we need an adequate theoretical and methodological framework.

How can we study psychoanalytic phenomena?

When we turn to consider the many places that psychoanalysis operates in popular culture, we see that it takes a variety of forms in our talk, writing and practice, and we need particular conceptual and analytic tools to uncover how it is constructed and how it operates.

Discourse

One useful way of exploring that talk, writing and practice is through an analysis of the patterns of statements or 'discourses' that define different objects, whether as things that are outside and independent of us or inside and part of us. One of the most powerful tricks of language, and something which is a source of human creativity, is the way it can construct a representation of an object at one moment and then seem to refer to that object as if it were something outside, 'out there' at the next. Human beings live in a world which is woven with language, and the different symbolic systems which comprise a human community are *organized* through different competing and cross-connecting discourses which produce a sense of the world as something which is independent of us. These discourses not only produce for us a picture of the world 'out there', but with the growth of the psy-complex, they also encourage us to talk about and feel that there are certain kinds of objects 'in here'. The array of drives, ego-defences and object-representations which make up psychoanalytic talk have, for many analysts and patients, acquired an even more solid status.

Discourses also carry specifications for certain kinds of extremely complicated objects, the *subjects* of talk, those things we feel to be the source of meaning, and, in psychoanalytic talk, those things, *our-selves*, are felt to be the origin of distress and cure. The reflexive capacity of the human being is viewed by discourse analysts as something quite historically recent, and it can be understood as a function of discourse in which discourse 'folds' around a body and gives the effect and power of consciousness (Foucault, 1966). We should be clear, however, that when 'subject positions' are laid out in discourse, especially those grounded in an institution as a discursive practice, certain powers are enjoyed by some speakers and denied to others (Bhaskar, 1989; Parker, 1992).

It is one thing to say that psychoanalysis is maintained in discourse, and another to give due weight to the ways it circulates and the power it enjoys. It is not, for a start, 'simply' a discourse, and it would be a mistake to think that it only exists as a type of talk or writing. A discourse, or network of contradictory discourses in the case of the psy-complex, subsists in a 'regime of truth' which makes it difficult for participants to challenge the 'realities' it refers to. Regimes of truth govern what can be spoken about, and they also define what will be seen as nonsense or madness. Because discourse-analytic work is often carried out in academic settings, it is tempting to describe 'discourses' as if they were only linguistic, only in language. However, Foucault's (1969) work, which has been an inspiration for critical perspectives on discourse in psychology in recent years, draws attention to the way that speaking, writing and other forms of representation are implicated in 'discursive practices', and the sanctions against nonsense or madness can be severe (Parker, 1992; Parker et al., 1995). Discursive practices are the sites in institutions like prisons and schools where patterns of meaning are embedded in techniques of discipline, where we are made to act and be in certain ways. To explore the way psychoanalytic subjectivity 'works' in culture, we need to elaborate discourse analytic approaches a little further.

Discursive complexes

The methodological device of the 'discursive complex' captures the twofold nature of psychoanalytic discourse. The term 'complex' is used quite deliberately here to evoke the peculiarly Freudian and post-Freudian nature of the subjectivity we live so much of the time, and are focusing upon in this book (notwithstanding the fact that Freud took up the term from Jung). Were we to study behavioural or cognitive notions conveyed in language and experienced by users, we would perhaps want to speak of 'discursive repertoires' or 'discursive templates'. On the one hand, the concepts that psychoanalytic texts employ are relayed through culture as components of a discourse, as objects that are circumscribed by definitions in academic and professional writing and used in advertising (Parker, 1995). In this sense, the discourse constitutes places for subjects to come to be, whether as a child with problems separating from the mother, as a teenager filled with frustration and resentment at authority, or as an older adult reflecting on an unfulfilled life and needs. The discourse thus *positions* the subject who is addressed by or who is employing the discourse to understand themselves or their troubling relationships. On the other hand, the discourse touches an already existing shape of subjectivity for those who write and speak about themselves and others, whether that is in the form of autobiography or in an advice column, in a television interview or on the couch with a therapist. It chimes with a theory of self that the subject has been invited to elaborate for themselves in this culture, and so it reconfigures each time some of the emotions that are available to them (Parker, 1997).

While psychoanalysis provides a reflection, compression and reduction of societal phenomena to the level of the individual, it does so in a way that also reveals something more of the nature of those phenomena. When we study the way discursive complexes structure cultural phenomena, we are also able to understand more of the way they attract and mobilize their subjects. The discursive complex not only exists for the individual subject, then, but it also provides a means for understanding how psychoanalytic language works in relation to specific cultural phenomena. We can then illuminate what is felt to be the 'sharing' of experience by those involved in those phenomena, the rendering of subjects one to another as having similar psychological properties.

Conceptual understanding and psychological critique

So far I have been referring to psychoanalytic discourse as if it were something singular and unitary. As with all discourse, and human 'nature' embedded in it, however, it is neither of those things. We are made of many things, descriptions and images, and those things are divided in many ways. Psychoanalytic discourse comes in many competing forms, and is constructed out of a range of concepts that are held loosely together, and which clash and mesh with other popular behavioural and cognitive theories of the self.

The notion of 'psychoanalytic discourse' plays a sometimes paradoxical dual-role in this book, and defines my two main tasks in the following chapters. First, to show how it is possible to read contemporary cultural phenomena with a psychoanalytic eye. I will be interpreting a range of texts using psychoanalytic concepts, and showing how these concepts enable us to illuminate them in such a way as to *locate* them. Here I follow in the tracks of writers of various theoretical persuasions who use psychoanalysis to make sense of individual experience and cultural phenomena (e.g., Rustin, 1991; Samuels, 1993; Young, 1994; Elliott and Frosh, 1995) and journals devoted to that task (e.g., *Free Associations* and *Journal for the Psychoanalysis of Culture and Society*). I am concerned not so much with what is going on inside the minds of individual writers as with the networks of discourse that give what they produce meaning, and with what that meaning reveals of culture and the conditions of possibility for being an author of one's self in this culture. Psychoanalysis can certainly be used to read and illuminate cultural texts, but I will be returning in each chapter to ask *why* it can be used in this way, and why certain versions of psychoanalytic discourse seem so appropriate to certain topics.

My second task, then, is to show how cultural phenomena are structured by discursive complexes, and the readings also provide opportunities for exploring the ways in which key concepts in psychoanalytic vocabulary have emerged in the writings of Freud and his successors. Here I am a little more sceptical about psychoanalysis as the master-key to open up the secrets of culture, and will want to show how psychoanalytic discourse itself has been constructed as part of the ideological mechanism which locks us into place here and now. Psychoanalysis encourages us to move below the surface to look at the ways in which meaning is produced, but here we will be looking at the way meaning is transformed and reproduced in culture rather than trying to find the sources of the meanings inside individuals alone. When the criminal psychologist in the film *The Dark Past* (quoted at the beginning of this chapter) looks out of the window at the young delinquents, for example, and transforms Freud's metaphor about the structure of the mind to distinguish between the good youth that can be salvaged from the bad who are the waste, he is simultaneously relaying a certain way of structuring a social phenomenon to the audience. Psychoanalysis then circulates as a form of representation and practice which positions subjects as they use and reflect upon what it is possible for them to say. But where did this discourse come from?

Freud's psychoanalytic discourse

Freud's contribution to the development of psychoanalysis was, of course, vitally important, and we should pay some attention to that contribution before turning to the cultural and economic forces that allowed his ideas to bear fruit. How we tell the story of an individual life formed by competing cultures and embedded in conflicting economic conditions will always be framed by certain theoretical and methodological frameworks.

Rather than simply trace Freud's biography – from birth in 1856 to the death of his father and his first use of the term 'psychoanalysis' in 1896, to the foundation of the International Psychoanalytical Association in 1910, and so to death in exile in 1939 – it will be more helpful here for the main themes of this book to focus on Freud's lifework as *located* in a series of events. His writing, professional activities and the mobilization of colleagues for the cause of psychoanalysis can be considered as governed by, and to some extent constituted by, these events.

Materiality of mind

Freud's training as a medical doctor served to reinforce a materialist approach to the body and mind that had impressed itself upon him at quite an early stage in his career. A visit to Manchester in 1875 provided him with the opportunity for a close reading of English empiricist works on science, a view of inquiry as rooted in the discovery of observable facts and the connections between them, and at the time Freud was strongly opposed to speculative metaphysics. The medical positivism he absorbed from Ernst Brücke, his mentor in the physiological laboratory where he worked from 1876 to 1882, mapped this empiricist frame of mind upon a trenchant critique of any variety of romanticism. Romanticism at the time was popular in biological theory among researchers looking to mysterious forces in nature to explain development and offering vitalist explanations for biological processes. Freud's first book, published in 1891, *On the Conception of the Aphasias: A Critical Study*, focused upon organic problems which affected language production, and which were thought to lie in lesions in the brain, and re-described them as relationships between systems of representation. This then paved the way for a view of hysteria as operating as if it were 'the lesion of an idea' (Forrester, 1980: 30).

Freud had by this time met Wilhelm Fliess, who travelled from Berlin in 1887 to hear Freud lecture on neurology, and by 1894 Fliess was, as Freud put it, 'the only Other' (cited in Gay, 1988: 56). There is a tension in his relationship with that 'Other' right from the start, and Fliess's rather mystical ideas about the significance of certain numbers in the female and male reproductive cycles – which provoked in Freud abiding anxieties about his own death at the age of fifty-one, sixty-one and then sixty-two – sat alongside what were then radical theories of constitutional bisexuality and more fantastic speculation about connections between the nose and the sexual organs (Gilman, 1993). Despite his attempts to escape romanticist notions, throughout Freud's career the duality of vital forces (in the drives) and physiological mechanisms (as mental structures) remains, though the discussions with Fliess set a context for the elaboration of an account which tried to ground the psyche in biology.

The *Project for a Scientific Psychology* (Freud, 1950) was written in 1895 following one of the intimate 'congresses' with his friend in Berlin in September. The still incomplete manuscript was sent to Fliess at the beginning of the following year. The editor's introduction to the *Project* in the *Standard Edition* notes that it 'contains within itself the nucleus of a great part of Freud's later psychological theories' and that 'its invisible ghost' 'haunts the whole series of Freud's theoretical writings to the end' (Strachey, 1966: 290). It laid the basis for a reading of psychoanalysis as a cognitive psychology, and for the reduction of therapeutic and cultural explanation to the frame of natural science (Pribram and Gill, 1976). The *Project*, which Freud called his 'Psychology for Neurologists', contained specifications for the accumulation, retention and discharge of quantities of excitation, and many of these themes, particularly that of grounding mental processes in the brain, ran through to one of his last reviews of a general analytic theory of mind over forty years later in *An Outline of Psychoanalysis* (Freud, 1940a). The recurring problem with a strict natural science account of psychoanalysis, however, is that human desire always reaches beyond biology, and Freud struggled over and again with a sense of the self as something trapped in the body and as attempting a trans-formation of itself and its relations with others.

Levels of representation

Freud's awareness in his aphasia studies that the mind was not only riven by different representations, and that it may be possible to speak of levels of representation as marking different regions of thought and varieties of mental process, led him, eventually, to the unconscious. A visit to Paris from October 1885 until March 1886 to study with Jean Martin Charcot at the Salpêtrière Clinic brought Freud to a place where hypnotism was lifting hysteria from the female body. A portrait of Charcot presenting one of his female patients to an audience of colleagues and students hung on the wall of Freud's consulting room in Berggasse 19 in Vienna until 1938, and then took pride of place over the analytic couch in 20 Maresfield Gardens in Hampstead. Freud also visited the hypnotist Hippolyte Bern-heim – who argued against Charcot's assertion that only hysterics are sus-ceptible to hypnosis – in Nancy in 1889, and he translated works by both Bernheim and Charcot into German. Charcot's argument that hysteria occurred in men as well as women, and that the hypnotic state reproduces in some way the hysteric condition, combined with Bernheim's claim that the phenomenon spanned the divide between the normal and the abnor-mal, fashioned abnormality and femininity into keys to unlock hidden processes in the normal male mind.

Here too was further evidence of a separate unconscious system of meaning in the mind, for the complaints of Charcot's hysterics could not be neatly mapped onto the contours of the body. Hysteric and hypnotic paralysis did not correspond to nerve pathways, to physiologically cir-cumscribed areas of stricken arms or legs. Something else was happening for the patient, and something could be produced or relieved in the patient by suggestion, suggestion at some level of awareness that was not con-scious. Charcot looked to times of traumatic shock which might have pro-voked these states of mind, and there was a good deal of attention in the Salpêtrière at the time to the prevalence and consequences of child sexual abuse. It was as if there was a packet of experience which suffered and retreated from things to then remain trapped under the surface, and a realm of consciousness which could speak of experience only when the suffering had been pushed underneath. The condition for everyday dis-course seemed to be that the shocking things must have been locked out of it.

Freud (1895a) later elaborated an account of the unconscious as consisting of 'thing presentations', a level of representation divided from an everyday consciousness which comprised the 'word presentations' of language. The very ability to use language, to consciously communicate with others and participate in a common discourse, was to be predicated, in mainstream psychoanalysis, on the existence of 'another place', an unconscious mental life in which creative work on the past and present was confused and combined in different disturbing and exciting ways.

Sex, seduction and fantasy

Freud's enthusiastic report on Charcot's demonstration of the existence of male hysteria and the *psychological* nature of the complaint to his Viennese colleagues in 1886 did not go down well. Here too was a confusion of discursive frames for making sense of psychopathology, with Freud caught between different cultural and academic representations of abnormality and sexuality. Freud's return to Vienna was also a journey between competing images of childhood. The 'Seduction Theory' Freud described some ten years later to colleagues, in April 1896, probably owed something to his reading of lurid reports in the French press of the extent of child sexual abuse as well as to Salpêtrière research when he was in Paris, but that theory jarred with stories of the manipulative lying child popular in German-speaking culture. Accounts of physical torment were disbelieved, and instances of sexual abuse all the more effectively concealed thanks to these images of children. It has been argued that Freud retreated from his 'Seduction Theory' because of the incredulous and hostile reaction it provoked in Vienna (Masson, 1984), though that he should then propose something a good deal *more* provocative – that we are all well-springs of perverse fantasy – does not sit easily with that charge. Whatever Freud's own reasons, the shift of focus from actual 'seduction' to infantile fantasies was a founding moment for psychoanalysis.

Images of sexual perversion have cut both ways in psychoanalysis, legitimating *and* combating abuse (Glaser and Frosh, 1993), though the strong association between mature development and normative heterosexuality meant that the more challenging aspects of Freud's work were often muted or buried. Fliess provided, for example, the idea of constitutional bisexuality which would make psychoanalytic sense of the phenomenon of male hysteria as well as break a strict essentialist distinction between the genders and the way that this was conventionally mapped onto the biological difference between the sexes. Freud's (1905a) *Three Essays on the Theory of Sexuality* made it clear, and clearer still in a famous footnote added in 1915, that biological differences between the sexes needed to be distinguished from differences between male and female gender identities in society, and distinguished again from the difference between activity and passivity. Freud goes on to insist though, even in this footnote which is often quoted by feminist writers sympathetic to psychoanalysis, that the 'libido' is 'masculine', 'for an instinct is always active even when it has a passive aim in view' (Freud, 1905a: 141). This is why Freud asserts in the passage to which the footnote is appended, 'the sexuality of little girls is of a wholly masculine character' (ibid.).

What Freud gives with one hand, then, he snatches away with the other. Sexuality is severed from biology, and so can become a plastic pleasure to be enjoyed as much by women as it is by men, but it is then stitched back onto masculinity, to become only enjoyable by women as if they were men. The decomposition of the 'drives' – into the charge or '*pressure*', the part or process of the body as '*source*', the '*aim*' always considered as the erasure of tension at the source, and the '*object*' by means of which the aim is realized – also performs a contradictory effect in the development of psychoanalysis as a form of sexual politics. Now it becomes possible to open up questions of perversity, and what Freud termed the 'polymorphous perversity' of infantile sexuality, to consider how homosexuality might be considered alongside heterosexuality as an equally confused and understandable response to the confusion and trauma of infantile sexual helplessness and wishfulness. The practice of psychoanalysis has often dealt with this, though, by ratifying current child-care arrangements and sexual identities in the 'normal' nuclear family rather than questioning whether the brutal assaults and compulsory heterosexuality which often mars it might not be seen as symptomatic of an 'abnormal', albeit culturally dominant, structure.

Infantile sexuality also plays a subversive and a conservative role in discussions of the unconscious lives of patients and analysts, for as well as pervading everyday life, sexuality must then riddle the therapeutic relationship. The analyst is confronted over and again with descriptions and questions about desire which *reproduce* patterns of sexual relatedness at the very moment they are talked about. 'Transference', conceived as the replaying of attachments from earlier significant objects onto the figure of the analyst, became one of the milestones in the development of psychoanalytic practice, and seen as structuring the route to the cure rather than as being an inconvenient blockage in channels of communication. It did not take long, perhaps by virtue of the role of psychoanalysis as an incitement to confess within the analytic community itself, for the sexual fantasies of the analyst toward their patients – their 'counter-transference' – also to be considered by 'object relations' analysts to be a necessary part of the process (e.g., Heimann, 1950). Fantasy keeps appearing in the process of cure, then, but it must be harnessed in order to turn that process into a properly creative and therapeutic endeavour.

Civilization and rationality

Freud saw psychoanalysis as a science as well as a therapeutic and cultural pursuit. Sometimes it was clear that by this he meant that it should be a natural science, one of the *Naturwissenschaften*, and that the circuitous and lengthy 'talking cure' might then eventually be shortened with medication to alter the chemical basis of neurotic or hysterical problems. The neuropsychological descriptions in the 1895 *Project* reappear in distinctions between primary process and secondary process thinking, and between the corresponding pleasure principle and reality principle. The notion of repression – Freud's 'cornerstone' of psychoanalysis – is often set in this natural science framework (Grünbaum, 1984). At other points, when Freud is referring to the cultural and literary background study that a trainee psychoanalyst should engage in as being more useful than a medical training, it is easier to accept claims that Freud saw psychoanalysis as one of the human sciences, the *Geisteswissenschaften*, sciences of the spirit in which criteria of understanding and experiential resonance are more important than hypothesis generation and empirical testing (Bettelheim, 1983). In either case, rational appraisal is accorded a high value; rationality as one of the hallmarks of psychoanalysis itself is to be found on the side of the secondary process, the reality principle and in the type of 'advanced' civilization that would make psychoanalysis possible.

Psychoanalysis also takes the side of reason when it comes to debates over the role of religion as a belief system in a civilized society. Freud himself, as a Jew living in Vienna, had good reason to be suspicious of Christianity as an irrational, and potentially pathologically dangerous enemy of rational thought. The mayor of Vienna, Dr Karl Lueger, for example, was a populist who had secured election by upping the stakes in anti-Semitic rhetoric. Freud was determined to ensure that his identity as a Jew should not hinder the development of psychoanalysis.

This determination is something that has also been used against Freud in anti-Semitic arguments that his cultural identity must necessarily have entailed a secret adherence to Judaism, and in characterizations of him as responding to Christian culture as a 'Jewish avenger' (Szasz, 1979). It is possible to find traces of Jewish mystical thought – particularly Kabbalist notions of text and sensuality – in psychoanalytic writing and practice (Bakan, 1958), but it is also possible to find Catholic themes emerging, with the trinity of id, ego and super-ego sometimes cited as one example, and seen as deriving also perhaps from his early experience with his nurse (Isbister, 1985). What is important here is the way that Freud's marginal position simultaneously provided him with a critical distance from the dominant culture and with some alternative cultural resources to forge a model of the rational individual which would be capable of both adapting to and challenging taken-for-granted social mores (Klein, 1985). Psychoanalysis often seems to trace its way along a knife-edge of conformity and revolutionary critique, and many of the most vibrant debates have been over its 'real' character, on which side it must fall, as if it must fall eventually on one side or the other.

Christian anti-Semitism came to bear repeatedly on the choices Freud made, from a career in medicine to the development of the psychoanalytic movement. Freud's hopes for Carl Jung, for example, as the Christian crown prince of the psychoanalytic movement were also conditioned by anti-Semitism. If Jung, the son of a Swiss pastor, would take over as figurehead of the International Psychoanalytical Association (IPA), then it might have been possible, he hoped, to break the isolation that Freud felt in Vienna. These hopes were tied yet again to an image of psychoanalysis as a rational, civilized enterprise, and it is ironic that Jung's own mysticism (which was always a serious liability) was eventually to be one of the reasons why he had to break from Freud. It is perhaps, however, also a saving grace that Jung did not remain in the leadership of the IPA, for his ideas were always in some ways diametrically opposed to psychoanalysis. Instead of a careful materialist attempt to unravel the complexities of adult experience by way of an examination of the past of the individual, Jung offered facile appeals to a 'collective unconscious'. It was then a short step to themes of religious salvation, and appeals to racial, and anti-Semitic, fellow feeling (Samuels, 1993).

Cultural improvement

Freud often mapped the development of scientific rationality onto the development of culture, and the development of individual rationality was also often seen as recapitulating a progressive movement in the civilizing process toward better mental functioning and self-understanding. His characterization of psychoanalytic practice in the famous quote about the Zuider Zee at the beginning of this chapter makes this link quite explicit, and self-improvement proceeds alongside and is modelled on cultural improvement in an image of the ego being strengthened and colonizing the id. In the various descriptions of the psychical apparatus in Freud's writing, the ego comes to assume pride of place as representative and guarantor of rationality in the individual and principle upon which cultural growth depends.

Whether the ego is seen as a function of an engagement with reality and as mediating between the social order and the unconscious, or whether it is assumed to precede social relationships as assessor and filter for language and other cultural material, it is always – with the paradoxical exception of Freud's account of narcissism – at the 'centre' of psychic life. The ego emerges through the various models of mind in the development of Freud's work as regulator, manager, focus point and rational locus of the self. It is possible to trace a path in Freud's writing through: (i) the dynamic model (in which libidinal energy flows from one site of the mental apparatus to another, investing 'ideational representatives' along the way), to (ii) the economic model (in which hydraulic metaphors come into their own in accounts of the 'exhaustion' of energy suffered by hysterics), to (iii) the topographical model (in which the key distinction is between the unconscious and conscious as separate regions of the mind), and so to (iv) the structural model (so beloved of psychology textbook writers with its simple compartmentalization of the mind into 'id', 'ego' and 'super-ego'), which crowns the ego as the rational centre and hero of Anglo-American 'ego-psychology' (e.g., Hartmann, 1939). Each model remains through Freud's work, but it is the structural model that is often taken to exemplify the 'final state' version of his theory (Greenberg and Mitchell, 1983). There, against Freud's (1925a) own insistence that the unconscious finds its way into *every* perception, it is assumed possible to conceive of the ego as a 'conflict-free' region of the personality, present from birth and rationally guiding the individual through the demands placed by the other two internal agencies and by the outside world.

There is an uneasy partnership here between the ego and the pleasure principle, and the early phases of Freud's writing revolved around the tension between the ego as container of the individual 'self-preservative' drives faithfully following the reality principle and the unconscious and disruptive effects of the pleasure principle which also facilitated the repro- duction of the species. Here in these early accounts it is as if the partner- ship keeps foundering on sex. In the later phases of Freud's writing, with his discussions of narcissism in 1914 as a hinge point (Freud, 1914a), sex helps glue the ego together as the site of the drive for self-preservation and Eros, and these now closer partners are faced with a new threat from deeper within the unconscious with the 'return of the repressed', with something 'beyond the pleasure principle', with death (Freud, 1920). Eros is then matched by Thanatos as a drive for self-destruction that wells up from the interior of the body, from every single cell to attack the integrity of the self and suck it back to an inorganic state.

Civilization is increasingly depicted by Freud as developing through a diversion of sexual and aggressive energies, through 'sublimation' as an improvement on what those energies would be in their raw state. It seems as if the appearance of violence on a massive scale in the First World War was interpreted by Freud as an expression of what had always already lain underneath the veneer of culture. As what seemed to lie underneath appeared more and more destructive, so it became all the more necessary to strengthen the veneer, to laminate more layers of culture upon the ego to make sexual pleasure as well as self-preservation part of its *raison d'être*. Freud was certainly isolated by the war, and the difficulty he faced in maintaining an international community of psychoanalysts through national rivalries became a focus for his energies after the war was over. The psychoanalytic movement itself had long been plagued by minor civil wars, with the split by Adler in 1911 and then by Jung just before the war started. The First World War intensified the struggle between life and death in the psychoanalytic community, and this struggle became central to the model of the individual described in psychoanalytic texts, in Freud's last writings.

The series of events that punctuated Freud's life also marked his theor- etical and organizational struggle for a coherent dynamic view of the mind and for a community of analysts to understand it, and the events still stay stuck, represented in the system of concepts that comprise psychoanalytic debates today. Notions of the materiality of mind, the unconscious, infantile sexuality, civilized rationality and cultural improvement in psychoanalysis carry with them, unresolved, the many political questions which prompted or framed them. This is partly because Freud struggled with each theme, reflecting on their meaning and consequences. Freud was an acute observer, and he discussed and elaborated many of his observations with others. Such intensely focused analysis, self-analysis and then psycho-analysis condensed each theme and pressed them together into the service of personal preoccupations, of Freud, patients and colleagues. Although the 'self-analysis' he undertook in 1896 following the death of his father is often portrayed as a lonely journey to the interior, his active reflection on family, institutional and political events was in most cases carried out in a variety of professional networks, as public activity. In this sense, those individual deep-felt concerns were still also cultural matters.

Cultural conditions of possibility

The themes that flowed into Freud's writing were not as so many currents mingled together in the smooth sea of a common culture. The forty-four years stretching back from the beginning of the twentieth century and the forty forward were marked by turmoil, intellectual and murderous. This was a time of strange ideas and mass movements that sent shockwaves through the different cultures of Europe and beyond; they inform and impel psychoanalysis as a dynamic modern practice of the mind, as well as how we are able to understand it and to account for how it emerged. These cultural themes often precede and precipitate, inform and intersect with Freud's work, and they are then often in turn framed by psychoanalytic discourse. We will find them reappearing time and again in the course of this book in relation to particular versions of analytic theory. I will review ten key cultural themes here.

Evolution

Evolutionary theory, as a first case in point, offered a 'scientific' account of the development of humankind but there was more than one evolutionary theory around and there was a surfeit of popular anthropological work that had less certain claims to scientificity. Freud admired Darwin's account of 'selection' of species, in which the best adaptive mutations survive and so spread through a population over time, but he was also influenced by Lamarck's argument for the inheritance of qualities obtained during a parent's lifetime, and such notions were employed in psychoanalytic description of the transmission of human memory through history. The Oedipus complex, for example, would, at times, be traced to events in the 'primal horde' of pre-history as if they were acquired and carried in genetically-coded memory to the present. Freud also repeatedly tried to locate individual development in the context of species development with appeals to the dictum 'ontogeny recapitulates phylogeny'.

The account of Freud as a 'biologist of the mind' (Sulloway, 1979) relies heavily on his preoccupation with this causal link between a general theory of human psychology and its place in evolution. While Freud opted for certain rather conservative readings of the emergence of history from nature, alternative theories were already in circulation for his colleagues to pick up and develop. Accounts of an early matriarchal form of social organization which preceded present-day patriarchy, for example, were being mobilized as a warrant for critique and for changes in relations between women and men, and between men.

Marxism

The early socialist and communist movement, which drew on evolutionary accounts to warrant alternative ways of organizing society, was also looking at the time to contemporary gender relations as symptomatic of an economic system which prioritized individual choice over the wider community. In *The Origin of the Family, Private Property, and the State*, for example, Engels (1884) traced the emergence of class society to the appropriation of agricultural surplus by men, their attempts to protect that surplus from others by force, and their control of women to safeguard inheritance of what they had personally accumulated. 'Primitive communism' was seen not so much as an early golden age – though it was that too for many writers – as evidence that things could be different and could prefigure something better than capitalism.

Evolutionary notions were also present in prescriptions for change, with the Marxism of the socialist and then social democratic parties of the Second International being interpreted as an account of the inevitable decline of capitalism and the gradual emergence of classless society. Freud was sympathetic to the moral claims of the socialists, but pessimistic about the possibilities of change. This pessimism was intensified with the ascendance of Soviet 'Marxism' and the Third International under Stalin, and it was left to a second generation of radical psychoanalysts in Germany (such as Wilhelm Reich and Erich Fromm), to use Marxist notions in their description of the authoritarian personality, and to keep alive the possibility of an anti-authoritarian Marxism in the sphere of psychology. Later Marxist writers in the French structuralist tradition, such as Louis Althusser in the 1960s, were queasy about essentialist and humanist notions, and so concepts from psychoanalysis, such as 'the unconscious', were treated carefully, with suspicion, but they still felt that Freud had tapped something true about the nature of human subjectivity.

The unconscious

The notion of the 'unconscious' has long been important in many Marxist accounts of repression at a personal level as something which accompanies and perpetuates oppression at a social level. Freud elaborated a description of something 'other' to everyday experience, picking up ideas about alienation and false consciousness which already lay as background assumptions in socialist politics, and ideas of creative mental activity outside immediate awareness which were prevalent in European philosophy and literature (Whyte, 1960). The sense that there were important and determining cognitive processes outside the realm of consciousness went back from Marx and Engels to Kant in the eighteenth century, and earlier to other writers. Unconscious aspects of instincts, emotions and imagination can be traced back beyond Shakespeare writing in the sixteenth century.

Pathology as an expression of unconscious motives and wishes was already central to Charcot's and Bernheim's hypnotism research and to their precursors working on magnetism, most importantly in Anton Mesmer's work at the end of the eighteenth century. The unconscious as a vital natural force was captured at the beginning of the nineteenth century by the German novelist Jean Paul Richter in the evocative and signal phrase 'the inner Africa' (cited in Whyte, 1960: 132), and captured here also as an index of a particular colonial moment. Consciousness as a problem, as a superficial and dangerous layer of deception, ran through Friedrich Nietzsche's writing toward the end of the century. Freud deliberately avoided Nietzsche's work, partly because of the very similarity of concepts between the two writers, and he found the existence of competing views of the unconscious and the 'It' while he was developing his own theory, in Georg Groddeck's (1923) *The Book of the It* for example, most discomforting.

Language

Language was becoming increasingly important to the attempts by various writers toward the beginning of the twentieth century to demarcate conscious from unconscious processes. Language was already central to Freud's work on aphasias, and there was to be a continual preoccupation with the ways in which language excludes and then provides the site for cure, the 'talking cure' (Forrester, 1980). After Freud's death, some of the most passionate debates around Jacques Lacan's 'return to Freud' in France revolved around the relationship between the unconscious and language, with the standard psychoanalytic view of the relationship – the unconscious as a precondition for language – being turned upside down; language now being seen as a precondition for the unconscious (Archard, 1984).

Lacan's appeal to structuralism, in which the system of language is seen as cutting the amorphous mass of thought into manageable discrete concepts, sometimes obscures the equally important resource for him in Hegel's (1807) writing, in which 'the word is the murder of the thing'. What is important here is the way that structuralism and post-structuralism as theories of language sit alongside a phenomenological tradition which is mortified by the thought of what language excludes, a tradition which goes back well beyond Freud. Saussure, the father of structuralism – and whose son was to become a psychoanalyst – was already in 1907 in Geneva giving the lectures on language that were later reconstructed by his students as the *General Course in Linguistics* (Saussure, 1974). Psychoanalysis was already, independently of Saussure's work and well before the rise of structuralism, a kind of semiology, a 'science of signs'.

Sexuality

For critics of psychoanalysis and many of its enthusiasts all the signs led to sexuality. One of the reasons why a 'Standard Edition' of Freud's writing was produced in English translation (Freud, 1953–1974) was as a response and corrective to the sensationalized accounts of psychoanalysis that were appearing in the United States. By the 1930s the editor of the *American Journal of Psychology*, for example, declared his horror at a new 'invasion' of 'immigrant subjects' which included psychoanalysis as 'a lurid doctrine of lust in little children' (Bentley, 1937: 464). Sexuality, by the time psychoanalysis emerged, certainly seemed to be the worrisome repressed secret at the heart of bourgeois creativity and misery. Images of children were all the more contradictory by now, for as much as people idealized the infant as innocent, they suspected that it was also knowing of sexuality and culpable in its own 'seduction'.

There is a recurrent switch back and forth from different sides of the split image of the child as good or bad, and this is evident too in the way some psychoanalysts take fright at the abuse they feel they too have sanctioned in their accounts of infantile sexuality and so they now insist that the child is essentially innocent (A. Miller, 1985). Sexual fantasies are, after all, assumed to lie at the core of every modern subject, and psychoanalysis is only one of the invitations to speak about what lies within us to ease our guilt about what we think, or might think, or think even without knowing it (Foucault, 1976). Psychoanalysis helps tie sexuality to confession, but it also opened the possibilities for liberation when the infant, and so potentially the adult, could be viewed as 'naturally' polymorphously perverse and constitutionally bisexual.

Feminism

Even while the unconscious was an undiscovered land that was succumbing bit by bit to psychoanalytic map-making, Freud never ceased to be puzzled by feminine sexuality, and he described women's sexual life on occasion as 'a *dark continent*'. His question 'What does woman want?'

was being answered increasingly by women themselves, and the emergence of the women's liberation and feminist movements posed some difficult questions to psychoanalysis. Feminism upped the stakes for descriptions of women's sexuality and the fate of their passage through the Oedipus complex. It was now no longer good enough to match, as Karen Horney (1967) had tried to do, women's supposed penis envy with the 'womb envy' suffered by men. Feminists were not so interested in constructing men's sexuality as a mirror of their own, as in reconstructing for themselves how sexuality could exist outside reproduction and demands of a nuclear family.

Feminism also provided women with a space to think through questions of sexuality outside psychoanalysis, and then to decide, for example, whether it was indeed the case that Freud was 'the strongest counter-revolutionary force in the ideology of sexual politics' from the 1930s through to the 1960s (Millett, 1975: 178). Hostility to psychoanalysis in the women's movement reached a peak during the 1960s, and even with the re-readings of Freud (through Lacan) that argued that psychoanalysis was 'not a recommendation *for* a patriarchal society, but an analysis *of* one' (Mitchell, 1974: xv), there is still understandable suspicion, suspicion which is politicized all the more with the visibility of lesbian critique inside and outside psychotherapeutic practice (O'Connor and Ryan, 1993; Maguire, 1995).

Romanticism

Psychoanalysis participated in the wider obsession and celebration of mental and bodily fragmentation in nineteenth-century culture. That fragmentation has continued to the present day, now under the sign of 'postmodernism' where it is treated as something peculiar to the late twentieth century. For every attempt to restore a sense of integrity and unity to experience, and for each search for innocence and purity at the heart of the self, there was a corresponding attention to the broken and fallen quality of humanity and nature. In this sense, postmodern 'new romantics' and 'goths' repeat cultural motifs from the last century but without their anguished depth and dark decay. German varieties of romanticism had been particularly marked by such themes from late seventeenth-century *Sturm und Drang* writing, and this mixture of torn and dejected worry at the storms and stresses of the world suffered by poets was advertised and then projected into every individual by the time psychoanalysis appeared.

The fate of Gothic fiction from the mid-eighteenth century also reflects an encounter with proto-psychoanalytic notions and then a more full-blown participation in Freudian notions of subjectivity and otherness. Gothic horror encapsulates a historical transition from the marvellous to the uncanny that parallels Freudian encounters with romanticism and musings on death; there is 'a progressive internalization and recognition of fears as generated by the self' (Jackson, 1981: 24). The romantic movement, of which psychoanalysis must be considered to be a part, despite Freud's best efforts to develop a scientific account of subjectivity as an alternative to vitalism, was, among other things, a testament to the attempt to combine a sense of disintegration with a striving to return to the organic, to Nature.

Surrealism

The Surrealist movement picked up many romantic themes but also sought to systematize inquiry into the creative mind which lay, it was thought, under the surface of bourgeois culture. There was a contradictory double-movement in Surrealism that ran from its Dadaist precursor in the 1920s through to its Situationist inheritors in the 1960s. Dada had revelled in the nonsense and madness of unconscious creativity and then Situationism rebelled against the crafted mystifying nonsense of the 'society of the spectacle' (Plant, 1993). On the one hand, there was an attempt in Surrealism to realize direct spontaneous desire, and here the movement repeated gestures of despair and defiance at the way language must necessarily misrepresent the world – to be 'the murder of the thing' – that Hegelian phenomenology and Sartrean existentialism revolved around. The way that the reality principle misdirects and sabotages the primary process at the same time as it helps the individual to participate successfully in society was often addressed in Freud's writing, and the problem was to recur in Marcuse's (1972) descriptions of 'repressive desublimation' under capitalism, for example, or, in a worse scenario, in Lacan's (1977) account of mis-recognition at the core of identity in every symbolic order.

On the other hand, Surrealists carried out detailed research on 'automatic writing' and dreams in order to discover the royal roads to liberated subjectivity. André Breton, leader of the Surrealist movement, was one of the first to take up Freud's ideas in France, and the 'Second Manifesto of Surrealism' in 1929 declared that Freudian criticism was the only one to provide a secure basis for the work of the movement (Rosemont, 1978). Lacan participated in the Surrealist movement in Paris in the early 1930s, and it is said that Salvador Dalí owed his paranoiac-critical method of painting to an engagement with Lacan's work (Macey, 1988).

Modernity

Different writers from various philosophical traditions describe cultural changes toward the end of the eighteenth and beginning of the nineteenth century using a range of terms, but all capturing something of the same reflective and self-transformative dynamic. Psychoanalysis tends to be seen as part of 'Modernity' or the 'Modern age', and evaluated negatively for that, by French structuralist and post-structuralist writers such as Foucault (1966). While Descartes – splitting mind from body and the rational from the irrational – is seen as one of the intellectual centres for modernity, it is the French Revolution of 1789 that stamped rationality into the heart of modern practices of surveillance and control. The concept of 'ideology' comes, for example, to be seen then as the operation of false ideas that can be dispelled by rigorous analysis and political persuasion, and the coercive character of this endeavour to define and implement a truth about society and individuals is described in Foucault's histories of the present and accounts of the emergence of new 'regimes of truth'. Marxism, for example, which offers enlightenment and liberation, is seen as of a piece with Freud's promise that hysterical misery might be allevi- ated by the subject looking inward and so coming to really know them- selves.

Freud is also seen as being a key actor in parallel descriptions, mainly by German historians, of the 'Enlightenment', though here the evaluation tends to be positive, and Marxism is also a reference point for the achieve- ment of something valuable by Western culture. This is something which enables critical reflection on the way people individually and collectively make meaning and on those social structures which restrict full human freedom. Psychoanalysis is, of course, an expression of beliefs in the value of personal meaning, cultural progress, and scientific rationality. While these ideas might be scorned as old, modern, out-of-date 'grand narra- tives' by French postmodern writers (e.g., Lyotard, 1979), they are vigor- ously defended by the second and third generations of German Critical Theory (Habermas, 1971; Honneth, 1995). Critical Theory takes Freud's ideas and transforms them as it radicalizes them, though there are some even more radical transformations by French writers who seem to make psychoanalysis postmodern.

Narcissism

There is a price to be paid for enlightenment, and each individual loses connection with other people, and from their own desire at the same time as they gain the ability to reflect critically upon themselves and rationally appraise different courses of action. Even within the German Critical Theory tradition, psychoanalysis is seen as both a solution and a part of the problem in this process of mastery of, and separation from, nature (Adorno and Horkheimer, 1944). The subversive impulses of psycho- analysis, reflected in the uptake of Freud's ideas by Surrealism, for example, were seen as squashed back into the prevailing order of things by the Anglo-American 'ego-psychologists' who hastened the reification of the mind and the adaptation of the person to society (e.g., Hartmann, 1939). Freud worked with the symptomatic fall-out from flourishing capitalism at the end of the nineteenth century where the ills of the time erupted in hysterical disorders. Later psychoanalysts, including the American ego-psychologists, theorized these as problems of ego develop- ment and functioning, noting an increase in narcissistic and 'borderline' personality disorders (e.g., Kernberg, 1975).

Again, parallel analyses of the malaise in contemporary culture have been traced by both 'postmodern' and 'post-Enlightenment' writers. Those working in the tracks of Foucault's (1976) work, on the one hand, will look to the *end* of psychoanalysis as those modern practices of discipline and confession that helped provide its conditions of possibility also seem to dissolve. A quite different, and more pessimistic description is found, on the other hand, in writers who use psychoanalytic concepts to help us to understand how the Enlightenment has spawned a new 'culture of narcissism' (Lasch, 1978). Narcissism is both more and less than the simple self-absorption its name would suggest; it is obsessive in its attention to the self at the expense of relationships and despairing in its sense that nothing of worth lies within as a source of strength and value. In place of the fullness of personal growth at the dawn of psychoanalysis, we are now faced with a yawning emptiness of the self, and this happens at the very moment that psychoanalysis saturates culture more than ever before.

Although psychoanalysis has now moved to the centre of culture, it developed on the edges, and, paradoxically, was stronger as a source of *critical* self-reflection for that. Vienna was one of the crucibles of modern culture, and a focal point for modernist reflections on the values and uncertainties of late nineteenth-century Europe (Mitchell, 1974). Freud was at the margins of this kaleidoscope of cultural innovations and social movements, but his writing made a particular sense, albeit a sense he would not always wish, in the context of this contradictory meshwork. The sense psychoanalysis carries today is still tightly bound to these myriad cultural forms, and even the most rigid clinical practice is tied to publicly available theories of the self and other that enrich and inhibit the things that individuals think and feel. Freud compressed these cultural themes further as he identified and explored them in his patients' minds and lives. Each of his patients had to manage the tension between self-absorption and involvement in social relationships, each struggled with the impulse to be both spontaneous and seriously reflective. Every case study shows the traces of cultural representations of sexuality and Freud's views of femininity, and in each case we find a tension between cure through speech and an awareness of things that cannot be rendered into language. Freud's reports are structured by attempts to find cause, meaning and possibilities for change. The cultural context saturates psychoanalytic attempts to describe and relieve hysterical misery and common unhappiness.

Economic preconditions

Specific cultural forms were undoubtedly important in moulding certain descriptions and experiences of subjectivity in Europe and then America in the late nineteenth and early twentieth centuries, but we need to pursue this review of cultural conditions further to address the role of broader *economic* factors, and the way these are played out in the forces and relations of production. Descriptions of the civilizing process in Western culture and the production of a new 'economy of instincts' (Elias, 1994) or of the individualizing of experience in new modes of confession (Foucault, 1976) can then be located in the tension between historical driving forces of industrial development and the various sets of social relations between people that facilitate and then hinder those forces. Three factors are particularly important here.

SPEED AND PLACE   Nineteenth-century middle Europe was a place where the pace of economic development had accelerated, where it was as if time itself was racing forward at an ever-increasing rate, and where people were wrenched from geographical locations that had theretofore provided a fairly stable source of identity. The 1848 *Communist Manifesto* described the development of capitalism as a vortex of change: 'All that is solid melts into air' (Marx and Engels, 1848: 37). This striking phrase has become emblematic of the way our ostensibly 'postmodern' sensibility was inaugurated at the *beginning* of capitalist modernity (Berman, 1982). Notions of progress, and the stretching of horizons to the future, were now to be found at a societal level and in personal experiences of the past and an ever-changing present. This civilization was marked by technological achievement and hopes for the future, but at the same time discontents multiplied for individuals reflecting on their own uncertain development and trajectory.

Time and space, hitherto settled and governed by the gods, were now disrupted by the imperatives of rapid progress and fragmentation: 'All fixed, fast-frozen relations, with their train of ancient and venerable prejudices and opinions, are swept away, all new-formed ones become antiquated before they can ossify' (Marx and Engels, 1848: 36). We can discover each of these dimensions of uncertainty – time and space – in the way that social identity under capitalism is disrupted and reconstructed (Harvey, 1989). Psychoanalysis expresses these disturbances in narratives and places of identity, and it reconstructs out of the fragments of the old images of the self a new subjectivity that carries within it to the core a sense of ambivalence and anxiety. This was a kind of psychoanalytic subjectivity *before* Freud captured it in his patients' free associations and self-descriptions.

COMMODITY AND IDENTITY   At the very moment that modernity breaks apart all 'fixed fast-frozen relations', the burgeoning market economy appears to solve problems of identity by fixing attention upon the objects that pass between people rather than on human nature itself. This new economy is built around the commodity form – something that can be separated from human labour – and this form becomes the template not only for the objects a human self may create in the working day, but also for the kind of self that sells itself to another for a certain period of time and then only escapes for sufficient time to recuperate and reproduce itself away from work. Work and play are split apart, and each self is split from others. Just as the dynamic of innovation set in play by capitalism has both an exciting and threatening side, so the economically driven shift of attention from human essence to social relationships is both helpful and mystifying, enlightening and obscuring. Each self must participate in the social order to survive, but only on condition that each self markets itself against the others. Again, all the uncertainties of the postmodern condition turn out to have been with us from the birth of the modern, and the modern self is split between the hope that things may change for the better and the fear that all may be lost as change overwhelms it (Frosh, 1991).

On the one hand, this is an economic climate in which it makes some sense to say, with Marx (1845: 423), that the human essence is not something pre-given but 'is the ensemble of the social relations'. On the other hand, the circulation of commodities – products, pieces of money and workers – gives to this social world the appearance of being only a world of things, objects to be bought and sold. For human beings, this brings into play a tension; between their status as a commodity in a machinic system of production and consumption on the one side, and their experience of creative engagement and enjoyment of the fruits of that system on the other. There is a second compounding aspect to the puzzle of identity, then, which is where we look to external objects as the only real things in the world and we define the self in relation to those things. Psychoanalysis, of course, revolves around the attempt to locate subjectivity in relation to others as 'objects', the struggle to incorporate those objects into a sense of self, and the transference relationship to others (in psychoanalytic psychotherapy) as the route to self-knowledge. Others must then be experienced as separate, but it is only through relationship with them that healthy separation can be accomplished.

UNCERTAINTY AND SELFHOOD   This economic system insists that individuals are free to sell their labour to whoever bids the highest price. There is a necessary measure of economic coercion here, of course, in so far as the workers must give over their time to another in another place in order to get money to live. However, the guiding ideological assumption that underpins this relationship of power between master and wage-slave is that the contract is entered into as if it were between sovereign individuals. It is made to seem as if selling and bidding are expressions of free choices. Again, this ascription of agency to the individual, with a vision of the person as capable of idiosyncratic feeling and rational reflection, is both progressive and reactionary. This image of the self is quite local and late-arriving on the stage of human history, and is a valuable achievement. At the same time there is an idealized notion of an independent and self-contained, an undivided and unitary self being produced here which is not always so helpful.

For every moment when that self feels secure, there is a moment of uncertainty about what the foundations for the self might be. For every success story of possessive individualism, there are agonized attempts to find what has been lost, and to define where that intangible centre of the self may be found. Capitalism poses questions to its subjects, then, about where they have come from and where they are going, about what their nature is in relation to others, and how they might reflect on and solve those problems as individuals. These questions structure how people are invited to think about themselves, and although they cannot ever be answered as such, they repeatedly provoke identity puzzles which people then struggle to answer. Capitalism constructs a place for people to experience their economic distress as a *psychological* problem and to look into themselves as if *they* were the cause of social ills.

The psychoanalytic endeavour is a quintessential reduction of public economic phenomena to the private space of the individual mind. The spirits of capitalism are rediscovered time and again in the vagaries of the human psyche, and personal distress in most descriptions of psychopathology tends to be seen as the cause rather than an effect of alienation, commodification and reification (Parker et al., 1995). Psychoanalysis reflects, compresses and reduces societal phenomena to the level of the individual. Freud read cultural processes of dislocation and fragmentation in the texts of his patients' complaints about familial and sexual relationships and looked for the sources deeper down. At the same time, there has always been a suspicion within the analytic community that essential features of unconscious psychic life are actually *collective* symbolic phenomena (Jacoby, 1977; Samuels, 1993; Wolfenstein, 1993). This book is part of an attempt inside and outside psychoanalysis to ground Freud's account of the unconscious and the talking cure in culture and to understand how that account took root. The review of concepts in psychoanalytic discourse in each chapter and the analysis of cultural phenomena which are structured by that discourse are designed to help us see why psychoanalysis needs to be taken seriously and why it feels so true to so many of us now a century after it began.

PART 1
OBJECT RELATIONS THEORIES: SELF AND SOCIETY

Yes, 'normals' who are eccentric, unhappy, and ill-adjusted are also in need in therapy. Their needs will, in time, be recognized, for they are actually the needs of our entire civilization, so that group psychotherapy with these 'normals' actually has significance for our entire social structure.

J.W. Klapman (1948: 23) *Group Psychotherapy: Theory and Practice*

Psychoanalytic clinical theory in the English-speaking world has been heavily influenced by concepts introduced quite late on in Freud's own writing. One important example is the claim that the ego itself can be 'split' by a psychical trauma, and that this would allow a kind of flight from reality that could occur in patients not otherwise thought of as psychotic (Freud, 1940b). This type of defence had been anticipated by Freud (1923a) in his description of 'disavowal' – in which there is a refusal and inability to perceive something traumatic – and then in his account of 'fetishism' – in which it is the absence of a penis on a woman's body which is felt to be traumatic, and so disavowed (Freud, 1927a). This modification of the structural model (of id, ego and super-ego) in psychoanalysis supported the idea that the ego as an internal apparatus of self-representation could be fragmented, and that this kind of psychotic distribution of 'identity' might maintain, in adult life, investments in a variety of different objects from early infancy.

Freud's writing has tended to be viewed as if it were always logically developing toward a 'final state' version, a systematic theoretical apparatus in which his descriptions of Oedipal conflicts, narcissism and the death drive could be slotted neatly into place. In the process, of course, the ambiguity and tentativeness of psychoanalytic speculation in the original German was pressed into precise technical specifications of normality and abnormality at different ages and stages. One advantage for psychoanalysts in Britain and the United States of seeing Freud in this way was that it supported their claims to be engaging in a properly scientific study and treatment of the mind. The authorized translation of the *Standard Edition*, which distorted Freud's writing to embed it more easily in natural-scientific and medical discourse, reinforced this final state version of the theory.

'Object relations theory', which is one of the termini for this train of intellectual work, has developed accounts of individual and group behaviour which run smoothly along the tracks of bourgeois humanism and empiricism: bourgeois humanism because a version of psychoanalysis was forged here which set a concern with the balancing of perceptions and preferences at the heart of the self in the context of a taken-for-granted division between individual and society; empiricism because this attention to felt conflicts inside the subject was assumed to be able to be studied by way of direct observations of infant behaviour.

The elaboration of models of internal cognitive mechanisms alongside detailed observation of infants in the United States (e.g., Stern, 1985) and Britain (e.g., Miller et al., 1989) has also made object relations psychoanalysis more attractive to Anglo-American psychologists who have long combined an empiricist preoccupation with things they can actually see with an attempt to map out something inside the head which might explain human behaviour. The object relations tradition has also, it must be said, been concerned with moral development and the defence of ethics in a hostile world, and in this respect it has worried away at some of the concerns of bourgeois humanism, at how the self can be maintained against oppressive relationships in the social world *and* be elaborated with others as part of a community.

There is no single 'object relations' theory, and as well as differences in the uptake of object relations approaches in different countries (including in the translation of the theories into French, Portuguese and Spanish, for example), there are disagreements within the psychoanalytic community as to which theorists should be included. Some North American writers are happy to gather together Melanie Klein and Donald Winnicott from Britain with Margaret Mahler and Harry Stack Sullivan under the object relations umbrella (e.g., Greenberg and Mitchell, 1983) because these writers focus on the infant's relationship with 'objects' (that is, other people or bits of people). Some see Klein as being concerned rather too much with internal processes of splitting which operate regardless of actual relationships with parental objects for her to be considered as an object relations theorist proper (e.g., Frosh, 1987), and there certainly is something grimmer and more irremediably destructive about Klein's subject than someone committed to an optimistic humanist vision of the person might be happy with.

Nevertheless, Kleinian psychoanalysis has developed alongside and in tension with the writings of object relations theorists, and it does stretch almost to breaking point some of the speculations about infant experience that we find in Winnicott and in Wilfred Bion's work. The theoretical field of 'object relations' is itself fragmented, but we can trace some common themes in Bion, Winnicott and Klein and find representations of the 'self' from these analysts circulating through the wider culture. There is, first, a concern with structure – as an internal and external matrix of relationships which anchors, contains and sustains the developing ego – and we find this extended most fruitfully in the writings of Bion in his account of groups and the 'groupishness' of human nature. Bion was a key 'Kleinian' influence on the development of psychoanalytic group psychotherapy in Britain, and we will see, in Chapter 1, that the notion of containment and the tension between the leader and the group played an important role in picking up and transforming Freud's writings on 'mass psychology'. Bion also describes images of mental state and containment that we find in institutional discourses and practices. There is, secondly, an attention to the ways in which belief systems function to maintain structures, and the role of belief as a positive, potential, 'transitional' space for thought as well as a system which locks people into place in repeated individual and group patterns, and this issue is explored in Winnicott's work. There is a tension here between how these processes might be understood and reproduced as forms of pathology or comprehended and supported as self-activity and empowerment. The Winnicottian infant is also conceived of as a site and source of care, and, as Chapter 2 demonstrates, our discourses of charity are laced through with some of the themes that Winnicott delineates and celebrates.

Thirdly, there is an analysis of structure and belief as forms of action. The structures of group mentality that Bion describes, for example, and the transitional spaces that Winnicott describes are not static but continually mutating, and they are sites of conflict and development. Klein brings to this a particular energetic pulse in which the instincts pull and tear at the inside and outside and wrench the ego and its objects in many contradictory directions at once. Kleinian work, then, holds the activity of explanation in tension with an attempt to prevent certain processes getting out of hand. Containment here operates at the interface of different lines of force, and so there is a particular attention to violence – internal, external, interpersonal and social. The Kleinian infant is at war, and we find, in Chapter 3, the Kleinian self and its projected images of society written across the texts of war in forms of psychoanalytic discourse.

1

Groups, Identity and Forms of Knowledge

among the special characteristics of crowds there are several – such as impulsiveness, irritability, incapacity to reason, the absence of judgement and of the critical spirit, the exaggeration of the sentiments, and others besides – which are almost always observed in beings belonging to inferior forms of evolution – in women, savages, and children, for instance.

Gustave Le Bon (1896: 36) *The Crowd: A Study of the Popular Mind.*

We are all members of groups, many groups. Our identity is constructed out of our engagement, willing or not, with groups that pull us simultaneously in different directions. The structure of these groups structures our sense of self, and psychoanalytic theories of group identity can help us make sense of this core of 'social psychology'. Much academic social psychology is concerned with what we do in groups, but its categories are insufficient for understanding our *experience* of being part of a larger mass (Turner et al., 1987). A psychoanalytic approach effectively deconstructs traditional oppositions in social psychology as an academic discipline; between primary groups (where we relate face-to-face with the other members) and secondary groups (where we relate only indirectly, if at all), and between reference groups (those we look to for guidance) and membership groups (those we simply happen to be a part of). For psychoanalysis, the vicarious and fantastic aspects of experiencing others in primary groups are at work just as powerfully second-hand, and the annoying compelling deference we feel toward our reference groups operates as powerfully in relation to those collections of people we want to avoid as those we choose. Freud, and psychoanalysis generally, sees all perceptions as mediated by *representations* of relationships, and those representations construct group categories as the deepest centripetal forms of relationship we will meet. A secondary group is always already a primary group, and a membership group is always already a reference group.

At the heart of group structure is the family, and that social unit determines the development of other types of group. In Western societies that family will more than likely be the dominant nuclear family form, and the imaginary reference group at work here will contain representations of the working father, the mother at home, and brothers and sisters who emulate and duplicate their parents' attributes and powers. This constellation of objects surrounds us in our own home perhaps if we have a family like that, and in the media whether we do or do not actually live in that type of household. It is this constellation of emotionally charged representations that organizes our perceptions of others. To say that this is the dominant family form is not at all to say that it is the most widespread (Gittins, 1993). It is dominant as an *image*, and that image structures our perceptions of our own 'incomplete' or 'broken' family groups. The relationships within the family are constructed as if the family were, or could be, or should be a nuclear structure. That structure is always already there, then, in secondary groups when we may never have experienced it directly in a primary group as a child, and it is always already there as a point of reference when we may never have been a member of a family.

Templates of group structure operate across a range of social arenas from school classes to work-groups to parties to crowds, and Freud (1921) attempted to show that the patterns of action in formal organizations such as churches and armies could also, once an 'understanding' of unconscious libidinal ties was developed, throw light on other apparently chaotic forms of mass action. Psychoanalytic 'understanding' also *recreates* group structure in terms of depth and energy though, and we need to keep in mind that this is powerful artificial light. This psychoanalytic view of things may seem to limit what we would like to think of as our free and spontaneous activity in groups, but groups are never simple containers with people just slopping around in them. To pretend that there is no structure at work can mystify the distribution of power, and lead to a 'tyranny of structurelessness' in which those who control the group do so covertly and without contest (Freeman, 1970). There is always structure, and it includes the structure of imaginary family groups.

Psychoanalytic group theory has shifted over the years from an account of disorganized mass behaviour, understood as underpinned by invisible and powerful structures (Freud, 1921), to studies of tightly organized rule-bound institutions which contain chaotic and unconscious desires (Trist and Murray, 1990). If we look at how it has shifted and *locate* those accounts in a cultural context, we can also locate social psychology as the discipline which constantly claims but continually fails to understand groups. The development of psychoanalytic theory can help us to understand a striking paradox in social psychology. Group psychology unwittingly reproduces, in the form it has taken in European social psychology, ideological representations of *individuality*, of what the individual can know, and how they can know it. We can use psychoanalytic theory to explore anxieties about disciplinary distinctions between social psychology and neighbouring fields and relationships within those institutions that have helped condition these conceptual problems in the discipline. We will start, then, with Freud's formalization of apparent chaos before moving on to look at work on fantasy in formal organizations, and the way that knowledge and identity are manufactured and destroyed in groups, in representations of groups in film, and then in representations of relationships in academic institutions.

Freud, the father, and the leader

Freud's (1921) *Group Psychology and the Analysis of the Ego* includes discussion of large conglomerations of people. There are problems with direct translation of Freud's German word *'Massenpsychologie'* into 'group psychology', for the phenomena he was concerned with were not at all restricted to small organized groups in the way the English title of the book would suggest (Bettelheim, 1983). The term 'mass psychology' is a little better in so far as it covers crowd behaviour, but we still need to bear in mind that Freud also included organized groups in his account. The Christian church and the army are the two main examples he focused on, but he also referred in passing to races, nations, castes, professions, and institutions (Freud, 1921: 96). Freud discusses a range of organized and disorganized mass behaviour, and the declared aim of his book is to understand a person's mental life in which 'somebody else is invariably involved' (ibid.: 95).

Billig (1976) points out that there are three levels of explanation in Freud's writings: individual processes, where Freud is describing conflict as deriving from interplay between the drives; interpersonal processes, where it is the present or past relationship between the person and others which is seen as the root cause; and social process proper, in which cultural and societal factors and properties of groups are studied. Although Freud sometimes reduces events to a biological, and so to an individual level, in *Group Psychology and the Analysis of the Ego* he explicitly attacks such attempts. He does not succeed in producing a fully social account though, for the three types of explanation he considers are still restricted to instincts, development and evolution. Each of these explananda has come to imbue the way that people in Western culture think about their relations to others in groups.

Instincts

The simplest variety of explanation in academic and popular psychology, and one at which all further explanation effectively comes to a halt, is instinct theory. All that is required here is a description of the phenomenon, and then the assertion that it is wired into the organism in some way. Anglo-American varieties of psychoanalytic psychology often jump straight to this too-convenient type of explanation. Freud developed his own theories of 'instincts', but these theories were concerned more with the complicated and changing inter-relationships between physiology and psyche than with the direct expression of the workings of biological matter on the mind. This is why Freud preferred to refer to 'drives', a better translation of the German term *'Triebe'* than instinct (Bettelheim, 1983). Psychoanalytic accounts of social action have contributed to reductionist explanations, but they are also the opposite of traditional instinct theories in that Freud and his followers *prolong* the process of explanation. Psychoanalysis sometimes seems to be the most complex variety of explanation we could find, and this is largely because human experience is necessarily the most complex thing we could try to understand, and it is continually mutating such that our explanations could never actually come to an end. Freud (1921) attacked instinct theories when they are used directly to 'explain' mass behaviour. Two writers he singled out, largely because he wanted to extract the best elements for his own account, are Gustave Le Bon and William McDougall. A third writer in the instinct tradition, Wilfred Trotter, is then discussed when he turns to evolutionary explanations.

LE BON   Gustave Le Bon is a particularly important figure, and his writing both reflected and contributed to popular cultural images of crowds (Reicher, 1982). He also had a powerful impact on early North American social psychology. Le Bon was an ambulance driver during the Paris Commune uprising of 1871 when the communards threatened the authority of the French State and the property of the French ruling class, of which Le Bon was a member. It is not surprising, then, that Le Bon was left with an abiding hatred of mass behaviour, and he set up seminars for French politicians on the threat of 'mobs', and how they could be controlled. His theories were immortalized in *The Crowd: A Study of the Popular Mind* (1896), which was to become a best-seller among US social psychologists and framed how they thought about collective action as a threat to individual rationality.

Le Bon describes a 'collective mind' at work in people when they gather together and he sees crowds of all types, all the types of group Freud is concerned with, as consisting of individuals as if they were cells in an organism. For Le Bon (1896: 28) there is 'an unconscious substratum created in the mind in the main by hereditary influences'. He identifies three characteristics of this unconscious substratum, and Freud agreed with much of the description that Le Bon provides at this point.

First, Le Bon claims that instincts are released in the crowd so that it develops a sense of invincible power such that even a 'cultivated individual' becomes a 'barbarian'. The group mind is impulsive, changeable, and irritable; it thinks in images, it knows no doubt or uncertainty, contradictory ideas coexist side by side; it hallucinates, and demands illusions. Words have an irrational magical power, and the crowd is guided by fantasy. Freud disagreed here with Le Bon's conception of the unconscious as a 'racial mind' (which is closer to Jung's rather static and mystical conception of the collective unconscious than Freud's notion of a dynamic unconscious consisting of repressed ideas). Secondly, the crowd is subject to contagion which operates like a type of hypnosis. Freud pointed out that in this account Le Bon neglects the role of the hypnotist, and this complaint will be developed as the main burden of his argument against Le Bon. Thirdly, alongside the hypnotic contagion, there is a 'magnetic'

influence of suggestion which, Le Bon says, 'gains in strength by reciprocity'. But what are the dynamics that enable this reciprocity to take
shape?

Freud agreed with Le Bon that unconscious factors are crucial, of course,
and he also agreed that the unconscious manifests historical throwbacks,
evolutionary vestiges. He even accepts Le Bon's argument that the person
in the crowd 'descends several rungs in the ladder of civilization' (Freud,
1921: 103). His main disagreement was with the insufficiency of Le Bon's
account, and there are two points here that he focused on. He claimed that
Le Bon concentrates on groups of 'short-lived character' (ibid.: 111).
Freud's argument here is actually not entirely correct, for Le Bon does take
pains to say that his descriptions apply to organizations and parlia-
mentary assemblies. Freud then made the point that Le Bon neglects the
way that 'creative genius' does not only arise individually but also sometimes collectively. This argument is similar to Wilhelm Wundt's well-
known view at the time in German social psychology that 'higher mental
processes' are present in the language and culture of the *Volk* rather than
in individual minds (Haeberlin, 1980; Danziger, 1990).

McDOUGALL   The second instinct theorist Freud tackled is William
McDougall, one of the founders of social psychology, and author of one of
the first textbooks for the discipline (McDougall, 1908). McDougall's
(1920) account goes beyond Le Bon, Freud argued, for it discusses stable
groups. To concentrate on 'mobs', as Le Bon does, neglects enduring structures: 'Groups of the first kind stand in the same sort of relation to those
of the second as a high but choppy sea to a ground swell' (Freud, 1921:
112). McDougall describes the ways in which the organization of the
masses structures their instinctually given propensities, and the role of
emotion, intensification and 'induction' of emotion in which 'the perception of the signs of an affective state is calculated automatically to arouse
the same affect in the person who perceives them' (cited in Freud, 1921:
112). Stable organization also facilitates the meting out of punishments to
those who transgress the rules of the group. These aspects of McDougall's
account will be drawn into Freud's own version of group psychology.
McDougall then goes on to argue that there are five conditions for the
raising of collective mental life to a higher level: continuity of existence; a
definite 'idea' to bind the group; interaction with other groups; the existence of traditions and customs that the group shares; and the differentiation of specific roles for constituent members.

Freud was unhappy with McDougall's account because the collective
realm here seems to have assumed a thing-like status, and he went on to
offer his own explanation which emphasizes factors which work
somewhere between the social and the individual. He criticized Le Bon
from a social angle and McDougall from an individual angle, and what
this delicate rhetorical balancing act leads to is a middle position in which
'there is a reduction of complex social phenomena, which might form the

basis of a "mass" psychology, to an individual or interpersonal psychology, in which the family becomes the prototype of the social group' (Billig, 1976: 24). However, the repercussions of this go further, for Freud then tried to explain how it is that we experience ourselves as cells in a collective body *and* how we are able 'to equip the group with the attributes of the individual' (Freud, 1921: 115). This led him to a *double reduction* of social phenomena in which what goes on in the individual becomes the explanation for group behaviour, and in which the group can be treated as a self-sufficient level in so far as it functions like a giant individual. The family as prototype of mass activity is explored further when Freud turned to a developmental account.

Development

Freud wanted to take seriously, and explain, some of the phenomena which Le Bon and McDougall drew attention to, such as contagion in groups: 'something exists in us which, when we become aware of signs of an emotion in someone else, tends to make us fall into the same emotion' (Freud, 1921: 117). He did this by using the concept of 'libido', but we have to bear in mind that Freud used this concept in different ways at different points in his writings. Libido is sometimes talked about as an energy, an 'instinct', or a drive. It is sometimes used as a word for love in the widest sense of the term, as 'Eros', and it is also sometimes given a wider explanatory meaning as a love which 'constitutes the essence of the group mind' (ibid.: 120).

Freud draws attention to the structure of two enduring groups, the Christian church and the army, in order to arrive at an adequate account of the way in which the libido is structured. In both of these groups there is a head, or if there is no head there is at least a 'leading idea', and there are two sorts of tie; a tie which unites each individual with the leader, and a tie which unites each with another. This means that with regard to Christ or the captain 'everyone has an equal share in his love' (ibid.: 123). There is always panic when the structure of the group breaks down, and the panic follows the break-down because the 'disintegration of the group' means the 'disappearance of emotional ties' which hold the group together, and there is persecution when someone attempts to leave the group, together with a continual intolerance of outsiders. Freud then explored the nature of the libidinal ties in the group by drawing attention to three other processes or mechanisms.

The first is *narcissism*, in which we attempt to regain, and we regress to, the fantasized point of fusion with the mother. The ego-ideal (the heir of narcissism) is regulated by the development of the super-ego (the heir of the Oedipus complex), but we cannot help loving those who replace our earliest love objects, and we resent those who threaten to disrupt that first most intense love. There is 'a sediment of feelings of aversion and hostility, which only escapes perception as a result of repression' (ibid.: 130), and so we have to take account of the 'ambivalence of feeling' (ibid.: 131) in group relations. One manifestation of this is in the way we actively have to turn our narcissistic love for ourselves outwards and transform it into a love which binds people together: 'Love for oneself knows only one barrier – love for others, love for objects' (ibid.: 132).

The second process is *identification*, which follows on developmentally from narcissism and the disruption to narcissism that the experience of separate others provokes. Here Freud ran through three permutations of relationships in a family to show how group processes follow patterns of symptom formation: The child may identify with the mother to gain the father's love ('the complete mechanism of the structure of a hysterical symptom', ibid.: 136); the child may identify with the loved father to gain the father as love object ('object-choice is turned back into identification – the ego assumes the characteristics of the object', ibid.); or the child may identify with one of the siblings so to have the father's love ('the mark of a point of coincidence between the two egos which has to be kept repressed', ibid.). Each pattern of relating to the father is a pattern of relating to a leader in a group.

The third process which Freud described alongside narcissism and identification is *idealization*, in which we construct our ego-ideal. The leader of the group is a powerful invested object in which 'the object serves as a substitute for some unattained ego-ideal of our own' (ibid.: 143). At an extreme point, the ego subordinates itself to an over-evaluated object so that 'the object has, so to speak, consumed the ego' (ibid.). This relation, Freud says, is a hypnotic relation, and it is as if the hypnotist has stepped in the place of the ego-ideal. With this he arrives at 'the formula for the libidinal constitution of groups' (ibid.: 147). The group is 'a number of individuals who have put one and the same object in the place of their ego-ideal and have consequently identified themselves in their ego' (ibid.).

Evolution

Freud then supplemented his developmental account with an evolution-ary account. Here he drew on some of the anthropological material he used in his explanations of religion (which we will discuss in Chapter 2). The main figure he took on here to clarify the role of evolution in the struc-ture of groups is Wilfred Trotter. Trotter's (1919) book *Instincts of the Herd in Peace and War* reduces group behaviour to an individual level, as do Le Bon and McDougall, but Trotter argues that the 'herd instinct' is a positive attribute of people in groups, and manifests the gregariousness of human nature. Again, though, it is the neglect of the role of the leader which Freud concentrated upon. Children are afraid when they are alone, but whereas Trotter would say that the 'herd instinct' is responsible for this fear, Freud argued that the fear flows from the infant coping with jealous rivalry of siblings for the attentions of the parents by identifying with them: 'So there grows up in the troop of children a communal or group feeling, which is then further developed at school. The first demand made by this reaction-formation is for justice, for equal treatment for all' (Freud, 1921: 151). One way of ensuring that others cannot have what we want for ourselves is to advocate the principle that we should all be equal, have the same, and maybe then, if necessary, have nothing. Freud also corrected Trotter's characterization of the human being as a 'herd animal', by saying that it would be better to say that the human being is a 'horde animal, an individual creature in a horde led by a chief' (ibid.: 153).

Freud then developed this argument by turning to anthropological work on 'primal hordes'. The events in the primal horde, which are relayed through to the present day as an 'archaic heritage', form a bedrock for the child's perceptions of the parents, and of the father as the leader, and so 'the psychology of groups is the oldest human psychology' (ibid.: 155). The primal father in the horde is both feared and loved by the sons (and here Freud characteristically slips from explanations of human psychology into a psychology of men), and this primal father reappears in the hypnotic relation between a leader and followers in a group: 'The primal father is the group ideal, which governs the ego in the place of the ego ideal' (ibid.: 160). Freud is quite deliberately adopting, then, a Lamarckian theory of evolution in which he supposes that it is possible to transmit characteristics acquired during one's lifetime to one's offspring. Freud's key supposition, then, is that the leader is vital to any account of group psychology. The relationship between members of the primal horde, and the 'primal father' is repeated in mass behaviour, and provides its underlying structure. In *Civilization and its Discontents* (1930) Freud argues that leaderless groups are psychologically impoverished.

Group structures and social structures

There are a number of problems in Freud's account. The anthropological evidence is challenged by present-day researchers, and to develop the line that the history of the primal horde is a 'Just-So Story', as he suggested it might be taken to be (Freud, 1921: 154), would have severe repercussions for his argument that this history is inherited as part of the biological make-up of human beings. We could say that a potent myth of the 'primal horde' operates in culture, and so structures our unconscious as we develop as individuals, but then we would also be saying that human psychology is not *necessarily* of this kind, and that the human being is not at root a 'horde animal' at all. Freud's account does also slide from talking about human beings into talking about men ('the brothers'), and he fails to address points in Le Bon's description of regression in crowds to lower stages of evolution (quoted at the beginning of this chapter) in which women (along with savages and children) are treated as lesser. Le Bon had noticed that many of the participants in the Paris Commune were women, and was horrified by this. If the answer lies in evolution, how do we account for the experience of women in groups? Again, a reworking of this in terms of powerful myths of the horde would allow us to address the question of how male and female psychology has changed over history, but it would severely undercut Freud's attempt to explain group psychology as an evolutionary and developmental process.

Perhaps we would then have to lay more emphasis on what actually does happen in the infant's relations with the parents, lay more emphasis on the developmental story, and include an account of the differential treatment of boys and girls and the theories about themselves that they acquire from their culture. Although it has been argued that because Freud neglects 'sex differences' in his developmental account, and does not specify how the girl negotiates the Oedipus complex, he cannot explain how women relate to leaders of the same and opposite gender (Billig, 1976), this is really not so much an issue for psychoanalysis, because it is the *structural* qualities of that relation – self, desired other and threatening other – that affect later perceptions of a leader. Our task would then be to examine how men and women are constituted as members of groups differently in various cultural contexts.

Freud's account of group psychology should also be seen in the context of contemporary political events. At the time of his visits to France toward the end of the nineteenth century (in 1885 to 1886 and then in 1889), there were countless scares around in the press about revolutionary mobs, and there were a number of examples of the assassination of state leaders and the end of regimes. In Vienna, Freud had the powerful example of 'sons murdering fathers' in the name of justice in 1916, when Friedrich, the more radical son of socialist leader Victor Adler assassinated Emperor Franz Joseph's prime minister, Count Stürgkh: 'Friedrich Adler (instead of Victor Adler) shot Premier Stürgkh (instead of Emperor Franz Joseph). Psychologically speaking, it was exactly the parricide in the name of fraternity which Freud considered as the core of every revolution' (Van Ginneken, 1984: 403). Following the October Revolution in Russia in 1917, there had been uprisings in many cities of Eastern and Middle Europe (with communes springing up in Berlin and Budapest in 1919). The memories of these events were very recent, not at all part of an archaic heritage, and fresh in Freud's mind. Alongside the pattern of the nuclear family which Freud appealed to in his account of development, then, were particular patterns of 'mass psychology', and he naturalized these patterns while trying to avoid a straightforward instinct explanation which would tie human behaviour and experience too closely to a biological bedrock.

The descriptions Freud offered were meant to apply to the *Masse*, and to crowds as much as to small groups, and a further problem here concerns the effects of describing crowd events as regression, whether evolutionary or developmental. Some recent social psychological writers on crowds would argue that Freud provided a better theory than Le Bon, but that the image of the crowd as chaotic and subject to contagion masks the *rational* activities of crowds (Reicher, 1982). It may, of course, be more helpful in some contexts to emphasize irrational aspects of crowd behaviour, and the ways in which people are not always responsible for their actions, and there have been some bitter debates over the role psychological knowledge has played in political trials under apartheid in South Africa (Colman, 1991a). The political consequences of images of crowds as rational or irrational will be affected by the circumstances in which the crowds form and act (Colman, 1991b; Reicher, 1991). Some writers have drawn attention to the general crowd-like experience of human beings in mass-society, in which individuals are addressed as if they were in a crowd even when they are on their own. The work of Moscovici (1986) on 'the age of the crowd', for example, draws attention to the 'social representations' which are shared among a population, and the ways those representations structure subjectivity. The 'Just-So Story' about the primal horde is relayed through these kinds of representations, or, I would prefer to say, through discourses and discursive complexes.

The social psychological theory of 'social representations' was part of a sustained attempt by the discipline to develop fully *social* explanations of identity and shared knowledge. It is, in many ways, compatible with the framework used in this book. It has failed, however, to prevent the recent return of interest in *individual* behaviour and cognition. To understand why that is so, it will be instructive to look at how psychoanalytic representations of the group have affected social psychology, and how a sense of panic was spread in the discipline in the last quarter century which provoked social psychologists to draw in closer as a group and protect their boundaries against alien forms of knowledge. First, however, we need to look at developments in group theory in psychoanalysis which focus upon individual identity as a *product* of threatening experiences in groups. These developments harvest and disseminate representations of groups which function far more powerfully now than Freud's accounts.

To the mother, object relations and Bion

Freud's (1921: 95) assertion that 'somebody else is invariably involved' in what appear to be individual private mental activities is a corner-stone of object relations theory. The tradition of research in and around the Tavistock Institute of Human Relations in the UK includes use of object relations theory, and it reflects a shift of emphasis from the infantile relationship to the father to the relationship to the mother in British Psychoanalysis generally. This was later the case for each of the three recognized tendencies in the British Psycho-Analytical Society (the followers of Anna Freud in the B group, now the 'contemporary Freudian group', the Kleinians in the A group, now the 'Klein group', and the Independents in the Middle group, now termed the 'Independent group'). There is also a corresponding shift from seeing the rational individual as at risk in groups to saying that irrational desires are *contained* by groups.

This does not mean that groups are now necessarily seen as 'good things', but that the organization of the group is seen as improvable, and with that improvement will come benefits for the individual.

In some ways the shift of emphasis in British object relations group psychology picks up Freud's own statements about the importance of narcissism in groups which do suggest that events before the Oedipus complex have an important bearing on group behaviour, and his acknowledgement, for example in his consideration of McDougall's work, that properly structured groups are helpful and necessary to human development. While Freud provided a theoretical account of group psychology, those around the Tavistock tradition attempted to develop an account which was part of their practice in organizations. Varieties of action research were used alongside psychoanalytic theory, and the Tavistock tradition also turned its attention to work. For Wilfred Bion (1961, 1970), the 'work-group' was the fundamental unit of analysis in psychotherapy too (Bléandonu, 1994). This attention to work as a key activity in group (and individual) experience is helpful, but at the same time the bulk of the Tavistock's research looked at things from the point of view of managers rather than the workforce (a problem which also plagues much early social-psychological action research in Britain and America).

Freud provides an historical account of the development of *individual* psychology in a postscript to *Group Psychology and the Analysis of the Ego* (Freud, 1921: 167–178), in which the group is seen as the 'primitive' basis of human psychology, and individuality arises over the course of time in pre-history as the travelling poet, who is a relayer of myths of nascent human culture, identifies with the exploits of an increasingly differentiated hero figure. His listeners then identify with the poet, and so they also become differentiated from the group. In this account, separate individual identity is a secondary and fairly recent phenomenon. This is an account of the emergence of the individual from the group, which Bion takes further.

Bion's knowledge

Bion's work on group cohesion and individual defence can be understood against the background of problems of group identity at a time of war, and the training of individuals to lead others. Bion's ideas were developed in a powerful institution, that of military training and rehabilitation in Britain during the Second World War. Psychiatrists from the Tavistock Clinic (which was originally founded in 1920 as the 'Tavistock Institute of Medical Psychology'), including Bion, joined the Directorate of Army Psychiatry in 1941, and it was from this that a number of innovations in psychoanalytic practice were developed, including 'command psychiatry', 'social psychiatry', the 'therapeutic community' and 'cultural psychiatry for the analysis of the enemy mentality' (Trist and Murray, 1990: 4). The strength of the home forces organization and morale was the focus in the experiments at Northfield Military Hospital in Birmingham which started in 1942, and this was the seed-bed of Group Analysis in the UK (Pines, 1985). At the same time as providing an important theoretical elaboration of psychoanalytic group psychology, then, Bion's work was embedded in an institutional climate in which the individual was a key focus as a source of strength against forms of 'group' mentality.

Knowledge, for Bion, is produced through processes of digestion, abstraction and construction in which raw psychic material, meaningless sensations, perceptions and words, are worked into a form that will help the person to understand the outside and the inside and the relation between the two (Grinberg et al., 1975). What Bion calls the 'alpha function' of thinking turns nonsense, a morass of so-called 'beta elements', into sense, but that process is not an easy one, and the task of building connections is fraught. The presence of others in the external world and the fragmented character of the internal world give rise to blocks and frustrations to the development of knowledge, and contradictions in the way we understand the world. Bion uses the term 'link' to capture the ways in which relations with others or parts of the self structure knowledge.

For Bion, knowledge is not a possession but a process, it is not an individual property but a function of a *relationship*. In the process of thinking, we attempt to contain the process of the acquisition of knowledge, and look to an 'other' to contain ourself. For Bion, knowledge is produced in a relationship between container and contained. Knowledge about oneself, what has been termed 'the psychoanalytic function of the personality' (ibid.: 37), is always constituted within a group. This form of knowledge is the 'K link'. Bion is employing a notion of knowledge as something that is changing, dynamic and provisional, and to 'learn from experience' is to engage in a process of continual reflection and transformation:

> It is necessary to distinguish between the 'acquisition of knowledge' as a result of a *modification* of pain and frustration in the K-link (in which case the knowledge acquired will be employed for further discoveries) and the 'possession of knowledge' that is used to evade the painful and frustrating experience.
>
> (Grinberg, 1985: 183)

It is a mistake to imagine that we can 'have' knowledge as something that is fixed and permanent (Bion, 1962). Whether we are giving and receiving sensations and meanings to one other in a two-person group in early infancy, or to many others in a larger group in later life, thought is completed and constructed as a form of knowledge which is formed as the contained within a form of container. Catastrophic change occurs when the relationship between container and contained breaks down, and when the boundaries are destroyed. Chaos and pain in the catastrophe produce an attempt not to know, an epistemological figure in which knowledge is evacuated, offloaded, passed on, forgotten. This is what Bion calls 'minus K'.

Minus K is both the opposite of knowledge, and a substitute for it. The running loose of minus K can be seen as a form of psychopathology in which the activity of knowing is turned around against itself. Bion saw minus K, or the 'minus-K-link', as the psychotic area of the personality, and this minus-K-link is charged with envy and greed, a spoiling and destruction of the very container it tries to save (Grinberg, 1985). For, like other psychotic processes, the apparent fragmentation and disorder belies a desperate attempt to reconstruct a form of order, and minus K is a form that can be highly functional in institutions. Minus K, as well as being a mass of non-knowledge, is also an injunction 'not to know', and the celebration of deliberate and studied stupidity, the pushing away and ruin of knowledge. To avoid knowing is also to avoid responsibility, and so the evacuation of knowledge can operate as an efficient shared defence against information or ideas that are threatening.

Studies of hospital wards by Menzies-Lyth (1959) illustrated the ways in which bureaucratic and nonsensical procedures function as shared defences against anxiety. The presence of death, for example, can be hidden from the nurses when the patients are treated as collections of symptoms or body parts (such as 'the liver in bed ten') rather than as very ill human beings. A lot of the talk which structures the life of the ward, and in particular the continual relaying of useless information from nurse to nurse, from shift to shift, can be understood as minus K (Bell, 1996). Whenever we are being subjected to someone offloading things they 'know', which they do not want to know, and which it will not help us to know, we are in the presence of minus K.

If Bion is right, then attempts to define strict group boundaries should be seen as a response to anxiety, the fear of an impending catastrophe. This provides a further context for the development of preoccupations with group identity, and the emergence of the individual in the group can be seen as a defence. Rather than individuality being seen as eroded by groups, Bion's work leads us to view the figure of the individual as a *product* of difficult group states.

Bionic man

A fantasy that holds a group together as a group with a task, a group behaving rationally, is that it is simply a 'work-group'. The work-group is a kind of mental state. The work-group is an important and productive fantasy, but a fantasy nonetheless. Against the wish that there is only a work-group are unconscious collective forces that Bion (1961) calls 'basic assumption states', and he identifies three: 'dependency', 'fight–flight', and 'pairing'. The operation of these basic assumption states also occurs at an institutional level; when we are dependent on the leader as an individual who will save the group, when we attack or flee from other individuals who threaten the group, or when we wait for a couple in a group to produce a magical idea which will solve the group's problems.

Each basic assumption state helps us to constitute our-selves as individuals as a defence against the group; as a leader or as singled out by the leader for special attention, as a distanced observer of the madness of the group as it fights or escapes, or as the saviour of the group in the couple that will produce the solution.

There is a fundamental theoretical point here in Bion's work where he insists that the human being is a group animal, and this point is picked up by analysts using Bion to describe the way in which the individual emerges as a product of group fantasy (Wolfenstein, 1990). The work of object relations theorists in psychoanalysis helps open the way to a reconceptualization of the relationship between individual experience and group behaviour. Such a reconceptualization goes beyond the dichotomy of the individual versus group levels of explanation and the fiction that looking to an interpersonal level of explanation somewhere between the two resolves that dichotomy. Wolfenstein (1990), for example, using Bion's work, argues that an understanding of group psychology could also help us to understand how it is that individuals both feel alienated in groups *and* submerge themselves in groups. Freud (1921) argues that group psychology is the most basic form of human psychology, and it is this point that is taken forward by Bion:

> The individual is, and always has been, a member of a group, even if his membership of it consists of behaving in such a way that reality is given to an idea that he does not belong to a group at all. The individual is a group animal at war, both with the group and with those aspects of his personality that constitute his 'groupishness'.
>
> (Bion, 1961: 168; and quoted in Wolfenstein, 1990: 160)

Like Bion, Wolfenstein looks to the relationship of the infant to the mother to explain experiences in groups: 'The ontogenetic foundation of group psychology is the relatively undifferentiated union of mother and infant' (Wolfenstein, 1990: 174). Groups provoke fantasies, and the idea that to be an 'individual' who might be responsible and free of the frustration and anger projected into a group (and possibly experienced by it as if it were an undifferentiated mob) is a form of defence. In a culture which pathologizes collective action (Reicher, 1982), such a defence is all the more likely. The member of a group may retreat into his or her 'individuality' as a form of escape, or a special 'individual' may be formed as 'leader' (or as someone specific inside or outside to be attacked), and in this way '"The individual" is an element in a group fantasy' (Wolfenstein, 1990: 174). Such fantasies are not only important to small groups, but, as in the case of Freud's writings on groups, these ideas are seen as applicable to organizations of all kinds. There is, argues Wolfenstein, a powerful fantasy at work in groups of all kinds that there are such things as individuals who exist independently of society, who could be separate from it: '*"the individual" (a self conceived outside of society and essentially constituted from the inside out) is a group phantasy*' (Wolfenstein, 1990: 154).

This theoretical account of the way the individual erupts from group experience is useful, but we also need to *locate* Bionic versions of object relations theory to understand why they work this way in this culture. Bion crystallized a particular way of talking about what he calls 'the psychoanalytic object', and it is necessary to read him alongside the argument that discourses constitute the objects of which they speak (Foucault, 1969; Parker, 1992).

Culture, crises and heroes

Psychoanalysis has percolated into the popular imagination of the West through a variety of media, one of the most powerful being film (Sekoff, 1989), and images of war and internal cohesion and conflict in groups have been important cultural settings for, and means of, transmission for Bion's ideas. The key genre here is the disaster movie.

In the disaster movie, a small group faces death, usually as a result of natural forces out of control or as a result of a breakdown of technological support. The characters must resolve the interpersonal tensions in the group to survive; they must work together, and typically the lives and foibles of each individual weave together as the drama unfolds. The disaster movie is actually quite a short-lived phenomenon. There are anticipations of the genre in the plane crash scenarios, in which a group of survivors battle against the elements, tribesmen or wild animals. These run from the late 1930s when Bion was first starting his War Selection Board work using group tasks. A first example is *Five Came Back* in 1939, and this sequence continued sporadically through the 1950s and 1960s, with *Back from Eternity* in 1955, and *Sands of the Kalahari* and *Flight of the Phoenix* both from 1965. The preoccupation with the effects of plane crashes is symptomatic, perhaps, of an unconscious military sub-text in these films, and strong leadership is usually a crucial ingredient to the group succeeding in reaching civilization.

The disaster movie's heyday was in the 1970s. One listing of 'Disaster movies' in a British film guide published in 1991 (Milne, 1991) includes *Krakatoa – East of Java* (1968) and *Airport* (1969), but the other fifteen films listed, apart from *The Last Voyage* (1960), which is about a luxury liner exploding, are from the 1970s. (Krakatoa, incidentally, is West of Java.) The first in the 1970s cycle was *The Poseidon Adventure*, about an upturned sinking ship. It is interesting to note that this appeared in the same year as two of the first texts in what is referred to as the 'crisis' in social psychology: Israel and Tajfel's (1972) *The Context of Social Psychology: A Critical Assessment* and Harré and Secord's (1972) *The Explanation of Social Behaviour*. The success of *The Poseidon Adventure* led to a number of films in 1974 set in exploding ships, fragmenting cities, burning skyscrapers and airborne passenger jets – *Juggernaut, Earthquake, The Towering Inferno* and *Airport 1975*, which was actually released in 1974. These films appeared in the same year as the two other key 'crisis' texts in social psychology: Armistead's (1974) *Reconstructing Social Psychology* and Marsh, Rosser and Harré's (1974) *The Rules of Disorder*.

The sky disaster movies carried on with *Airport '77* before petering out with *The Concord: Airport '79*. One of the last films in the genre, *Meteor* (1979), connected with science fiction and cold-war themes, but by this time the series had run its course. One would need a broader and more thorough cultural and political analysis to explain exactly why the disaster movie died in 1979. It was the year Margaret Thatcher seized power in Britain, and it would be possible, perhaps, to argue that the gradual incubation of individual identity in small groups on the screen was succeeded by the eruption of a charismatic individual on the political stage. What is important here is that what appears to be a social form, the group, actually contains and embeds a form of *individual* identity.

It should be remembered that the quintessential disaster movie brings together as a group an assortment of stars, and the distinct individual quality of each person is played out in their struggle together, and their struggle against irrationality in the group. Once again, the individual emerges as a group fantasy in the viewer's identification with them projected on the screen. This is a form of narrative in which the viewer is left watching a broken group, perhaps with the remaining individuals clutching to one another, in a repetition of the way in which characters in the film are left watching a broken physical form, of a plane, ship or building. And the group itself is left as a meaningless shell, like the physical container that dissolved around it, leaving the audience with a feeling of not having learnt from experience, being left with minus K.

Social psychology and identity

If we turn to academic social psychology to see what it has to say about these issues, we find a paradox. For although it is a discipline which has group behaviour as one of its key topics, it seems unwilling or unable to account for its own structure as a discipline, its own forms of thinking and organization. We can now throw that paradox into sharper relief by tracing the ways in which academic social psychology exemplifies and reproduces many of the group phenomena described by psychoanalytic writers precisely by virtue of its denial of the possibility of those phenomena being real. The remainder of this chapter will illustrate Bion's approach to groups, use that approach to explain how social psychology struggles to understand groups and fails, and locate this version of psychoanalytic theory as cultural matter.

The discipline of social psychology has its origins in the United States, and there was in the early years of the century a concern with the efficiency of rational individuals working together and against the threat of an irrational group spirit taking over (Parker, 1989). Although there was some opposition to this individualism, it was only in the 1960s that an alternative tradition developed, in Europe, that seemed strong enough to resist it. It was then thought that the thorough re-evaluation of the objects of study and research goals of the discipline at the end of the 1960s and beginning of the 1970s, during the so-called 'crisis' in the discipline, had accomplished a double shift away from the traditional North American and reductionist assumptions which had hitherto held sway (Israel and Tajfel, 1972; Tajfel, 1972). A necessary and progressive shift of attention from North American research (Moscovici, 1972; Doise, 1978) was to be accompanied by a rejection of the individual as the focus of research (Billig, 1976; Tajfel, 1979). Out-dated North American social psychology, which reduced explanation to the level of the individual, would be replaced by a new European social psychology focused on the group.

For a while this shift seemed to have done the trick. In Europe, the emphasis on groups as the source of social identity and individual self-hood was exemplified in the work of Henri Tajfel and co-workers on minimal groups (Tajfel, 1970; Tajfel et al., 1971), and the European tradition, which links this group focus with work on social representations and ideological processes (Doise, 1978; Farr and Moscovici, 1984) is institutionalized in, among other places, the *European Journal of Social Psychology*. The *British Journal of Social Psychology* has been heavily influenced by this tradition, in part because Tajfel was based at Bristol while the key work and intellectual cadre for social identity theory was being accumulated (Billig, 1976; Turner et al.,1987; Condor, 1989), and the tradition has found an echo in North America, where it appeared to provide an alternative to reductionist research (Brewer, 1979; Wilder, 1981).

After two decades of group research, however, European social psychology is showing signs of embracing, once again, *individual* psychology as the core of research into group behaviour. If one compares the spread of articles in the *European Journal of Social Psychology* between the 1970s and the 1990s, for example, one finds a striking change of emphasis. The image of the individual has become progressively more important inside those very group frameworks that challenged reductionism in social psychology. To take some examples from 1992 and 1993: one finds cognitive models of stereotype change replacing group identity notions (Hewstone et al., 1992), and minority group status being represented as the background for individual action (Ellemers et al., 1992); the 'power-distance reduction' framework is used to study individual power bids (Bruins and Wilke, 1993), 'egocentric' social categorization is used as an explanatory concept in ingroup bias (Simon, 1993), and even class is conceptualized as if it were simply a collection of individual cognitive processes (Evans, 1993). It is possible to put this change of emphasis down to wider political transformations in the cultural landscape in Western Europe over the last twenty years, with more interest in the individual as locus of action than in the collective. However, the particular way in which the image of the individual emerges again within group studies that took so much care to challenge individualist explanations is still a puzzle. One way of solving that puzzle is to attend to anxieties about knowledge in social psychology and basic assumption states in academic institutions.

Social constructionism and minus K

As well as provoking a 'turn to the group' in the European tradition, the debates during that crisis period in social psychology can also be viewed as stimulating a 'turn-to-language' (Parker, 1989). The early 1970s 'new paradigm' social psychologies (e.g., Harré and Secord, 1972; Gauld and Shotter, 1977) have been transformed in recent years by a broader and more thorough-going 'turn-to-discourse'. The mixture of symbolic inter-actionism (Mead, 1934) and dramaturgy (Goffman, 1959) in 'ethogenic' social psychology (Harré, 1979, 1983) and hermeneutic approaches (Shotter, 1975, 1984) have given way, through the emergence of discourse analysis (Parker, 1992; Burman and Parker, 1993) to a view of social reality and individual identity as constituted by language. The common thread in these developments, one which also underpins this book, and which has been pushed to the limit in recent writing on 'postmodern' psychology (Gergen, 1991; Kvale, 1992), is the idea that psychological phenomena are socially constructed. This turning point, a revolution in knowledge, is one significant setting for debates over individual and social identity. The stakes are very high when such claims are made about paradigm changes, for a scientific revolution is a transformation in epistemology, in ways of knowing (Kuhn, 1970). Once the possibility of epistemological rupture was broached, it seemed to many that the discipline of social psychology could never be the same again.

The idea that social psychology should 'turn to language' did not simply fall from the sky, of course. Changes in knowledge are anchored in discursive practices, and there was something in the nature of the institution and in the cultural and political forces that pressed upon the institution during the 1960s that we need to take account of. A social constructionist account needs to attend to such forces to understand how academic knowledge is itself socially constructed at particular points in history. It is significant that the key ideas in this paradigm revolution flooded in from other disciplines; symbolic interactionism and ethno-methodology from sociology, a focus on ordinary language and language games from philosophy, semiotics and deconstruction from literary theory. It is also striking that with every celebration of interdisciplinarity there was renewed anxiety about the integrity of the discipline of social psychology among its practitioners (Eiser, 1980; Zajonc, 1989). The proper field of study of social psychology as a science was under threat as the boundaries of the group, of the group of social psychologists differentiated from colleagues doing much the same or more interesting work in neighbouring disciplines, seemed to dissolve.

One way of accounting for the rise of the study of minimal groups and social identity theory in the 1970s would be to stress the role of the group in theory as an emblem of the social psychology research group, and the re-marking of boundaries as the recasting of academic identity at a time of uncertainty. The focus on differentiation from others, the marking of identity in relation to outgroups, and the function of group membership as a natural and universal property of human cognition can be interpreted as a warrant for the particular differentiation and separation of *social psychology* as a group, and its comparison with adjacent groups of researchers. Again, as a theory of social representations opens up the boundaries between psychology and sociology (Farr and Moscovici, 1984), all the more effort is channelled into surrounding each cluster of social representations with the ringfence of a group. The reception of social representations in Britain, for example, has been marked by an attempt to integrate it with Social Identity frameworks (Hewstone et al., 1982). It could be argued that social representations can only be conceptualized by experimental social psychologists when they are held by securely delimited group boundaries. In this respect, Moscovici plus Tajfel equals a new 'container' for safe research.

Social constructionism, a new relativism, is not necessarily radical as such, but in this discipline now it is very subversive (Curt, 1994). It cannot be contained by the dominant group which is tightly wedded to positivism and feels its identity to be under threat, and it is attacked by the group as a form of nonsense, as non-science or a bizarre object called 'deconstructionism', for example (Secord, 1991). Because social constructionism has been associated with post-structuralist theory and even psychoanalysis (Parker and Shotter, 1990), the fear may have been that the entry of one idea would permit a flood of more extreme notions. The revival of interest in psychoanalysis in academic institutions in Britain has been a further particular source of tension, and although this revival has been, as yet, mainly in neighbouring disciplines, experimental social psychologists have found this a worrying development, and on occasions have tried to stop it (Stanton, 1990).

It is sometimes difficult to imagine what exactly the traditionalists think would happen if this epistemological revolution ran its course. It does seem as if a host of dangers are associated with the success of relativist ideas, and that the increase of such ideas will eventually produce a crisis of massive proportions, leading eventually to the disintegration of the discipline. The consequence, while difficult to formulate, is that something awful would happen. The social constitution of research objects throws into question the whole experimental apparatus, and social constructionist conceptions of knowledge threaten the accumulation of data and careful empirical testing of theories. The important message which appears to run through such anxieties and complaints is that an *absence* of knowledge is better than this type of knowledge. Much positivist social psychology is so removed from real life that it does sometimes seem as if readers of journals and textbooks are being subjected to minus K, and that researchers in the discipline would prefer to continue circulating nonsense rather than engage with social constructionist critiques of what they have been doing.

The crisis as a turning point in the history of the discipline, as a turn to the group or a turn to language, is compounded, then, by the anxieties among social psychologists that disciplinary group boundaries may be threatened. It has been suggested so far that such anxiety over the nature of academic identity may have been one of the factors in the development of a research interest in groups as a source of social identity, but this argument can be pressed further if the ways in which the organization of knowledge may be affected at times of crisis are explored, and notice is taken of the corresponding fear that the crisis in social psychology is part of a more general disruption to intellectual work. Here it is necessary to consider the institutional context for knowledge generation.

Basic assumptions in academic institutions

The interest in 'social comparison' in academic social psychology as the basis for group identity can be understood as the reflection of anxieties about the breakdown of differentiation from other disciplinary groups. Bion's work can also throw light on the ways in which the *individual* emerges as a defence against the breakdown of the group at times of crisis. The figure of the 'individual' emerges from the group at times of threat as a defence against the group, and particular forms of group behaviour provoke individual responses, and the formation of individual identity within and against the group. Now we can elaborate Bion's account of the production of minus K in work-groups with particular reference to academic institutions. The example presented here also, ironically, pertains to the context within which much group research is carried out, and it highlights the importance of psychosexual dynamics in academic work. This, then, is a particular context for the re-drawing of group boundaries as a response to anxiety, the fear of an impending catastrophe.

The distinction between the container and the contained appears, to some writers at least, to be breaking down in some British universities as arenas within which knowledge is reproduced and transmitted from tutor to student. The particular anxiety is that professional boundaries are being disrupted as male staff sleep with female students. Notwithstanding the occasional successful and non-exploitative relationship in this context, the overall pattern of behaviour is made possible and provoked by a blend of sexual inequality and academic power. There is no doubt that such behaviour constitutes an abuse of power, and the issues that this raises for women over their position in predominantly male teaching institutions in relation to sexual harassment has been discussed openly in the feminist movement since the 1960s (Paludi and Barickman, 1993).

Now there is increasing concern, and calls by many students and lecturers for the question to be tackled. Articles have appeared on the issue recently in the journals of both major UK lecturers associations (AUT and Natfhe) following debates at national conferences (Barbour, 1993; Kirsch, 1993), in the main weekly higher education newspaper (Brookman, 1993), and in the Sunday broadsheet press (Martin and Flanagan, 1993; Smith, 1993). It appears that Britain is not peculiar in this respect, and debate over the issue from North America has also, for example, appeared recently in the British press (Kerrigan, 1993). The problem has been related explicitly to the abuse of power in therapeutic relationships (Rutter, 1992), and parallels concerns in therapy over the extent of sexual exploitation in professional relationships (Russell, 1993). Similar worries have been expressed among doctors (Gwyther, 1993), lawyers (Dyer, 1993), followers of gurus (Finnigan, 1995), and driving instructors (Prynn, 1996).

A composite case example

In University Psychology in Britain most lecturers are men, and most students are women (Burman, 1990), and the breaking of professional boundaries has come to the fore as a problem in a number of psychology departments. It should be noted that the focus on recent events is not meant to imply that the phenomenon is more prevalent now, and the particular focus on psychology departments here is not because it is a worse problem than in other departments. The anxiety is particularly important now because, to an increasing extent since the 1960s, it has been identified and re-experienced by students and staff within a language, within a newly available discourse that names it as sexual exploitation. Psychology departments are the case in point here also because in psychology academic research is about the very phenomenon, human action, that academics are part of. The naming of one particular department would be unhelpful here, but a composite picture of recent parallel events in different departments over a five-year period will serve to highlight a pattern. This composite department will be described in the singular, as if it were a single case. This pattern can be understood using Bion's (1961) description of work-groups and 'basic assumption states', and this will then be related to his account of knowledge and its opposite, minus K.

In this example, the psychology department where this was a problem attempted to grapple with this issue as a work-group. The task was clear, but the process by which it should be carried out was not. Basic assumption states quickly took over, as forms of defence. Basic assumption states do not neatly follow one from the other as a rule, but in this case example they do. Dependency is where members of the group look to one powerful figure to come to the rescue, and any sense of responsibility disappears. In this case the group looked to the head of department to solve the problem, and this state of dependency, in which nothing happened, went on for a year. The advantage of the dependency basic assumption state is that one particular person is charged with tackling the issue, but the disadvantage is that anxiety grows as it becomes apparent that one person cannot perform what is a group task. The state of anxiety increased in this case to the point where the group developed the idea that there was a 'witchhunt' against certain members. Instead of being treated as a structural problem of male–female and staff–student relationships, the problem turned into one that could only be understood as one of individual culpability, or, in this case, of individuals being victimized.

This is where the group moved on to the second fight–flight basic assumption state. The flight from the task was reinforced by the notion that certain members of the group were simply intent on persecuting others, and the fight emerged as an aggressive counter-assault on 'politically correct' thought police who wished to deny staff and students the right to be friendly to each other. This second basic assumption state paralysed the work-group for another year. The accompanying anxiety resulted eventually in a second phase of this basic assumption, a phase which eventually inaugurated the third basic assumption state. The flight from the problem was augmented by an attack on staff who were identified as sleeping with each other, and it was claimed that this was a worse problem. Although this could be easily written off as a diversion from the original task, the function of this idea, that certain staff were paired with one another, was able to lead to a fake 'solution' – pairing, as the third basic assumption.

From the idea that certain staff were paired, and that this presented a worse danger than staff–student relationships, the idea developed that each member of the teaching staff should be linked with another, a critical friend or 'pal' who would sensitively discuss with them ethical concerns of any kind, including worries about professional misconduct. Now all discussion would be confined to individual counselling, and the group task, never tackled, was seen as unnecessary. This last basic assumption state of pairing was thus effective in sabotaging the attempt of the group to address the problem.

This solution averted the catastrophe that everyone feared. This convoluted procedure guaranteed the integrity of the work-group, but the attempt to link what was happening as a learning process, to produce knowledge, had to be abandoned. Instead, the relationship between the awareness of the problem among the teaching group as container and the anxieties of the students as contained was rendered meaningless, as 'minus K'. What had originally been presented to the group as a form of knowledge had been turned into its opposite, and the group itself had decomposed into separate individual elements.

The individual as a group fantasy

One important aspect of this example is that the group imagined that it was only a work-group. The fantasy that it was only this type of group and so that there could be no unconscious dynamics at work to be addressed, did two things. First, the basic assumption states were able to run unchecked, and the task of the group was frustrated. Secondly, rationalist free choice arguments were mobilized to attack those staff concerned about abuses of power on the grounds that they infantilized the students by treating them as unable to make relationships with whom they wished. It is not insignificant that this department was a psychology department, in two respects. First, the arguments by an external group facilitator, who pointed out that abuse by someone in power was especially traumatic, were discounted as 'too psychodynamic' and thus just plain 'bad psychology'. Secondly, a commitment to cognitive explanations of individual activity in groups sanctioned a retreat by the members at each point when emotions ran high into individual experience; either in dependency on the head of department as a powerful individual who would sort out the problem, or in attacks on those labelled as particular puritan individual troublemakers, or in pairing with some other individual they felt they could trust to behave rationally. Here it is possible to see how an individual emerges from the group at times of threat as a defence against the group, and how particular forms of group behaviour provoke individual responses, and the formation of individual identity within and against the group.

In the composite case example discussed here, the individual emerges out of the impending catastrophe presented to the academic staff group as boundaries between staff and students seem to break down. It is a defence against the group as a chaotic mass, and the work of the group is accompanied by the production of individual solutions for each member of staff to help them cope. The question may arise as to what extent this is a local and specific problem and to what extent it is a general one. It is not being suggested here that this is a group process that has been played out in every department. However, even if it is not a problem that has beset every department conducting research into group processes and feeding research into the academic journals, the shared cultural preoccupation with these issues frames how each researcher will conceptualize the relationships between self and other, and how they may draw group boundaries around them as a form of protection. The point here is that such a form of protection is one which gives birth to the individual, not to a sense of group solidarity or collective action.

The psychoanalytic group in discourse

I have described some group processes in academic institutions to illustrate Bion's contribution to group psychology, and used Bion's account of basic assumption states and minus K to explain why social psychology seems so fixated on the individual as explanandum of group processes. The psychoanalytic discourse that Bion traced in his writings did not simply pop out of his head though. The version of psychoanalysis that he elaborated circulates through culture and then frames the way we understand how groups work in disasters on film and crises in the academic world. This discourse then frames the way social psychologists in crisis talk about and experience their relationships with each other, and with their students. This analysis is plausible for you (if it is) because the phenomenon is constituted through shared cultural resources which explain to us how we should comprehend ourselves in groups.

Using Bion's work it is possible to see how particular forms of group behaviour provoke individual responses, and the formation of individual identity within and against the group. Such images surround researchers carrying out research into group identity, but they provide a model of group experience which will always eventually be sabotaged by individuals who protect themselves against the very group they want to save. The images frame the behaviour of social psychological researchers in their relationship to those they teach in the academic institutions, and again, *individual* responses have been the outcome of group activity. The cultural and institutional pressures build upon a discipline which has faced its own identity crisis. One response to the crisis was a turn to the group, but in this cultural and institutional context, it was a turn that failed, that ended in catastrophe, that was a disaster for social conceptions of psychological behaviour.

It is also possible to see how psychoanalytic conceptions of group and individual identity which saturate the culture that social psychologists work in come to frame their own theoretical development. The structure of the group is not so much, then, something which lies hidden inside an individual's mind or floats in a mysterious realm ready to afflict individuals when they get together. Rather, group structures are carried in the cultural images we have of groups, and in the systems of discourse and institutions which define who we are and how we should understand our relationships with others. We turn to look at some of the powerful beliefs that are carried in these structures in the next chapter, and we can then also develop some alternative analytic frameworks to comprehend how those systems of discourse work.

2

Religious Belief, Charity and Crooked Cures

Babies need to grow into awareness of relationship, of reciprocity and therefore of sacrifice. God is the Lover who draws us out of ourselves, whose Love makes demands of us for response, for commitment.

Heather Ward (1996: 9) Myers-Briggs and the concern with techniques, *Myers-Briggs: Some Critical Reflections*

Group structures would be unable to operate without systems of belief to glue people into place, and to help them feel that what they believe was not open to question. Psychoanalysis provides some insight into the way people are recruited into belief systems, and the way those systems enter them and lock them into something bigger and deeper than they can comprehend. However, there is also a risk for those wanting to use psychoanalytic explanation in this way. A critic of Freud's group psychology pointed out that 'psychoanalysis offers the possibility that important facts lie hidden beneath the surface of everyday reality. Nevertheless claims to "hidden truths" must be investigated rigorously if one is to avoid the short fall from theory to mysticism' (Billig, 1976: 7). Nowhere is this more true than when psychoanalysis simultaneously explains and embraces religion. As well as using psychoanalysis, then, we have to be able to comprehend how it emerges and functions as something big and deep itself.

Religious ideas are contradictory. As systems of belief which hold communities together they also hold together groups with disparate interests, and there is a narrow dividing line between a group *illusion* that gives meaning to the group or provides a sense of community, and a group *delusion* that mystifies the members of the group or leads it to erupt in sectarian communalism. Religious beliefs are often myths which tie subordinate groups (the working class, women, cultural minorities) to dominant groups (the bourgeoisie, men, whites). Then mysticism can be seen as a buttress for ideology, with the members of the subordinate group becoming victims of false consciousness. The irrationality of religion here is not only a problem of the individual being unable to see things as they are, but also a problem of their group being unable to help them understand what their true interests are. Religion here obscures the real structures of power that distribute rights to material goods and rights to speak. Religious ideas may mask interests.

When systems of belief hold together one community with the same interests, however, the story might well be different. The group illusion may correspond to reality in the sense that the group is able to capture and represent to itself symbolically the varieties of oppression it suffers and the different routes to emancipation that are available. As Freud (1927b: 213) points out, an illusion need not necessarily be incorrect, for it may express a wish and *still* correspond to the way the world is. There may be no other way of expressing the identity of the group than in religious terms, and religion will operate here not only as an account which informs its members about spiritual matters, but also as an account which empowers them to understand and change social conditions. The strength drawn from their spiritual existence may be a way of combating the poverty of the 'real' world. A subordinate group which turns to religious explanation, and is able to identify the sources of evil may also be understanding more and expressing better possibilities for emancipation. Religious ideas may, then, also reveal interests.

This chapter is about the different ways psychoanalysis opens up religion as mystification, the ways it sometimes colludes in that mystification, how some theological arguments open up psychoanalysis, and the way psychoanalytic belief can be contextualized and studied. After tracing Freud's scathing analysis of religious belief and the modifications of the psychoanalytic position in his writings and that of other analysts, we will turn to the way religious beliefs structure patterns of care in Western culture. The methodological device of the discursive complex will be described later in the chapter and used to explore discourses of charity in English culture.

Myth, evolution and enlightenment

Alongside his developmental account of the structure of groups in *Group Psychology and the Analysis of the Ego* (1921), Freud discusses, as we saw in the previous chapter, an evolutionary account. The postscript to that book deals with the way in which the 'individual' became separated from the mass as part of a progressive historical process. The poet travelled around recounting the activities of a 'hero' figure who, as time and retelling proceeded, became more individuated. The poet telling this kind of story identified with the hero: 'The myth, then, is the step by which the individual emerges from group psychology' (ibid.: 170). This account of the emergence of the individual is also a narrative of the progress of human history and civilization. However, as social beings become *individuals* they pay for this progress.

One of the costs of this progressive individuation of human beings, and their separation one from the other is that *neurosis* appears as a particular problem which may afflict the person and become a source of their unhappiness, an unhappiness experienced as private distress. The cultural evolution of a human society consisting of people separated from one another and so always suffering some degree of neurosis as a result will then be played out in the evolution of distress in an individual in the course of their life; thus, 'a neurosis should make its victim asocial and should remove him [sic] from the usual group formations. It may be said that a neurosis has the same disintegrating effect upon a group as being in love' (ibid.: 176). Membership of a group may provide a therapeutic return to the company of others, but it is, at a fundamental level of humanity in 'advanced' Western culture, simply too late to undo how we have learnt how to be. The damage has been done in the way culture has prepared people to live alone in all too ordinary unhappiness.

At the same time as people are pulled apart to suffer in silence, however, there is still another powerful need to bond with others and to speak and share and find relief. Group membership provides a source of identity, and an opportunity to get and give care, but a group can only function in this way when it has some meaning, some system of belief to envelop and sustain its members. The beliefs that tie people to many of the groups they belong to are often religious beliefs of some kind, and so these beliefs operate in a contradictory way. They are simultaneously expressions of distress, our privatized pain, and responses to this distress: they are 'crooked cures of all kinds of neuroses' (ibid.). Freud's account of religion is clearly ambivalent: religious ties are both 'crooked' and 'cures', they are distortions of people's need to be close but they do, even then, provide that closeness. The emphasis in his writings is on the 'crooked' side of this formula. There are a number of reasons for his opposition to religion. One reason is his overall view of the development of civilization and rationality.

The evolution of human culture

Freud (1912–1913) outlined an evolutionary schema for the development of humankind which follows a sequence of stages. The first is *animism*, which is reproduced in every individual's development as a stage of childhood omnipotence. The infant at this point is unable to distinguish parts of the world endowed with agency from parts which are mere objects, and they are unable to distinguish words from the world. To speak something is to make it happen. The second stage is that of *religious thinking*, which we find in the child who attributes to the adult the power to change the world. The child now attempts to use incantations and other magical language to invoke authority figures, and their abject submission to these figures is an expression of their feeling of helplessness in the face of greater power. Finally, we reach the third stage of *science*, which is achieved by each individual child in civilized society as they become adapted to the logic of the reality principle. This is the state of an 'advanced' technological culture which has outgrown animism and religious myth. The Western Enlightenment, and psychoanalysis as an exemplary signal expression of that, belong to the third stage. This three-stage evolutionary scheme underlies Freud's use of anthropological work on events in human pre-history, anthropological descriptions which also map on to his explanation of the structure of groups in general. The three-stage view of the development of civilization also explains how we accumulate an understanding of the past as a way of coping more rationally – in a more 'civilized' way – with the present: 'An unconscious understanding . . . of all the customs, ceremonies and dogmas left behind by the original relation to the father may have made it possible for later generations to take over their heritage of emotion' (Freud, 1912–1913: 222).

The main burden of Freud's account of the origins of religion rests on a phylogenetic account, and this is outlined in a series of essays first published in 1912 and 1913, and together as a book in 1913 under the title *Totem and Taboo: Some Points of Agreement between the Mental Lives of Savages and Neurotics*. It is no accident that 1913 was also the year that Jung finally split from the International Psychoanalytic Association, for his interest in anthropological tales was used to give a very different account of the sources and functions of mythology than that preferred by Freud. Freud claimed that he was giving an analytic account of the development of 'folk psychology', and he characterized his endeavour here in terms that deliberately follow Wilhelm Wundt who wrote about higher mental processes as being a property of a collective mind, a *Völkseele*. Wundt, ironically and mistakenly, is remembered today by psychologists as a founder of their experimental discipline which routinely reduces phenomena to individual minds (Danziger, 1990). Freud argued that changes in culture can be understood as if they were changes inside an individual; there is some kind of 'a collective mind, in which mental processes occur just as they do in the mind of an individual' (Freud, 1912–1913: 220). He also claimed that he was unearthing a real history based on anthropological evidence rather than simply offering another mythical account which speculates, as Jung does, about what may or may not be in the 'collective unconscious'. Freud also argued that we have to adopt a Lamarckian conception of evolution to account for the way we relive in our individual development (ontogeny) the cultural development of humankind (phylogeny). The Cuvierian formula 'ontogeny recapitulates phylogeny' is here extended from biology to explain the transmission and reappearance of archaic cultural phenomena.

Freud discussed anthropological material on the primal horde and the symbolic residues of conflicts in the horde. His account draws heavily, selectively, and rather uncritically upon anthropology of his day (Hirst and Woolley, 1982), and we should note that his use of contemporary examples of exotic other cultures to illustrate what he claims happened once upon a time is a device strongly opposed by present-day anthropologists (Hobart, 1993). He includes material on the primal horde (which he then used in accounts of group psychology), the development of clans, and then, as the title *Totem and Taboo* suggests, the role of taboos which were to become organized around totemic icons.

TOTEMS   The primal horde is, Freud argued, the basic building block of earliest human society. The hordes were organized groups controlled by one old strong male who prevented the young males from gaining access to the females. There was, then, enforced exogamy in which mating had to take place out of the horde. The young males were driven out to mate and set up a horde of their own. If one of these males was able to set up a new horde, then he would be the leader until he was deposed. Exogamy imposed by force was then given a set of cultural meanings as the hordes became *symbolic* as well as physical entities, and so prepared the development of human culture as a system of representation and self-representation. The hordes were thus transformed into clans.

In the clans, one object came to 'stand for' or represent the identity of the group. The symbolic representation of enforced exogamy – a material representation which came to warrant and obviate the exertion of brute force and to allay the leader's jealousy – was also, then, the sign of the distinctiveness of the clan. This sign of the clan was an object regarded with superstitious respect and was a collective mark of identity; this was the clan totem. Most often the totem was an animal, and the clan would develop a story to explain the uncanny power of the totem in which they would describe how they were descended from the animal. Freud gave examples of the clan totem's power; that you could not hunt, kill or eat the totem, that sometimes you could not touch, or even look at it, and that sometimes you could not call it by its name. The fear, respect and awe of the totem enforced exogamy and it prohibited incest, for to have a relationship inside the clan would be to make some kind of symbolic contact with the totem. An additional, crucial, function of the totem was that it contained the anxiety of the horde; the fear, rivalry and hatred of the horde chief was transferred, displaced, on to the totem. The clan leader's power, then, was augmented by an association with the totem, and the totem was the clan's repository for mixed feelings toward the leader. Both leader and totem were the objects of powerful, inhibited, ambivalent feelings, feelings of love and hate. With every totem came taboos.

TABOOS   The taboos were the prohibitions on men killing the totem, and so also the leader, and on men having sex with the women in the clan because women were the property of the leader. The *ambivalence* of the taboo is, Freud argued, its key property, for it carries a double meaning of being both sacred and unclean. This double meaning had already been noted by Wundt as an essential property and explanation of its power.

This ambivalence is dynamic, for a taboo expresses a rejection of a wish. There is repression of desire here, and so the attempt to escape and the circling around the object of love and hate is underpinned by a magnetic fixation on the taboo. It is fascinating and feared because it signifies something that is desired. Examples of taboos which Freud described are those which require that cruelty toward enemies is tempered by acts of appeasement, that there should be restrictions on the slayer after victory, and that the victor should perform obligatory purification rituals and other ceremonies of remembrance. Other taboos may concern rulers who must not be touched. Freud also discussed taboos on contact with the dead (such as Palawan widows either being restricted to their huts or knocking on trees with a stick to warn others of their presence, the Masai changing the dead's name so that it will not touch them as they speak it, North-West American Indians changing the names of the dead's relatives, and the Guaycurus changing the names of each member of the clan after the death of the chief). The power of words is noted by Freud here as a manifestation of 'pre-religious' animism, and he also drew attention to the operation of projection – the putting into another what one cannot bear in oneself – in the fear of the dead: 'The survivor thus denies that he has ever harboured any hostile feelings against the dead loved one; the soul of the dead harbours them instead' (Freud, 1912–1913: 117).

Taboos became devices for holding the group together centred on the clan totems. Then those totemic taboos manifested the ambivalence which was felt toward a revered and feared icon in the periodic sacrifice and communal eating of the totem animals. Contemporary examples Freud cited at this point are the Bear Clan in Ottowa and the Aino in Japan who eat bears, and the Zuni in New Mexico who revere and consume turtles. The eating of the totem animal is followed by mourning. Freud argued that we can explain this sequence of killing, eating and mourning by seeing it as a repetition of events which occurred once upon a time back in the primal horde.

Murder in the horde

The brothers who were driven out of the primal horde banded together, so this story goes, and killed the father. The father, as a figure who was feared and envied, was then devoured in order to accomplish identification with him and to acquire a portion of his strength, but there are a number of complications for the brothers. They had to band together, and so access to the women was not available to any single one of them; that it was necessarily a collective act meant that the wish which fuelled it could not be realized. A second problem for the brothers was that the devotion to the father, and the repressed desire they felt for him, erupted in guilt after his murder. There was such guilt on having killed him that 'the actual father became stronger than the living one had been' (Freud, 1912–1913: 204). In order to cope with the guilt and to revoke symbolically the crime, the fear of the father was displaced on to the totem, and the killing of it was forbidden. The fruits of the act were renounced, and exogamy was enforced by the injunction not to 'touch' the totem. The totemic meal was then experienced both as a repetition of the act, and as an attempt to atone for it.

The events in the primal horde have left symbolic residues in mythologies which not only tie humankind together, but also tie it to imaginary powerful and omnipresent beings. They also, for Freud, operate as the historical source of a child's murderous feelings toward their father in the Oedipus complex, with those distant memories transmitted and relived over and again. The obsessional nature of contemporary religious practices is underpinned by an attempt to deal with this archaic heritage. The process of killing, eating and mourning is found in present-day Christian mythology. It is found in the notion of original sin, in which the devout have each betrayed the father, and the sin is against the father in 'the guilty primaeval deed' (ibid.: 216). It is relived in the expatiation of that deed through the sacrifice of another life, where another dies for the Christian's original sins. It is expressed in the concern with renouncing desire, sometimes to the point of complete celibacy. Christianity maintains the ambivalence of the sons in the primal horde in their relation to the chief in the believer's identification with Christ the son as defiant and the way in which 'He himself became God, beside, or, more correctly, in place of, the father' (ibid.: 217), and all Christians relive the totemic meal in the Eucharist in which the sons consume the body and blood of the son and father who is thus incorporated into their body and mind.

Present-day psychopathology

There is also another more specific reason why we should be wary of religion, according to Freud, and this is to be found in the striking similarity between religious practices and contemporary psychopathology, particularly obsessions. As Freud pointed out in his paper 'Obsessive Actions and Religious Practices' (1907), there are some significant differences between obsessions and religious practices. There is greater individual variability in obsessions, and they are usually private. These differences reflect the creeping privatization of distress over the course of history. The similarities Freud notes are that there are qualms of conscience if the practice is neglected, there is some isolation from other actions as well as there being a taboo on interruption. We can note the conscientiousness with which the practice is carried out in both cases, and the minutiae of the practices are full of significance. In both there is a feeling of guilt at the temptation not to perform the practice, and there is a fantasy of being tempted. The fantasy of being tempted is, for Freud, one of the keys, for this fantasy indicates repressed desire.

Freud argued that the guilt at the fantasy which accompanies the repression of desire – desire which, of course, has hidden, unacknowledged significance – is alleviated by the practice, but the practice functions in two ways. The practice functions as a defence against something *and* as a covert expression of that something. This double function, a double function we also find in the dreamwork and in jokes, is to give a yield of illicit pleasure in the carrying out of the practice. There are examples of this in Freud's case studies of obsessional practices, and he included one in his 1907 paper which concerns the woman who repeatedly straightened a stained tablecloth in the presence of her maid and so revealed a stain which represented, for her, another stain from her wedding night which was visible in the wrong place on the sheets. The similarities, and an underlying identity of function led Freud to argue that we can understand 'obsessional neurosis as a pathological counterpart of the formation of a religion' (Freud, 1907: 40). So, neurosis is 'individual religiosity', and religion is 'universal obsessional neurosis'.

Religious counter-discourse

Freud appears more conciliatory in 'The Future of an Illusion' (1927b) in which the 'illusion' is not seen as mere mistake but as the attempt to fulfil a wish, and so to serve some fairly healthy functions. These functions include exorcizing the terrors of nature, reconciling people to the cruelty of fate and compensating for the sufferings and privations of mental life: 'A store of ideas is created, born from man's need to make his helplessness tolerable and built up from the material of memories of the helplessness of his own childhood and the childhood of the human race' (ibid.: 198).

Christianity and spirituality

Although Freud was very critical of religion and he adhered to a rationalist and evolutionist explanation of the pernicious grip of spirituality on people's minds, he was still open enough to invite his friend Oscar Pfister, a fellow analyst and Christian pastor, to respond to 'The Future of an Illusion'. In his response, *The Illusion of the Future*, Pfister argued from within a Freudian and Christian framework that Christian religion was now unlikely to be displaced, and that it did have positive functions in the maintenance of civilized society (Gay, 1988). Freud clearly was not hostile to individuals simply because they believed. He was, however, hostile to people who used religious ideas in a deliberately mystical way. *Totem and Taboo* was, in part, a response to Jung, and there is an irony here that the historical explanation that Freud gave of the formation of the Oedipus complex in events in the primal horde took on board key Jungian concepts in a literal rather than a metaphorical way. It was under the influence of Jung that Freud took to referring to these conflicts as part of a 'complex' (Forrester, 1980), and then, many years after his description of those kinds of conflicts in infancy, the term 'Oedipus complex' started appearing in his writing (Freud, 1910).

Freud's rationalist reaction to religion may indeed have been exacerbated by his aversion to Jung's mysticism, and Jung's work is still often an explicit or implicit counterpoint to Freud's work as far as spirituality is concerned. Theologians wanting to adapt psychoanalysis to their own belief system have often ended up supporting Jungian versions of analysis against Freud's (e.g., Philp, 1956). This is partly because Jung himself was religious, and he also seemed to see acceptance of religion as a necessary part of the analytic 'cure', arguing at some points that of all his patients 'there has not been one whose problem in that last resort was not that of finding a religious outlook on life' (cited in Masson, 1988: 156). Jung is willing to concede that Christianity is not perfect, and that there is some cultural 'relativity of the gods', but he argues that acceptance of such relativism has its limits, and should not be confused with 'a stupid error like atheism' (Jung, 1983: 242). While Freud described himself as a materialist, Jung was always opposed to the 'materialist error' (ibid.: 244), and to the 'urban neurosis of atheism' (ibid.: 245).

There is something deeply and deliberately mystical in Jungian thought, and his explanation for the transmission of belief across generations is as dubious as Freud's. While Freud resorted to Lamarckian accounts of heredity because he thought this would provide support for a materialist account, Jung posited a realm of the 'collective unconscious' which floats free of any particular culture or historical process. Some later 'post-Jungians' have argued that the contents of the collective unconscious – the 'archetypes' – may be transmitted on DNA (Samuels, 1985), but this is a rather desperate claim which runs against the guiding spirit of Jung's work.

Neurosis and psychosis

There have been responses recently by psychoanalytically inclined theologians who want to counter characterizations of religion as a kind of obsessional neurosis: 'there is more to religion than the analogies to psychological pathology recognized by Freud' (Westphal, 1990: 132). One point that is often made by them is that religion need not be 'wrong' or 'incorrect' even if one adopts a strict psychoanalytic worldview. Freud distinguished between illusion and delusion. Illusion is the product of a wish, and this wish may have some basis in reality. This reality may only come to be by the remotest chance, as in Freud's (1927b) example of a girl dreaming of a prince coming to marry her and being lucky enough to find it happen. A delusion, on the other hand, is a wish which contradicts reality, and which expresses beliefs about the world and what may happen which are impossible. Religion, then, may both be an illusion and be *true*. Another point made by theologians is that *anti*-religious views can be just as susceptible to psychoanalytic explanation as religious views. Anti-religious views can be understood as the expression of a wish that there is no deity. An example may be what has been termed the 'adolescent response' to religion, in which 'it would be much nicer if there was no one on whom we are dependent and to whom we are responsible' (Westphal, 1990: 119).

ILLUSION   Theologians using psychoanalysis are quite happy to concede some ground to psychoanalysis, but with the eventual aim of rehabilitating religion. Two kinds of circumstance have been identified where psychoanalytic accounts may be acceptable to religious believers. One is where religious belief may be driven by a wish, and this will be, in effect, an illusion, and an example here may be in 'the belief of the child or the theologically naïve' (Meissner, 1990: 110). Another example may concern individuals who are driven by wishes relating to infantile relationships: 'the naïve believer, whose God-representation is determined in large measure by the transferential derivatives from parental figures' (ibid.: 111). Here, then, the theologian will accept that there may well be cases where the believer turns to God for the wrong reasons.

Meissner (1990), for example, is concerned with the relationship between that which is objective, generally agreed to be a reality independent of the person, and that which is subjective, as merely a reality for the individual. Standard psychoanalytic accounts, in line with dominant accounts of the self in Western culture, often split reality into two halves, an objective public collective knowledge and a subjective private individual belief. Meissner flips these oppositions over into their opposite. Religious belief, he asserts, lies on the *objective* side of the equation. Religious beliefs are on the 'objective or extrapsychic dimension' (ibid.: 98), and there one finds 'demonstrable objective evidence or realities' (ibid.: 100). It is necessary, then, to try to distinguish the 'authentic religious impulse' (ibid.: 108) from inauthentic illusion, or merely subjective reality. Behind the illusion there may actually be 'revelation with the presumption of a divine presence and action behind it' (ibid.: 109). This means that the distinction between the objective reality of God discussed, for example, by 'scientific theologians' and subjective perceptions of religious objects entails going beyond the stance of the 'theologically naïve' to truth: 'faith ultimately renounces the imperfection and finitude of basic trust in order to reach beyond it and thereby recapture it more profoundly. This is the creative moment of faith' (ibid.: 113).

DELUSION   Another set of circumstances, more serious than simple naïveté or illusory wish, concern psychopathological beliefs, and this is where we move into the realms of delusion, from neurosis to psychosis. One of Freud's (1911a) cases, that of Judge Schreber, whom Freud analysed through the Judge's autobiographical account, is a good example here. Schreber fantasized about being persecuted and sexually abused by his doctor, Dr Flechsig, and this eventually developed into a full-blown paranoid fantasy of being penetrated by the 'rays of God' and thus being turned into a woman so he could redeem the world. Schreber was never on the couch with Freud, but the case still functions as an early example of an attempt in the psychoanalytic clinical literature to grapple with psychosis. Freud traced through the delusions, and concluded that it is Schreber's desire to be turned into a woman which is primary and that this then may be represented in fantasy either physically as a transformation of sex or through adopting a role in sexual intercourse as a transformation of gender. Freud also used the case to develop his own theory of paranoia, in which it is homosexual desire which has been deeply repressed which lies at the root. This desire is transformed by defence mechanisms of projection, reversal and denial (and we will meet this account again in theories of war paranoia in Chapter 3). The delusion provides Schreber with moral legitimacy for his homosexual desire, the freedom to love rather than hate his father, and it also gives him some not insignificant status as redeemer of humankind.

Westphal (1990) argues that it is possible to redeem the religious elements even from Schreber's paranoid delusion. For Schreber, there is patently a problem of a relationship to the father, and the relationship to Dr Flechsig repeats that relationship (and Schreber's psychosis should really be understood, as anti-psychiatrists later pointed out, as a consequence of what his father actually did to him, and not just what he fantasized (Schatzman, 1973)). God functions as a representation within the delusion, but as a representation of the father and the doctor. The problem does not lie with religious belief as such, Westphal claims, for that religious belief is not the source of the psychosis. It is also necessary, he argues, to draw attention to the distinction Schreber makes between the 'upper God' and the 'posterior realms of God'. Schreber's problems seem to revolve around his relationship to these lower demonic components of the God fantasy, and there is a homology between that distinction Schreber makes and the difference between real theological forces of good and evil. Schreber does take for granted, then, 'the truth of religious belief' (Westphal, 1990: 118). Westphal also takes this 'truth' for granted here, of course. There is an underlying assumption in these theological responses to Freud that it is possible to bracket off the reality of God from the various ways in which an individual accepts that reality or defends themself against it. For these writers the truth they take for granted is the reality of their deity as a Christian God.

Judaism and Kabbala

The problems with Jung and with other universal claims for what should be seen as *situated* knowledge are highlighted by the focus on Christianity in much psychoanalytic debate over the psychological functions of religious belief. Freud himself was most concerned with Christian religion, for it was all around him as a dominant cultural form and as a powerful influence in his own childhood (Isbister, 1985). Although it is often argued that Freud opposed religion from a strictly scientific atheist viewpoint (Sulloway, 1979) and that Freud's strong Jewish identity had little bearing on his clinical work (Gay, 1988), the picture becomes more complicated if we look at alternative strands of Jewish religious thought in the development of psychoanalysis generally. Freud, quite under-standably, displayed an ambivalence to religion, and we see this ambiva-lence not only in his account of the development of monotheism in general and Christianity in particular, but also in his own identity in relation to Judaism. The notion of religion as a 'crooked cure' is not, of course, only negative, for there are still valuable curative and cultural aspects.

Bakan (1958) argues that 'Freud, consciously or unconsciously, secular-ized Jewish mysticism' (ibid.: 25). This argument is one pole in a debate over the role of Judaism in psychoanalysis (Klein, 1985), and the way Freud expressed and repressed, revealed and concealed his identity as a Jew in clinical practice (Billig, in press). There are implications in Bakan's account for the ways in which mysticism could be seen not only as mys-tification but also as *revelation*. Bakan draws attention to the emergence of a tradition in Jewish religious thought called Kabbala which has often come into conflict with mainstream Judaism. Modern Kabbala dates from the thirteenth century and centres around Abulafia, who was born in Spain in 1240 and who advocated an interpretative method which involved juggling around letters, each of which was thought to have some mystical significance, and a method of 'skipping' quickly from one concept to another to arrive at a reading of a text. Bakan points out that this method shows some striking similarities with psychoanalytic 'free association'. Kabbalistic doctrine became important as a Messianic move-ment in the seventeenth century around Sabbatai Zevi. He pronounced himself the Messiah in 1648, and was both a point of resistance and celebration during the pogroms in Poland, in which 300,000 Jews were murdered in that one year alone.

The Kabbalistic movement was able to point to these events as confir-mation of the prophecy that the Messianic era would begin in 1648, and it celebrated mystical revelation and sensuality – expressed explicitly, for example, in one of the key texts of Kabbala, the *Zohar* – against community leaders who preferred to see the Jewish tradition as a scholarly one based on interpretations of the Torah. While the transmission of the Law is through writing in Torah studies, the Kabbala runs underneath as an alternative subversive *oral* tradition, and this is expressed again in Freud's work:

> he was motivated, consciously or unconsciously, to hide the deeper portions of his thought, and . . . these deeper portions were Kabbalistic in their source and content. . . . The Kabbalistic tradition has it that the secret teachings are to be transmitted orally to one person at a time, and even then only to selected minds and by hints. This is what Freud was doing in the actual practice of psychoanalysis.
>
> (Bakan, 1958: 35)

Freud obtained some of his key ideas from his colleague and only 'other', Wilhelm Fliess. 'Fliess, in his major thought, combined three important Kabbalistic elements: the notion of bisexuality, the extensive use of numerology, and the doctrine of the predestination of the time of death – the doctrine of "life portions" ' (ibid.: 62). Some of these ideas were to be found later in psychoanalysis, but the particular ideas are less important than their form, and the way they coexisted with and contradicted mainstream Jewish religious thought. For Bakan:

> The subject matter of classical Kabbalistic interpretation was the Torah. . . . With the social development of Kabbalistic modes of thought . . . the idea gradually took hold that the Messiah was a Torah. . . . Later the person of Zaddik, the Holy Man, the center of Chassidic groups came to be regarded as a Torah. . . . We may say that Freud carried this transition one step further. . . . Not only is Zaddik a Torah, but each person is a Torah!
>
> (Bakan, 1958: 246)

The implications of this are not so much that there is a hidden Kabalistic religious core to psychoanalysis, but the idea that we are all texts to be interpreted, and that these texts can be read for a religious sub-text. Psychoanalysis is a form of thought which could then permit religious readings. We should also be aware here that Freud himself explicitly repudiated claims that he was drawing on mainstream or oppositional Jewish religious thought (Oxaal, 1988). However, there are a number of consequences of Bakan's claim if it is correct. One is that it could be possible to be religious *and* psychoanalytic. Another important consequence is that such a religious engagement with psychoanalysis could have a democratic and humanist form, for if each person is a Torah, a text, then each person's truth deserves to be read and respected. Just as Kabbala survived as a sub-text in Judaism, as another hidden and more democratic alternative to Talmudic scholarship, so it may be possible to conceive of a spirituality which is positive and empowering running underneath and against all varieties of organized religion. Despite Freud's hostility to religion as 'universal obsessional neurosis', then, psychoanalytic ideas are embedded in systems of religious iconography and ethics.

Divine objects of desire

Although it is tempting to try to build a universal covering account to describe the way religious belief works, this is not terribly helpful if we want to understand how this belief actually operates in particular cultures. What is at stake here is the way religious iconography structures the way we represent what we are doing and feeling in this particular culture (e.g., Höpfl, 1996). I also want to show how certain psychoanalytic notions are interwoven with religious ideas such that they help structure the way we feel about relationships and the self, and so in this part of the chapter I will focus on the specific ways in which religion and psychoanalysis operate in English culture, and then bring the focus down still further to look at representations of how people are encouraged to help others who are less

fortunate than themselves. Despite psychoanalysis drawing upon subal-
tern religious traditions such as Kabbala, the dominant mystical systems
which enclose and rework much psychoanalysis now in the West are still
usually varieties of Christianity. Christian belief is one of the most powerful religious systems in the UK, and it lies as a dead weight on the minds
of the living now as a kind of prototypical super-ego, or 'above-I'. There
are, again, both negative and positive sides to this.

Recent debates over the introduction of the vernacular into prayer
books saw the Archbishop of York arguing that 'It is important to have in
worship some things we cannot understand' (*The Guardian*, 11 July 1994:
3), and these notions are clearly endorsed by some of his flock: 'What do
you mean, do I believe? What do you mean, what do I think? We don't
have to think about such things, they are given and laid down for us. They
are a part of the few things in life that require no thought at all. It's a very
dangerous question to be asking at all' (Mrs Bradley, retired, in 'Do people
in Godley believe in the virgin birth?', *Guardian on Saturday*, 19 December
1992: 59). Here, religion is used as an injunction not to know. Religious
ideas are the unthought which define and limit what questions might be
asked, and they prevent reflection.

On the other hand, most of the main charity organizations in the UK
are religious, and in most cases they are inspired and fuelled by forms of
Christianity. Many of the major British overseas aid charities, such as
Oxfam, are Christian in origin and still structured by Christian moral
codes (Black, 1992). These codes are then reflected upon and developed
to accommodate political movements, and even to support, for example,
trends in liberation theology in Latin America. Restrictions on the political activity of charities have made this kind of support difficult, but
groups like Christian Aid have tried to broaden the meaning of 'charity'
to include empowerment work in the Third World (Burnell, 1991).
'Empowerment' and 'helping' are, of course, themselves difficult concepts when the helpers will always have many more resources than those
they help.

Charity is a particular kind of response to poverty which carries with
it certain assumptions about who is responsible (Harper, 1996), and it
also tends to carry a moral stance in which 'the needy are to be pitied for
their treatment at the hand of fate' (Radley and Kennedy, 1992: 126). In
the context of the attempts to aid the 'development' of the Third World,
and much charity having that work as its reference point, help may
indeed, as Marianne Gronemeyer (1992: 53) writing from within the tradition of liberation theology claims, be 'a means of keeping the bit in the
mouths of subordinates without letting them feel the power that is
guiding them'. This complicated relationship of care and power also
structures how people become helping subjects in the First World, in the
UK as the case in point. It seems particularly important when we consider the appeal and function of charity to take into account the discourses and forms of power which mobilize subjects, and their symbolic

debt to Christianity. This means that we need an approach that can situate accounts of spirituality in psychoanalysis in a cultural context.

DISCURSIVE COMPLEXES One way of reworking psychoanalytic themes as collective social constructions rather than as individual deep and inevitable psychic truths is to use the notion of the 'discursive complex'. A discursive complex is a set of statements about a psychic object which is organized around psychoanalytic preoccupations such that the object simultaneously looks like an item in a psychoanalytic vocabulary and the subject is defined as a psychodynamic subject. Discourse reproduces and transforms the social world in texts, and a discursive complex simultaneously reproduces and transforms the psychic world of the subject as addressed, recognized and transformed by texts in accordance with psychodynamic principles. The discursive complex is an analytic device, then, which brings together the study of discourse as it pertains to the positioning of subjects and the study of psychodynamic processes as they are constituted in language and structured as collective cultural forms. But this coupling of discourse analysis and psychoanalysis really only gives us the shell of a device to help us read a text. It is still a rather abstract notion, and to fill it out we must elaborate a specific appropriate analytic framework for the phenomenon in question.

In psychoanalytic psychotherapy, one develops a particular dynamic story which makes sense of the patient's life-world. That is why, in psychoanalysis, there is really no such thing as a 'case' from which other cases can be extrapolated. But we do have available many frameworks which elaborate different psychoanalytic stories about the nature of sensuality and the unconscious, and these are useful as templates to help us think through an interpretation. In analytic discourse research we see those templates as cultural forms, and they inhabit the talk, writing and imagery which cluster around certain social phenomena. We 'discover' them as we rediscover the writings of analysts whose ideas either seep into the contemporary social imagination or crystallize concepts that have already arrived from other places, or both. The story we tell in our analysis, then, is driven as much by our theoretical understanding of the phenomenon as it is by the patterns that are really there in the text we are analysing. Discourses and discursive complexes are never actually or only there in that single text. The analysis I present in the next section moves backwards and forwards from puzzling over the way charity images work to explorations of the internal shape of religious thought, Christianity in particular, and then sideways to writings in the Winnicottian object relations tradition. But why Winnicott?

Winnicott and the English self

One of the most English of psychoanalytic theoretical systems and practices has been that produced by D. W. Winnicott from within the object relations tradition. The way he explains how caring and dependency work between mother and child draws upon and filters back into cultures of concern for others and conceptions of charitable giving. A number of writers have also drawn on Winnicott's writings to reassess Freud's dismal view of religion and to support the argument that religious belief can be valuable as a source of comfort, or even of 'truth'. The interaction between genuine religious faith and illusion has been interrogated using Winnicott's work in order to distinguish the 'authentic religious impulse' from inauthentic illusion (Meissner, 1990: 108).

There is something of the atmosphere of the fantasy of cosy English family relationships in Winnicottian object relations theory, and the comfortable fit between the theory and its culture makes it possible for one writer sympathetic to Winnicott to argue that it is an 'ordinary-language psychoanalysis' (Phillips, 1988). Winnicott himself was very influential on the shape of 'ordinary-language' accounts of family relationships in England through popular BBC broadcasts on mothering during the 1940s (Winnicott, 1957) and through lectures to midwives, child welfare offices and social workers in the 1950s (Winnicott, 1965). His descriptions of the mother's state of 'primary maternal preoccupation' with her infant, the child's discovery of its 'true self' in relation to the mother, and the role of 'transitional objects' in the gradual detachment of the infant from the mother as it becomes an independent child, tapped into the English imagination.

Psychoanalysis traditionally revolves around infantile fantasy, but what Winnicottian theory does is to emphasize what the mother *actually* does to her infant, how it is so difficult to escape that dependency on the mother, why independence is at such a terrible cost, and the ways in which the grown-up child may infantilize the mother and others in a mistaken strategy to gain autonomy. In this story, mother is the source of the child's self, and the father is a distant figure in the background operating as little more than a protective envelope for the mother–child couple. We can thus rephrase Freud's dictum about the ego and the id and the work of culture as 'Where the Id of the infant is, there the mother's Ego must be also' (Phillips, 1988: 100) The developmental story here is one of the provision of love and elements of a self *and* potential psychic suffocation and the ruin of something originally and essentially good. Winnicott had no time for Freud's theory of the death drive, and for him it is, rather, the mother that helps rupture the 'pre-ambivalent dependence' of the infant through *her* violence: 'The mother hates the baby before the baby hates the mother, and before the baby knows the mother hates him' (Winnicott, 1947: 200). It is what the mother does to the child that enables it to love or makes it hate. The infant's own destructive 'drive' is, as far as Winnicott is concerned, something that expresses its ruthless love, but which the mother experiences as hateful.

It is vital that the mother is there for the infant as a secure point from which the infant can explore the world around it, and Winnicott collaborated with Bowlby on the research on 'Forty-four juvenile thieves' which was to emphasize the importance of early secure attachment to later civilized well-being (Bowlby, 1944). The mother must be an object that is 'real' so that the infant can use it as a baseline for its understanding of the world and other people. The infant's experience of what is real is mediated by 'transitional objects'.

Transitional objects are the original 'not-me' possessions that the child adopts sometime in the first year of life so that it might both be comforted by them because it is immersed in its own inner world and might use them to learn to negotiate its way around unfamiliar objects. It must move out from its own separate universe where it hallucinates objects into being and wishes them away, and learn to participate in a universe of enduring objects in the outer world in order to develop into an adult. Transitional phenomena are both part of the realm of illusion and the 'real' world. Again, those who care for the child have a special responsibility to enable this to be so: 'This early stage of development is made possible by the mother's special capacity for making adaptation to the needs of her infant, thus allowing the infant the illusion that what the infant creates really exists' (Winnicott, 1953: 16). As the infant attempts to grasp what is objective in the world, it hallucinates objects into being. The mother is among those objects, and when the infant destroys the object in fantasy but discovers that the mother is *still* there, it develops an understanding of the difference between subjectivity and objectivity: 'it is the destructive drive that creates the quality of "externality"' (Winnicott, 1969: 110). Transitional objects lie between the two spheres of the subjective and the objective as bridges, links between inside and outside, and between sleeping and waking. The Winnicottian version of psychoanalytic discourse contains images of mother and infant, powerful and powerless, which resonate with wider concerns in English culture around religion and forms of care for others.

Object relations in Christian culture

Winnicott's family background in Plymouth was Wesleyan, and he attended a Methodist church when he was at Cambridge until he converted to Anglicanism, to the Church of England. He was not especially devout, nor concerned to use psychoanalysis in the service of religion, but in recent years his work has been employed by Christian theologians anxious to rebut traditional Freudian characterizations of religious thinking as psychopathology. The advantage of Winnicott's work for some theologians is that it is concerned with 'illusory experience' as a necessary part of the infant's grasping what is inside and what is outside, what is real and what is not (Meissner, 1990). The image of God, or the sense of God can be thought of as a 'transitional object'.

The communion, for example, is then seen as 'concrete symbolic action', and the objects in the communion bridge the abstract (God) and the concrete (things that can be touched). For Winnicott, 'illusion is not an obstruction to experiencing reality but a means of gaining access to it' (ibid.: 106). Thus, 'Only in the transitional realm is it possible to articulate the doctrine in terms of the metaphorical, symbolic, spiritual, and credal sense that it intends' (ibid.: 114). The truth of God is treated in these writings as an objective reality, but one that an individual cannot hope to grasp directly in itself. Internal objects operate as representations of this 'Truth', and transitional objects in the sacrament mediate between the internal sense of God and the external truth of his Being. When one tries to deny God, to destroy him in fantasy, he will still be there holding the subject, as a power that can be returned to. As the fluorescent sign on the church near me has it, 'God's love will never let you go'. The point here is not whether this Winnicottian account is correct or not, but the representation of self that it maintains, and the image of the self as a carer and cared-for being in relation to others. This is why Winnicott's elaboration of psychoanalytic discourse is powerful in structuring the way images of charity circulate among the English.

Advertising charity

Let us turn to three specific charity texts. I trawled through every English national daily newspaper on one day, 7 June 1993, and this turned out to be a day when there were no Oxfam appeals, nothing in fact that related to the Third World or overseas aid. This was a surprise, and it is important to note this as an absence, for the absences on that particular day will still condition our reading of what did actually appear. There were only three charity adverts in total. Again, this was a surprise, and a surprise that drew attention to my expectation that a charity advert appears on almost every page of every paper. One advert was in *The Times*, and two were in the *Daily Express* – a third surprise, for I expected those newspapers to be read by people who would never give anything to anyone. The advert in *The Times* was for the 'King George's Fund for Sailors' (Figure 1), one in the *Daily Express* was for the 'Royal National Lifeboat Institution' (Figure 2) and the other was for 'The Mental Health Foundation' (Figure 3). What discursive complexes might be at work here? I will focus on anxiety and identification.

ANXIETY   The appeal for money face-to-face in the street or to a reader faced with a newspaper advertisement sets in play a tension between donor and recipient. That anxiety in the donor is mobilized as the advertisement addresses them as a particular kind of subject and demands recognition and response. The notion of anxiety changes in the course of Freud's writings from being the result of an accumulation of sexual tension which has not been processed effectively (Freud, 1895a) to being a 'signal' which functions as a symbol of danger so that the ego may defend itself against internal or external threat (Freud, 1926). It is this

Worse things happen ashore

Disaster at sea is something we all learn to live with. But worse things can happen ashore – when sailors grow old, become disabled, fall on hard times, leave widows to be cared for and children to be educated.

King George's Fund looks after Royal Navy and Royal Marines widows and orphans from two World Wars and the Falklands Campaign to the present day. It is also the vital safety net for the many organisations serving the Merchant and Fishing Fleets. In 1992 alone, over 80 maritime charities received more than £2·1m in help from KGFS.

All these charities rely heavily on us – as we need to rely on you. Your gift and your legacy will be their lifebelt in a very special sense. Please give us your support!

KING GEORGE'S FUND FOR SAILORS

The Safety Net for *all* Seafarers

1 Chesham Street. London SW1X 8NF
Tel: 071–235 2884   Charity 226446

Figure 1

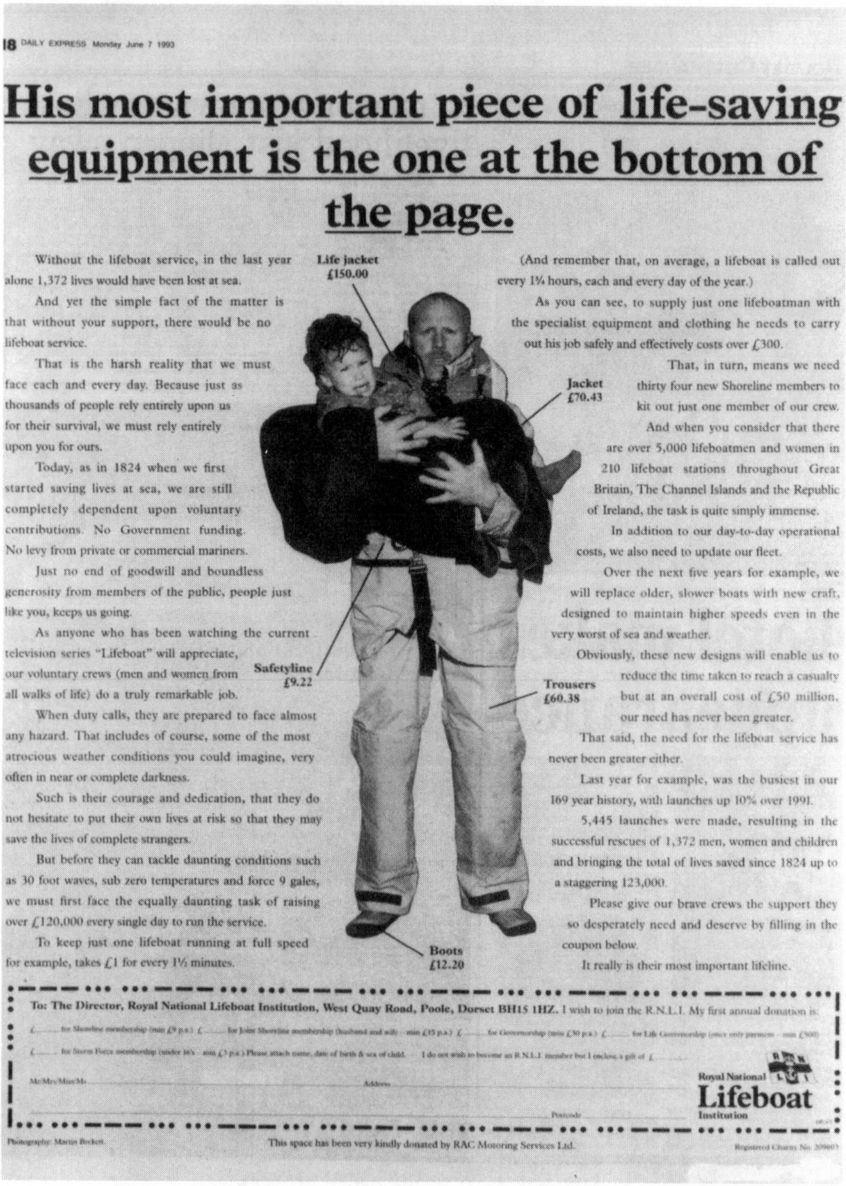
18 DAILY EXPRESS Monday June 7 1993
His most important piece of life-saving equipment is the one at the bottom of the page.
Without the lifeboat service, in the last year alone 1,372 lives would have been lost at sea.
And yet the simple fact of the matter is that without your support, there would be no lifeboat service.
That is the harsh reality that we must face each and every day. Because just as thousands of people rely entirely upon us for their survival, we must rely entirely upon you for ours.
Today, as in 1824 when we first started saving lives at sea, we are still completely dependent upon voluntary contributions. No Government funding. No levy from private or commercial mariners.
Just no end of goodwill and boundless generosity from members of the public, people just like you, keeps us going.
As anyone who has been watching the current television series "Lifeboat" will appreciate, our voluntary crews (men and women from all walks of life) do a truly remarkable job.
When duty calls, they are prepared to face almost any hazard. That includes of course, some of the most atrocious weather conditions you could imagine, very often in near or complete darkness.
Such is their courage and dedication, that they do not hesitate to put their own lives at risk so that they may save the lives of complete strangers.
But before they can tackle daunting conditions such as 30 foot waves, sub zero temperatures and force 9 gales, we must first face the equally daunting task of raising over £120,000 every single day to run the service.
To keep just one lifeboat running at full speed for example, takes £1 for every 1½ minutes.
Life jacket £150.00
Jacket £70.43
Safetyline £9.22
Trousers £60.38
Boots £12.20
(And remember that, on average, a lifeboat is called out every 1¾ hours, each and every day of the year.)
As you can see, to supply just one lifeboatman with the specialist equipment and clothing he needs to carry out his job safely and effectively costs over £300.
That, in turn, means we need thirty four new Shoreline members to kit out just one member of our crew.
And when you consider that there are over 5,000 lifeboatmen and women in 210 lifeboat stations throughout Great Britain, The Channel Islands and the Republic of Ireland, the task is quite simply immense.
In addition to our day-to-day operational costs, we also need to update our fleet.
Over the next five years for example, we will replace older, slower boats with new craft, designed to maintain higher speeds even in the very worst of sea and weather.
Obviously, these new designs will enable us to reduce the time taken to reach a casualty but at an overall cost of £50 million, our need has never been greater.
That said, the need for the lifeboat service has never been greater either.
Last year for example, was the busiest in our 169 year history, with launches up 10% over 1991.
5,445 launches were made, resulting in the successful rescues of 1,372 men, women and children and bringing the total of lives saved since 1824 up to a staggering 123,000.
Please give our brave crews the support they so desperately need and deserve by filling in the coupon below.
It really is their most important lifeline.
To: The Director, Royal National Lifeboat Institution, West Quay Road, Poole, Dorset BH15 1HZ. I wish to join the R.N.L.I. My first annual donation is:
Mr/Mrs/Miss/Ms
Address
Postcode
Royal National Lifeboat Institution
Photography: Martin Beckett
This space has been very kindly donated by RAC Motoring Services Ltd.

Figure 2

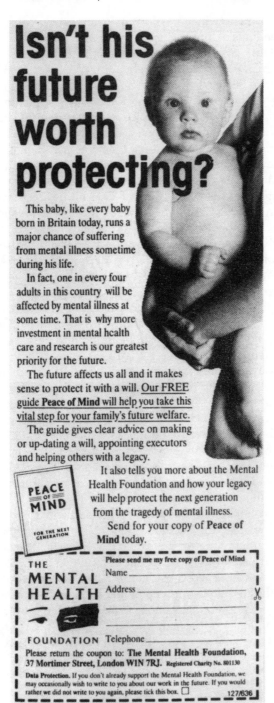

Figure 3

second sense of anxiety that one finds in Winnicott's account; he combines everyday meanings of anxiety as a sense of uneasiness with an account of what the infant will feel if the mother is intrusive, and anxiety then becomes a signal of impending annihilation (Winnicott, 1953).

As soon as we begin reading the King George's Fund advert (Figure 1) we are being warned that the 'disaster at sea' in the picture is not something we can keep at a distance. We see a ship floundering, but we are told that 'worse things' than this happen ashore, where we are. We are drawn into a scenario of impending disaster where each danger out at sea is matched by even worse things around us, and the problems of the past, from 'two World Wars', come closer to us in 'the present day'. The Lifeboat advert (Figure 2) evokes the sense of impending disaster through the written text in the crescendo of tasks facing the charity as it supports those dealing with 'the most atrocious' weather conditions, the 'very worst' of sea and weather, 'near or complete' darkness and 'sub zero temperatures', and we are told that it is faced with a 'quite simply immense' task where the need 'has never been greater'.

We can also note that in both the Lifeboat and Mental Health adverts we are face to face with those who need help gazing out at us. The Lifeboat advert has a distressed child imploring us to help and the lifeboatman is holding the child as if he is about to pass it over to us. The baby in the Mental Health advert (Figure 3) gazes at us more in an attitude of curiosity, but the text reframes this so that we are aware of their message too as a warning. Here, we are all seafarers. There is a 'major chance' of this child suffering from 'mental illness', and 'one in every four adults in this country' will be affected. They will be affected at some time, and so the advert reaches out and includes the reader in that one in four chance, a point which is made more explicit when we are invited to send for the booklet for 'your' family's future welfare. The device of impending disaster, and the advert as a signal of anxiety is thus constructed in each of these three texts.

Gronemeyer (1992: 54) points out that modern help 'is much more likely to be guided by a careful calculation of one's own advantage than by a concerned consideration for the other's need'. The crucial task of the charity advertiser, however, is to cut through this calculation, and to ensure that even concerned consideration does not permit the viewers to decide that they are safe enough not to need to give. The sense that something might go badly wrong mobilizes the readers to protect themselves, but the trick of the advertisement must be to draw the readers in so that they are also impelled to protect others. Children are particularly powerful emblems of powerlessness in charity advertising, and they also function as reminders of the powerlessness of all charity recipients in the 'Third World' (Burman, 1995).

IDENTIFICATION   There is a progressive shift in Freud's writing to seeing the self as built up out of the variety of identifications with significant others in childhood. In *Totem and Taboo* (1912–1913), Freud describes this process of identification as occurring through oral incorporation, and the ego will later be seen as consisting of bits of the parents that have been taken in and patched together through the trials of Oedipal love and hate (Freud, 1924). This impetus is continued in the object relations tradition, and Winnicott (1969) describes the way in which infant is given a self by the mother and may even fabricate a 'False Self' out of bits of mother for the time when it will take her position to mother her. It is this process that gives 'peace of mind'.

'Identification' in these adverts is invited through the rhetorical trope of 'people like you'. Identification encourages the self-less giving over of part of one's-self to another. The Lifeboat advert describes the ways in which 'people like you' keep them going and how they save the lives of 'complete strangers'. The reader is a complete stranger, but is addressed as a stranger who helps other complete strangers in an identification with the organization. The Lifeboat advert puts it this way: 'Because just as thousands of people rely entirely upon us for their survival, we must rely entirely on you for ours'. A similar device is used in the King George's Fund advert, which reads 'All these charities rely heavily on us – as we need to rely on you'. The Mental Health advert runs rapidly through a series of identifications to arrive at the reader from the headline to a point in each paragraph: 'Isn't his future worth protecting' to 'This baby, like every baby' to 'In fact, one in four adults' to 'this vital step for your family's future welfare'.

This identification is two-fold. First, there are reminders of dependence, powerlessness and passivity. The child is a potent sign for each of these things. The child being held in the Mental Health advert is fairly placid, but the child in the Lifeboat advert is distressed, and the man holding the child gazes helplessly at the reader too. A semiotic displacement from child to floundering ship occurs in the King George's Fund advert. Secondly, there is the promise of autonomy, control and activity. The Lifeboat advert is particularly interesting here, for we have a Winnicottian mother–child dyad appealing for support from the father as protective envelope, but we take the position of the father while we simultaneously identify with the man who is positioned also now as a kind of mother.

If we read this in the context of charity adverts in general – and it is important to be aware that these three adverts asking us to help local causes must be located in the wider signifying chain of charity advertising – we may also understand how a normative and normalizing discourse frames modern help: 'Its essential impulse nowadays is to overcome a deficit, the important deficit to be precise. It conducts a struggle against backwardness' (Gronemeyer, 1992: 59).

Choices about the placing and frequency of adverts negotiate a fine line between readers' altruism and their annoyance. There is a powerful ambivalence among readers of newspapers like these about giving money with no return. It is uncomfortable to be reminded of our ambivalent feelings of helplessness and love for others and hatred of those who lack. The process of identification between the reader of the advert and those who need help is premised on the possibility of sidestepping that ambivalence and returning the objects of care to a state of pre-ambivalent dependence where we need not hate them so much for calling upon us in our homes at breakfast.

Spirituality and materiality

Some would argue that this kind of advertising expresses a distortion of genuine caring which is of a piece with the reification of relationships in contemporary Western culture. Charity is perfume in the sewers of capitalism, and 'aid' to the Third World binds the colonized all the more tightly into relations of dependence on those with power (Hayter, 1971). As far as the charity advertisements that begin at home are concerned, 'care' is turned into part of a commercial machinery which reduces recipients to powerless objects. They are also captured as objects of the gaze of the giver in texts that are mechanically reproduced millions of times and circulated out of their control: 'Whoever desires help is "voluntarily" made subject to the watchful gaze of the helper. This gaze has nowadays assumed the place of the compassionate' (Gronemeyer, 1992: 54). That aside, or precisely because of that, it is important to understand how those texts work when they meet the readers who are turned into *subjects*, and so into powerful objects of another kind. The relationship between the readers as givers and the objects in the charity texts is infused with anxiety and fixed by processes of identification. These patterns of meaning reconfigure representations of care so that the viewer is simultaneously positioned in the realm of religious ethics and psychodynamic care. This realm is constituted by, among other things, the versions of psychoanalytic discourse which Winnicott picked up and popularized, and this means that when we are subjects of charity advertising we are also, in some sense, Winnicottian subjects.

This analysis raises broader ethical considerations about our sensitivity to the political consequences of attacking or defending religious ideas in different cultural contexts. Such considerations have also led some analysts to reconsider the standard psychoanalytic position. Freud intended psychoanalysis to be a materialist critique of all forms of theology but it too has often been incorporated into the church as priests draw upon psychotherapeutic discourse to reach deeper into the soul of the penitents. This is reinforced by the argument advanced by some analysts that they are simply occupying the priest's domain today when they minister to sicknesses of the modern soul (Fromm, 1967). Foucault's (1976) critique of psychoanalysis as a continuation and intensification of the Catholic confessional draws attention to this, even if it has been claimed by some writers that his account is compatible with Christianity precisely because it leads us to a possible view of caring and giving to others without expectation of return (Fox, 1995). Foucault's account of 'pastoral power' may now even be seen as a recommendation for as well as a description of Christianity.

Writers such as Kovel (1988), who have identified themselves with not one but two materialist traditions of thought hostile to religion, psychoanalysis and Marxism, have now shifted their position under the impact of events in liberation movements that have appeared to gain strength from religion rather than been weakened by it. The notion of religion as a 'crooked cure' is a dialectical notion, in which relief is both obtained and frustrated. Kovel points out that the well-known formula which proclaims that religion 'is the *opium* of the people' (Marx, 1844: 244) is also dialectical, and more so if we read back in Marx's invective to the sentences before that slogan where we find that he also characterizes it in this way: '*Religious* suffering is at one and the same time the *expression* of real suffering and a protest against real suffering. Religion is the sigh of an oppressed creature, the heart of a heartless world and the soul of soulless conditions' (ibid.): the drug gives solace and perhaps some strength. Kovel is also writing against the background of our experience of Stalinist 'scientific' socialism, which was as much a nightmare for a culture as the most oppressive scientific psychology is for the individual. Societies that tried to blot out spirituality not only failed, but we find now that they are collapsing and that worse forms of mysticism are erupting as a result of that failure. For Kovel,

> Mystical experience is self-reflection on the spirit; it is to make the spirit densely present, the spirit-self as deity: God is within you; you are God; for the Buddhist it is the insight that all beings are already Buddhas, except they don't know it.
> (Kovel, 1988: 327)

Kovel argues that spirituality is not the same as organized religion. It may operate as an expression of transcendence which allows desire to take on new objects and so it enables the individual to realize the possibility of new social relations. It is bound up, then, as much with the transformation of our awareness of our-selves as with the reproduction of power relations between ourselves and others. Although Kovel offers examples of progressive reformulations of spirituality from religions such as Buddhism, he argues that when people are empowered they can rework even the most conservative religious institutions. It might even be possible, as the experience of the liberation theologians in Latin America indicates, for something progressive to emerge from the very Catholic Church which was, of course, Freud's object of scorn and favourite example of the sedimentation of psychopathological religiosity. In this view it is not individual transformation which accomplishes the destruction of religious neurosis, as Freud thought, but social transformation which accomplishes the spiritual transcendence of our need for neurosis. Neither a psychoanalysis of religion or a discourse analysis of charity texts should be seen as sufficient responses to the issue. Marx puts this well in a passage which follows that phrase about religion being an opium:

> The abolition of religion as the *illusory* happiness of the people is the demand for their *real* happiness. To call on them to give up their illusions about their condition is to *call on them to give up a condition that requires illusions.*
>
> (Marx, 1844: 244)

There is thus a tension in Freud's writings which is stretched almost to breaking point in the writings of some later psychoanalysts; between wanting to save rationalist critique of mystification *and* to value alternative forms of belief that people may find helpful. Such beliefs which hold people together in groups become harmful or helpful when they are put into practice, and we will turn to look at what fantasies are unleashed in cultures faced with 'others' they fear and what action that might entail in the next chapter.

3

War Breaking Out, in Inner and Outer Space

Lord Goddard, the late judge who sentenced Derek Bentley to hang in 1952, got sexual gratification from sentencing young men to death [...] 'His clerk, Arthur Smith, told me he used to take a spare pair of striped trousers round for Goddard because he knew that Goddard always had an ejaculation when sentencing youths to be flogged or hanged,' writes Mr Parris, the only surviving counsel in the case.

The Guardian (10 June 1991)

Psychoanalytic descriptions of group structure (seen as operating through identification with the leader or through the interplay between basic assumption states) and descriptions of religious belief systems which hold groups together (seen as operating through some obsessional neurotic pathology or through a sharing of transitional spaces of devotion) also key us into particular ways of understanding conflict between groups and the eruption of violence as groups defend their own belief systems against those of their rivals. Freud, and those following him in the object relations tradition all the more so, tended to see such violent conflict as being on a kind of war-continuum. The war which breaks out at an international level is interpretable because it is seen as an expression of war raging inside the mind of the individual. Thus, 'the psychoanalysis of war is continuous with the psychoanalysis of peacetime' (Richards, 1986: 24). The violence that erupts from inside the person can lead to conflicts between people, and these conflicts can then escalate into civil war, and thence to war between nations. Just as Freudian accounts of group identity and religious practices can be traced down to the intricacies of identification and obsession, so the dynamics of war can be reduced to murderous licensed varieties of acting out. The State might sanction war, but it draws upon reserves of violence that are ready and willing to spill out from each citizen.

Some social psychologists (e.g., Billig, 1976) have argued against psychoanalytic explanation because it always seems to reduce violence in society to aggression deep in the unconscious of each person. Psychoanalysts (e.g., Kovel, 1983) have also challenged this sort of reductionist tendency, and have argued that there is something qualitatively different about the nature of conflict at the level of the State, whether that is in the way the State provokes and manages the violence that exists inside the borders of one nation or in the way the State mobilizes the violence of its population against other States. It is possible to go a little further in this critique of reductionism in psychoanalysis, however, if we look at the ways in which psychoanalytic accounts have themselves emerged from conditions of extreme violence, and the ways that images and metaphors of violence have come to be embedded in Freudian and in some versions of post-Freudian theory. Freud's explanation of violence was elaborated in the context of the carnage of the First World War, and some of the most extreme representations of the infant at permanent war – in the writings of Melanie Klein – were spun as the Second World War brewed and erupted and threw forth images of cruelty that surpassed what many imagined could have been possible in twentieth-century Europe.

Freudian representations of interpersonal violence as the repetition of destructive impulses in the human constitution have flowed through cultural images of war, and these representations have played their part in framing the way people account for war. This is not at all to say that psychoanalytic discourse has become the dominant mode of explanation for war, merely that representations of the self at conflict with itself and others chimed with prevalent appeals in the West to innate aggression and the sense that there was something wrong with human nature. Freud was not the source of all we know today as 'Freudian discourse', and many people speak that discourse about their selves and their violence and how important it is to understand it and work it through without knowing that it is at all psychoanalytic. Few people outside the psychoanalytic world have heard of Klein, but she too crystallized and informed, sucked in and spat out into the culture a certain kind of discourse about the self and what lies inside it. Kleinian representations of the infant torn in rage at itself and at its objects twist this psychoanalytic discourse a demonic turn beyond Freud, and these representations have also fed into a cultural climate deeply pessimistic about the depths of natural and essential human depravity. Kleinian representations make sense to a generation of psychoanalysts now working in the object relations tradition, and despite Winnicott's more comforting story about the infant frightening the mother with its relentless love, Klein's ruthless hateful child has sunk its roots into the demotic circulation of psychoanalysis in child-care training, nursery provision and so into the way many people talk and think about welfare and warfare (Riley, 1983; Rose, 1993a).

This chapter tracks the road from First World War Freud and the death drive to Second World War Klein and death instincts. The chapter then turns to ways Kleinian images of death in the inner space of the child help structure discursive complexes in the talk of people preoccupied with death in outer space and their investment in it. This exploration of psychoanalytic discourse in accounts of sightings and meetings with UFOs and aliens will serve to illustrate key tenets of Kleinian theory, *and* to show how that theoretical system permeates and so gives a peculiar psychoanalytic flavour to contemporary preoccupations with aliens. While 'real' wars have certainly broken out around the planet since the Second World War, the fascination with extraterrestrial attack helps to constitute the population as one ready for another big war, and the transmission of talk about conspiracy and vigilance is one of the ideological sites for framing and priming groups in the West for action.

Freud's war

Freud's own comments on the topic of violence after the start of the First World War prepared the ground for a reworking of the first dual-drive model that had structured the early years of psychoanalysis. That *first* model had been organized around a polarity between sexual instincts and ego instincts, and aggression toward others was then seen as resulting from the ego asserting itself. Although in *Three Essays on the Theory of Sexuality* (1905a) Freud had suggested that aggressiveness might be one of the 'component instincts' of the sexual instinct, the possibility that aggression might be instinctual is dismissed; it is viewed as a manifestation of the 'instincts of self-preservation' (Freud, 1909a), and in *Instincts and their Vicissitudes* he argued that 'Hate, as a relation to objects, is older than love. It derives from the narcissistic ego's primordial repudiation of the external world with its outpouring of stimuli' (Freud, 1915a: 137). In the same year, in his paper 'Thoughts for the Times on War and Death', he writes of the way in which 'the primaeval history of humanity is filled with murder' (Freud, 1915b: 81), and the grim message here is that this murder has its roots in our attempts to cope with destruction around us, and in destructive impulses from deep inside. We will review Freud's first dual-drive account of death-threat from our images of what lies outside us first (focusing on themes of ambivalence and paranoia, and suggestions as to how these may be tackled), and then turn to second dual-drive psychoanalytic accounts of death-threats from the interior (focusing on the death drive and innate aggression, and discussions of how best to ameliorate these).

Threat and defence

Freud described certain processes which may give rise to interpersonal violence and then to war as the result of inadequate or insufficient developmental working through in which the ego is formed. Although Freud's account is deliberately and thoroughly reductionist, it has been possible for some later analysts to retrieve his explanations and try to re-situate them in contemporary culture as social processes.

AMBIVALENCE   The notion of ambivalence can be used to account for simultaneous feelings of affection for and identification with an enemy, and so for the way hatred can coexist with empathy, and so open the way to the possibility of forgiveness. Freud's (1915b) rumination on war also describes the tortuous route by which ambivalence works to reinforce unconscious fantasies about the nature and power of an 'other' who cannot be seen and about threats that cannot be rationally assessed. Freud argued that the twists and turns in the perception of violence, defences against it and the attempt to pre-empt it by violent attack on the enemy, often run through the following four steps.

First, the murder of enemies evokes an identification with those murdered others as being like the self, and so there is some feeling of empathy. However, secondly, this in turn evokes fears about one's own mortality, for one cannot face the fantasized annihilation that one wishes on the other and the idea this provokes that one's own life will come to an end. This fear leads, thirdly, to a defensive fantasy in which one is consoled by the notion that the spirit will live on after the body has perished. An implication of this, of course, is that the spirits of the enemy will also live on. This sense of the dead continuing to live is fuelled by our experience of those we love always 'living' in our memories. The fourth and final twist, then, is that our hatred and fear which has been projected out at the enemy – as actually dead, or as fantasized into a state where it 'will-be-dead' – reinforces the perception of that enemy as uncannily powerful and persecutory. The most powerful fear and hatred of the 'other' rebounds, then, to create in us an experience of enmity and a fantasy of imminent death which borders on and feeds paranoia.

PARANOIA   Freud's (1911a) discussion of Judge Schreber's delusions sets out the basic mechanism of paranoia. Paranoia results from the experience of threats from within, and the defence mechanism of projection is activated to an extraordinary degree because of complex internal dynamics. Another typical logical sequence is set in train through this mechanism. The account also anticipates Freud's (1914a) discussion of the stage of narcissism in which an internal love object is constructed which is based upon the self. This internal love object is a mental agency which Freud (1921) will later term the 'ego ideal' when he discusses group psychology, and this agency is then seen as the heir to narcissism (while the 'super-ego' will later come to be seen as the heir to the Oedipus complex). The narcissistic state lingers on in our desire for others who are the same sex as ourselves – a homosexual desire that is 'normally' repressed as a precondition for emerging as a healthy boy or girl from the Oedipus complex – and this kind of same-sex desire is thus assumed by many analysts always to take a narcissistic form.

The reasoning here is that we are looking for another to love who is like ourselves, and that we thus take a position as the lover who will love another very much like our mother loved us. However, this desire is felt to be threatening, and so it is important that it stay repressed. A consequence is that the internal representation of love for another like ourselves is projected; that is, it is experienced as being *outside* the body who is doing the desiring and who is wanting to be desired. This manoeuvre will still not solve the problem though, for it would be difficult to accept this desire even when it comes from outside because of deeply internalized sanctions against homosexuality. The sense that someone who is the same sex as ourselves may love us or be loved by us is, for many 'normal' folk, unthinkable, and so a 'reversal of affect' occurs such that the fantasized external lover is *hated* and experienced as *hating*.

By this point we have been drawn into a psychopathological spiral, but we can also turn psychoanalytic discourse against itself at this point to deconstruct the homophobia that runs through most psychoanalytic theory and practice. Although Freud repeatedly described homosexual object choice as if it were an abnormal arresting of development at the narcissistic stage, and it is still treated as a perversion by contemporary analysts (e.g., Chasseguet-Smirgel, 1985a), one of the lessons of Freud's account of paranoia is surely that it is the *repression* of ubiquitous homosexual desire that is the problem. Because those feelings of love are turned into hatred, and those feelings which we have attempted to throw out still feel glued to us, inside us, there are then delusions that the 'other' knows what is going on inside, and so an uncanny and unshakable sense of persecution follows. We arrive, then, at the main characteristic of paranoia as a conviction that we are being observed and that others know our innermost thoughts.

SOCIETAL PARANOIA   This account does help us to comprehend the way in which a powerful enemy is often also fascinating, and even loved, and it may even be possible to reframe such a narrative about denial and reversal so that what is being described is as much a distorted social process as one rooted in the faulty development of the individual. Certain cultural conditions and patterns of authority can constitute paranoia as a frightening experience of real persecution and provoke in the victim such dependency that the oppressor enters their life-world as a kind of love object. We see this described and explored well in fictional representations of persecution, for example in the way that Winston Smith both fears and loves O'Brian in George Orwell's *Nineteen Eighty Four* (Easthope, 1984). This image of the persecutor and persecuted locked into love and hate also draws attention to the way this pattern can just as well bind men together as it can men and women. It has been argued, for example, that there are close links between contemporary masculinity, homophobia and militarization because masculinity is a form of gender identity which is predicated on a precarious separation from the mother which is then shored-up by attacks on gay men who evoke that early closeness (Easthope, 1986). Armies operate as collections of men which express unconscious desire and threat as a symptom and 'crooked cure' of this homophobia. The army is bound together by unconscious homoerotic libidinal ties, but the anxiety this closeness to other men provokes can only be defended against through an all the more vicious destruction of 'others' who are perceived as the more evident threats to masculinity. In peacetime, then, soldiers will want to attack men who are out as gay to affirm their own masculinity, and in wartime representations of the enemy will be soaked in sexual ambivalence, as was apparent during the Persian Gulf War (Levidow, 1995).

NUCLEAR PARANOIA   In such states of mind the person is deeply attached to the persecutor, and the existence of a weapon that may annihilate everyone, and which is mobilized by the State to maintain a tension between fear and trust is also a phenomenon which is qualitatively different from everyday paranoia. Kovel (1983: 106) claims that 'nuclear strategy ... induces paranoia', and that it produces both an active hatred of the enemy and passive acquiescence to authority at home. At the time of greatest nuclear threat, when the Soviet Union was portrayed as the 'evil empire', the basic psychic structure of the West was 'the perfect culture medium for the bacillus of paranoia' (ibid.: 110). The fantasized image of the other was bound up with fascination and fear. Now the focus is shifting. At one moment it is centred on dictatorships in the Third World who cannot be trusted with nuclear technology, and at another it is on terrorists at home who may steal a nuclear device and destroy us all. Wherever it shifts, it is continually mobilized through images of the enemy and what the enemy knows, it is produced and energized through our discourse about the other.

AFFINITY GROUPS   Kovel (1983) does offer some suggestions as to how this process might be challenged, and he attempts to apply psychoanalysis not only to the psychodynamics of war at an intrapersonal and interpersonal level, but also to the social level. He tries to explain the paranoiac grip of the State on individuals in 'nuclear' culture, as well as to explore possible ways of resisting that. One solution rests on the way that people might organize together to challenge the power that paranoid ideology enjoys when they are isolated from other people. Affinity groups are seen by Kovel as one solution, and these groups would consist of people sharing a specific aim – to get rid of the Bomb. The dissolution of paranoia would be brought about through identification with other members of the group. This building of emotional ties with others of the same as well as the 'other' sex would also serve to challenge the homophobic roots of paranoia. Desire would thus be re-channelled to bind rather than separate people from each other.

This process would not operate, then, through the development of an abstract 'reason' or rationality to oppose and repress further 'unreasonable' or irrational feelings. Contemporary 'reason', for Kovel, is the bureaucratic reason that produces nuclear technology in which people are reduced to numbers and 'kill factors'. Instead of the triumph of reason, the joining with others would be 'the work of Eros' (ibid.: 223), and 'Otherness no longer remains locked away in paranoid projections: it, too, rejoins and empowers the self even as the self joins others' (ibid.: 224). Psychodynamic processes are thus located in specific patterns of rationality in modern society and in the context of particular kinds of destruction. The strategies Kovel presents are designed to transform our relationship with each other, and with death threats that appear from without.

Death from within

Freud's theoretical shift to his *second* dual-drive theory after the First World War opened the way for descriptions of more deeply rooted irrational and destructive forces. These forces are not produced through a failure of development or full formation of the ego. Rather, they boil as an ever-present threat from within the unconscious, and then further down from within the body. Here it is much more difficult to rework Freud's account as a social story, and the tendency has been for later psychoanalytic writers to draw on this to embed descriptions of violence even more firmly in an instinct model of human behaviour.

THANATOS   The notion of the death drive was introduced by Freud after the First World War. There are a number of reasons why Freud might have been led to propose the existence of a death drive. Two oft-cited but untenable reasons are that he was suffering from cancer of the jaw (which was not diagnosed until four years later) or that he was overwhelmed by the death of his daughter Sophie from influenza in 1920 (which was after he had completed the manuscript). Freud's preoccupation with death might be relevant, and he is reported as thinking about dying every day (Fromm, 1974). Good reasons to do with the internal logic of psychoanalytic theory would include his attempt to solve the 'regression paradox' in which some force could be posited which would draw the libido back to an earlier *aim* as well as to earlier objects, and the 'evolution/involution paradox' which would ground the tendency to recapitulate old reactions to new events in material biological processes (Sulloway, 1979). The new dualism between Love (*Eros*) and Death (*Thanatos*) also reasserted psychoanalysis as a theory which was structured around a polarity, something threatened by Freud's (1914a) work on narcissism as a monist account which would lose the sense of internal contradiction in psychodynamic processes (Fromm, 1974; Sulloway, 1979). Freud (1920) also described his efforts to account for the tendency of dreams not only to engage in the wish-fulfilment of pleasant things, but also to return us to times of fright. The First World War also provides more than a backdrop to these theoretical transformations, and was a major explosion of violence in Europe after years of stability.

Freud later argued that such violence was a projection outward of the death drive, and in *Beyond the Pleasure Principle* (Freud, 1920) he saw this as counterbalancing the drive for life: 'besides the instinct to preserve living substance and to join it into ever larger units, there must exist another, contrary instinct seeking to dissolve those units and to bring them back to their primordial, inorganic state. That is to say, as well as Eros there was an instinct of death' (ibid.: 299). In later papers this is elaborated so that violence toward others can be accounted for as the channelling of the destructive impulses to the external world through 'a special organ': 'This special organ would seem to be the muscular apparatus; and the death instinct would thus seem to express itself – though probably only in part – as an instinct of destruction directed against the external world and other organisms' (Freud, 1923b: 381).

The *Standard Edition* turns Freud's *Todestrieb* from a 'death drive' (which is how it should be correctly translated) into a 'death instinct', and this interpretation of Freud's concept has been further vulgarized by psychologists who then think that it is equivalent to their own descriptions of innate aggression (Richards, 1989). Notwithstanding the attempts at re-translation and theoretical re-framing to rescue what he originally meant, Freud's account here is much more difficult to rework as a social process, and even radical psychoanalytic writers like Marcuse (1955), who tried to locate Eros and Thanatos in the development of civilization, still presupposed the existence of those two figures of Love and Death as huge metaphysical forces which had always and would always power history and society.

AGGRESSION   Freud's notion of the death drive also slots all too conveniently into popular ideological motifs of instinctual violence, and the notion that it is impossible to build a peaceful society because aggressive impulses will always eventually burst out. Biological explanations for violence are integrated into psychoanalysis here in the work of writers influenced by ethology. Key figures in the Independent tradition of the British Psycho-Analytical Society, such as John Bowlby (1973), for example, drew on the writings of Konrad Lorenz (1966). In this kind of account, 'the "causes" attributed by historians to the wars of the recent past are not really causes at all, but merely the triggers that set them off' (Stevens, 1986: 2). The appeal to aggressive instincts can then be elaborated in a number of ways. Organized group hostility, for example, is then seen as an 'inherent characteristic of the species', with the problem reduced to being that of 'activating the inborn neuropsychic complex responsible for co-ordinating aggressive experience and behaviour' (ibid.: 3).

Stevens (1986) also appeals to the work of Alfred Adler (1930), who split from Freud in 1911 and went on to elaborate an alternative drive account based on the 'power principle', and he argues that warfare arises through the specialization of functions in human groups in which aggressive impulses are evolutionarily advantageous: 'Disease germs are the most important microparasites humans have to deal with. . . . Our only significant macroparasites are other men who, by specializing in violence, are able to secure a living without themselves producing the food and other commodities they consume' (McNeil, quoted in Stevens, 1986: 6). This hotch-potch of wired-in explanations ranging from mysticism to ethology even embraces Jung to argue that 'archetypes' are similar to 'innate releasing mechanisms', and so they explain phenomena as varied as male bonding, hunting and killing, in which a process of 'pseudo-speciation' (a concept drawn from yet another analyst, Erik Erikson) sanctions the murder of others who are thus represented as sufficiently different from ourselves. Ingroup–outgroup distinctions are also explained in this way, as indeed anything and everything could be, because it is then 'natural' to construct an image of the other to support one's own group identity.

AWARENESS AND SUBLIMATION   All that can be hoped for in this grim picture of innate human aggression is that we might reflect on what is driving us and try to channel it in less harmful directions: 'If we wish to prevent nuclear war, then we have to confront a set of archetypal imperatives which are of great phylogenetic antiquity' (Stevens, 1986: 14), and so the degree to which we can be optimistic 'depends on which possesses the greater power – consciousness or the archetypes' (ibid.:15). Freud's own suggestions provide little more comfort.

In Freud's debate with Einstein, they agreed on the need for a special body to oversee conflicts. Einstein (1933: 347) suggested that this might help us cope with the 'lust for hatred and destruction' in people. Freud (1933b: 352) argued that violence could be overcome 'by the transference of power to a larger unity, which is held together by emotional ties between its members'. Given that the death drive could not be wished away, the question was how to channel it, and so how to provide a way of sublimating it in an organizational form: 'The ideal condition of things would of course be a community of men who had subordinated their instinctual life to the dictatorship of reason' (ibid.: 359). This solution rests on a belief in the ability of delegated bodies to represent interests without being affected by the drives and a belief in the power of reason, of the positive progressive character of the reality principle.

Sublimation, which in the original German includes meanings of 'improvement' (Bettelheim, 1983), would thus be one way of channelling the drives. Another way which Freud considered was that the death drive could be contained by mobilizing alternative forces. Here, in a proposal that Kovel was later to pick up, Freud (1933b: 359) argued that to counter the death drive we should 'bring Eros, its antagonist, into play against it' because 'Anything that encourages the growth of emotional ties between men must operate against war'. This solution rests on a belief in the contradiction between the death drive and Eros and a belief that the construction of 'emotional ties between men' would lessen the threat of war. While Freud's account is fairly joyless, there is little more hope in Klein.

Klein's war

There is a problem in the translation of Freud's term *Todestrieb*, but for some psychoanalysts in Britain, there were no qualms in referring to it as an 'instinct'. The notion of the death instinct is taken seriously by Kleinians who would see the movement between different infantile defence mechanisms against destructive forces as being the key to development (Segal, 1987, 1995). Although Klein describes the rudimentary ego and super-ego as structuring Oedipal relationships at an earlier age than Freud, hers is not so much a revision of a developmental account as the abandonment of traditional psychoanalytic notions of personal history and time. There is not so much a regression to a phase, but the re-adoption of a *position*: 'what she is observing, describing and theorizing is the very absence of history and of historical time' (Mitchell, 1986: 29). Klein is not so much interested in the unconscious as a system of thought following particular laws, as in the unconscious as a kind of container where representations of self and other collide, and she is interested not so much in the dream-work as in the *contents* of the dream (Mitchell, 1986). The narcissistic grandiose self which hides a hollow emptiness, an inside as a sparsely furnished space, is a common phenomenon that has been noticed by those who diagnose society now as having been transformed into a 'culture of narcissism' (Lasch, 1978). (This diagnosis is discussed in Chapter 6.) Klein is not a theorist of narcissistic disturbances, but her model of the mind does seem to fit with this sense of the mind that contemporary culture contains, the mind as container of objects.

The horror of being a child calls into play a variety of positions and defences which endure through adult life. Earliest psychotic anxieties of the infant psychically glue it to the first object, the mother's breast through the operation of certain key defence mechanisms. In this first paranoid-schizoid position, the defences simultaneously control and reinforce the anxiety: *Splitting*, the 'severance of love and hate', and of the 'frustrating breast' from the 'gratifying breast', is a process which tears at the ego as well as at the object; *Projection* throws the death instinct out onto the object but rebounds to persecute the infant; *Introjection*, the taking in of the good object, is 'a precondition for normal development', but provokes anxieties of dependence in which the ego is only a 'shell' for the object; and *Projective Identification*, 'the forceful entry into the object', connects ego to object through terrifying 'phantasies' of retribution and of imprisonment and persecution within the object (Klein, 1946). The attainment of the depressive position, the production of 'the synthesis between the loved and hated aspects of the complete object' (ibid.: 178), is attended by mourning, guilt and reparation. The paranoid-schizoid position and depressive position are not developmental stages, they are positions which we flee and revisit, and from which there is no escape.

Klein carries through to contemporary psychoanalysis the second dual-drive system that Freud tentatively outlined in *Beyond the Pleasure Principle* (1920), a model in which the libido no longer struggles with the ego instincts but in which there is a more deadly competition between the still sexual 'life' drive and the death drive. For Klein this really is the death instinct, a 'destructive impulse' which is projected outwards in oral, anal and phallic forms of aggression, in devouring, burning and cutting the object, but which repeatedly returns as 'hatred and persecutory anxiety' (Klein, 1946: 180). The fantasies of killing, eating and mourning that are expressed in the specific rituals of Christianity, and which were described by Freud as *pathological* phenomena, are fantasies that are similar to those described by Klein as operating in every infant (particularly in the way physical activities of eating are used as the model for psychic processes of incorporation). For Klein it is not necessary to return to events in the primal horde to account for them. These processes are played out in every group we inhabit, and Klein's work has been attractive to some researchers wanting to understand conflict in the workplace.

Class war

Klein's work was used in the 1950s to link individual and group phenomena at work. The starting point of Elliott Jaques's (1951, 1953) study of industrial conflict was the hypothesis that 'one of the primary cohesive elements binding individuals into institutionalized human associations is that of defence against anxiety emanating from the psychotic developmental level' (Jacques, 1953: 420–421). Kleinian accounts of projection, introjection and identification were used to expand Freud's account of group psychology. Freud's (1921) explanation of the tie bonding members with a leader rested on identification and the putting of the leader into the place of each of the members' ego-ideals, but Jaques argued that there is also a sense in which the members of a group are putting part of themselves into the leader and then identifying with that part of themselves they recognize there. This is the process described by Klein as projective identification, and its roots lie in early infancy when the the child projects parts of itself onto the mother and identifies with those parts. The ego, built up out of these identifications, is reconstructed out of the phantasized parts that were once part of the infant's internal world outside of their ego in the unconscious. The risk is that projection may be carried out to such a degree that *all* that is good is felt to be outside, and then there is a sense of loss. The panic in groups described by Freud, which, Freud says, follow the loosening of libidinal ties, may include panic at having lost the good parts projected onto the leader when the leader is lost.

In organizations, which always consist of different sub-groupings, an important aspect of group experience concerns the relationships between the groups that one is a member of and *other* groups (and these small groups also consist of sub-groups). Here, the projection of bad parts from a minority group onto a dominant group can provoke a 'real' persecution which, because it then becomes 'real' outside is able to rationalize and so gloss over painful awareness of conflict in psychic reality:

one of the operative factors ... is the consensus in the minority group, at the phantasy level, to seek contempt and suffering. That is to say, there is an unconscious co-operation (or collusion) at the phantasy level between persecutors and persecuted.

(Jaques, 1953: 428)

Jaques's case study concerned one department in a light engineering company. There were about sixty members in the department, and so they constituted, in therapeutic terms, what group analysts would now call a 'large group' (Kreeger, 1975). Conflicts broke out between workers' representatives (the shop stewards) and management over attempts to move from piece-work payments to flat-rate methods of payment. The dispute was over the administration of the payments rather than the principle of the move (which all parties had agreed to). There were conflicts between the workers and the shop stewards and between the shop stewards and management. These two forms of conflict were sharper than conflicts between the workers and management. Jaques explained this process using notions of defence against paranoid and depressive anxiety, and his concerns were not so much with projective identification as a form of alienation in capitalist society (cf. Hinshelwood, 1983, 1985, 1996) as in the way alienation might be made palatable in a new contract between workers and management.

First, the workers split management into good and bad (the good managers being the ones they had direct contact with), and destructive impulses were projected onto the shop stewards (who were directly in contact with the 'bad' management). The shop stewards, then, carried the hostility of the workforce. Because the shop stewards expressed hostility toward management, the workers were able to cope with their paranoid splitting of management into good and bad (and so they could work with the good). The collusion between the opposing factions can also be accounted for. The shop stewards were able to contain the hostility and destructiveness they felt toward management by experiencing these impulses not as their own property but as an expression of their members' wishes. The management were at the receiving end of these projections but had their own investment in this process. For them, guilt at wielding authority against the workers, with all the associated anxieties and phantasies of power that comes with such authority, could be assuaged by idealizing the shop stewards as the workers' representatives. The unconscious processes in each group thus complemented and reinforced each other:

> A circular process was set in motion. The more the workers' representatives attacked the managers, the more the managers idealized them in order to placate them. The greater the concessions given by management to the workers, the greater was the guilt and fear of depressive anxiety in the workers, and hence the greater the retreat to paranoid attitudes as a means of avoiding depressive anxiety.

(Jaques, 1953: 434)

War frames

Perhaps we should look to the experience of violence and symbolic violence in culture since Freud's death to understand the ways in which
images of life and destruction have become embedded in the conceptions
of self that people now weave and inhabit. Just as talk of a death drive
became plausible after the First World War, so Klein's bizarre and pessimistic account of the mind of the infant as torn between 'hallucinatory
gratification' and 'omnipotent annihilation' seem true after the Second
World War. The popular talk of innate aggression and projection, the mass
circulation of pre-war psychoanalysis in everyday consciousness also provokes a spiral deeper down into even more devastating phantasies of what
the infant must be, and so what we must really be. Even their preference
for the spelling of 'fantasy' as 'phantasy' serves to emphasize that what
Kleinians are concerned with are representations that inhabit the *unconscious* (and so it is the ph spelling that is often followed in this chapter).
When Klein talks of 'envy, greed, hatred and feelings of persecution in
relation to the primal object, the mother's breast, as largely innate' (Klein,
1956: 227), we can read her as describing potent *signs*, powerfully
cathected words and phrases in discourse in Western culture, the same
culture she obtained them from – even if she thought she simply saw them
in her children, in her child patients (Grosskurth, 1986).

The lifting of taboos on talk of sexuality and violence which the popularization of psychoanalysis has encouraged has not simply been a process
of revealing what was always there. This kind of discourse is, as Foucault
(1976) pointed out, *productive*. To talk of the infant's innate knowledge of
the penis, the vagina and womb, as Klein does, is to attribute to the infant
what we now all know, and know so well in the discourse of sex that now
surrounds us that we cannot imagine that it is possible not to know. And
because the discourse of sex is one that provokes us continually to know
more, it is not surprising perhaps that we project our obsessive desire to
know into the infant, as if it really were 'the epistemophilic instinct and
the desire to take possession' (Klein, 1928: 72).

Bion's work on groups and the application of Kleinian ideas in group
therapy were pursued as a direct result of war, and psychoanalysts were
drawn into the task of prosecuting war more effectively. We saw in Chapter
1 how psychiatrists from the Tavistock Clinic were concerned with staff
morale in the army and with analysing 'enemy mentality' during the
Second World War. Following the war the 'military wing' of the Tavistock
Clinic was transformed (in 'Operation Phoenix'), and a separate Tavistock
Institute of Human Relations was constituted in 1947 with a grant from the
Rockefeller Foundation (Trist and Murray, 1990). The analysis of enemy
mentality then focused on the Russian national character, with one key
study based on intensive interviews in 1952 with Soviet defectors (Dicks,
1960). Psychoanalysis itself as an institution was now caught up in forms
of war as the acting out of unconscious phantasies. The enemy was not only

seen as outside the nation state, but there was an ever-present threat to social order at home too. As well as continuing to prosecute a cold war for the State, then, the psychoanalysts at the Tavistock turned their energies to understanding and containing conflict in industry, and this too was the context for Jaques's (1951) therapeutic 'action research'.

Civil defence

These descriptions of the psychodynamics of internal war have consequences for how one thinks through responses to civil defence planning when war does loom. The threat of nuclear war until the late 1980s condensed these kinds of threats, and provoked some useful discussion of how threat and defence should be assessed. Government plans for war tend to feed the problem and call for critique and opposition, and this is all the more important because of the way the nuclear Bomb becomes the repository of destructive feelings. Using a Kleinian framework, Richards (1984a) argued that there is a two-fold phantasy that locks us into anxieties about death. On the one hand, the Bomb is filled with feelings of hate and destruction which we also identify with it, and this identification produces feelings of guilt. A consequence of this is regression to an omnipotent denial of the power of the Bomb. On the other hand, the incredible power of the Bomb is matched by a no less omnipotent belief in the ability of shelters to protect us, and in almost magical powers of survival and regeneration.

It would be tempting to conclude from this that civil defence planning should be rejected out of hand, but this would be to fall into a mirror-image of the first problem, and into the phantasies of the government preparing for war. A refusal to plan to survive could be interpreted as denial and as an expression of an intense inner conflict between fear and hatred of nuclear annihilation (a traumatic fright at the thought of the self being extinguished) and a desire for that annihilation (a wish to end conflict and to bring about an end to the struggle to survive). Any symbol of utter destruction will evoke this conflict between fear and desire, and the consequence is not only a splitting into 'good' and 'bad' projected into the outside world (and the division between the 'free world' and the 'evil empire'), but also a vacillation between two extreme and equally hopeless positions where we race from omnipotent faith in our ability to stop the Bomb to despairing powerlessness and back again. This kind of splitting is compounded by images of the government as part of a Welfare State which is charged with the protection of the citizens. The State is perceived as a substitute for the parents who nurture and care for us. The discovery that the State did not intend to protect us, but was only reserving places in the shelters for the administrators, is as traumatic as if we had made the discovery that our parents wanted to murder us – an old and powerful fantasy, of course, which recurs as a common theme in fairy tales (Bettelheim, 1976). These increasingly deeper levels of threat lead us into more elaborate strategies of denial, and Richards (1984a) argues that there is thus an imperative not to know, and so a refusal to put forward plans for any defence. For Richards, all of these factors are expressed in a refusal even to discuss alternative civil defence provision.

In these Kleinian accounts of the ever-present potential for war we also have some prescriptions for how we might cope when paranoid-schizoid splitting draws us into spirals of violence. We can also use Kleinian concepts to understand the *cultural* dynamics that keep this war drive on the move, and we can trace the way in which Kleinian concepts themselves structure anxieties about threat circulating through culture carrying representations of war with them.

Wars of the worlds

Let us move on now to accounts of meetings with aliens. The use of Klein's work will serve not only to illuminate some of the dynamics in these texts but also to show how the accounts are symptomatic of the emergence of a Kleinian sense of ourselves as something that has come to operate as if it were true. The descriptions of self and other that are elaborated in UFO discourse crystallize popular public fantasies. These have a mass audience. One of the biggest cinema hits of 1996, and the fastest-earning film to date (taking $100 million in six and a half days), for example, was *Independence Day*, released in the USA on 4 July. Following quickly in its wake were a number of other alien invasion movies (such as *Star Trek: First Contact* and *Mars Attacks!*). Meanwhile, the *X-Files* television series have led millions of viewers into the paranormal science fiction maze-world of agents Mulder and Scully.

This is a symbolic universe perpetually on the brink of destruction as the result of assaults from hidden forces from outer space and from inner space, with the individual at risk of being abducted by aliens from the stars and having their fate concealed by agents in the recesses of the State. We can track this universe by focusing on the discursive complexes of helplessness, family romance, projective identification and reality-testing. Unlike the previous chapter, this analysis takes a large corpus of text. I cite from the range of books, magazines and newsletters in the UFO community, and have been helped by interviews and discussions (that I don't cite directly here) about these themes with those attending some of the many conferences that community supports. These complexes turn the discourse that organizes the world of aliens into Klein's world, but the very possibility of reading those texts in this way is evidence of a Kleinian subjectivity circulating through them.

Helplessness

Infants are dependent on others to bring an end to the intolerable feeling of tension that biological needs produce. The biological basis for the powerlessness of human beings, then, is both embedded in and mediated by their first relationship with care-givers, and their helplessness also sets in play a structure for later traumatic situations and the production of anxiety (Freud, 1926). There is a recurring theme of subordination and submission in the 'contactee' literature. ('Contactees' are those who have been contacted by aliens.) Strieber's (1987: 24) description of his first meeting with aliens in his best-selling book *Communion* has him 'in a state of apparent paralysis', and of puzzling over his stillness, wondering at first whether it was part of a dream: 'Maybe this is why I continued to sit in bed, taking no action. Or perhaps my mind was already under some sort of control' (ibid.: 22). When the alien asks him, in a Midwestern accent, what they can do to stop him screaming, Strieber says:

> My reply was unexpected. I heard myself say, 'You could let me smell you'. I was embarrassed; that is not a normal request, and it bothered me. But it made a great deal of sense, as I have afterward realized. The one to my right replied, 'Oh, OK, I can do that', in a similar voice, speaking very rapidly, and held his hand against my face, cradling my head with his other hand. The odor was distinct, and gave me exactly what I needed, an anchor in reality.
> (ibid.: 28–29)

Although in this case the alien is male, it is normally the case that contactees meet with figures whom they perceive to be of the opposite sex. At one point, Strieber comments that 'I do not know why, but I had the distinct feeling this was a woman, and so I shall refer to her in the feminine' (ibid.: 25). In some cases the gender of the alien is important to the phantasies played out in the contact, as in the case of Antonio Villas-Boas who was abducted in Brazil and seduced by an alien with blonde hair and blue eyes (Vallee, 1988: 139). The relationship more often mutates rapidly into something more like enveloping and persecuting mothering. The polarities that underpin the accounts of the relation between alien and abductee are of male–female, master–slave, and of active–passive. These polarities also give space for the abductee, as a defence against helplessness, to shift into phantasies of omnipotence.

At the same time as the alien is powerful, it is also helpless: 'They are frail, limited individuals far from home' (Strieber, 1987: 290). Strieber is visited by a figure 'roughly three and a half feet tall, altogether smaller and lighter than my son' (ibid.: 22). Some contactee groups in the USA are now very protective of aliens, and prefer to use the more friendly term 'UFolk' (Hough and Randles, 1992). There are detailed discussions of the difference between the 'Grays' and the 'Reticulans' who are 'among the most benevolent of the extraterrestrials visiting this planet' (Stevens, 1992: 17).

Alien interference does also often include violent sexual imagery:

> two of the stocky ones drew my legs apart. The next thing I knew I was being shown an enormous and extremely ugly object, gray and scaly, with a sort of network of wires on the end. It was at least a foot long, narrow and triangular in structure. They inserted this thing into my rectum. It seemed to swarm into me as if it had a life of its own. Apparently its purpose was to take samples,

possibly of fecal matter, but at the time I had the impression that I was being raped, and for the first time I felt anger.

(Strieber, 1987: 30)

There are now debates in the alien contact literature as to the significance of actual abuse by parents of those who later report being abused by aliens (e.g., Basterfield, 1991; Brookesmith, 1995). It is the anger as defence which is most often expressed in science fiction in displaced forms of racism, the alien as 'other', and although the message in some accounts is of a meeting of worlds, the fantasy of knowledge is more often of a war of the worlds in which the thing to be known has to be thoroughly dismantled and mastered.

The polarized phantasies of helplessness and omnipotence are supported by those of maleness and femaleness, of mastery and slavery and of activity and passivity, and these are then given an additional dynamic through the science fiction polarities of technology and nature. One of the participants in a contactee discussion group says:

When I get to thinking about it alone, by myself, I get a little angry, and I begin to think, Who the hell do they think they are that they can just do what they want to us, as though we were nothing. And that really disturbs me, so I turn it off.

(Strieber, 1987: 258)

Being 'nothing' is to be annihilated, feminized, enslaved, pacified and treated as nature. But the technology which is experienced in so persecuting a form is also a technology which can make something special out of someone who is 'nothing'.

Family romance

Among the Oedipal phantasies we weave to attack our poor parents and to find better people to model ourselves upon, some of the most appealing are found in those 'family romances' in which we may imagine that we really are the biological product of another superior couple (Freud, 1909b). The idea that our parentage really lies in outer space is one of the most extreme, but also now one of the most widespread forms of family romance. While the pleasure and resolution of the family romance, the idea that we are the product of a better class of being than our parents, was once relayed to the child through fairy tales (Bettelheim, 1976), it now also appears in science fiction narratives. In some cases, the phantasy is displaced on to the thought that God was really a space man (Däniken, 1976).

Claude Vorilhon, contacted in France, was told that human beings were created by scientists of an advanced civilization in 'a fantastic scientific experiment' (Letourneau, 1992: 25). The notion that those responsible for the interference and abduction are, in some respect, our real parents compounds the anxiety, and the sense of violation and internal violence carried by these narratives. This also brings to the surface anxieties about reunion with them and their intentions to subject us once again to the terror of separation. A question often asked by contactee groups and UFO experts is:

> Do the UFO occupants want to lessen the distance between our race and theirs in order to land, eventually, and join us on our planet? ... Or do these aliens merely wish to enrich their own stock and then depart as mysteriously as they arrived?
>
> (Budd Hopkins, cited in Vallee, 1988: 131)

The 'Direct Investigation Group on Alien Phenomena', based in Bolton in the UK, believes that the human species is being subjected to a vast experiment by the ninety-eight different forms of alien they have catalogued, and that human females are being used as part of an alien breeding programme. Phantasies of exclusion and of envy here position the aliens as male, as fathers who are inside the 'mother ship', inside the enveloping and persecuting generalized alien other which is female, is mother. The phantasies are also then about how such aliens may come to be inside the feminine part of ourselves, of our 'species'.

A contactee group at Stanford, USA, called 'Human Individual Metamorphosis', was told that they were entering a period in history in which they could overcome human nature and then physically leave the planet. The leaders of the group, known as 'The Two', had been born in the United States and it was not until they were in their thirties, and married, that

> suddenly they began to have the feeling that there was something that they were here for. Circumstances eventually brought them together. And it was a couple of years before they began to realize that they had come from a different level, a level above the human level, an actual physical level out in space.
>
> (Vallee, 1979: 73)

The contactee group which ran in elections in California on the 'Space Platform' ticket argued that the US Constitution and the Magna Carta 'were sparked by the Saucer People – invisibly but absolutely by them, and they can prove that it is' (ibid.: 112). The impulse to know this invisible system, as the penetration of the secrets of the inside of the generalized alien other, alien mother, further fuels phantasies about what more there is to know.

The common themes across history and culture of visitation from superior beings, and sightings of their space ships or chariots, raise questions about the contents of a collective and universal unconscious, and Strieber discusses these, including with reference to Jung's (1959) comments on the topic. But to ponder on this when one takes the phenomena themselves as true then invites issues of parentage: 'Maybe you and I are larvae, and the "visitors" are human beings in the mature form' (Strieber, 1987: 224). In hypnotic regression sessions Strieber recalls the alien voices telling him 'You are our chosen one' (ibid.: 83). 'Being special' here includes both the revelation of hidden knowledge to the person who has been abducted, and the giving up of secrets to the invader. The abduction is carried out in order that human beings, or this particular human being, can be studied. One researcher has commented that 'These cases have become so common as to be one of the defining elements of abductions. You get a peculiar emphasis upon the reproductive and neurological functions to the apparent neglect of everything else' (Bullard, 1991: 47). In one account, a woman called Kathy recalled, under hypnosis, that the beings touched her and kept her in a 'quasi-anesthetized state' as they operated and removed an ovum from her (Vallee, 1988: 9). Betty Hill reported, also when she was under hypnosis, that when she was abducted along with her husband in 1961, a long needle was inserted into her naval as part of a 'simulated medical test' (ibid.: 122). Bruce Cornet reported an encounter with the 'Tans' 'where I was taken, stripped naked, slapped on a cold table and had devices attached to my genitalia and then they took a sperm sample!' (Cornet, 1995: 65).

In some cases, the contactee has been singled out, and will be responsible for the knowledge or abilities they are given by the aliens. This was the case for Uri Geller, who walked into a UFO in the desert near Tel Aviv and received his powers at that point (Vallee, 1979: 133). In a story typical of those charged with a mission by the aliens, one of Geller's friends, Jim Hurtak, described the magnetic pull of a UFO, his contact with 'the higher intelligence', his body being penetrated by a beam of light, and the presentation to him of scientific codes in a manuscript called 'The Biocomputer Keys to Our Consciousness Time Zone, Revealed to Me by Master Control Messengers Metatron and Opthanim' (ibid.). George King was chosen in London in March 1954 while he was washing up, but the first contact was only a voice which told him 'Prepare yourself. You are to become the voice of [the] Interplanetary Parliament' (Evans, 1973: 150). King went on to found the Aetherius Society which has thousands of members in different countries who believe that King is the 'primary terrestrial channel' for an advanced civilization based on Venus, and whose parliament has met on Saturn. Now the Society relays, through King, the edicts of 'Mars Sector 6' (Shaw, 1994).

Alongside the destructive phantasies – of the alien directed to the insides of the body, and of the self directed toward the alien and wishing to obliterate it – are reparative phantasies. But such depressive anxieties, of destroying and being destroyed, take a manic turn in the narcissistic and omnipotent accounts of those selected by aliens to change the world. Claude Vorilhon was contacted by space craft near Clermont-Ferrand, and was told that he had been specifically chosen. The alien life form told him that it was 'For many reasons. First we needed someone who lived in a country where new ideas are well-received. France is the country where democracy was born, and her image on the entire Earth is that of the land of freedom' (Vallee, 1979: 142). Being singled out is a phantasy of narcissistic omnipotence, but being singled out for attention carries with it the subordination to a higher intelligence. Although this repeats the submission to the alien, it also provokes the defence of being 'chosen', of 'the sense of omnipotence for the purpose of controlling and mastering objects' (Klein, 1935: 133).

Projective identification

Freud (1911a) describes the pathological projection of material from inside the self to the outside, usually onto other people, as part of the mechanism of paranoia, and Klein (1946) follows the bizarre logic of this process to show how the interior which is expelled and located in others is *still* attached to the self. What is projected is also identified with so that all that has been thrown out returns, and the violence of the expulsion and penetration of the mother's body, as a paradigm case, is matched by the violence of the invasion of the self when the bad objects strike back.

Strieber includes transcripts of hypnotic regression sessions, and these produce further memories of the experience of the encounter:

> She was undeniably appealing to me. In some sense I thought I might love this being – almost as much as I might my own anima. I bore toward her the same feelings of terror and fascination that I might toward someone I saw staring back at me from the depths of my unconscious.
>
> (Strieber, 1987: 105)

The comforting image of the 'anima' is quickly twisted into a phantasy of penetration, and the confusion between inside and outside is experienced as terrifying, as something that seems irresolvable: 'Her gaze seemed capable of entering me deeply, and it was when I had looked directly into her eyes that I felt my first taste of profound unease. It was as if every vulnerable detail of my self were known to this being' (ibid.: 106). To simultaneously know and be known is operating as projective identification in which the 'epistemophilic instinct' is projected into the alien and taken back into the ego as the alien attempts to know what the victim knows.

In one of the contactee groups there is discussion of 'the sexual intrusion experienced by some of the men, involving extraction of semen with a probe, or having it drawn out with a sort of vacuum device' (ibid.: 273). The penetration into the body and the scooping out of the insides, a phantasy which preoccupies the infant and which is directed against the mother (Klein, 1955), is also, in many cases, a penetration into the mind. The physical taking-in of the alien and the forcible removal of bits of the body by the alien is the symptomatic expression and model among contactees for mental incorporation and cutting out. Two of the most celebrated contactees for some years in the USA were Barney and Betty Hill. While Betty Hill reported that the aliens spoke to them in English 'with an accent' near the Pease Air Force Base in New Hampshire, her husband Barney reported that:

> I did not hear an actual voice. But in my mind, I knew what he was saying. It wasn't as if he were talking to me with my eyes open, and he was sitting across

the room from me. It was more as if the words were there, a part of me, and he was outside the actual creation of the words.

(Vallee, 1988: 121)

The insertion of objects and of thoughts is also the intrusion of feelings: 'They can also create words inside the center of their heads. One occasionally feels from them powerful emotions' (Strieber, 1987: 250). In a contactee group, one bit of discussion goes as follows: 'Fred: "I felt like slapping one of them. There was always one you felt comfort under, security under". Jenny: "Like he was part of me. In me". Mary: "There's a little part of him in me all the time".' (ibid.: 262)

The eyes are important to the inter-penetration of self and other, with the creatures being reported variously by contactees around the world as having eyes that are:

with horizontal slits; large and sensitive; no pupils and no eyelids; huge, round with no eyelashes or eyebrows; large and slanted; blue and slanted; large; large, round and glowing red; reddish-orange; huge, round, prominent, yellow-green; protruding, with small irises; like human eyes; frog-like; small, bright like burning coals, like cat's eyes; or in the forehead.

(Vallee, 1988: 297)

The eyes are points of contact and points of entry: 'Her gaze seemed capable of entering me deeply. . . . I could actually feel the presence of that other person within me – which was as disturbing as it was curiously sensual' (Strieber, 1987: 106). This invasion connects with something inside, as something that can be 'curiously sensual', but this is also something that disrupts the boundaries between inside and outside.

Contactees may be drawn into conspiracies that also include specifications of enemy forces that must be defeated. *Cosmic Voice*, the journal of the Aetherius Society, reported that an attempt by highly intelligent fish creatures on the planet of Garouche to 'annihilate all humanoid life on Terra' was only just thwarted by Martians (Evans, 1973: 158). Sometimes the accounts are of submission to a good object who is loved as well as hated, and sometimes there are good and bad objects. But the phantasy of destroying the bad object is still also often combined with the phantasy of merging with the good. Claude Vorilhon, for example, was told at Clermont-Ferrand that:

You must eliminate elections and votes of mankind. Men are the useful cells of a large body called Humanity. A cell in the foot doesn't have to say whether or not the hand should pick up an object. The brain decides, and if the object is good, the cell in the foot will profit by it. . . . A world government and a new monetary system must be created. A single language will serve to unify the planet.

(Vallee, 1979: 143)

One of the contactees in a support group says 'they are us and we are them, so if you call them "them", but say "They are looking at us, they are doing this to us", it's not right. They are us and we are them' (Strieber, 1987: 253). Although these are aliens from outer space, once they enter inner space the terrors of persecution and imprisonment, of them in us and us in them, multiply.

Reality-testing

Freud's (1911b) discussion of the process by which we disentangle perceptions of the internal world from the external world, and so arrive at some sense of what social reality is, produces more problems than solutions in psychoanalysis. The object relations tradition addresses this through describing a particular kind of mental linking of elements (in Bion's work) or through making the mother responsible for being 'real' in the face of infantile hallucination of what is and is not (in Winnicott's work). Kleinian accounts of phantasy and reality also revolve around the making of links, but in such a way that it is difficult to see how the infant escapes from the nightmare world it constructs around itself.

It seems to be in the nature of UFO research that conspiracy theories proliferate. Objectivity and subjectivity flip over in some accounts such that reality-testing is no longer the basis for, and can even be the opposite of truth: 'my conscious life was nothing more than a disguise for another reality' (Strieber, 1987: 113). This account will not fit with a standard Freudian 'reality-testing' model of ego development, for the 'reality' that is tested continually threatens to disintegrate. Later Strieber says 'I can discern a visible agenda of contact in what is happening. Over the past forty or so years their involvement with us has not only been deepening, it has been spreading rapidly through the society' (ibid.: 290). The connections between things, between symbols, are ways of coping with anxiety here, not for coping with what we take to be reality.

The interference by aliens can often only be inferred, with typical acts which are not directed at human beings being the abduction or destruction of animals. The theme of the cutting of the object, of phallic aggression, is linked with phantasies of masculinized technology, projected onto the aliens and then displaced onto images of them cutting animals, not us. Cattle mutilations, with specific organs cut away and blood drained from the animal, have been widely reported in the United States, in the UFO literature at least, and attributed to aliens: 'In an eighteen month period before January 1977, there were 700 mutilations in fifteen western states. More than 180 cases occurred in Colorado alone in 1975' (Vallee, 1979: 164). The more mundane the answer seems to be, the more sinister the conspiracy: 'Perfect squares or circles were taken from the hide. In one incident a scalpel had been left behind; it was an ordinary article of military surplus' (ibid.: 176).

The paranoid-schizoid splitting that structures such attempts to make sense of such strange happenings fuels and blocks the making of links between different symbols. There is a sense both that there are connections, conspiracies, and that there are attempts to hide the connections. The anxiety that provokes the symbol development in this realm, then, is intensified by the anxiety that phantasy and reality cannot be disentangled.

One writer proposes that cattle mutilations are performed by 'covert agencies of the U.S. Government' and that this must be 'in fact the most believable theory of all, even with its lack of perceivable logic' (Amendola, 1992: 17–20). Alongside the hidden influence of the aliens is an account of hidden conspiracies by those in power not to acknowledge that the aliens are here. One typical case is the reproduction of court documents in the article 'Covert Operations of the US National Security Agency' in *Nexus: New Times* (1995: 3 (3): 17–20). There is a problem in 'refusing to take the matter seriously. Many people of the highest reputation have been sucked into this stance' (Strieber, 1987: 234). It is a recurring theme in the UFO literature that there is a cover-up by the US government and Air Force. Some of the explanations for this secrecy and concealment have been that the governments in the West suspected that there was a connection with the Soviet Union, where there had long been a strong research interest in UFOs (Ostrander and Schroeder, 1970).

Reality-testing is a process that is deliberately sought after in the alien-contact world, with calls for 'sensible research' in the UFO community (Randles, 1992a: 3). One way it is guaranteed is through the links that are made with natural scientists who have become interested in UFOs. When these people start discussing abductions and telepathic contact, for example, a certain kind of 'knowledge' can then be presented as bedrock of sensible inquiry. An example is the interview with 'Dr Bruce Cornet, geologist, scientist, searching for a way to explain the knowledge that has been placed within him' (Cornet, 1995: 57). ' "[A] team of extraterrestrial psychologists," said Dr James Harder, Professor of Engineering at University of California, Berkeley, "are evidently at work among us, killing and dissecting livestock and kidnapping young and healthy humans." ' (Ribera, 1992: 19). These assessments of the probability of alien invasion have also recently been connected with the debates on 'false memories' in psychotherapy, with claims that certain UFO researchers have been too zealous in their questioning of victims, and that they may have 'implanted' memories of alien abduction (Schnabel, 1994; Brookesmith, 1995).

The UFO community also finds itself bedevilled by the attempts of the authorities to disrupt their work. Alongside the calls for close rational investigation of alien phenomena, there is an awareness, as one leading investigator puts it, that 'this is what a government agent would do' (Randles, 1992a: 3), and there have been calls that 'serious allegations of spies in our midst be adequately aired' (Randles, 1992b: 11). Appearances by those claiming to be sympathetic experts on UFOs who then discredit UFO research are subjected to close scrutiny (e.g., Banyard, 1992; Roberts, 1992), and commentaries on the *X-Files* have often been hostile to the series because it 'trivialises it's [sic] subject matter, and casts a paranoid, irreverent light upon the whole community' (Carter, 1996: 44). There is understandable frustration at those who use alien-abduction networks for their own ends. Strieber (1987: 13) claimed that the account he presented in *Communion* 'is the story of one man's attempt to deal with a shattering assault from the unknown. It is a true story, as true as I know how to describe it'. He had written a number of best-selling novels dealing with themes of horror and the unknown already, and sceptics did suspect that this was simply a marketing ploy for the book, and their suspicion was confirmed when Strieber eventually confessed that he had made it up (Schnabel, 1994).

The conspiracy theories seem to proliferate inside the UFO community to such an extent that the stories of alien visits themselves are sometimes seen as conspiracies. Jacques Vallee, one of the leading researchers on the phenomenon, for example, argues that UFOs are real, but not in the sense that contactees think they are: 'UFOs appear as an outgrowth of a large-scale, worldwide manipulation operation rather than as a visit by space beings' (Vallee, 1979: 21). His earlier view involved speculation about a 'strange force' and a 'machinery of mass manipulation' that, he argued, was the result of the use of 'psychotronic technology' here on earth. There were 'physical devices used to affect human consciousness' (ibid.: 20–21). This argument failed to specify who operated this technology, so now it has been revised, and Vallee talks of a 'spiritual control system ... [in which] ... mythology rules at a level of our social reality over which normal political and intellectual trends have no real power' (ibid.: 277). Symbolism is 'the foundation of all phantasy and sublimation' (Klein, 1930: 97), but the paranoid twist here is that the symbols cannot be mastered, for as part of a 'control system', *they master us*.

Science fiction war

In some ways the sheer variety of reports makes the text of alien encounters seem like a giant projective test. The explanations of sightings and traces of UFOs have also been varied, including that they are brought about 'By the wind moving the stars around; by waking dreams; by herons or cranes; by crocodiles in love; by shrimp-size meteorites; by cylinders of electricity; by the urine of sheep; by atmospheric effects; or by cognitive dissonance' (Vallee, 1988: 297). When the narratives are examined, however, there does seem to be an underlying set of patterns, and the urban legends of alien abduction both express something of our anxieties about our selves and others and they reinforce those anxieties. They also feed into other narratives, most significantly into narratives of war. For the hidden war against the aliens from outer space is, as well as being a projection of an infantile war in our inner space, also a displacement from other types of war – war in the Third World, with the Third World, in the Middle East, or nuclear war. If it operates in its displaced form without being recognized for what it is, it can then always feed back again into the wider political domain in ever more dangerous ways. A question that the alien abduction phantasies raises is how does this system of delusions function in the body politic, and of what is it symptomatic?

The paranoiac themes of the *X-Files* were anticipated thirty years ago in the television series *The Invaders* which was first screened in the USA in 1966, and cancelled a year later without a final episode (Halliwell, 1980). In that series the hero David Vincent cannot convince anyone else that the aliens he saw outside Bud's Diner one night are already here on earth, for each time he locates their headquarters they have moved on, there is nobody there. Worse, those who seem most sympathetic to Vincent in many episodes turn out to be aliens themselves, and each time Vincent just escapes after having recognized them. The claim that there are hidden persuaders has been a part of Western culture for many years (e.g., Packard, 1957), but the preoccupation with hidden forces seems to have recently become magnified.

One magazine included a checklist in its first issue for readers to identify aliens at work: odd or mismatched clothes, strange diet or unusual eating habits, bizarre sense of humour, frequently off sick, keeps a diary, misuses everyday items, constant queries about co-workers' customs, secretive about personal lifestyle and home, frequently talks to themself, and change in mood or physical state near certain high-tech hardware (*Encounters*, October 1995). More chilling were the trailers for *Independence Day* which set the three-day countdown to threat and defence: 'Day One, they arrive; Day Two, they attack; Day Three, we fight back'. Aliens are others of a particular type, and our relationship to them brings into play processes of splitting – many contactees both love and fear their aliens – and projective identification – many contactees are both loved by and persecuted by their aliens. The repetition of these images, and associated paranoiac phantasies, can be connected with the images of the state of potential war which the development of weapons of mass destruction have provoked, what Kovel (1983) calls the 'state of nuclear terror' based on paranoiac phantasies of the other. This is the structure of war with aliens, and it then feeds into the structure of wars now between the West and its others, and the proxy wars of the West fought in the Third World – relentless, pitiless.

Such a description of paranoia need not lead us to discount *real* conspiracies. People living under conditions of real dictatorship may *also* need to be able to explore the phantasies of persecution that make their lives so intolerable and which inhibit them from fighting back. In Argentina during the dirty war of the early 1970s, for example, psychoanalysts who were on death lists had to both assess when they should take practical steps to hide or leave *and* how they should address the phantasies of persecution provoked by the military which made any such rational assessment difficult (Langer, 1989). (Argentina also presents a special case here in being a civil society that has been drenched in violence and a culture which is saturated with psychoanalytic discourse.) The question in conditions like these, then, is not how we choose between political analysis and analysis of discourse, but how to pursue both. Likewise, in the case of extraterrestrial assault, there are undoubtedly government cover-ups and attempts to marginalize and pathologize those who challenge State secrecy. It is possible that such secrecy is either the result of a fear on the military's part that aliens are abducting people or a certain knowledge (as well as fear) that this is happening. Again, whether it is actually the case that UFOs have visited or not is neither here nor there to the analysis developed in this chapter, which has been focusing on the circulation of *fantasies* in the Kleinian form of psychoanalytic discourse which frames our understanding of what is happening (and now we will return to the everyday spelling of fantasy, for we are concerned with the reproduction of notions of the self in everyday discourse). This discourse helps to obscure our understanding of it, but it at least tells us a story about our helplessness, fantasies of parentage, projective identification and reality-testing in times of war and, it would seem, at times of 'peace' in the Western world. We turn in Part II to look at the discontents this apparent state of peace provokes.

PART II
CRITICAL THEORIES: INDIVIDUALITY AND CULTURE

> The angel of history's eyes are staring, his mouth is open, his wings are spread. His face is turned towards the past. Where we perceive a chain of events, he sees one single catastrophe which keeps piling wreckage upon wreckage and hurls it in front of his feet. The angel would like to stay, awaken the dead, and make whole that which has been smashed. But a storm is blowing from Paradise; it has got caught in his wings with such violence that the angel can no longer close them. This storm irresistably propels him into the future to which his back is turned, while the pile of debris before him grows skyward. This storm is what we call progress.
>
> Walter Benjamin ([1939] 1973: 259) Theses on the Philosophy of History

Psychoanalysis was first conceived by Freud as a clinical theory and technique for self-understanding, but he very quickly turned it into a social theory and tool for cultural critique. This aspect of psychoanalysis, which was crucial to its appeal for those who read Freud in the original German, was filtered out in the process of translation into English (Bettelheim, 1983). In the hands of the Frankfurt School, psychoanalytic social theory was also a key to unlocking the forms of culture that had constituted people as isolated individuals. This miserable and dangerous alienation of individuals from each other and from culture had to be understood as part of a dialectical historical process. In this way psychoanalysis could be recruited to *Critical Theory*. The Frankfurt School response to Freud's descriptions of basic structures in groups – which were still often assumed to reflect essential biological categories – was to question, then, the very notion of human 'essence' which these descriptions presupposed. The German tradition of psychoanalytic social theory, with the Institute of Social Research as its central institutional site, offered an account of an historically produced '*second nature*' which appears no less real to individuals than the biological drives. In modern society it feels natural to us to be masters and possessors of our own selves and needs, but this nature is produced by the development of class society and intensified by capitalism. A rigorous programme of research was required to comprehend this.

The initiative to set up the *Institut für Sozialforschung* (Institute of Social Research) came from Felix Weil (whose father provided the initial finance) and Friedrich Pollock. The original name *Institut für Marxismus* was rejected for diplomatic reasons, to make it easier to affiliate to the University of Frankfurt. The founders and early participants were all sympathetic to Marxism, and some form of Marxist humanism drawing on phenomenology underlies all Critical Theory, whether that is in Walter

Benjamin's dabbling with Kabbala and hopes that the angel of history might signal the flash of liberation at any historical moment, or in Jürgen Habermas's research as part of the School's second generation with a more cautious search for free and transparent communication. The Institute was officially founded on 3 February 1923. The first director, Carl Grünberg, whose period of rule was marked by strict economically based versions of Marxism, was replaced by Max Horkheimer (who was chosen in 1929 and officially installed in 1931). Horkheimer had a more open sociological view of the task of the Institute, and he was responsible for bringing in psychoanalytic ideas. For Horkheimer, the 'social philosophy' which was needed should not adopt one scientific worldview, but use different disciplines to propose theories which could then be connected with empirical work. The first task, Horkheimer argued, should be a study of workers' and employees' attitudes toward social issues, using public statistics and questionnaires supplemented by interpretations of the data from a variety of disciplinary viewpoints (Roiser and Willig, 1996).

Theodor Wiesengrund-Adorno joined in the late 1920s, and a new journal appeared in 1931 – the *Zeitschrift für Sozialforschung* – and included in its first issue articles and reviews by Pollock, Horkheimer, Adorno, Erich Fromm, Kurt Lewin and Wilhelm Reich. Herbert Marcuse, then a student of Heidegger, joined in 1932. Most of the founders were Jewish, though, in the main, assimilated (and there was surprisingly little emphasis in the early research on anti-Semitism, which was seen as but one symptom of the degeneration of Western 'civilization'). Not all of the key figures in the Institute escaped in 1933 when the Nazis took power. An office had been opened in Geneva while the funds were transferred to Holland to prevent them being seized. The *Zeitschrift* was then published in Paris, and a decision was taken later, when key personnel were in the USA, to continue publication in the German language. The Institute was refounded in New York, attached to Columbia University in 1936. It became known as the 'Frankfurt School' when it returned to Germany after the war.

The Frankfurt School tradition of research was dominated by Max Horkheimer and Theodor Adorno with their work on the Western Enlightenment (Adorno and Horkheimer, 1944), but is only known to many social psychologists through later empirical work on the 'authoritarian personality' (Adorno et al., 1950). Two important strands of work which later became detached from the main body of the Institute provided the key psychoanalytic input and then the terms of debate which the other researchers used and argued about. These strands of work were elaborated by Erich Fromm and Herbert Marcuse. Chapter 4 reviews how these writers used psychoanalysis to understand the powerful psychologizing impulse of modern Enlightenment culture, and it then explores the way the peculiar versions of psychoanalytic discourse employed by them may help us to understand the way the disciplinary apparatus of modern psychology works. Psychology makes us feel that what we are and what we want at our core cannot be changed. Fromm's and Marcuse's critical account, however, then prompts a question as to the reality of human needs in 'first nature', and how far these needs are biological or existential.

This kind of critique means, of course, that a psychoanalytic interpretation of culture should not be content with describing the development of different belief systems. Certain beliefs operate as forms of *ideology*, and those caught in those forms were seen as suffering from 'false consciousness'. Ideology-critique and the stripping away of false consciousness underpinned the Institute's work in the tradition of Western European humanist Marxism (Lukács, 1923). The most devastating forms of false consciousness were lived by those who thought that Nazism would provide a final solution to the degeneration of capitalism, and the politically active analysts working with the first generation (with Reich the most important) and academic theorists in the second generation of Critical Theory (with Habermas as the central figure) focused on the rise of authoritarian ideologies. Chapter 5 describes Reich's and Habermas's work, and then turns to the way authoritarian motifs are now surfacing among men trying to find their strong core selves.

A question that has run through Frankfurt School writing after the Second World War is whether we are now still living in an Enlightenment culture, or whether something worse has befallen us, with the emergence, perhaps of an age of narcissism. This question parallels debates over modernity and the postmodern condition. Chapter 6 reviews these debates, and the ways psychoanalytic discourse is implicated in modern Enlightenment culture and its narcissistic postmodern successor. We then turn to 'new age' responses to crises in contemporary culture as a symptom of these uncertain times. Baudrillard is part of this tradition as exemplar and symptom of its decay and excess (even though he is often lumped in with other French theorists as if his concerns were the same as theirs). He both celebrates and sabotages the attempt by the Frankfurt School to go beyond action to *praxis*, to a committed progressive linking of theory and practice.

There are no simply technical solutions to cultural crisis, and it is just as much a mistake to romanticize nature as an alternative to technology. Among the top five per cent most-visited Internet Web Sites in 1996 was 'Decapitate An Angel' (http://www.halcyon.com/maelstrm/angel.html) where you can click on the angel's head and see it reappear at her feet while her dress is stained in blood. For Frankfurt School Critical Theory, *Vorsprung Durch Technik* ('progress through technology') was a dead-end, and unless capitalism was destroyed human culture would collapse into barbarism. The spread of Western consumer culture still carries with it a deadly virus of cynicism and self-destruction, and a successful challenge to it has yet to develop.

4

Individuality, Enlightenment and the Psy-complex

You're going to meet three troubled and tormented people . . . not mental cases mind you (for the insane cannot be helped by psychoanalysis), but people who are plagued by the same type of emotional disturbances that may be plaguing you or us. . . . If an outsider was given the privilege of listening in on an actual analysis, the main effect upon him would be boredom beyond all endurance. Therefore, for dramatic effect and entertainment value, we plan to telescope each analysis into three to five issue-sessions, according to the severity of the particular patient's problems. . . . At the completion of each analysis, a new patient . . . with new problems . . . will be introduced. (Who knows, you might eventually meet YOU!)

Editors (1955: i) Id bits. *Psychoanalysis*, 1 (1). New York: Tiny Tot Comics Inc.

Psychoanalysis is a powerful form of self-knowledge in Western culture, but it *makes* the very things it illuminates. When you read psychoanalytic or self-help texts you must fashion yourself into the kind of subject described in those texts for their prescriptions to make sense. Psychoanalytic discourse threads its way through the various popular representations of what it is to be a self and how one may achieve happiness, and it does not simply bring aspects of the self to light that were hidden away before. Rather, it operates by throwing certain kinds of shadow on parts of the mind which then feel obscure when we speak that discourse and direct its beam upon our-selves. Psychoanalysis emerged at a particular historical point in the development of capitalism in the West, and it is a reflection of Enlightenment hopes that sustained reasoned examination of individuals and culture would lead to the improvement of both.

Enlightenment thought gathered pace in Western Europe and North America in the eighteenth century and promoted the value of scientific reason, historical progress and personal self-understanding. The Enlightenment (which is often also referred to as 'Modernity' in post-structuralist writing, as we shall see in Chapter 6) requires a sense that it is worth hoping for social improvement and that each individual will find something valuable in themselves (Giddens, 1992). The work of the Frankfurt School stood in the Enlightenment tradition, but Adorno and Horkheimer (1944) produced a *dialectical* analysis of the Enlightenment such that the best and most progressive aspects of it would be turned against what was worst and most regressive. Fromm and Marcuse were recruited to the work of the School, and each used psychoanalytic ideas in distinctive ways to assist this critical dialectical task.

Freud laid the basis for a psychoanalytic understanding of culture and the individual, and this chapter starts with a review of one of his key texts on culture where we find him using metaphors for the self and the state which will return to haunt Fromm and Marcuse. We will then turn to the development of Critical Theory in the Institute of Social Research as the context for Fromm's and Marcuse's work before showing how the forms of psychoanalytic discourse they used now circulate in modern psychology. The kind of analysis we will need to develop for this will also require us to move from a focus on what is going on inside separate 'individuals' to the ways *subject positions* are set up in discourse which people may then inhabit. It is ironic that the very forms of discourse these writers elaborated to understand the social construction of psychology now informs the *libidinal structure* of modern psychological institutions. It is all the more ironic when these institutions spend so much energy trying to combat psychoanalytic ideas. Our task in this book is to analyse the way different psychoanalytic conceptions of social institutions and individual selves, including Fromm's and Marcuse's, are part of the fabric of Western culture. First, though, we need to trace the way those accounts were conceived by Freud.

Civilization

Freud's (1930) *Civilization and its Discontents* laid out a psychoanalytic perspective on the relationship between the individual and society. By the time he published this book Freud had come to the conclusion that psychoanalysis as a therapeutic 'cure' was much less important than psychoanalysis as a theoretical system to comprehend culture. The development by the Frankfurt School of a psychoanalytic social theory was not, then, so different from Freud's own project at the time, but the crushing of psychoanalysis in Europe and its replanting in English-speaking culture does make Freud's and the Frankfurt School's work look different now (Timms and Segal, 1988). The Frankfurt School did stamp their own distinctive mark on Freud's view of civilization and individuality, and so it is worth reviewing Freud's own proposals and then the development of Critical Theory before looking at how Fromm and Marcuse developed their own versions of psychoanalytic social theory.

Civilization and its discontents

Freud's title *Civilization and its Discontents* (1930) should be translated from the German *Das Unbehagen in der Kultur* as 'The uneasiness inherent in culture' (Bettelheim, 1983), and there are a number of important nuances of meaning in the re-wording of the title which we should take note of before we go on to look at the sources of the 'discontents' and Freud's account of the channelling of the drives.

The original translation of Freud's title fudged the distinction between civilization and culture. Bettelheim (1983) argues that while *Kultur* should be taken to refer to moral value systems and intellectual and aesthetic achievements, *Zivilization* refers to material and technological accomplishments (though other writers have argued that Freud does not himself make such a distinction, e.g., Mitchell, 1974). For Freud, it appears as if the development of one does necessarily entail the development of the other, and so there is a deliberate adoption of the Enlightenment view of progress linked to scientific reason. Frankfurt School theorists try to disentangle 'cultural progress', which always has a moral-political evaluative component, from technological advance for its own sake, and they are concerned with the way the relationship between the two is confused in modern attempts to apply a value-free technology to cultural issues. The distinction between the two is crucial, for those working in the Frankfurt tradition argue that the idea that it is possible to find technological solutions to cultural questions is one of the sources of Nazism and the Holocaust (e.g., Baumann, 1989). The British Psychological Society's (1988: 69) assertion that 'We believe absolutely in the power of knowledge for its own sake' would, then, be anathema to Frankfurt School writers and evidence of the dangerous ideological role that positivism plays in modern psychology.

The tension between the civilization and the discontent (whether as a state of mind or a segment of the population), or between the culture and the unease is not seen by Freud as something to be solved. It is, rather, a problem which is *inherent* in the relationship between individual desire and social prohibitions. The Frankfurt School theorists struggled with the implications of this rather pessimistic position. They often subscribed to the view that the tension could be resolved, though they did so in different ways. Fromm (1956), for example, looked to socialist self-management humanism, while Marcuse (1955) evoked a polymorphously perverse liberated utopia. (We will see in Chapter 5 that Reich aimed for a genitally focused sexual communism, and Habermas advocates that present-day distortions of communication should be measured against an ideal speech situation.)

There are also differences in the way we may conceptualize our dissatisfaction with present-day culture in the different translations of the title of Freud's book. The use of the term 'discontents' evokes an intellectual, rational, dissatisfaction with the world, and a relationship with 'civilization' to which, perhaps, we may not be adequately adjusted. There is a danger here that psychologists might be given the task of addressing our discontents by fitting us better to culture rather than questioning what it is about present-day society that makes it an uncomfortable place for human beings. 'Uneasiness', on the other hand, is concerned with feelings which are underpinned by unconscious responses and discomfort with the organization of cultural life (which would include the arts as well as science, and the varieties of representations of self that are available to us in different communities). Frankfurt School theorists focused on exactly these kinds of discomfort as symptomatic not only of what was going wrong, but what hopes there might be for resistance and the development of alternative cultural forms. There was also a strong trend in Frankfurt School writing, and for Marcuse more than Fromm in this case, to see in the aesthetic sphere a place for resistance and more genuine enlightenment.

Freud's title makes it clear, however, that whatever the nuances in translation, he is still holding to a stage model of development of culture and/or civilization in the book (with animism succeeded by religious thinking, which is then followed by a scientific stage and the triumph of rationality). Frankfurt School theorists also place a strong value on this third stage, which corresponds to the overall Age of Enlightenment, but they stress the self-deception which this metaphor of 'enlightenment' as illumination conceals.

The uneasiness inherent in culture

For Freud (1930), there are three sources of uneasiness, an uneasiness which is felt as 'suffering' by the individual. The first is 'the superior power of nature', in which the arrival at a scientific stage also gives rise to a degree of helplessness in the face of an external nature, which is always imperfectly mastered. Frankfurt School theorists saw this helplessness as resulting from the separation from nature which is accomplished by the triumph of technological reason. The second source of unease is, according to Freud, 'the feebleness of our own bodies' and our susceptibility to suffering and death. Again, while Freud saw this as resulting from our growing awareness of what we cannot accomplish with technology, the Frankfurt School theorists argue that this sense of weakness in the face of death is heightened by the very technological fantasies of beating nature which Enlightenment culture encourages, and the consequent distaste in this culture for illness and old age. The third source of unease is 'the inadequacy of the regulations which adjust the mutual relationships of human beings in the family, the state and society' (ibid.: 274), and so the way in which society deals with contradictory desires. Frankfurt School theorists see this problem as being largely to do with intolerance of 'others' which the rigidity of modern thinking produces. Again then, rather than simply being a failure to cope with some aspect of modern culture, as it seems to be for Freud, the problem is seen by the Frankfurt School writers as one which is provoked by modern culture and exacerbated by the forms of individuality which are produced for us within it.

Freud argued that the drives are employed to maintain a state of civilization or culture, and that they are thus 'used up' in different ways (ibid.: 285). The first way the drives are used is through the production of 'character traits', and a channelling takes place through the 'cathexis' or investment of the drives at different stages and in zones of the body such that a 'fixation' of the drive gives rise to character types. There are two aspects to this process of investment. One aspect is where *particular* character traits emerge from an obsession with control, cleanliness and order: an 'example of such a process is found in the anal erotism of young human beings' (ibid.: 286), and this kind of fixation is something that will later become important to Frankfurt School attempts to explain closed rigid thinking styles and authoritarianism. A link is being made here between an interest in 'the excretory function, its organs and products' and parsimony, compulsiveness and domination – anal characteristics of the personality in adult life. As well as Fromm's (1942) use of these ideas to account for the peculiar character structure of followers of authoritarian movements, other Frankfurt School theorists used these notions to discuss cultural phenomena, such as the development of certain kinds of music (Adorno, 1973).

The other important aspect of the development of 'character', though, is where *individual character* as such results from these kinds of fixations, and this is seen by both Freud and the Frankfurt theorists as a cultural process whereby notions of individuality are produced at a certain point in the development of civilization. This point also recalls the account Freud gave of the emergence of the individual out of the primary 'groupishness' of humankind (which was discussed in Chapter 1). Frankfurt School theorists argued that this sense of individual uniqueness is dangerously overblown in Enlightenment culture, and it is one of the deep institutional blocks to collective action against capitalism.

The second way in which the drives are channelled is, according to Freud, through the operation of the psychic defence of sublimation. Freud and the Frankfurt School theorists saw sublimation as necessary and progressive, and a dialectical view of the development of modern culture would recognize that some sublimation is crucial. A critical evaluation of culture requires that there has been some degree of sublimation on the part of the individual who is carrying out the evaluation and this would then permit that necessary and potentially liberating intellectual work. The third way the drives are channelled is through what Freud called 'renunciation': 'This "cultural frustration" dominates the large field of social relationships between human beings' (Freud, 1930: 286–287). There have been many debates among Frankfurt School theorists as to how far it is possible to distinguish between necessary and culturally oppressive renunciation, over what is and what is not, in Marcuse's phrase, 'surplus repression'.

'A garrison in a conquered city'

Freud argued in *Civilization and its Discontents* that 'the most important problem in the development of civilization . . . is the heightening of the sense of guilt' (ibid.: 327), and this includes guilt over our resentment toward those who enforce restraints on the drives, over a resentment at authority which is, at its root, Oedipal. In particular, aggressiveness is introjected, internalized, directed against the self. This account of the turning of destructive energies against the self is, of course, being developed after Freud wrote *Beyond the Pleasure Principle* (1920), and so he is concerned with the way the death drive emerges from within the unconscious as a threat to the self and then to others if it is channelled out via the muscular apparatus.

Freud employs an interesting metaphor of the social here with an account of the self being developed on the model of military occupation and an account of the polity operating as a hydraulic mental system. Freud argues that at the wider social level it is possible to conceptualize the turning back of hostility against the population it comes from, and an agency, the State, being formed to direct this force. The super-ego, he argues, is then 'like a garrison in a conquered city' (Freud, 1930: 316). This agency can contain revolutionary forces, but there will always be fears that the outside world will carry out reprisals if it finds out that there are those in the city that have violent intentions. This means that it is necessary to increase the grip of the agency, and to engage in continuous surveillance. Not only must the revolutionary forces be contained, but their very existence must be repressed so that the outside world will not use their claims as a pretext to attack. This process is then replayed at the level of the individual, where 'instinctual renunciation' creates 'conscience' 'which then demands further instinctual renunciation' (ibid.: 321).

Freud's metaphor of the garrison in an occupied city is also an image of a trap from which there is no escape: 'A threatened external unhappiness – loss of love and punishment on the part of the external authority – has been exchanged for a permanent internal unhappiness, for the tension of the sense of guilt' (ibid.: 320). The relations that the city-state strikes up with the outsiders will always be fraught by the possibility that they might find out that somewhere in the city there are those with disruptive intentions, and so, however peaceful those relations with the outside are, there will always be a state of barely repressed misery, 'permanent internal unhappiness'. One of the further consequences of this state of affairs is that each sector of the city-state culture will find itself trapped in the same logic, when it attempts to keep quiet anybody or any desire which might disrupt the false peace: 'the community, too, evolves a super-ego under whose influence cultural development proceeds' (ibid.: 335). At best, the demands of the cultural super-ego could be relaxed to reduce the danger of 'communal neurosis' but, as Freud points out, 'as regards the therapeutic application of our knowledge, what would be the use of the most correct analysis of social neurosis, since no one possesses authority to impose such a therapy upon the group?' (ibid.: 338).

Discontents

The Frankfurt School theorists, who were revolutionaries inside the city-state of the Western Enlightenment, saw the ego itself as being the garrison. At the level of the State, it was not necessary to wait for an overt military occupation to bring into play an apparatus of repression and surveillance. The State was already, for them as Marxists, essentially a body of armed men devoted to the protection of the property of the ruling class. Any threat to the most liberal State would provoke military defence. At the level of the individual too, the ego itself had been so thoroughly colonized by bourgeois culture and psychically beaten into submission that very little was left beyond miserable subjection, resentment at authority and guilt at the thought that authority could be but was not challenged. Although super-ego prohibitions were important, they could not be seen as peculiar extras. These repressive processes were built into the modern ego. The penetration of the forces of oppression and repression into the ego also intensified, of course, the problem of how to conceptualize liberation and to imagine where that liberation might come from. The problem would be exacerbated through the imposition of a 'solution' from above, and the real solution had to be through a critical account which worked *within* and from the base up. Critical Theory, then, was developed as an 'immanent critique' (Dews, 1987), or as a 'negative dialectics' (Buck-Morss, 1977) which shows some similarities with later notions of deconstruction in French post-structuralist theory (Ryan, 1982).

Critical Theory

The philosophical framework for the Frankfurt tradition set in place by Horkheimer and Adorno can be summarized in six theses about the historical development of society (Jay, 1973). First, a 'Critical Theory' worth its name was seen as necessarily opposed to positivist notions of value neutrality in social science. Those accounts that pretend to be 'objective' are still developed from a particular standpoint, and scientists who try to remain distant from their objects of study in social science will therefore develop an account which is distorted in certain ways because of that distance. Each theoretical position involves a viewpoint that should be made clear to a reader. Rather than pretend to offer an objective account then, Critical Theorists were working from a moral-political position (with a theory of history and opposition to oppression under capitalism). Secondly, it was necessary to shift from crude economic determinism (in, for example, Second and Third International Marxism) to the way consciousness affected the social world. Cultural forms could not be explained away by reducing them to economic structures or class positions. Although there may be certain characteristic ideas about property under feudalism and capitalism, for example, or differences between the way the bourgeoisie or the working class viewed the world, a specific detailed analysis of the development of culture was needed. Struggles over culture and ideology would affect how the bourgeoisie defended its property and how the working class might develop a challenge to private property.

Thirdly, Western capitalist culture was marked by the individualization of people (their isolation and privatization of feelings) which, while vaunted as personal enlightenment, was actually destructive and alienating. The more people try to cut themselves off from nature and, from each other, the more miserable they become. The Enlightenment had encouraged the development of a feeling of individuality and creative reasoning, and this was a valuable achievement, but it was necessary to remember that these properties were still developed as a particular kind of relationship to others, and should only be maintained with others rather than against them. Fourthly, the splitting of the individual (as isolated and repressed) and culture (as alienating and incomprehensible) had a dynamic which would lead to barbarism, unless deeply repressed human potential was recovered and redeemed. Nazism was seen as one of the expressions of the degeneration of capitalism – a combination of technological reason (solutions separated from their human consequences) and romanticism (the idealizing of the blood ties and fantasies of race). Fifthly, the experience of individuality was false, but felt to be true, and lived as if it were true. The needs, desires and ways of relating to others in Western culture were constituted as a second nature which had to be understood and challenged by a process of interpretation – and psychoanalysis, which was itself a product of this culture, was the key for this lock.

Sixthly, within each dominant cultural form, or set of ideas, there was a Hegelian dialectic at work, and the course of history is marked by this dialectic which follows a progressive sequence of thesis, antithesis and synthesis. The Hegelian dialectic is a metaphysical 'master narrative' or 'grand theory' which tries to comprehend the way history unfolds itself. Marx, and the Frankfurt School in the Hegelian Western Marxist tradition – exemplified by the work of Lukács (1923) – saw the sequence of different class societies over the course of history as proceeding in dialectical fashion. An example would be the aristocracy as thesis being challenged by the bourgeoisie as antithesis, with the conflict being resolved by capitalism as a new synthesis. The hope was that the proletariat would act as antithesis to the bourgeoisie as thesis, and that socialism would emerge as a synthesis which would be a *sublation* (negation, preservation and transcendence all at once) of capitalism in a dialectical qualitative leap.

Freud and Frankfurt

Erich Fromm joined the Institute of Social Research in 1929, recruited by Horkheimer who had briefly undergone psychoanalysis to improve his lecturing style and was impressed by it as a therapeutic technique. Fromm was responsible for the psychoanalytic input into the Institute (Jay, 1973). Other psychoanalytic members included Fromm-Reichmann and Landauer (who was the most senior psychoanalyst attached to the Institute, and who failed to escape when the Nazis took over and perished in one of the concentration camps).

Fromm's work

Fromm was brought up in a Jewish religious family, and remained influenced by Jewish messianic religious themes (which were also around in the Institute through Walter Benjamin's work on history, technology and his use of Kabbala). This religious background is an important resource for the development of Fromm's reading of psychoanalysis and implications for his account of individuality, enlightenment and modernity (Burston, 1991). Fromm was concerned with the development of selfhood through relation with others, and of the possibility, the potential for this human nature rather than its actuality at any particular time. This meant that he had an optimistic picture of the 'progression' of human nature and was concerned with the *potential* of human beings rather than with trying to discover what that nature was as if it were static. His humanism was a socialist humanism which provided the measure of what was distorting and destructive about capitalism, and which provided the source of resistance to oppression. This also meant, however, that Fromm was sceptical about the value, in itself, of 'tolerance', and, like the rest of the Critical Theorists, was suspicious of the way a façade of neutrality was often a cover for accounts which protected the *status quo* (and psychoanalysis was not exempt from this criticism). His search for expressions of spiritual longing as signs of a challenge to capitalism led him to sympathetic explorations of different religious belief systems (Fromm, 1967).

Fromm employed a Marxist notion of alienation from human potential, and saw one of the main theoretical tasks of the Institute to be a synthesis of Freud and Marx (Fromm, 1962). The Soviet Union was proving to be a big disappointment to Marxists by this time, and Fromm was sympathetic to Trotskyism in the late 1920s and retained an admiration for Trotsky throughout his life (Rickert, 1986; Burston, 1991). During his time with the Institute he defended Freud's first instinct model (with sexual instincts working alongside and pitted against self-preservative instincts), and argued that 'Psychoanalysis is a materialistic psychology which should be classed among the natural sciences' (Fromm, 1932: 478). He agreed with an ideal of non-repressed genital sexuality, and held to a stage model of development with distinctions between characters fixated at oral, anal, and phallic stages (in which the anal stage was particularly dangerous, and the phallic or genital stage was associated with 'independence, freedom and friendliness'). He eventually abandoned libido theory and was opposed to hydraulic models of the mind, and his later work was concerned with forms of relatedness to others. In this respect there is some convergence with the perspective of British and North American object relations theorists (Greenberg and Mitchell, 1983).

There were two respects in which he differed quite sharply from Freud, and the more so from the later Freud. He was opposed to the notion of the death drive, and he saw human destructiveness as a distorted relation to others rather than the expression of underlying drives or instincts

(Fromm, 1974). He refused to employ the notion of the 'Oedipus complex', and preferred to refer to Oedipal-like relationships to fathers and then to authority as something specific to forms of patriarchy and to capitalism structured by the nuclear family. This family was crucial to the reproduction of this particular social system: '*The family is the psychological agency of society*' (Fromm, 1932: 483). Different societies have their own 'libidinal structures', and Oedipal relationships were restricted to patriarchal societies.

Anthropological work held the key to a theoretical and practical political understanding of different cultures and forms of child-rearing which might offer alternatives to the nuclear family, and Fromm looked to accounts of early matriarchal societies. These anthropological theories were quite popular in Germany at the time Fromm was writing, and there was interest in the research of Bachofen and Morgan from the end of the nineteenth century. It was important, however, to distinguish between two varieties of matriarchal theory. There was a popular right-wing version which was then used by the Nazis with a celebration of the 'Mother' as a mystical figure and with a romanticizing of women as mothers (and these notions were also to find their way into Jungian archetypal accounts). Fromm was more interested in the left-wing accounts which had already been discussed extensively by Engels (1884). These were studies which stressed the solidarity and happiness which marked matriarchal clan society before men took over in order to enforce private property. Motherly trust and compassion had then been replaced by paternal guilt and authoritarian morality.

Fromm's ideas found expression in the psychoanalytic ideas employed by the Institute, and in his *Studien Über Autorität und Familie* (Roiser and Willig, 1996). Fromm broke from the Institute in 1939, and in later years came closer to the North American ego-psychologists. He acknowledged similarities between his position and those of Karen Horney and Harry Stack-Sullivan, and this was to be one of the grounds on which Marcuse (1955) was to attack him. Ego-psychology in America drew on the ideas of Anna Freud (1936) and Heinz Hartmann (1939), and it emphasized the way in which a person adapts to different circumstances. Fromm is often unfairly lumped together with the ego-psychologists, and not only by Marcuse (e.g., Jacoby, 1977), but his view of the potential for human freedom was inspired not so much by American individualism as by existentialist ideas in German philosophy.

In *The Fear of Freedom* (1942), Fromm's humanist perspective was reinforced by an employment of existentialist themes in which he set up a conceptual opposition between 'freedom from' and 'freedom to', and an opposition between the biological rootedness of the human condition and attempts to transcend it. These oppositions were then overlaid by an opposition between isolation and relatedness. Sadism and masochism were false solutions to isolation in which the self attempted to lose itself in a relationship to the other, by dominance or submission. The *Fear of Freedom* traces the traps of the Enlightenment (and its culmination in Nazism) to the individualizing and competitive Protestant ethic. Here, restrictions on displays of wealth combined with the compulsion to produce more exacerbate anal characteristics and lead to the development of a 'character type' peculiar to authoritarian capitalist society.

This development of character was *dialectical*:

> capitalism . . . contributed tremendously to the increase of positive freedom, to the growth of an active, critical, responsible self. . . . However . . . at the same time it made the individual more alone and isolated and imbued him [sic] with a feeling of insignificance and powerlessness.
>
> (Fromm, 1942: 93)

The feeling of economic and social freedom encouraged by the Enlightenment was felt as a threat, and this could be 'escaped' from in three ways. The escape could be through authoritarian sadism or masochism, in which 'the frightened individual seeks for somebody or something to tie his self to' (ibid.: 130). The escape could be through destructiveness, through 'the removal of all objects with which the individual has to compare himself' (ibid.: 155). A third possibility for escape could be through automaton conformity, in which there is abject submission which evades the responsibility to think, or to distinguish one's self from others.

Fromm's critics argued that his humanist hopes were evidence that he did not recognize the depth to which culture embedded itself as 'second nature' in the individual, and the way in which 'humanism' itself was part of this 'second nature'. In this view, despite his good intentions, Fromm is portrayed as one of the 'conformist psychologists' (Jacoby, 1977). One of the harshest critics was Herbert Marcuse.

Marcuse's critique

Marcuse did not develop an interest in psychoanalysis until after his arrival in North America. He worked for the war effort in the US State Department as part of the OSS (which was the forerunner of the CIA) before emerging as one of the leading thinkers of the 1960s 'New Left'. His work also reflects his interest in Freud's 'metapsychology' rather than psychoanalysis as a clinical practice. While Fromm was a practising psychoanalyst, and was accused by Marcuse of being complicit in the practical adaptation of individuals to an oppressive society, Marcuse was accused by Fromm of not being able to fully understand psychoanalysis because he did not work clinically.

Marcuse's development of psychoanalysis as a social theory is exemplified by *Eros and Civilization* (1955). The death drive is taken seriously, but Marcuse also attempted to historicize this 'Thanatos' as a drive which was not necessarily destructive, and so he emphasized the tension-reducing aspect which Freud (1920) discussed in *Beyond the Pleasure Principle*. The 'Nirvana principle' which underlies the death drive only becomes dangerous when it is inhibited, and when it is projected outwards. The drive's objective is the termination of pain, and so the conflict between life and death would result in, and facilitate, the reduction of tension. What was needed then, was an alternative to tension-producing alienated labour under capitalism, an alternative found in childhood and child-like 'aestheticized play'.

An important aspect of this return to something approaching the tranquillity of inorganic nature was the escape from the 'performance principle' in which sexuality becomes an activity to be compulsively engaged in always to achieve an end point. This 'performance' of sexuality was a reflection of an instrumental means-end form of reason, and while it was advertised and incited as a form of pleasure, it was actually one of the elements of an all the more pernicious sexual misery under capitalism. A key aspect of the 'performance principle' was the focus on genital satisfaction, and so Marcuse thought that Fromm was seriously mistaken in advocating this as if it could be an index of mental health and human happiness. (Reich was even worse than Fromm in this respect, as we shall see in Chapter 5.) Instead, the ideal should be the enjoyment of 'polymorphous perversity' in which there would be a recovery of pleasure in parts of the body that have undergone repression. In this way the alienated, and so threatening, sexuality of modern life would be transformed into Eros.

Marcuse sometimes appears to be promoting a regression to childhood polymorphous perversity as an alternative to the oppressive maturity of modern culture, and is accused of this by Fromm and by other later writers, of 'never growing up or moving beyond childhood' (Chodorow, 1985: 296). Marcuse is seen as celebrating 'the psychological stance of the infant' (ibid.: 294). He is, however, at the same time trying to assess how modern culture incites individuals to give themselves over to sexual pleasure in ways that are not at all liberating. His notion of 'repressive desublimation' tried to capture the way in which critical thought can be dissolved in the pretence that repressions are being lifted:

> This mobilization and administration of the libido may account for much of the voluntary compliance, the absence of terror, the pre-established harmony between individual needs and socially-required desires, goals and aspirations ... satisfaction in a way which generates submission and weakens the rationality of protest.
>
> (Marcuse, 1972: 71)

The problem is that the more he is critical of the repressive ways in which 'desublimation' is managed, the more he is tempted to appeal to some libidinal force that is deeper down below the grip of culture as a source of protest.

Marcuse argued, as did Freud, that while there was a need for a degree of basic repression for a society to be able to function, modern capitalist society operated on 'surplus repression'. Surplus repression kept the individual in place as a subordinate to those in authority and isolated from colleagues or work-mates. One crucial sphere which prefigures an utopian state in which Eros has replaced the 'performance principle' (and where 'surplus repression' is not employed) is the aesthetic sphere: 'The truth of art is the liberation of sensuousness through its reconciliation with reason' (Marcuse, 1955: 184). Marcuse looked to this 'reconciliation' as evidence of a still dialectical conception of separation, conflict and the possible resolution of historical and social tensions.

Marcuse's Epilogue to *Eros and Civilization* is a 'Critique of Neo-Freudian Revisionism', and here he points to a 'fateful dilemma' for psychoanalysis as a form of cultural critique. Fromm's early work is applauded, but then Marcuse argues that the 'affirmative attitude' Fromm promotes is 'compatible with prevailing values' (Marcuse, 1955: 244–245). Many of the quotes Marcuse gathers to condemn Fromm as one of the 'Neo-Freudian revisionists' are actually from Horney and Stack-Sullivan, and Marcuse overlooks aspects of Fromm's work that would not fit Marcuse's image of him as a conformist (Rickert, 1986). Nevertheless, Marcuse does draw attention to a problem that besets all progressive psychoanalysts and psychologists who aim to make people happier in a society that is founded on repression and on the production of a deep misery as a condition for functioning as a productive individual in it. As he points out,

> In such a society, the self-realization of the 'personality' can proceed only on the basis of a double repression: first, the 'purification' of the pleasure principle and the internalization of happiness and freedom; second, their reasonable restriction until they become compatible with the prevailing unfreedom and unhappiness.
>
> (Marcuse, 1955: 259)

Marcuse's work has been an important resource for those who have wanted to challenge 'conformist psychology' (Jacoby, 1977). When contemporary culture is not challenged, then behaviourist and humanist forms of psychology simply push people into shape; 'it doesn't matter *what* one expresses so long as one is aware of what is being expressed', and psychologists forget that 'the liberated person will be that of a spontaneous, honest and loving member of this culture and will express the contradictions and frustrations of capitalist society' (Ratner, 1971: 63).

It is not clear that there is an escape from this trap. On the one hand, Fromm needs to appeal to the potential for integrity of the self against unconscious destructive processes that are provoked by oppressive social relations under capitalism and to a reasoned therapeutic reflection on the sources of unhappiness, and he wants to use the notion of mature genitality or capacity for relatedness as the measure of happiness that is frustrated and sabotaged by modern culture. On the other hand, Marcuse wants to retain some source of resistance to the colonization of the ego by capitalism, and he looks to unconscious desires which still escape the reality principle, and to political action outside therapy and polymorphously perverse childhood resistance to the culture children are forced to submit to as they develop. The trap holds both Fromm and Marcuse in the thrall of modern forms of individuality, as either confirming it or as simply attacking it within its own terms. We can see the power of this trap in the forms of discourse which now structure how professional psychologists account for themselves.

Chartering the future of the psychological sciences

Psychoanalytic discourse has a peculiar relationship with the rest of the theories and practices that constitute the disciplinary apparatus of psychology in Western culture. This apparatus, which operates as a network of speculations about the behaviour and mental states of individuals and as a range of attempts to regulate how people behave and think, is the 'psy-complex' (Ingleby, 1985; Rose, 1985). 'Psychology' here includes, then, the activities of academic psychologists carrying out experiments or conducting interviews and the work of a host of professionals working in agencies ranging from child-care to social work. It includes all the weird jargon of cognitive-behaviourists, humanists and psychodynamic folk as they deal with individuals who are unhappy or who do not fit in and attempt to turn them into self-monitoring, self-regulating subjects. Psychoanalytic discourse is one powerful version of psychological discourse in the West, but those who call themselves 'psychologists' and organize in their own professional associations to oversee teaching and training in the colleges and clinics are often very hostile to psychoanalysis.

Cognitive and personality psychologists worry away at the effect of non-conscious mental processes on their models of reasoning, but they refuse to engage seriously with psychoanalytic notions of the ego and unconscious. Instead, rather bizarre experimental studies are set up which are designed to make any psychoanalytic explanation look foolish (e.g., Eysenck and Wilson, 1973). Social psychologists try to conceptualize the way relationships and group phenomena operate out of rational individual control, but they are determined to contain social behaviour within the confines of the laboratory-experiment if they are old-style positivists (Turner, 1975) or to deny that anything might be happening beyond people's accounts if they are new-style social constructionists (e.g., Varela, 1995). Developmental psychology tries to incorporate psychoanalytic conceptions of early life stages, but it shuts out any exploration of the infant as a sensual being entering and struggling with the harsh adult world. Although psychoanalysis has had a long and complicated relationship with psychology, and many well-known psychologists (such as Boring, Luria and Piaget) were very sympathetic to Freudian ideas, psychoanalysis now operates as a kind of 'repressed other' of psychology (Burman, 1994).

At the same time, however, the discipline of psychology is suffused with psychoanalytic discourse, and this is no more apparent than when the discipline is taking steps to define and protect itself against outsiders. Fromm's and Marcuse's psychoanalytic work is particularly pertinent here because the concepts that they explored and debated are those that structure the way psychologists now talk about themselves and their institutions. We can also see Freud's image of the garrison in the city and his concern with the development of mature defences appearing in different metaphorical guises over and over again in the way psychologists talk about disciplinary professional regulation. Their discourse is structured by the tension between Fromm's emphasis on the value of rational thought, the integrity of clinical work and the value of mature defences on the one hand, and Marcuse's celebration of unconscious impulses, political activity which breaches institutional boundaries and infantile pleasure as model and source of liberation on the other. A useful way of unravelling the way in which these notions circulate in psychology is to highlight the operation of discursive complexes in self-representations of the discipline.

In this analysis, phenomena like 'egos' and 'ids' are seen not as structures inside the head of any particular individual but as *forms of discourse*. These forms of discourse then *position* individual speakers in certain ways, with certain rights to speak or write in certain locations and cultures (Davies and Harré, 1990; Tan and Moghaddam, 1995). So, when psychologists speak or write within forms of discourse that are structured by discursive complexes, the way they speak or write will position them as being rational or irrational, as respecting the rules of the institution of psychology or not, or as being mature or infantile. Speaking and writing always takes place in certain practices, and in this case we are concerned with the institutional settings which frame how psychology is practised. The intersection of the different discourses and discursive complexes in an institution means that to step out of 'normal' subject positions will entail costs for the speaker or writer. These costs will range from being misunderstood or labelled as a trouble-maker to being disciplined or expelled. Most psychologists live so comfortably in the subject positions that are laid out for them in the psy-complex that even reflection on the consequences of these ways of speaking and writing will seem strange or pointless to them. To understand how that happens we do also need some account of ideology and false consciousness (and we will turn to that kind of account in Chapter 5).

I will illustrate the operation of six discursive complexes which are organized into three different pairs in the libidinal structure of the psy-complex by focusing on some of the documents of the British Psychological Society (BPS) as it has attempted to professionalize psychology. The late 1980s saw significant changes in the regulation of members of the BPS and attacks on the 'charlatans' outside who would not or could not join. The BPS has been developing a 'Charter' of professional psychologists which would include those who practise in clinical or educational settings, for example, and those who teach psychology in universities. The hope has been that eventually the BPS will obtain a 'Royal Charter' which would enable the organization to determine who can and cannot call themselves a 'psychologist'. Other national psychological organizations, such as the Australian Psychological Society, which tightened up on registration to stop Scientologists from calling themselves psychologists, moved earlier and faster than the BPS, and the BPS has tried to replicate the success of the Australian organization. The BPS Register of Chartered Psychologists is the first step, then, to the total policing of what psychology is and who should be allowed to do it. There have been similar attempts by psychotherapists in Britain to develop a registration process that would satisfy European regulations, and there is now a United Kingdom Council for Psychotherapy (UKCP) which includes many psychoanalytic psychotherapists (as well as the Lacanian analysts). A rival British Confederation of Psychotherapists was set up by the British Psycho-Analytical Society (the local section of the IPA) after the UKCP refused to allow psychoanalysts their demand that they should be the top tier of a two-tier professional body. These registration moves do seem to be designed to protect professionals rather than clients (Mowbray, 1995).

The three texts I will be drawing upon here are: a document prepared in 1988 for the Scientific Affairs Board of the BPS, *The Future of the Psychological Sciences* (British Psychological Society, 1988); an article by Ian Howarth (then President of the BPS) in the Society's house journal, *The Psychologist* (Howarth, 1988); and an open letter from Howarth to BPS academics encouraging them to join the Charter (Howarth, 1989). The three pairs of discursive complexes are the ego versus the id, working through versus acting out, and stages of development versus polymorphous perversity.

The ego and the id

The BPS sets itself up as the rational reflective guardian of the discipline, as the kind of well-adapted entity that Fromm spent much of his time trying to encourage individuals to develop. At the same time, however, it finds itself having to deal with unruly forces that might disrupt its good work, the kind of irrational impulses that Marcuse championed. If the psy-complex is to be turned into a civilized city-state, then the BPS wants to make sure that it knows the layout of the garrison.

EGO   A separate self-conscious apparatus must be necessary, according to Freud (1923b), for individuals to assess the demands of an external reality as well as to cope with pressure from internalized prohibitions (which become located in the super-ego) and from the unconscious drives (which become located in the id). The ego is also the site of the various defence mechanisms which enable the individual to operate independently of those significant others from childhood who were a formative influence (and were also an influence on the development of the ego itself).

The rhetorical figure of the ego in this case refers to the way the BPS as the key institution for governing those who work in the psy-complex in Britain represents itself as if it were a mental apparatus maintained by a system of defences. The Working Party set up by the Scientific Affairs Board noted, for example, that 'At every meeting of the Board there has been discussion of some new threat to the psychological sciences' (BPS, 1988: 2). A dense network of rituals, procedures and safeguards for the defence of the institution of psychology has been building up in the BPS as Charter-fever increased during the 1980s. The self-image of the Society, as the representative of 'British Psychology', revolves around defence, and around an anxiety about the effects of unfair attack, as well as anxiety about behaviour that might provoke such an attack: 'Too many professional organizations have protected their members rather than the public. If we behave in the same way we shall be easy targets, less able to defend ourselves' (Howarth, 1988: 96). One thing that is striking about the document *The Future of the Psychological Sciences* is the notion that the health of psychology depends upon an acceptance of debate but that care must be taken that there should not be any loss of integrity as the discipline faces the outside world. Howarth (1989) also argues that 'it is important to preserve the unity of the profession of psychology'.

The BPS is constructed, then, as if it were a kind of ego for the profession, and the discursive complex of the ego – a psychoanalytic notion reproduced here in the way that psychologists talk about themselves – governs the way internal unity might be maintained. Chartering is seen as providing a guarantee of this unity: 'Chartered status is a signal to our students and to others, that we share their concern for the preservation and development of the profession of psychology' (Howarth, 1989). What is at stake here is the collective professional identity of psychologists. It is not surprising, perhaps, given the way psychologists usually try to make individuals responsible for everything else they do, that there should be injunctions here that it is the responsibility of *individual* psychologists to act in ways compatible with that collective identity. As well as cautions about not provoking attack from outsiders, calls for the unity of the discipline and for the protection of the next generation of psychologists, there is a concern with healthy flexibility and self-control that any ego-psychologist would be happy to endorse, for, as the BPS (1988: 12) puts it, it is important to value 'Variety combined with orderliness'.

ID   The ego is pitted against the 'id' in psychoanalytic theory, and this mental agency became for Freud (1923b) a way of referring to a pulsating, demanding subterranean part of the mind which consists of innate instinctual drives and those drives which have been felt and then repressed. The drives from the id then power the ego and super-ego and lead it into conflict with these agencies when they attempt to prevent or divert it.

The counterpart to the discursive complex of the healthy ego of the BPS is the discursive complex of the unruly id, conjured into being as a source of threat. Just as repression as one of the defence mechanisms of the ego often serves to intensify a threat from the id rather than to destroy it, so the attempt of the institution of mainstream psychology to deal with what it perceives to be irrational threats from outside confirms and strengthens the fantasy of those threats. Outside the BPS, then, lie irrational forces incarnate in those charlatans who not only have 'false perceptions' of psychology, but who may employ psychological knowledge in irresponsible and dangerous ways. It is symptomatic that psychodynamic approaches are explicitly mentioned as a potential problem here. The BPS (1988: 28–29) notes that 'psychodynamic approaches and the associated notion of intra-psychic conflicts, continue to be taken seriously by non-psychologists' and it argues that 'experimental and clinical psychologists should take up the challenge of developing appropriate and relevant research methodologies' (ibid.). There is the spectre of a threat again if they do not: 'If such research is not carried out there is an increased risk that a multitude of practices, all announcing themselves as "psychotherapy", will proliferate without regard to its validity or effectiveness' (ibid.).

The irrational outside is constituted, then, as an incomprehensible unreasonable 'it', and an additional correlative fear that is often expressed in the BPS document is that internal dissent could also be disruptive and destructive: 'The psychological community could be its own worst enemy', and so 'energies directed at conflict should be diverted to constructive endeavour' (ibid.: 3). Overt disagreement over questions of method in psychology, for example, could be seen as constituting a 'threat', and then this could give rise to a destructive 'conflict'. When such conflict occurs, certain internal forces are seen as responsible, and as breaking the unity of psychology and provoking worse attack and disorder from the outside. This self-image of the institution constructs certain kinds of restricted subject positions for individual members of the BPS. A consequence of the dichotomy operating here between the rational ego of the professional institution and the uncontrolled, unregistered, unchartered outsiders is that real responsible psychologists should stay inside the institution and guard the boundaries. Individuals are invited to experience activity outside the BPS forums as risky. Because the BPS is employing a rhetoric which presents itself as a collection of civilized citizens engaged in rational debate, a subject position is constituted for members such that those occupying this position will feel that the 'outside' is dangerous. We are warned that 'when away from the laboratory, the psychologist should not feel that he or she is somehow a stranger in an alien land. The psychological scientist should not feel ill-at-ease when invited to offer advice on other people's home ground' (ibid.: 24).

There is a powerful image here of the psy-complex as a territory, with the discipline of psychology as the city-state and the BPS observing and regulating from within the garrison. This is not at all the state of affairs that Fromm would have wanted to endorse, but his concerns about the development of internal coherence and forms of relatedness with those outside the self are uncomfortably close to the images of the individual self that the BPS employs to constitute itself as a collective entity. The opportunities for the kinds of libidinally charged resistance to the garrison in the city-state that Marcuse championed are positioned in these discursive forms as much too risky. It is as if the id has become invested with all the power Marcuse wished for it, and then demonized all the more so because it holds that power. Psychologists have that power conjured up as a threat which might erupt from inside the BPS or which might beset them when they step outside the gates.

Working through and acting out

The division between the rational secure inside and the irrational risky outside which is set up by the discursive complexes of the ego and the id is compounded by a distinction between appropriate and inappropriate behaviour, between what members of the BPS can talk about with each other and what it would be right to discuss with outsiders. Here there are echoes of the debate between Fromm the clinician and Marcuse the radical theorist, and what each thought the other could not understand because they were 'inside' (Fromm) or 'outside' (Marcuse) a clinical setting. The rhetorical figures of 'working through' and 'acting out' are more than just echoes of old debates, however, for they help to condition how psychologists relate to each other and to the 'others'.

WORKING THROUGH   Psychoanalysis requires a notion of mental work undertaken by a patient as they deal with unwanted attention to defence mechanisms by the analyst, and to the consequences of having these made salient. To 'work through', understood clinically, is to carry forward the therapeutic work in its proper place, to reflect upon and feel the implications that mutative interpretation and painful self-reflection provokes. It is not enough to remember something traumatic. The reasons why it was forgotten, and the process of forgetting and remembering have to be addressed in the process of working through (Freud, 1914b).

Although the discursive complex of working through is derived from clinical work, it functions as the specification of boundaries and proper times and places for issues to be spoken about and acted on. For the BPS (1988: 7), there is just such a concern with appropriate arenas for discussion, and it argues that 'The psychological community should seek to establish mechanisms which ensure mutual communication between such groupings [with common interests within the psychological sciences] and opportunities for synthesis'. It is advisable, then, to conduct debate within the institutional structures, and such debate is advertised as a proper scientific way of establishing points of difference and resolving them. This is then counterposed to the activities of those errant psychologists who get too closely involved with the 'outside'. There is a concern that such entanglement with outsiders will give rise to divisions *inside*, and the BPS (ibid.: 52) points out that 'an unproductive distinction between scientific (not 'professional' or 'applied') and professional (not 'scientific') issues' has opened up, and that this unproductive distinction 'has distorted the development of the scientific aspects of psychology, by failing to acknowledge its application to real-world problems and the benefits that may ensue'.

Rather than seek a different kind of relationship between those in the BPS and those outside who may have different ideas about what psychology is about, *The Future of the Psychological Sciences* is concerned with an internal solution: 'an alternative division of functions might well be between issues of membership, training and professional regulation (essentially internal issues), and issues of psychological science and practice (with both internal and external dimensions)' (ibid.). As with the distinction between the discursive complexes of the ego and the id, this discursive complex requires that BPS members should not only respect the boundaries which surround the community of 'psychological scientists', but that they should also actively inhabit and fulfil the rights and duties of a certain kind of subject position. Participants should not only acquiesce, but should *speak*, undertaking the process of working through with enthusiasm, in a self-motivated way. Thus, there is a concern that 'the Society develops a strategy for encouraging more active involvement in the affairs of the Society by members who are relatively passive in their relationship to it' (ibid.: 7).

ACTING OUT   Alongside the invitation to 'work through' issues in a carefully circumscribed clinical setting, psychoanalysis is quick to pathologize attempts by the patient to do that kind of thing outside. There is always a temptation for the patient to refuse to understand the meaning of unconscious wishes or to defer gratification by talking about meanings on the couch. To seek immediate expression in activities outside analysis instead, then, is to act out (Freud, 1914b).

Against the appropriate working through of disagreement in the BPS, then, to 'act out' means more than simply speaking outside appropriate professional forums. In the discourse of this institution, it sometimes seems tantamount to betrayal to speak with outsiders, and there are warnings about the dangers such activities might present when the psychological scientist is in an 'alien land'. *The Future of the Psychological Sciences* reproduces an image not only of things having a proper place in certain channels of communication, but also of the necessity for the ability to dissimulate. It reports on the suggestions made by some of the participants at the Harrogate Conference (which was set up to help it address 'The Future'), and displays worry that some speakers 'insisted that psychologists had better learn to give unequivocal answers', and it insists in turn that 'We believe that this is overly simple' (BPS, 1988: 24). There is a particular problem here, of course, for those critical psychologists who engage in action research (Lewin, 1946), let alone participant action research (Jiménez-Domínguez, 1996), for those kinds of research activities require openness about what the psychologist is up to and encouragement for members of a community to set appropriate agendas and goals for the study themselves.

Those who do want to do critical action research will, when they are positioned by this discursive complex, be seen as separating themselves from the discipline. The discussions of Chartering in the BPS function to set out such positions when their document on the future argues that 'We believe that the discipline should resist splintering of psychological knowledge into groups which identify themselves as separate from the mainstream of psychology and deny their psychological origins' (BPS, 1988: 7). In addition to images of irresponsible abandonment of the younger generation, 'our students' who are looking to us to preserve and develop the profession, the Society member is urged, then, not to desert or 'deny their origins'. The position of the mature parent is comple-mented, here, with the position of the dependent child, the one who needs to live in the extended family of the psy-complex and become active in the nuclear family of the BPS. The security offered by respons-ible self-governance can only be maintained if a steady pattern of growth is aimed for: 'It is surely self-destructive to insist prematurely on criteria which are far more rigorous than other well-established professions are willing to accept?' This self-destructiveness is conjured up as an ever-present threat when it is argued that 'In certain contexts scepticism can be destructive if it undermines initiatives for new developments' (ibid.: 70). Once again, this pair of discursive complexes – working through and acting out – not only locks BPS members into place in relation to out-siders, but also requires them to behave themselves inside the institution. It is always possible to be pathologized for varieties of 'acting in' as well as acting out.

Marcuse was worried by exactly these kinds of conservative impli-cations of institutional policing. He saw Fromm as advocating psycho-analysis as a therapeutic technique operating as a self-contained clinical practice which not only pathologizes certain symptomatic behaviours outside analysis (as acting out) but also pathologizes certain desires which are viewed as symptoms when the patient is on the couch. Psychoanalysis was, for Marcuse, 'a course in resignation'. While Fromm did attempt to develop psychoanalysis as a critical practice, the discourse of working through and acting out still maintained the boundaries between behav-iour seen as appropriate and that which was seen as infantile. In turn, Fromm accused Marcuse of advocating 'infantile' gratification and not respecting the value of healthy development.

Stages of development and polymorphous perversity

The conceptual distinction between the ego and the id and between working through and acting out is given a further conservative moraliz-ing twist when images of infantile behaviour and mature development are stirred in. These images are crucial, of course, to the way Fromm saw adult relatedness to others, and to the way Marcuse championed the healthy impulses of the child before it has been subjected to the reality principle.

STAGES OF DEVELOPMENT Psychologists tend to find Freud least threatening when they read him as simply describing the different stages a child must travel through to become a healthy adult. Freud (1905a) was actually concerned more with the particular ways in which different aspects of sensual experience became important to the infant and then to the adult than with a set sequence of oral, anal, phallic, latency and genital 'stages', but the stage model has still haunted psychoanalysis.

An image of the institution of psychology in relation to potentially dangerous outsiders is reinforced by its account of its own history and the way it imagines dangers of fixation on, and regression, to the past. The BPS even applies the narrative of every-child's travel past certain developmental milestones to the discipline, and it asserts on the first page of *The Future of the Psychological Sciences* that 'A key purpose of this Report is to identify growth points for the future of the psychological sciences in Britain' (BPS, 1988: 1). A link is made between the striving for 'variety and order' and the 'well-being' of the psychological sciences, and the balance between these things confirms an image not only of the institution but also of each individual member. The idea that this process of self-reflection is bound up with a healthy sequence of stages of development is also supported by the images of learning and community spirit that members are invited to participate in. BPS members are told that 'Each individual who works for the benefit of the Society constitutes part of the Society's memory and immediately becomes invaluable; the more such people there are, the better' (ibid.: 52).

For each healthy adult member of the Society, 'The toleration of variety in psychology encourages flexible thinking' (ibid.: 48). Alongside this nostrum runs a warning, a warning that once again concerns what the outsiders might see: 'There are, however, disadvantages in a public show of diversity within a discipline' (ibid.). These 'disadvantages' concern what might happen if others perceive that the straight and narrow path of development is being deviated from: 'To outsiders the appearance can be one of immaturity and self doubt' (ibid.), and the suggested solution is that 'greater emphasis on the cumulative acquisition of psychological knowledge would help to counterbalance the negative results of disputes among proponents of different approaches to psychology' (ibid.). There is a rhetorical shift of focus at points in *The Future of the Psychological Sciences* where the stages of development are not only given a normative flavour, but also linked to debates over whether psychology should be an art or a science. The transition from non-rational activity (here assumed to be the realm of the 'arts') to a kind of research which the BPS is now able to support (here represented as 'science') is mapped onto the development of psychologists from their incomplete past, and so 'The Society should seek to publicise the fact that psychology may be used as a means of transferring students from arts to sciences' (ibid.: 9).

POLYMORPHOUS PERVERSITY   Freud (1905a) provides a description of the infant as having no conception of gender or sexuality, but as being driven by pleasure and pain regardless of kinds of object or parts of the body. To speak of the infant as being 'constitutionally bisexual' and 'poly-morphously perverse' opens up the possibility for different modes of development and different forms of personality in the adult, though psychoanalysis as a practice has typically endorsed culturally dominant ways of escaping the earliest free plays of desire that these terms connote.

If the BPS is following certain stages of development, its vision of 'The Future' must be certain and secure. In contrast, the discursive complex of polymorphous perversity helps the BPS to narrate the past as a state of untutored sensual being that *must* be left behind. This narrative then func-tions as a warning to those who lag behind or those who may refuse to follow a normative developmental route toward a more mature rigorous science. Those who are critical of psychology may then be seen as wilfully regressing, and their attempts to question the direction of growth are seen as evidence of inadequate development. The BPS (1988: 12) is keen to point out that 'At present, the psychological sciences are in many ways frag-mented', something remedied only if acknowledgment of this fragmen-tation is combined with a vision of a correct developmental path for 'psychological science' to follow. The rhetoric of self-discipline and scien-tific growth places a responsibility on members of the BPS to care for those who will come next. The two discursive complexes of stages of develop-ment and polymorphous perversity together emphasize security and maturity, and they warn against infantile demands and failure to provide a safe environment for others to grow. There is an appeal to this sense of responsibility in the declaration by the then BPS President to academic members that 'Chartered status is a signal to our students and to others, that we share their concern for the preservation and development of the profession of psychology' (Howarth, 1989).

In this context, those psychologists who are critical of the cumulative positivist model of research and who are working with phenomenologi-cal, post-structuralist, discursive or feminist perspectives are positioned as being in favour of uncertainty, and so they are unscientific and imma-ture. The BPS document asserts that 'We believe absolutely in the power of knowledge for its own sake and that scientific advance is likely to be inhibited if immediate and obvious utility is the sole criterion of worth' (BPS, 1988: 69). Furthermore, this contextualizes in a rather unhelpful way the attempt to make good some of the ways in which the institution of psy-chology has excluded certain categories of people (Burman, 1990; Howitt and Owusu-Bempah, 1994). People from 'ethnic minorities', for example, could be positioned as lagging behind, and will be recruited in much the same way as students might be recruited from the arts to science: 'The

Society should gather information from other professional bodies about the strategies they use to increase recruitment of members of ethnic minorities' (BPS, 1988: 10). There are similar problems in the way that issues of sexism are framed by these discursive complexes and in the suggestion that 'the Council considers steps which could be taken to redress the imbalance in gender representation, including the positive encouragement of women to take a full part in the Society's business' (ibid.).

The theoretical–political tension between Fromm and Marcuse allows us to see how notions of maturity and infancy structure the discourse of psychological institutions, and how questions of healthy relatedness and repressive desublimation apply not only to the individual that Western culture fabricates to make society run smoothly, but also to the professional bodies that oversee the psy-complex charged with this work. When the libidinal structure of a society and its constituent organizations has been set in place, invitations to participate function not so much as signs of openness but as threats of recuperation. Those who have been excluded will now be admitted on certain conditions, with certain subject positions set out for them to speak and act. At the same time, we need to keep in mind that the reason why Fromm's and Marcuse's versions of psychoanalysis are so pertinent to images of psychology and psychological science is because the aspects of psychoanalytic discourse they elaborated now wash through the self-representations of individuals and professionals in the psy-complex. We are not so much concerned, then, with searching psychological texts for hidden unconscious contents, but with reading the texts closely with an eye to the way they produce the unconscious as something unbearable and then try to push it away.

Dialectics of individuality and culture

Cultural processes of self-representation in the Western Enlightenment need secure institutional sites where images of the individual can be practised and elaborated upon so that the discourse of individual responsibility and separation from nature can be made to work. The individual self, governed by the ego as if it were the captain of the soul, is one institutional site, and the psy-complex governed by professional soul-servers is another. There is a necessary mutual reflection and identification at work between these two institutional sites, with each modelling itself on the other so that the theory of self that is produced by one becomes the theory which is acted upon by the other (Harré, 1983).

The trap Fromm often fell into was to see an appeal to humanism as a solution and to forget that Enlightenment culture makes us interpret humanism as a property of the individual. Fromm did insist that humanism was a potential that was realizable only in the context of certain kinds of open undistorted social relations, but what is at issue here is the way that his radical hope can be so easily recuperated into bourgeois individualism.

Marcuse, too, fell into the trap of trying to escape individualist illusions of human freedom by turning to sources of liberation outside the conscious self, and by intensifying the fear and romance in the West of things unconscious and 'natural'. The appeal to Eros and Thanatos confirms images of the body and nature, and an appeal to these as essential sources of critique and freedom also buttresses discourses of rationality as the only alternative. The mirror-work between the professional psychological institutions and the self we each feel we possess is accompanied by another kind of mirror-work, between how we feel we must reason to stay sane and how frightened we feel we would be if we stopped reasoning.

Both Fromm and Marcuse tried to develop a dialectical account which would work with the conceptual oppositions which provide the libidinal structure and second nature of the Enlightenment and then break with those oppositions, an account which would be able to develop an antithesis to the modern individual and culture which would not simply provide a negative mirror but which would lead to the possibility of synthesis. As we shall see in the next chapter, when we turn to the development of authoritarianism, a simple refusal of cultural forms that feel oppressive to the individual constituted by this culture can be just as dangerous as deliberate collusion.

5

Authoritarianism, Ideology and Masculinity

He went from Mr Right to Mr It. It was as if I was confronting Satan himself.

Edwards, a near victim. In Dvorchak and Holewa (1991: 23) *Milwauke Massacre: Jeffrey Dahmer and the Milwauke Murders*

A sense of individuality is closely tied to authority in modern Enlightenment culture; as the ability to author the narrative of our own lives, and also to have power over others or to resent the power others hold over us.

Our experience of ourselves as separate and isolated from other people means that we have particularly hostile and fearful relationships with others, and these feelings are exaggerated when we relate to those in authority. The beliefs that we have deep down about our own nature and about those lesser and greater than ourselves are forms of *ideology*. The second nature that is embedded in who we are under capitalism functions as ideology, and it buttresses beliefs about human nature and social relations which prevent us from changing things which are exploitative and oppressive. Psychoanalysis can help us interpret ideology and reveal its power, but *how* psychoanalysis can do that is disputed. A key question here has been whether ideological forms should be seen as grounded in physical coercion and in the repression of biological needs (in which case liberation will be to do with the release of repressed unconscious forces) or whether ideological forms are distortions of language, and the repression is of alternative meanings (in which case liberation will come through the unravelling of those distortions so we can see things clearly).

Wilhelm Reich and Jürgen Habermas addressed this question, but do not solve it. They share an allegiance to the Frankfurt School (Jay, 1973); Reich through his brief association in the early years when the School was attempting to connect Freud and Marx, and Habermas from the 1950s as the School was distancing itself from both Freudian and Marxist traditions. That link with the first and second generations of the School lingers in a task both Reich and Habermas addressed, which is how to build an account of subjectivity that connects the individual with culture, how to a build a bridge over the modern rift between the inside and the outside. A concern with understanding authoritarianism is also evident in both writers' work, for the isolation of the individual from others is bound up with power and with mistaken ways of striking out against authority (Reich, 1934a; Habermas, 1969). In contrast to Fromm and Marcuse, both

Reich and Habermas abandon a dualist model of the drives (or of a tra-ditional Freudian 'pair of opposites'), but they do so in very different ways. Reich, like Marcuse, held to the view that it was biological needs that were crucial, but, unlike Marcuse, did not take notions of the death drive seriously. The libido, and its expression in orgasm was a manifes-tation of the *body* which had to be freed from the constraints of modern society. Habermas, on the other hand, is concerned, like Fromm, with *meaning*. Unlike Fromm, however, he sees meaning as an intersubjective function of communication, and the role of reflexivity is as an endeavour which would dissolve the defences employed in language and the history of the individual.

These quite different conceptions of repression and freedom – what it is that distorts and what it is that resists – entail different accounts of the development of authoritarianism, and of ideology generally. These differ-ent conceptions of authoritarianism also take forward the well-known Frankfurt School empirical work on prejudice (Adorno et al., 1950), and each could help us to understand the way in which prejudice is reinforced and transformed in societies that do not appear, at first sight, to be authori-tarian. Reich was concerned with the most vicious aspects of fascist authoritarianism that was erupting around him in the 1930s from within both society and the individual, and his account was an exaggeration of themes in psychoanalysis to counter extreme events. Habermas, on the other hand, is concerned with the distortions that constitute prejudice and which lie buried in the rhetoric that individuals use in times of peace, and his version of psychoanalytic social theory is a more liberal response to a more liberal post-Second World War Western society. Although Habermas seems more reasonable, however, it may be that Reich's account better captures something about the underlying dynamics of liberal society, and this may be because 'in psychoanalysis only exaggeration is true' (Adorno, cited in Jacoby, 1977: 20).

Reich and Habermas appeal to something 'true' that will resist the insid-ious grip of false consciousness, our mistaken investment in ideology. However, as we shall see when we turn to contemporary masculinism which has emerged as a counterpart and reaction to feminism, the truth of the drives or of free communication can also operate ideologically. In this chapter, then, we will review Reich's and Habermas's use of psycho-analysis to dissolve false consciousness, and then turn to Robert Bly's (1990) *Iron John* to show how Reichian and Habermasian versions of psychoanalytic discourse thread their way through this masculinist text and reproduce authoritarianism while having once been used to challenge it. The fantasies at the core of the image of the new wild man that Bly celebrates are two-fold. They are structured by the development of par-ticular notions of nature (supplying, particularly for men, the well-springs of heterosexual libido pushing against social constraints) and culture (diverting the attempts at genuine communication between men and men, and men and women). We can also see then how subject positions that are available for speakers can also be invested with such emotion that they feel as if they must be true.

Reich: energy

There are problems in understanding Reich, and this is partly because when he changed his mind he would rewrite his manuscripts, leaving the same titles for very different books. The later rewriting also functions to cover up his early political involvement, especially the Freud / Marx phase of 1929–1934, with a reinterpretation of communism as being as bad as fascism (as a 'red fascism') (Ollman, 1972). Reich became a clinical assistant in Freud's Psychoanalytic Polyclinic in Vienna in 1922, and at roughly the same time he started to become involved in radical movements, eventually joining the Austrian Communist Party in 1927. Reich's career traced a trajectory through training as an analyst in the late 1920s, a break with Freud over the physical and measurable reality of the libido, activity in and then expulsion from both the psychoanalytic and communist movements in the early 1930s, the discovery of 'atmospheric (cosmic) orgone energy' (Reich, 1942: 358) in the 1940s, and a slide into paranoia in the 1950s (Sharaf, 1983; Boadella, 1985). The nature of repression conceived as a process that locked energy in the unconscious and in the body led Reich to believe that relief from neurosis required the recovery of orgastic potency, of release of the energy (Reich, 1942). There is a strong enduring theme in Reich's work of the perversion of natural heterosexual libido; perversion wrought through the imposition of patriarchal order upon a natural matriarchal pre-historical state of being, and through the imposition of the father's rage upon a natural genital character. This cultural-historical and individual-developmental process reinforces the ego as a repressive agency. It is possible to trace a direct line of descent for this vitalist theme in his work from the first disagreements with Freud to the last tragic days (Chasseguet-Smirgel and Grunberger, 1976). His earliest interest, as a psychoanalyst, was in the *reality* of libido.

Reich's libido

The libido, for Reich, was not only a metaphor. For Freud, 'libido' was a term for hypothetical 'energy' for which a hydraulic description was the one which was most convenient. For Reich, it was a material force, and it was measurable. This meant that it was necessary to actually release this energy in sexual activity, and not merely to experience the release. Blockages in the libido may occur in 'normal' sexual behaviour, but these blockages become psychopathological when they result in the loss of ability to surrender to the flow of the libido. Reich argued as early as 1923 that this surrender was necessary for 'orgastic potency'. The libido, then, was a physical energy which was more important than the meanings attached to it, and this meant that a 'talking cure' was insufficient – it was *physical* release that was crucial, and this meant that therapy also had to have a physical component. This emphasis on the body is reflected in contemporary 'neo-Reichian' bodywork and bio-energetic therapies (e.g., Boadella, 1988).

Rather than impotency being an effect of neurosis, then, it was seen by Reich as the cause, and so an ability to recover orgastic potency was a necessary part of the recovery from neurosis. Reich subscribed to the 'repression' hypothesis, in which liberation comes about through the release of the blocked up energy (and although this notion appears in his psychoanalytic writing, there are very similar appeals to the body as a direct site of resistance in Foucault's critiques of psychoanalysis, Keat, 1986). The libido is contained by physical repression as opposed to the mere exclusion of threatening ideas from consciousness, and becomes part of the personality and bearing of the person as 'character armour'. Character armour consists of bodily habits – stance, posture, gestures and patterns of muscular tension – which inhibit the natural 'genital' character all people are born with, and are capable of regaining (Reich, 1942).

Reich's other divergences from Freud

Reich's work on character armour and character analysis is still referred to in mainstream psychoanalytic clinical writing, but his differences with Freud over libido were compounded by other innovations which took him away from psychoanalysis as it is usually understood. For Reich (1932a), civilization was not necessarily antagonistic to the desires of the individual, and he argued that there was a time before modern civilization in which our social and sexual discontents did not exist. Like Fromm, then, Reich looked to early matriarchal society as a kind of 'primitive communism' in which private property was unknown, and he looked to Marxism to unlock present-day capitalist society and so to when 'the original conditions of primitive communism return once more on a higher economic and cultural level as the sex-economic management of sexual relationships' (ibid.: 248). There is an emphasis in Reich's work, then, on *external* constraints. For Reich it is the repressive outside world which forces us to build defence mechanisms, and these then affect our ability to experience psychical and bodily needs. For Freud, the ego develops as a sense of self to mediate between the unconscious and the external world, and for later neo-Freudians the ego develops independently through 'normal' socialization from a naturally occurring 'conflict-free sphere of the ego' (Hartmann, 1939). For Reich, though, the ego itself is a product of sexual repression, and character armour is effectively part of the ego.

Reich also departs from the Freudian framework of a 'pair of opposites', in which libido was counterposed to the ego instincts (in Freud's first model) or to the death drive (in his second model). Reich argues that there is one fundamental drive, and it is on this basis that recent critiques of his approach locate him within a narcissistic tradition. Chasseguet-Smirgel and Grunberger (1976), for example, argue that Reich's theoretical framework is stuck at a narcissistic stage, and that this leads him to the delusion of an utopian 'Illusion' as the solution to all conflict. Reich certainly had a naturalist conception of what sexuality was as a single driving force. Sexuality was seen as unitary, as being of a single uncomplicated nature and seeking a direct release rather than as mediated by active or passive aims. His account rested on the assumption that there was a natural state to aspire to, and this was the 'genital character'. This meant that he saw 'perversions' as unnatural and incapable of leading to orgastic potency, and he argued that the expression and release of the libido had to be in a heterosexual relationship. He refused to have homosexuals as patients (Sharaf, 1983). Natural healthy sexuality was seen as being genitally focused (as the term 'genital character' suggests). Despite his political agitation for the free expression of childhood sexuality, he also viewed masturbation as an inherently unsatisfactory practice.

Reich on the family

Reich linked the individual and culture by focusing on the structure of the family. The family for Reich was 'the ideological nucleus of society', and he cited Malinowski's (1927) anthropological studies of the Trobriand Islanders as proof that sexual life started to be restricted when the chief had an interest in the inheritance of property through the male line. It is only then that paternity became an issue. Matriarchal society has no need of this notion, and so matriarchy was seen by Reich as a type of 'primitive communism'. This rosy account of matriarchal society has three functions in Reich's writings. First, it gives a lie to the myth that human beings are naturally competitive and selfish and so well suited to capitalism. Secondly, it exposes the way in which human values and sexuality have become subordinated to the circulation of things as commodities. Thirdly, the 'garrison' in the city that Freud (1930) describes in Civilization and its Discontents is exposed as defending specific sets of interests – those of men and the bourgeoisie.

Our emotional lives are structured by class society and by gender oppression. Reich saw jealousy as one product of a patriarchal society, and the institution of marriage as cementing people into monogamy; the fixation on one partner for life was seen as as inappropriate as always wearing the same set of clothes. Marriage thus functions as an institution which also becomes an increasingly miserable unsatisfactory refuge from sexual scarcity in the world outside. Sexual misery under capitalism is then compounded by the transmission of alienation and disappointment to children through a compulsive spiteful strictness about their behaviour, and so these children also grow up to resent others who appear more carefree and uninhibited. Those suffering from sexual misery project fantasies of revenge into and against those who seem freer, and the most inhibited heavily-armoured sufferers thus become attached to authoritarian movements where they can obtain vicarious pleasure from repressing somebody else. This dynamic eventually gives rise to fascism, something analysed in *The Mass Psychology of Fascism* (Reich, 1946). Reich tried to give a particular Marxist inflection to the analysis by linking a 'Freudian' analysis of authoritarian character structures with an account which saw fascism as emerging from the disappointed and threatened middle class caught between the bourgeoisie and the working class (Trotsky, 1933).

Reich and society

In 1928 Reich helped found the *Sozialistische Gesellschaft für Sexualberatung und Sexualforschung* (Socialist Society for Sex Consultation and Sexological Research), and then in 1929 he started establishing 'sex-hygiene' centres. His movement, known as Sex-Pol, soon had 20,000 members. He published popular works such as *Politicising the Sexual Struggle of Youth* (Reich, 1932b) which were, among other things, simple sex guides. He campaigned for nursery provision to allow women to work, distribution of free contraception, a loosening of marriage and divorce laws, legalizing of abortion, lifting of restrictions on homosexuality, provision of free sex education, provision of places where young people could meet to have sex, for freedom of expression for young children and no restriction on infantile masturbation, for opposition to corporal punishment by parents, and for open discussion of sexuality (ibid.).

He fought for these reforms to be included in the programme of the communist parties, but by the 1930s the Communist Third International was in the grip of Stalin (who was reintroducing Tsarist restrictions on abortion, divorce and homosexuality that had been repealed after the Bolshevik Revolution). Reich had discussions at one point with revolutionary Marxists, supporters of Trotsky in Germany working to found a Fourth International (Reich, 1934a). He was expelled from the Communist Party (in Denmark, where he was then based) and from the International Psychoanalytic Association in 1934. His books were burnt in Germany, Russia and then in the USA – where he was prosecuted by the Food and Drug Administration for distributing, without charge, plans for 'orgone energy accumulators' (Reich, 1951) – and he died in prison there in 1957.

Habermas: meaning

Habermas's association with psychoanalysis was briefer, and Freud's work was one way-station on Habermas's journey through most of the major theories in Western intellectual culture. His work owes much to earlier contacts with the work of Chomsky, Austin and Searle, from which he develops the notion of a 'universal pragmatics', and with the work of Piaget and Kohlberg, from which he develops an account of the necessity of moral reasoning (Habermas, 1985: 77). His writings on Freud in the 1960s have to be set in the context of his interest in these other theories, and they draw upon a particular reading of Freud developed by the German psychoanalyst Lorenzer (1970: 150) which already saw repression as 'exclusion from linguistic communication'. At both the level of the individual and culture, Habermas views the main enemy as the twisting of meaning (Habermas, 1970). While language is the source for ego functions and reality-testing, it is also the source of misunderstanding and conflict; 'split-off symbols and defended-against motives unfold their force over the heads of subjects, compelling substitute gratifications and symbolizations' (Habermas, 1971: 255).

Habermas is a key figure in the 'second generation' of the Frankfurt School. He describes himself as a 'genetic structuralist' – that is, as a Piagetian – and there is a two-fold emphasis throughout his work on the way a human being becomes social and so necessarily breaks from early ego-centricity, and on the way the human being becomes able to reason logically and engage in formal operational thought. Herbert Marcuse (1972) dedicated *One Dimensional Man* to him, but Habermas is not a Marxist. Rather, he characterizes himself as a 'radical liberal' (Habermas, 1985: 94), and as someone who takes the rational egalitarian strand of thought from Adorno and Horkheimer's writings. Society will only function, and debates over such things as 'oppression' and 'exploitation' and 'unfairness' only make sense, he argues, by virtue of people's allegiance to the reality principle. For this reason Habermas (1969) argued against what he saw as the extremism and authoritarianism of far-left student activists in the 1960s, and he also opposes 'fundamentalists' in the Green movement who, he says, are 'unconcerned with norms of civic equality' (Habermas, 1985: 100). Three aspects of Habermas's work are important; the notion of enlightenment within enlightenment, his use of hermeneutics in psychoanalytic readings of text, and his discussion of the effects of distorted communication.

Enlightenment

For Habermas, *Dialectic of Enlightenment* (Adorno and Horkheimer, 1944) is a nihilistic book. It does not offer a way out of the condition it analyses. Instead, Adorno and Horkheimer's analysis leads to despair because it seems as if the very notion of enlightenment itself is a problem, and any attempt to reflect rationally on the Enlightenment – even in an 'enlightened' way – ineluctably becomes part of the problem. Habermas (1985: 82) acknowledges that Adorno did himself also champion the position that, in Habermas's words, 'there is no cure for the wounds of the Enlightenment other than the radicalized Enlightenment itself' (ibid.).

However, Adorno and Horkheimer seem to block off the possibility of there being anything progressive in the Enlightenment in their description of the way 'people develop their identity by learning to control external nature at the price of repressing their inner nature' (Habermas, 1982: 15–16). The unconscious becomes experienced as if it were a thing, as an 'it' or 'id', and there is a corresponding split between nature and culture, such that nature only becomes acceptable when it is made into a part of culture (in safari theme parks or package holidays to exotic locations, for example). Habermas adds his own interpretation to Adorno and Horkheimer's grim account: 'The process of Enlightenment leads to the desocialization of nature and to the denaturalization of the human world; Piaget describes this as the decentering of the world view' (ibid.: 19). So, this cultural development is positive as well as negative, for it signals the development of the very critical thought which allows us to understand the destructive effects of the Enlightenment.

Psychoanalytic depth hermeneutics

Psychoanalysis is one of the foundation stones, for Habermas, for the building of a critical movement within Enlightenment both as an example of enlightenment thought – with the notion that people should adopt the maxim 'know thyself' – and as an example of how the work of enlightenment can be extended and transformed from within. Psychoanalysis as a clinical practice is reflexive for it provokes self-reflection at the individual level, and the knowledge that an analysand (the patient in analysis) gains does not 'cause' a cure to happen. Rather, it is self-knowledge and self-reflection that *is* the cure: 'the act of understanding to which it [psycho-analytic depth hermeneutics] leads is self-reflection' (Habermas, 1971: 228). Psychoanalysis also operates in the same kind of reflexive way as a social theory, but only if it is read as an essentially hermeneutic enterprise. The aim in both clinical and critical social theory is then to ensure that 'the transparency of recollected life history is preserved' (ibid.: 233).

There are three aspects of hermeneutics that are important for Habermas. The first is that the task is not explanation but *understanding*. It is not possible to break down an object of study when that object is a meaningful human product or practice. It is only possible to gain a provisional holistic appreciation, or illumination, of the object. The second aspect is that the object of study is always a *text*. Originally, hermeneutics was a religious exercise in which biblical texts would be interpreted to uncover the true word of God. Speeches and conversations can be treated as texts, and ethnographic interviewing adopts a broadly hermeneutic approach when thematic continuities are identified. The third aspect of hermeneutics that is important to Habermas is that the approach can be taken further to apply to texts that are supra-individual, in which something beyond an individual's intentions are uncovered. Once this third step is taken, one moves toward something like psychoanalysis. There are two crisscrossing routes to psychoanalytic depth hermeneutics.

First, there is a tendency in even individually focused hermeneutics to move beyond what the author of texts consciously 'meant' to what they implicitly signify. For example, in everyday folk psychology the declaration 'I love you' may be interpreted as an expression of desperate and inauthentic desire which has been provoked by rebound from another failed relationship if it is uttered too soon after the speaker has broken up with someone else. There is a move, then, to understanding the 'real' meanings as residing somewhere else which is inaccessible to the speaking subject. Secondly, however, this type of interpretation is not a simple discovery of deep, hidden individual intentions, for it is paralleled by the recognition that any understanding to be gained can only be in the context of other meanings in texts produced by other people. It is only possible to uncover meanings by a process of empathy, by moving into the 'hermeneutic circle' in order to understand the 'horizon of meaning' the subject inhabits rather than by looking for objective 'facts'. What responsibility do people have for their actions if the meanings reside in the 'social text'? Habermas does argue that psychoanalysis encourages the individual to take responsibility for unconsciously present meanings, which is a problem identified by some of Habermas's critics (e.g., Lichtman, 1990), but that psychoanalytic depth hermeneutics can also be used to engage in a critical appraisal of the texts which hold society together, and which distort it.

Distorted communication

It is by virtue of the fact that human beings can speak that liberal rationality is possible, and the identification of, and opposition to, deception in human communication in all societies testifies to the prime function of communication, which is to tell the truth. Habermas posits the potential existence of an 'ideal speech situation' which is 'the set of general and unavoidable communicative presuppositions which a subject capable of speech and action must make every time he or she wishes to participate seriously in argumentation' (Habermas, 1985: 86). Although this 'ideal speech situation' may never actually be reached, it is the *aspiration* to achieve it that marks human consciousness as social. The Enlightenment has encouraged the development of this critical rationality and concern with truth: 'The release of a potential for reason embedded in communicative action is a world-historical process ... the number of cases is increasing in which interaction must be coordinated through a consensus reached by the participants themselves' (ibid.: 101). An examination of historical texts can be aided by hermeneutics, and so 'hermeneutics can help out the faulty memory of mankind [sic] through the critical reconstruction of these texts' (Habermas, 1971: 215). A psychoanalytic depth hermeneutics attempts to understand both the meaning of the texts, and the *systematic* nature of the distortions and the purposes they serve or the interests they conceal: 'The mutilations have meaning as such' (ibid.: 217).

On an individual level, repression involves the transformation of public communication into the unconscious as a hidden private communication, and so when they are 'repressed', 'motives' become 'delinguisticized'. When these repressed motives do find expression, it is as part of a private language which makes no sense to anyone else. On a social level, the repressed motives of a culture will be found in texts that have been excluded from the public arena. It is the ability to understand which is distorted, and the distortions themselves which are important, and the 'delinguisticizing' effects of the censor's blue pencil, for example, are less important than the systematic application of censorship and what it is trying to shut out of public communication: Thus, 'The analyst instructs the patient in reading his [sic] own texts, which he himself has mutilated and distorted, and in translating symbols from a mode of expression deformed as a private language into the mode of expression of public communication' (ibid.: 228).

Habermas reinterprets Freud's (1930) *Civilization and its Discontents,* and in particular the argument that the distortions cannot be cured. For Habermas, it is not necessary to have an omnipotent analyst providing interpretations. For Habermas 'The same configurations that drive the individual to neurosis move society to establish institutions' (Habermas, 1971: 276). Collective defence against imaginary outside threats, for example, leads to the rigidification of institutions, and so it is necessary to make a conceptual distinction between the *forces of production* (the level of technical control over natural processes, and material achievements), which for Freud (1930) are 'the knowledge and capacity' human beings have developed, and the *relations of production* (the way in which human beings are organized into social roles and classes), which Freud refers to as 'all regulations necessary in order to adjust' people to one another. For Habermas, 'the institutional framework consists of compulsory norms, which not only sanction linguistically interpreted needs but also redirect, transform, and suppress them' (Habermas, 1971: 279). Institutions are, then, 'a power that has exchanged acute external force for the permanent internal compulsion of distorted and self-limiting communication' (ibid.: 282). This leads Habermas to argue that 'power and ideology are distorted communication' (ibid.).

The defence mechanisms which are embedded in institutions need to be reflected upon, so that their unnecessary, limiting aspects can be unravelled. It should be possible to use psychoanalytic descriptions of defence mechanisms to decode texts – government communiqués, public documents, outlines of policy, court judgments and so on – as the symbolic and distorted communication bases of institutions. In Anna Freud's (1936) list of defence mechanisms these would include repression, regression, reaction-formation, isolation, undoing, projection, introjection, turning against the self, reversal into the opposite and sublimation as well as other defence procedures such as denial, idealization and identification with the aggressor. Klein (1946) added splitting of the object, projective identifi-cation, denial of psychic reality, and omnipotent control over objects, and later ego psychologists divide defences into 'narcissistic' defences (delu-sional projection, psychotic denial and distortion), 'immature' defences (projection, schizoid fantasy, hypochondriasis, passive-aggressive behav-iour and acting out), 'neurotic' defences (intellectualization, repression, displacement, reaction formation and dissociation) and 'mature' defences (altruism, humour, suppression, anticipation and sublimation) (Vaillant, 1971).

Habermas has been criticized for drawing upon the 'therapeutic alliance' celebrated by US ego-psychologists as a model for symmetrical free dialogue (Lichtman, 1990), and for focusing on language at the expense of a properly psychoanalytic account of embodiment in social relations (Keat, 1981). Reich and Habermas both tried to challenge authori-tarianism in modern Enlightenment culture, but it does seem as if the forces they thought would work as solvents – the release of the drives or equality of communication – have themselves become part of the discur-sive apparatus of oppression in present-day society. Masculine sexuality, for example, which feels so essential and so repressed to so many men in this culture, performs an authoritarian function when men try to find liberation, and when they imagine that women's liberation is part of the problem. We can see how ideology is able to absorb and neutralize those forces that threaten to disrupt it and turn them too into dangerous ideo-logical resources if we look at recent reactions to feminism among some new and wild men.

Man, myth and hairy subjectivity

The social shapes and meanings of masculine authority are being trans-formed and reproduced, and the wild man is an eruption into the body politic of a new version of psychoanalytic subjectivity. Robert Bly's (1990) *Iron John* is one symptom and contribution to accounts of masculinity which carry authoritarian prescriptions for male experience (cf. Edley and Wetherell, 1995). The Bly text, then, operates as a kind of 'gender practice' (Wetherell and Edley, 1997). Reichian and Habermasian notions of the self run through the Bly text, and an understanding of Reich's and Habermas's work can now help us unravel the way it sets up certain subject positions for men and invites them to pour emotional investment into it.
New men
One of the consequences of the growth of the women's movement in the 1960s and 1970s in North America and Western Europe was the appear-ance in the 1980s of New Man. Unlike the rough, selfish and sexist

traditional men that enjoyed patriarchal power until the arrival of feminism, the new men were supposed to be gentle, caring and supportive of
feminist ideas. The image of the new man has been important in Western
advertising, where it has been linked to changing views of women and the
family (Burman, 1992). The image of the traditional man produced in the
discourse of the new man is also an expression of some powerful middle-
class fantasies. If new man drives a Volvo estate, shops at Waitrose and
holidays in Siena (Carter and Brule, 1992), where is old man in the class
order? It is not surprising, perhaps, that new man was soon seen either as
a media fabrication, as a reaction to feminism, or as an attempt to get
access to the bits of power women seemed now to enjoy, or all three
(Moore, 1988).

If new man was to be treated as joke, and most of the media hype was
also laced with sarcasm, it was not surprising that new man should mutate
rather quickly into a man who liked a joke too, into New Lad. This, at least,
was the case in the UK. It is one of the characteristics of traditional heterosexual male bonding that friendly abuse and banter should be used simultaneously to hold men together close enough to have fun and to keep them
apart sufficiently enough to allay anxieties about the expression of mutual
desire (Easthope, 1986). So, after a hiatus of serious politically correct new
men imagery, we have men who like to do things together and tease each
other while they do it: 'The Wind-Up features prominently in the pantheon of New Lad pastimes' (Kershaw, 1991). New lads like motorbikes,
football and junkfood, and you may recognize in this celebration of stereo-
typical male pursuits another fantasy about the working class coming to
the surface. Appearing again as well are all the endearing qualities of 'old'
men which made it possible for women to cope with them by infantiliz-
ing them and regaining an (albeit fleeting) active role. At least there is
some sense of contradiction in New Lad, even if that means he can flip
into his opposite: 'he can metamorphose, at the flick of his psychic switch,
into an Old Lad when he's in the company of his ideal audience – his
mates' (O'Hagen, 1991: 23). Now, with another flick of the switch, we are
faced with something more serious again in the form of *Wild Man*. Wild
Man promises, like all the most transparently superficial fads, to be
looking very deep into a nature that does not need to be changed at all, a
nature that has been lost and can be found.

Wild man

Robert Bly's (1990) *Iron John* briefly traces the aggression and callousness
that marked the experience of men in the 1950s, and the attempt by men
in the 1960s to refuse violence and to connect with caring and intuitive
qualities of women, and then the sense of loss and passivity that resulted
from this flight into the feminine: 'In the seventies I began to see all over
the country a phenomenon that we might call the "soft male"' (Bly, 1990:
2). The problem, as Bly sees it, and his book distils the wisdom he has been

distributing to men in workshops since the 1970s and before the popular-ization of new men and new lads, is how men may recover the power they lost as feminism triumphed: 'In these early sessions it was difficult for many of the younger men to distinguish between showing the sword and hurting someone' (ibid.: 4).

It seems as if the appeal of Bly has stretched from one patriarchal culture to another, and a common Western preoccupation with threats to mascu-linity and power has allowed him to leap across the Atlantic and down to Australia. There has been a more mixed reception in Scandinavia and Eastern Europe (Hurme, 1995; Jovanović, 1995). The UK shares much more than a common language with America, of course, and there has been a lot of enthusiasm for the book in some quarters here in the UK. In radical mental health networks, one key cross-over point between therapy and anti-sexist work, Bly has struck a chord, with the book being described as 'a joyous stimulating potentially healing experience' (Hinchcliffe, 1992: 33). The men's workshops that Bly, James Hillman and other analysts have been visiting over the last ten years have prepared the way for this text; for some participants, *Iron John* is the eagerly awaited souvenir book of the weekend course. The book has also been anticipated by the rush of other writings on goddesses and gods from within the men's movement (e.g. Rowan, 1987), a movement that has developed in parallel to the media images of new men and their successors, images that tend to appeal to suc-cessful and more affluent men. The £300 three-day residential workshop in Dorset with Bly in 1991 was sold out for months (Horder, 1991), and was repeated the following year, a bit cheaper, with James Hillman (Anthony, 1992).

Although *Iron John* was heavily hyped in the UK, its real success has been in the USA as an American best-seller. The 'mythopoet movement' and wild man retreats are most prevalent in Southern California (Fee, 1992), though it has been pointed out by US scholars that the context in which the story of 'Iron John' was originally written is rather different from North American culture (Zipes, 1992). Men's groups in the UK and publications such as *Achilles' Heel* have tended to have a different, more progressive agenda than the masculinist movements in the USA such as the Men's Action Network (Lichfield, 1991). In the alternative therapy networks in the North of England, even those into such things as neo-Reichian body-work and shamanism, there is some suspicion of Bly men, or 'mythos' as they are known. In the Left press the reception has been lukewarm or hostile; one review claimed that the book portrays women as persecutors, that it has fascist overtones, and, most damning perhaps, that it is effec-tively in alliance with the psychoanalytic establishment (Anon., 1992).

Iron John's construction of the past

Bly claims that 'Iron John' reflects deep mythical truths about the male condition. In fact, the story of 'Iron John' was not discovered like many of the other Grimm tales, but *constructed* almost from scratch by Wilhelm Grimm, who was working through his own feelings toward his father (Zipes, 1992). Nevertheless, we are told that the solution lies deep in past myth, in a story that Bly suggests may be twenty thousand years old, and deep in each man: 'When a contemporary man looks down into his psyche, he may, if conditions are right, find under the water of his soul, lying in an area no one has visited for a long time, an ancient hairy man' (Bly, 1990: 6).

The 'Iron John' story from Brothers Grimm concerns a large man with reddish hair like rusted iron who is taken by the King from a pond and imprisoned in a cage in the courtyard, the key of which is taken and hidden under the Queen's pillow. The King's eight-year-old son accidentally rolls a golden ball into the cage, and he must confront the wild hairy man in order to get it back. Each turn of the story reveals the significance of the pillow, the golden ball and the rusted iron man, and through these Bly arrives at five necessary stages in male initiation: First, bonding and separation from the mother; secondly, bonding and separation from the father; thirdly, the meeting with the male mentor 'who helps a man rebuild the bridge to his own greatness or essence' (Bly, 1990: 182); fourthly, apprenticeship to the Wild Man or Warrior; then fifthly and finally, 'the marriage with the Holy Woman or the Queen' (ibid.).

Appeals to the aristocracy and fantasies of identification with Kings and Queens often accomplish a blurring of, an amnesia about, the nature of class power, and Bly's book is no exception. It also seems to resolve the class contradictions between the new man and the new lad. Bly appeals beyond the particular needs of men or women of any particular class, to the deepest possible universal category of the psyche and what the psyche wants, and he concludes the book with these words: 'what the psyche is asking for now is a new figure, a religious figure but a hairy one, in touch with God and sexuality, with spirit and earth' (ibid.: 249). This yearning for unity speaks to and within a tradition of thought in which the duality of experience is felt both as a productive tension and as tragic fact of the human condition; it is the romantic tradition. It is worth reviewing the place of analytic notions in that tradition to understand where *Iron John* is coming from.

Dualism and romanticism

A series of contradictions structure the masculinist literature on men, and these contradictions resonate with dominant cultural and analytic polarities in twentieth-century Western thought. Those dominant forms of knowledge cathect, invest, pick up and recycle the polarities of subjective personal experience versus objective social system which condition the ways we have been taught to understand the relationship between what goes on inside ourselves and what goes on outside. We learn that we are special but fragile, and although we are able to develop idiosyncratic perspectives on things, we are part of a social world which is locked together as if it were a sort of machine in which there is little room for manoeuvre or change. Psychoanalysis is one expression of this modern dualist conception of the relationship between the self and the social world.

Freud worked with the sense of the self as torn and struggling with a hostile world, and he challenged the romantic essentialist picture of the person as a stable core of experience. The infant is polymorphously perverse for Freud, and the ego develops by virtue of its fraught relationships with others, as a social accomplishment which also succeeds in setting down inside the self the structures of familial environments which must limit and channel the desires of the child. Psychoanalytic conceptions of the interplay between society and desire deconstruct a simple opposition between internal phenomenological free-play and external structural(ist) constraint, though it should also be noted that in so far as Freud (1930) does characterize the conflict between the drives and social rules, he subscribes to and reinforces the dominant oppositions between a chaotic inside and a structured outside.

The new masculinist sensibility reverses such a polarity and sets in motion a tension of a different kind, and it brings into play a different emotional register. It returns to pre-modern romantic images of the self as something that is true and pure, and which must assert itself in a world that is confusing and uncertain. Now the opposition is (once again) between what is experienced as fixed and essential to the shape of the interior world and what is understood to be merely the set of relative truths which hold together what goes on in the exterior. So, in Bly's account it is the inside which has a fixed form and which must struggle against an outside which is fluid. There is thus a celebration of the essential unitary energy form inside the person which has been blocked by things happening in the world outside, such as the arrival of feminism and the lack of an older man as mentor and initiator into the world of men. However, this is a world understood, and which Bly is quick to paint, as being relativist and pluralist, and as marred mainly by mis-communication and misunderstanding.

Bly's account repeats romanticist images of a true self at the mercy of a mistaken world, images popular in German culture a century ago, and that indeed is part of the problem, part of the authoritarian appeal they hold. This ideological vision of the strong self struggling in a weak world, and the individual striving for understanding as mastery over a social reality that is essentially plural, calls for an authoritarian politics, a politics that would put Nietzsche at the centre. The will to power is a will that drives one way of seeing to triumph over a multiplicity of possible visions, within the perspectival kaleidoscope that is culture (Nietzsche, 1977). There is a celebration of certainties, certainties that promise to bring some order to an uncertain world.

Jungian themes

While Freudian psychoanalysis made a detour from the royal road to an understanding of the romanticist self, this road was returned to by some of those who broke from Freud and looked to myth, most significantly by those following Carl Jung (1983). This is also the road that Bly treads in his search for the 'inner King' (Bly, 1990: 110). The overt analytic source for Bly's account is Jung, with the other main analytic reference points in the text of *Iron John* being James Hillman and Alexander Mitscherlich, followed closely by Alice Miller and D. H. Lawrence.

The book is, in some senses, part of the Jungian tradition. The Jungian rhetorical strategy of naturalizing the myths of other cultures as part of a common history of the West, and as part of a still potent sedimented memory in the mind of the West, is employed to the full by Bly. The orientalism which suffuses Jung's anthropology is also revived in the Bly workshops in the material link between European fairytale narratives and African drumming. Out of these myths the elements of the true hidden self can be recovered and rebuilt. This strategy also carries with it, of course, the racist architecture of much Jungian work (Dalal, 1988), and there are points in *Iron John* where Bly is able simultaneously to disclaim responsibility for, and confirm the 'truth' of Eurocentric images of White and wrong:

> White for the Ndembu and Ashanti peoples calls up semen, saliva, water, milk, lakes, rivers, 'blessing by flowing water', the sea, and priesthood. . . . For Europeans white *retains* the connection to blessing and to milk, and it does suggest some qualities of good fellowship and strength. It also calls up the purity of children and brides, and by extension persons with high moral purposes, such as the white knight, who fights for purity, the Virgin, and good.
> (Bly, 1990: 200–201, my emphasis)

It is worth noting that the problems with Jung's racism have been recognized by those within the Jungian tradition (Samuels, 1993), and that the relationship with the father as archetype, and work with men in groups can be conducted within a very broadly Jungian framework without necessarily repeating the worst excesses of Jung and Bly. The problem of essentializing the difference between masculinity and femininity runs as an unbroken thread from Jung to present work, but can be expressed in reactionary or progressive ways (Cathie, 1987; Tatham, 1991). Such essentialism is also sometimes employed within feminism, and it is possible to make connections between feminism and Jung's (1989) discussion of the anima and animus (Wehr, 1988). There have been 'feminist' Jungian hairy self texts for women too, such as *Women Who Run With the Wolves* (Estés, 1995). The search for deep archetypal forms that lie buried in myth to support feminism and anti-sexist men has also preoccupied some men with a history of activity in the Left (Rowan, 1987), though this does not solve the problem of how these contents are relayed to the minds and culture of those living in the twentieth century in the West.

Bly explicitly acknowledges his debt to the classical Jungian Marie-Louise von Franz, and ends the book with a résumé of her diagnosis of the ills of contemporary culture, and this debt is evident at those parts of the book that read like a parade of tarot card characters. In so far as the Bly book develops a Jungian picture of the self emerging out of the inter-play of mythic themes and archetypal forms of the King and the Warrior, it invites a sense of the self as a Jungian self. However, to stick with this *single* sense of self is to gloss the tension between images of inside and outside, a tension that Bly himself wants to emphasize. Furthermore, when we locate Bly in the context of other writings on men in the latest wave of masculinist writing, the tension becomes even more important. A reading of *Iron John* is produced through the circulation of many other texts before and around it, and those other contexts give it the appeal and popularity it now enjoys. Although Jung is an explicit reference point for Bly, the text is actually organized around *psychoanalytic* themes. Further-more, despite the Jungian romantic vision of a single true self struggling against a heterogeneous social world, the text operates with more than one image of the self.

Reich and Habermas: energy and meaning in the double-self

It is important to emphasize that the split between inside and outside entails not one but *two* models of the individual, two theories of what it is to be a person, one which revolves around energy and another which circles around communication. There is a tension between two models of the person which have been elaborated in the theories of two writers using psychoanalytic ideas in quite different ways. Lying in the background as resources for a reader to make sense of *Iron John* and then activated as a double-effect as the reader puts the text to work, are the theories of Reich and Habermas.

Reich and Habermas reflect culturally bounded ideas of what the self is like, and the conceptions of the self they elaborated have become part of the public realm to produce theories that we now adopt and make our own. The popularization of Reich's ideas and the debates over Habermas's work in the 1960s' student movements is important here (Brinton, 1970; Dews, 1992), and these ideas helped structure the sub-cultural milieu that now forms the new 'men's movement'. Reich's ideas, for example, have been taken up by some Trotskyist groups in the UK (Knight, 1974), and there have been attempts to adapt his analysis of fascism to the 'mass psy-chology' of Thatcherism in the UK (Chaplin and Haggart, nd.). Forms of psychoanalytic theory operate in this way as reflections of, and models for the way we remake ourselves. At the same time, the forms of rationality they appeal to and insist upon continually recreate forms of irrationality as other, forms of irrationality that Jung and Bly continue to feed upon and regurgitate.

It is worth pointing out that neither Reich (1929) nor Habermas (1985) have much time for Jungian variants of analysis, which are seen by them as slipping into mysticism. Reich argues that Jung 'stands the whole of analytic theory on its head and turns it into a religion' (Reich, 1929: 55), and that he acted as 'the spokesman for fascism within psychoanalysis' (1934a footnote, ibid.) For Habermas, Jung's work is one example of the kind of 'metaphysical obscurantism' that the early Frankfurt School struggled against, and which is rife again in the writings of Lacan and Guattari (in Dews, 1992: 212). For both, the hostility to Jung flows from their faith in rationality. Reich, for example, despite the biologistic and spontaneist impulse in his writing, is against attempts to 'spellbind' people or to appeal to unconscious processes to win them over; the task of the revolutionary movement is to 'disclose processes to the masses' and 'to develop one's own initiative means quite unequivocally to gaze upon life steadily and to draw the consequences' (Reich, 1934a: 362–367). A different translation in a UK libertarian socialist pamphlet is more direct still: 'Developing one's own initiative means nothing other than looking at life in an undistorted manner and drawing the conclusions' (Reich, 1934b: 75). It is the spread of these ideas through the political unconscious that is precisely at issue here. Habermas, too, is against encouraging intuitive or irrational action, and for the possibility of rational argumentation which will make it possible to allow the situation 'to come to consciousness, in an undistorted manner, just as it is' (Habermas, 1971: 18).

Iron John

Let us turn to an analysis of *Iron John* itself, and the discursive complexes that govern it. The discursive complexes in this text are each held in place by a tension between a notion of biological or psychic drive (as an essential force which pushes from within and which needs to find release), and the notion of disturbances in communication (as the twisting of speech such that argument is riven by misunderstanding). We also find this tension expressed in the opposition between essentialism and pluralism. Both of these notions are found in traditional psychoanalysis of course, but they are each elaborated separately as key tenets of Reichian and Habermasian theory, and they now operate as popular ideas about the nature of the human condition in masculinist writing, so governing the meaning of this text. I will take one small passage, and use this to illustrate how discursive complexes of separation, distortion and castration structure *Iron John*:

> The naive man will also be proud that he can pick up the pain of others. He particularly picks up women's pain. When at five years old he sat at the kitchen table, his mother may have confided her suffering to him, and he felt flattered to be told of such things by a grown-up, even if it showed his father up poorly. He became attracted later to women who 'share their pain'. His specialness makes him, in his own eyes, something of a doctor. He is often more in touch

with women's pain than with his own, and he will offer to carry a woman's pain before he checks with his own heart to see if this labour is proper in the situation.

(Bly, 1990: 64)

SEPARATION The first separation from the first love object occurs at the very moment when that object and the ego are experienced as distinct. Separation as the break from the mother is also the break from a primary narcissistic state which continues to exert some pull as a fantasy of union and completeness in the individual's past. The separation anxiety that is evoked at the loss of a later object or even an internal representation of that object calls into play the operation of defence mechanisms. The attempt to control the absence of the object is played out with reference to substitutes, and the experience of something being 'here' or being 'gone' can thus be mapped upon the memory of being separated from the object (Freud, 1920). The notion that the ego is produced at the moment of separation, and that it results from the drawing together and fusing of component drives, contrasts with the idea that the sending out of libido is as if it is sent from the ego operating as a kind of reservoir, where the more that is sent out, the less there is left. Both Reich's and Habermas's work is closer to the first of these notions, and the ego is reified, treated as a thing, as one separates oneself from others and from one's self. The production of the ego can then be seen either, as Reich saw it, as entailing the suppression of physical energy by a mechanism – the ego – which is reinforced by identification with horribly powerful others, or, as Habermas saw it, as the sedimentation of an apparatus that is necessary for reality-testing but which becomes entangled in the loops and gaps that mark social reality as plural matter.

The noting of a specific age, 'five years old', for the child sitting at the kitchen table appeals to a normative developmental story of childhood, and Bly will set out appropriate stages of initiation later on in *Iron John* in which the boy must separate from the mother, and then bond with significant others. The task of separating here is seen as a process of differentiation that is necessary with respect to one other before an appropriate bond with another can be struck. The theme of differentiation before integration is one that plays itself out in Bly's book in his comments on what happens if the stages of initiation are absent. For the stages to run their course, it is necessary that the mother be present, and if there is no father present, the boy risks sticking with, being 'in touch with', the mother, 'her suffering', and not able to focus on himself, on 'his own'. The dangers of failing to differentiate, and the importance of the physical presence of the father in this process of separation and the production of a sense of self and one's own pain, is driven home by Bly time and again, as in, for example, the comment that 'Between twenty and thirty percent of American boys now live in a house with no father present, and the demons there have full permission to rage' (Bly, 1990: 96). Bly argues that it is necessary for the father 'to stand up for his boundaries' (ibid.: 171), and that men at gatherings he presides over often say 'My father never stood up to my mother, and I'm still angry about that' (ibid.). For this to be possible, of course, there must be a father present.

A consequence of the stages of separation and bonding is that the closeness to each of the parents has a different quality. The mother's space is of a special kind, and is marked in this example by the 'kitchen table'. Bly often appeals to domestic imagery to evoke the relation with the mother, and agricultural scenes to describe work alongside the father. For Bly, one of the problems is that the male is a 'set apart' being, and the closeness he feels toward the father is only possible if that father is also 'set apart'; 'I say this to speak to many young men who want from the father a repetition of the mother's affection, or a female nurturing they haven't gotten enough of. Whatever the father gives us, it will not be the same kind of closeness that our mother offered' (ibid.: 121).

The failure to separate encourages inappropriate contact with others, a mixing up of one's feelings with others', so that to be 'in touch' with another's pain is to blot out one's own. The 'naive man' is then drawn too close to, is 'attracted later to', women who will threaten the distinction between him and her. Bly says 'It is our intuition that can tell us when the merging is appropriate or inappropriate; then it is the warrior inside who can teach us how to hold boundaries' (ibid.: 173). There is an ideal of complementarity in this later relationship between the man who is guided by his warrior inside and the woman he meets in the outside. The process of differentiation and merging is also a differentiation of the genders one from the other and the eventual reunion of the two. In Bly's work this is symbolized in the figure of the King and the Queen.

The ideal of the union and the dangers of inappropriate union are reinforced, of course, by the fantasy that the self itself can be reunited with itself, that it can become one once more. This is a narcissistic fantasy that Bly both evades and fuels. Among the responses to Bly's work which are still located in the mythic tradition of men's awareness are those which have drawn attention to the isolation of Iron John from others, and the lack of relationships to women in the course of the story (Rowan, 1987). Running through Bly's work, then, are notions of separation and unity that are both sexual *and* semantic.

DISTORTION   As the contents of the unconscious attempt to enter consciousness they meet a censor, and so they appear in disguised form. The model for the process of distortion that produces the disguise is the dream-work – condensation, displacement, considerations of representability, and secondary revision – and the defence mechanisms come into play as helpmates to these motivated and functional distortions. The core of the dream, which can be better understood when the distortions that the dream-work and the defences that constitute it have been decoded, can be conceptualized in a number of ways: as the latent content which is often merely material from the preconscious and is usually accessible; or as the more deeply repressed material from the unconscious in which Oedipal fantasies are replayed; or as the self who lies hidden within the unconscious and in the dream trying to make itself heard; or as the system of distortion itself and how that produces a meaning which misleads. The idea that hidden contents rest in the bottom of the preconscious or unconscious, or deeper in a collective unconscious, and that they are the core of the self, is present in Freud but is more important to Jung's work. Although Freud does refer to contents of the unconscious, it is the *distortion* itself in the dream-work which is the meaning of the dream (Freud, 1900). The idea that there is something underneath that seeks release is a powerful one, however, and, in a throwback to cathartic theories, this may be conceptualized both as repressed content and repressed energy. A focus on the repressed and an emphasis on distortion are both present in the psychoanalytic tradition then. In one approach it is what has been distorted and the unchaining of what lies hidden that is the key to cure. This is Reich's way. In the other approach it is the distortions themselves that are most important and the reflection upon the conditions that produced those snags in self-understanding is the curative process. Habermas takes this line. Let us return to the quote about the young boy at the kitchen table.

The man who can 'pick up the pain of others' is 'proud', but this pride is, of course, a distortion of the true state of affairs. That is, he does not correctly understand either the circumstances in which he was encouraged to feel special when he was 'flattered' by his mother or current circumstances in which he has a conception of his own 'specialness' which masks his pain and the way in which the pain of others operates as an unnecessary burden. That the boy is 'flattered' when the mother 'confided her suffering to him' is marked here not only as something which constructs for the boy and later in the 'naive man' a false sense of self, for he is not, in reality, a 'doctor'. It is also a type of communication that positions him sitting at the kitchen table in a kind of double-bind. The family pattern that is evoked here is one in which the boy is drawn into an alliance with the mother and against the father, for his mother's confidence risks having 'showed his father up poorly'.

The boy is then unable to check 'his own heart', and he is unable to distinguish between appropriate and inappropriate sharing of pain, unable to know when 'this labour is proper in the situation'. There is a double threat here: the boy represses his own pain, for he is no longer 'in touch' with it; and there is a systematic distortion of the messages that flow across the family, so he replays those distortions in relationships with other women. Bly comments 'How often every adult man has felt himself, when baffled by a woman's peculiar interpretation of his behaviour – so different from his own – go into a sulk' (Bly, 1990: 61). This comment again presupposes both a gap in communication, the sense that an interpretation is 'peculiar', and it treats as natural repressed affect, so the emotional response is to get mired in a type of anger that takes the form of a 'sulk'. What it is to be 'naive' here also operates as a contradictory blend of notions to do with essentialized feelings which are corrupted and with knowledge that the man has failed to reach.

The 'pain' is unspecified in this passage save when the mother's pain is described as her 'suffering'. The pain may flow from the inside to the outside such that problems in familial patterns are a consequence of the pain, or the suffering may be translated from the outside to the inside such that individual problems are caused by that suffering. Habermas attempts to steer a middle way between these options, arguing that 'The same configurations that drive the individual to neurosis move society to establish institutions' (Habermas, 1971: 276). There is a sense of this in Bly where he seems to be rooting the problems and healthy patterns in types of story, myths operating as configurations that cause individual and social ills. Reich also tries to connect the individual and the social, but in such a way that he thinks that a catastrophe will occur if they are split apart: 'society's sexual oppression undermines itself by creating a permanently widening divergence between sexual tension and the outer opportunities of gratification as well as the inner capabilities for gratification' (Reich, 1932a: 247). Bly also diagnoses a decline that has reached a crisis point.

Because the crisis point is located somewhere between the individual and the social, it is necessary to tackle it at both levels. It is not possible to appeal either to one or the other as the solution. In this sense, the man can only check 'his own heart' if he does it with others. The pride of the 'naive man' prevents him from getting in touch with his own feelings and working with others. There is an impulse to change that derives from the impulses in man that are repressed, a theme from Reich, together with a notion of truth which rests on understanding in itself. The aim, as Habermas puts it, is to ensure that 'the transparency of recollected life history is preserved' (Habermas, 1971: 233). Also running through Bly's text, then, is the argument that the way to truth for the 'naive man' lies in the release of energy *and* direct communication, in the accomplishment of discharge *and* transparency.

CASTRATION   When the child puzzles over the reason for the anatomical difference between the sexes, and arrives at the conclusion that the girl's penis has been cut off, a castration anxiety is set in action. The fear of castration is intimately linked to the Oedipus complex, but linked in different ways for girls and boys, and the difference between the two is compounded by the different points of entry to and exit from the complex: for the girl, the lack leads to Oedipal rivalries and the problem of how to regain what has been lost; while for the boy, the rivalry for the mother's love is put to an end by castration anxiety, and necessary subordination to the father (Freud, 1924). The sets of relationships which structure the beginning or end of castration anxiety can also be interpreted as relationships of power, and the sense of gender which is produced by this anxiety then revolves around the loss of infantile omnipotence forever for the girl and access to it only vicariously later through association with men, or the loss of omnipotence temporarily for the boy and the fantasy of regaining it when he becomes a man. The loss of power, and the repression of the hope of obtaining it again, can either be seen as the physical repression of genitality with sexual energy erupting in distorted forms as the boy looks back and at the father with anger, or as the constitution of webs of deceit in the family as the parents play out their own powerlessness in their relationships with their children. An emphasis on one aspect, with release of libido as the solution, draws upon Reichian notions, and an emphasis on the other, with direct and equal sharing of the facts of the situation, echoes Habermas.

In the case of the boy sitting at the kitchen table, the confidence that he is drawn into is about 'women's pain', and her 'suffering'. However, this suffering is also at issue here as she takes the position of a 'grown-up', but, by implication, not as securely in that position as the father, who may be shown up poorly. To carry 'women's pain' is thus to carry the pain of the powerless, the pain that is not rightly his. To have 'showed his father up poorly' would also make the boy complicit in the castration of the father. For Bly, it is necessary to be able to relate to the father as a powerful other, as the police in the family: 'The police chief of Detroit remarked that the young men he arrests not only don't have any responsible older man in the house, they have never met one' (Bly, 1990: 32).

The strength of the father is complemented by the qualities of the mother, but her power at the kitchen table is only to confide. For Bly, the father is attributed with power not because authority figures like police chiefs are men, but because of the operation of archetypes. For Bly, even the power of women to give birth must be put in question, for there are certain qualities that only men can give to their boys: 'only men can initiate men. . . . Women can change the embryo to a boy, but only men can change the boy to a man . . . boys need a second birth, this time a birth from men' (ibid.: 16).

There is a general necessary problem Bly is concerned with, then, a necessary pathology in the family, which is that power is given to the mother, and the boy must negotiate this. Bly says, 'All families behave alike: on this planet, "The King gives the key into the keeping of the Queen" ' (ibid.: 11). The problems that attend the absence of the father are compounded by the excessive power that accrues to the mother. In Bly, castration anxiety is displaced onto the figure of the mother, and the themes of initiation through bonding and separation mean that it is necessary for the boy to negotiate the loss and return of power a number of times as they join and break from the mother, father, mentor, and wild man. The absence of the father from the home creates an arena in which the mother castrates the boy: 'the culture does not take very seriously the damage caused by psychic incest between mother and son' (ibid.: 185). The boy at the kitchen table is castrated by the mother when she confides in him, and draws him away from his own pain. It is necessary to challenge the mother's power, to take that key the King has given to her, but at the same time as the mother is stripped of her power, she is idealized and feared for holding a peculiar power of her own. She is strong as Queen, too strong.

Whether it is the regaining of full maleness, or the ability to run with the hairy man, there is a duality at work. On the one hand, power is conceived of as something that can be possessed, in the form of the phallus or the sword which the young man can hold aloft without fear. Reich sees things this way, though the moral he draws is different from that drawn by Bly. For Reich, collusion with patriarchy derives from deliberate threat by the beneficiaries of patriarchy, and is then relayed unconsciously by those who have some smaller investment in its continuation: the 'patriarchate' 'initiates a battle against childhood sexuality and harms sexual structure from the very beginning in the sense of orgastic impotence . . . the same motives which originally created the basis for the castration complex maintain this complex today' (Reich, 1932a: 170).

On the other hand, power is understood as rights to speak, to give and receive confidences without getting caught in patterns which cause pain to all. In the Bly scenario, the boy, his mother, and the father all end up the poorer. The inability of each to understand their place leads to resentment, and the absence of dialogue leads the 'naive man' to 'carry' pain without understanding what the consequences are. The attribution and mis-attribution of power is the problem here, and the experience of power is tied up with the failure to even approximate Habermas's 'ideal speech situation', an ideal to which Bly also at points seems to aspire. There is also, then, a preoccupation in Bly's work with power that conceptualizes it as both possession *and* relation.

Resistance and reaction

The figure of the wild man also carries with it some authoritarian prescriptions for male subjectivity. Bly, for example, bemoans the decline of the United States since the 1950s which opens up 'the depressed road, taken by some long-term alcoholics, single mothers below the poverty line, crack addicts, and fatherless men' (Bly, 1990: 35); and he then attacks protests against that decline which he diagnoses as part of the problem, 'the son's fear that the absent father is evil contributed to student takeovers in the sixties' (ibid.: 21).

At times it seems clear that Bly is allied to the Right, and his statements on the role of the father, and the dangers to the boy's development if he does not have a strong father and mentor, chime in, of course, with conservative familialist rhetoric in the West since the 1980s. It does, then, seem like a short step from Bly to the attempts in the USA to breathe life again into the notion of 'husbandry' supported by activists in the Men's Action Network, and which the Jungian therapist Robert Mannis glosses as 'a sense of pride for men . . . in purposeful care for their families and communities' (quoted in Lichfield, 1991). Mannis goes on to suggest that one figure men could usefully turn to as their role model would be Norman Schwarzkopf, 'tough, competent, funny, articulate, warm but caring about his troops' (ibid.). Despite Bly's protests that his book is supportive of feminism, the political logic of *Iron John* is to fuel the masculinist protest at feminism and what men feel to be the power of women over them (Faludi, 1992). This is graphically expressed in the complaint by one masculinist in America that feminists 'poured this country's testosterone out of the window in the Sixties' (quoted in Lichfield, 1991).

The book may also lock into men's and women's different experiences of gender, and these may be the very differences that structure the book. That is, the difference between a Reichian and a Habermasian way of understanding the world may also be the difference between a masculine and a feminine way of understanding it. Reich's work is directed to men and reproduces male senses of themselves as driven by biological forces they have little control over. What Hollway (1989) describes as the 'male sex drive discourse' structures Reich's work. Habermas, on the other hand, with his emphasis on communication and talking things through, reproduces idealized characterizations of women as concerned primarily with relationships, and a way of talking about relationships which Hollway (1989) terms the 'have/hold' discourse. Habermas has been attractive to feminists, perhaps, because of this emphasis on communication (Benhabib and Cornell, 1987). The different voices of women and men may be structured by different emphases on the quality of relationships or the satisfaction of the individual, and Gilligan (1982) for one, has been willing to risk essentializing this difference to bring a stereotypically feminine value to relationships to the fore.

It is worth emphasizing again the point that our experience of sexuality is contradictory, as men or women, and that these descriptions are about the ways in which social representations of masculinity and femininity are constructed now and allocated to males and females. This analysis lays out aspects of the discursive field that men have to negotiate to be men (Wetherell and Edley, 1997). The versions of psychoanalytic theory discussed here do not reveal the essential unchanging 'nature' of masculinity, though they do help demystify currently dominant representations of men. Different forms of masculinity also reproduce forms of psychoanalytic knowledge, and so the task of the analysis is to demonstrate how that knowledge is now structured for us to talk about and understand ourselves. Whether the modern Enlightenment culture that spawned these notions of the self is breaking down or not, and whether it is turning into something better or something worse is an issue we turn to in the next chapter.

6

Culture and Nature After Enlightenment

In the past we have always assumed that the external world around us has represented reality, however confusing and uncertain, and the inner world of our minds, its dreams, hopes, ambitions, represented the world of fantasy and the imagination. These roles, it seems to me, have been reversed. The most prudent and effective method of dealing with the world around us is to assume that it is a complete fiction – conversely, the one small node of reality left to us is inside our own heads.

J.G. Ballard (1995: 5) *Crash*

The Enlightenment held open the promise of a transformation in the way that individuals might understand themselves and their relationships with others. Science, progress and personal meaning became linked such that it could now be possible for us to reflect on what we need and to develop a theoretical reflection on the moral-political consequences of our actions. There was an attempt to fuse reflection and action in Critical Theory, and to produce something which would approximate to Western Marxism's project of simultaneously understanding and changing the world through revolutionary *praxis*. However, a paradox haunted the Critical Theorists; while they developed a powerful tradition of intellectual work and radical analyses of the malaise of Western culture, this tradition was rooted in academic institutions rather than in movements of the oppressed. Reflection and action were still separate, and so praxis – a combined theory-practice – was impossible.

This was particularly the case for the founders of the Frankfurt School, Adorno and Horkheimer, who then, while in exile, tended to conceal their most radical work in cryptic philosophical writing while carrying out rather traditional social psychological questionnaire studies on prejudice (Billig, 1979, 1982). There was a well-founded fear among refugees during the Second World War that radical activity might lead to imprisonment or deportation. The crushing of critical work in psychoanalysis which had been started by the Nazis (with the banning of Freud's books and the use instead of Jung's work in Germany (Cocks, 1985)), and assisted by the IPA (with the expulsion of Reich and suppression of the views of other left-wing analysts (Harris and Brock, 1991, 1992)) was finished off by the terrorizing of psychoanalytic radicals in academic and clinical organizations in the USA by the ego-psychologists and medics (Jacoby, 1983).

It is understandable, then, that when it seemed that socialism had been defeated after the war (or marginalized and sealed off as a bureaucratic caricature in the USSR), the most pessimistic aspect of the Critical Theory intellectuals' worldview flourished. Not only had capitalism triumphed when they had made a diagnosis of 'socialism or barbarism' for the West, but Enlightenment culture seemed so much more secure and able to smooth over any contradictions within it after the war that it appeared as if it might even have turned from being the seed-bed of individualism and authoritarianism into something worse. Perhaps the absence of any significant alternative political movement now meant that the time of revolutionary praxis was over. The Hegelian dialectical movement of society through the clash of thesis and antithesis, which Marxists saw as embodied in the historical struggle of social classes, had ground to a halt, and the most radical theory was so efficiently absorbed that it ended up confirming existing practices rather than changing them. It is this grim prospect of the impossibility of change that underpins the work of psychoanalytic writers on the culture of narcissism (Lasch, 1978) and postmodernity (Baudrillard, 1988) as they bemoan or welcome life after enlightenment, or even, for some new conservative Hegelians, as they celebrate the 'end of history' (Fukuyama, 1992).

The dangers of this turn within Critical Theory have been identified already by Habermas. As well as the obsessive self-control, mastery over nature and hardfacedness that the Enlightenment encourages, there are two dangerous nihilistic *reactions* to the Enlightenment that Habermas (1982) identifies in the work of its critics, and he traces these reactions back to Adorno and Horkheimer's (1944) *Dialectic of Enlightenment*. The first problem is that these Frankfurt School tradition writers are preoccupied with 'the eclipse of reason', in which, it is argued, the Enlightenment has burnt itself out to the point that there is no possibility now, or no necessity, for any rational appraisal of society or resistance to it. Habermas argues that this position leaves us powerless in the face of present-day society because we feel that there is no possible way of improving it, and no point of purchase left from which to challenge it. The second problem Habermas identifies as a reaction to the Enlightenment is the alternative, more nihilist, position in which the critic supports 'rebellion against everything that is normative' (Habermas, 1982: 25). This is a position that Habermas traces back to Nietzsche (1977), and to a view of 'truth' reduced to a battle of wills, to the play of power. Here, any attempt to understand and be in control of the unconscious puts us on the side of the 'reality principle', an activity which is then assumed to be necessarily oppressive. Habermas is quite rightly worried by this licence for irrationality which claims to be the most anti-fascist position, but which could end up leading to something like fascism.

This chapter addresses two separate traditions of work which take the Frankfurt School analysis of pre-war capitalist society and twist it to describe contemporary culture. The transformation of the Enlightenment into a 'culture of narcissism' is discussed by Christopher Lasch (1978), and, overall, he sees this new culture as negative. This account turns Marcuse and Reich into symptoms of the way culture was going when they tried to understand and challenge it. Complementing this account, in a most

bizarre way, is Jean Baudrillard's (1988) argument that modern Enlightenment culture has now mutated into a 'postmodern condition', something
which he argues is positive. This is the kind of account which supporters
of modernity such as Fromm and Habermas had already anticipated and
condemned as deeply ideological, irresponsible and cynical. Lasch's
account includes reactionary appeals to the Western nuclear family form
that Critical Theorists so scorned, and Baudrillard's account leads to the
wholesale abandonment of any political critique of the family or any other
social institution.

Nevertheless, these two different descriptions of the culture of narcissism
or postmodernity do usefully capture *something* of the shape of contemporary society, and it is possible to see reflections of these kinds of change
in Western self-experience in some recent responses to modern technology
in the 'new age' movement. We will also see here how Enlightenment
technological reason analysed by the Frankfurt School provokes rather
romantic fantasies about the nature of 'nature', and these fantasies now
underpin a growing and potent sub-cultural milieu in the West. An analysis of the circulation of new forms of psychoanalytic subjectivity among
people who are part of the new age also provides the opportunity for a comparison with another older social movement which has seemed so far to
have remained untouched by psychoanalysis, that of naturism. This is a
movement that once attracted people who wanted to flee from modern
civilization back to nature, but one which is now dwindling fast. Thus the
argument running through this book, that psychoanalysis suffuses culture
and sets up certain kinds of subject positions around different social
phenomena, needs to be read with the caveat in mind that there are still
spheres of modern culture which have evaded psychoanalysis. Naturism is
a movement of people who like to work and play unclothed, and there is a
rhetoric of naivety and simplicity which appears to precede preoccupations
in psychoanalytic discourse. That naturism should now seem anachronistic,
on the other hand, is evidence that psychoanalytic discourse is rapidly
becoming a culturally dominant way of framing the way we understand
the self and its nature. Naturism was a place, then, where nature is very
different from the way it has become in the new age. While the new age is
dissatisfied with modernity and looks forward to some postmodern
notions, naturism knows that it will be satisfied only if it looks back. For all
the rhetoric of returning to nature in the new age, it seeks something new
and emerges now when modernity appears to many to be at an end. Naturism, meanwhile, has never wanted what modernity offered, and for all its
rhetoric of self-improvement it wants to go back to original nature.

Cultures of narcissism

After the Second World War the hopes of the Enlightenment seemed to
have collapsed into a kind of culture in which all contradiction was erased,

and no critical distance or potential for change remained. Adorno and Horkheimer (1944) indict manufactured mass culture as the ideological site for the smoothing over of conflict and the paralysis of any critical dialectic movement of history, and it sometimes seems in their writing as if Benjamin's (1939) angel of history has finally been defeated by capitalism, in an insidious but complete barbarism. The symptoms of this loss of critical distance at an individual and social level had already been identified and interpreted before the war by Frankfurt School writers, as a desire to wish away conflict and to pretend that conflict in the world did not exist.

The family and fascism

There was always a tension in Frankfurt School writing between two different psychoanalytic accounts of the power and decline of the Western nuclear family, and the way this ideological apparatus operated as part of the machinery in capitalist culture for producing obedient and then fascist personalities (Poster, 1978). In one account – adopted in one way or another by Reich and Fromm – a representation of the authoritarian father as a grotesque and incomprehensible bully was internalized by the child as the super-ego or embedded deeper still in the ego. Here, the male infant was first crushed and then placated by the illusion of triumphing by becoming someone like this father at the close of the Oedipus complex. Unconscious anger and resentment at the humiliation he suffered during this time was then regarded as directed by the young adult out onto others, onto anyone but the father. But this was in such a way that he could take the position of the father as he grew up into an authoritarian personality modelled on the very figure who had caused him so much pain. This kind of analysis presupposes the strength of the family.

An alternative account, however, is that because the family was breaking down in Europe in the early years of the twentieth century and fathers were absent or weak, the child was unable to find a secure point of identification and so he remained preoccupied with the imaginary state of narcissistic bliss which preceded the necessarily brutal awakening and entry into culture that the Oedipus complex forced. Because there was no strong father to break the infant out of the illusion that it was always possible to retreat to a narcissistic fusion with first-loved others, psychically represented in the ego-ideal, the young adult now became prey to dictators. These strong men then function as the ego-ideal and invite the weak to fuse with them and thereby find some power for themselves. Like the first account, and like much psychoanalytic writing, this focuses on the manufacture of *men*. The second account is also, of course, the one eagerly canvassed by those who wish they were wild men (Bly, 1990). This second kind of analysis presupposes the decline of the family (Benjamin, 1977).

This second account is adopted by Adorno (1951) in his description of the way fascist propaganda works. He uses Freud's (1921) work on mass psychology, and on the way the leader of the crowd stands in the place of the ego-ideal, and he argues that this process underpins the appeal of fascism. Adorno notes that fascist propaganda is directed to individuals, and seems personalized so that it is able to appeal to each particular self-interest. The fascist leader presents himself as a similar, flawed, being to each individual in the audience who feels he is the special recipient of the leader's love. This is important, for the leader must be just a little less than super-human for the follower to be able to identify with him. The follower then has the opportunity not only to submit to authority, but to be authority themselves, and so the beloved leader becomes almost part of their self. The language of fascist propaganda then works not so much by way of its rational meaning as through its evocation of early experiences of being comforted in a kind of lullaby repetition of soothing, fusing love.

The words in fascist propaganda, Adorno says, 'function in a magical way', and they trigger regression to a narcissistic state. This works because the listener has not learnt the hard lesson provided by the experience of submitting and surviving the Oedipal relationship in the family, and has not come to know deep down that it is impossible to overcome the separation between self and others. The person is transfixed by idealized images because they have never had to deal with the existence of a strong father in the family. They have not resolved the conflicts the Oedipal relationship provokes, and so they have not developed a super-ego which will help them to evaluate morally what they can and cannot do and to strike a critical distance from those who flatter them. Fascism before the war and consumer culture after the war both dissolve critical distance between the self and others and between the self and society, and narcissistic individuals are thus sucked into things they have no power to assess or from which they can escape.

The mirror of consumer culture

Mass culture stimulates and structures narcissistic kinds of experience, and it dissolves the struggle for personal or social enlightenment into a collective illusion that things can get better if you simply *wish* hard enough. Modes of experience which promise the end of all conflict through the assumption of a narcissistic fantasy are advertised and they act as models. The experience of viewing these models also works by a process of narcissistic mirroring such that the spectator is lured into a world where contradiction is absent or can easily be smoothed over.

Take the example of Disney's *Snow White and the Seven Dwarfs* from 1937, where the wicked Queen says 'Mirror, mirror on the wall, who is the fairest of them all' and sets up an idealized image of 'the fairest' – the ego-ideal. This case example, which illustrates and reproduces narcissism, requires the existence of mirrors as widely available artefacts and the mass duplication of images as commodities (Benjamin, 1936; Stockholder, 1987). The Queen wants the mirror to reply that it is she. There is an attempt, then, as a first aspect of narcissism, to close the gap between the ego and the ego-ideal, between the I and that which is idealized as perfect. She appeals to a mirror for the very good reason that the image the mirror presents is not only an idealized image, but is also still the Queen herself. Not only is the Queen wishing that she was the fairest of them all, but she hopes that the idealized image could be a perfect reflection of her self. The second aspect of narcissism, then, is the attempt to lose the self in images which flatter the viewer into believing that they are nothing but an extension of the self. When the mirror eventually replies that Snow White is the fairest, the wicked Queen recoils in horror for an *other* now separates her from the image, and this horror of separation evokes separation anxiety, which replays the anxiety felt by an infant broken away from the mother or from a representation of the first love object. The third aspect of narcissism, then, is an attempt to avoid the horror of separation, and to refuse to accept that separation is a fact of adult existence, and to continually strive to regain the fusion between the self and the other.

It would, perhaps, be possible to resolve the tension between the two competing accounts of the family by saying that while the first dangerous strong family form was in the ascendant during the heyday of the Enlightenment, the second equally dangerous weak family form became more prevalent as the Enlightenment suffocated and was replaced by a culture of narcissism. The problem with the logic of this argument is that it leaves us with a rather conservative nostalgia for what the ideal secure family *could* have been and a longing for the return of a time when Oedipus could do its job of saving us from Narcissus. This is the logic followed by Janine Chasseguet-Smirgel and Christopher Lasch.

Narcissism and ideology

One important theoretical source for psychoanalytic extensions of Freud's (1914a) account of narcissism to contemporary culture is Chasseguet-Smirgel's (1985a) description of the power of the ego-ideal. Other strands of cultural analysis which draw on Otto Kernberg's (1975) clinical work on borderline and narcissistic patients in the USA try to evade some of the more objectionable implications of this line of argument (e.g., Alt and Hearn, 1980). Chasseguet-Smirgel is so useful here because she shamelessly spells out those implications (and her work has been admired by Kernberg (1985) in the foreword to one of her books). She makes connections between the grip of ideology and group fantasy, and then links these in a poisonous psychoanalytic cocktail with accounts of creativity, homosexuality and perversion (Chasseguet-Smirgel, 1985b).

A central conceptual category in Chasseguet-Smirgel's work is that of 'Illusion', and she describes the narcissist's attempt to lose themselves in infantile Illusion in order to explain the irrational adherence of the individual to certain kinds of group, or their attempts to lose themselves in large crowds. She argues that the leading force is not the father in such cases, but that the leader is the person who brings back into play the wish for the union of the self and the ideal. The leader is, psychically speaking then, more of a *mother* figure. Groups can be based upon Illusion, and so they become arenas for the stimulation of narcissism as a form of perversion:

> in groups based upon 'the Illusion', the leader fulfils in relation to the members of the group, the role that the mother of the future pervert plays in relation to her child when she gives him to believe that he has no need either to grow up, or to identify himself with his father, this causing his incomplete maturation to coincide with his ego-ideal.
>
> (Chasseguet-Smirgel, 1985a: 91–92)

We should note that this also leads Chasseguet-Smirgel to argue that mother–son incest is more damaging to the child than father–daughter incest.

Ideology is a form of Illusion too for Chasseguet-Smirgel, for all ideology boils down to the attempt to abolish social constraints, to wish them away. This means that attempts to set up alternative forms of social arrangements as 'ideals' are also necessarily mired in ideology, and so are pathological. Ideologies are 'those systems of thought which ... promise the fulfilment of the Illusion' (ibid.: 91). Chasseguet-Smirgel explains the lure of socialist propaganda, for example, as keying into the desire to abolish all social distinctions, to level everything and to pretend that the world need not be the nasty way it is at the moment. Those who are suffering from Illusion have never faced up to reality: 'Behind the ideology there is always a phantasy of narcissistic assumption' (ibid.: 82). A crucial part of the resolution of the Oedipus complex is the recognition of castration, and this means that the infant has to recognize that she or he is not omnipotent. There are others more powerful, and the child has to accept the rules of society. A narcissistic person, however, still believes that society can be moulded to their own plans, and Chasseguet-Smirgel argues that egalitarian ideologies are defences against castration anxiety. This means that anyone, like Reich or Marcuse for example, who tries to challenge present-day society is accused of falling into narcissistic Illusion (Chasseguet-Smirgel and Grunberger, 1976).

Chasseguet-Smirgel is keen to root social problems in pathological individuals, and she deliberately pursues a reductionist account of the malaise in culture after Enlightenment. The narcissist, then, is also a kind of pervert, and is someone who cannot accept generational differences. The incest taboo has not been embedded in their conception of themself and their relation to others because they have not had to deal with the existence of a powerful other – the father – who stands between their desire and their first love object. The pervert is also someone who cannot accept gender difference, and they look for others like themselves to love instead of transferring desire to a different object. This is why, we are told, homosexuals are more likely to be perverts (Chasseguet-Smirgel, 1985b).

Narcissism as cultural malaise

The notion that the whole of culture has become narcissistic was taken a step further by Christopher Lasch (1978). Lasch indicts modern consumer culture for breaking down any secure site for the formation of identity and provoking individuals to seize upon commodities as idealized introjects to form the self. The narcissist constructs the self around objects for sale in the market-place that are empty and insufficient but seem full and perfect, and the self which is displayed to others may then appear to be happy and successful. The fear and rage that this surface self conceals, however, circulates in an interior which feels hollow and inadequate. The narcissist is desperate for 'relationships' but frightened of any connection with others of real depth (Kernberg, 1975). Lasch also contributed the foreword to the English translation of Chasseguet-Smirgel's (1985a) book on the ego-ideal, and despite claiming some sympathy for progressive causes, Lasch argued that the Left is very susceptible to this kind of pathology (Lasch, 1981). Despite attempts to defend Lasch by those on the Left in psychoanalytic theory (e.g., Richards, 1985), it is difficult not to read his work as little more than a complaint against the decline of the family and for the return of secure patriarchal structures. This is of a piece with attempts by US ego psychologists and English Anna Freudians and US ego psychologists to pathologize student unrest as an expression of narcissistic disturbances (e.g., Wangh, 1972; Badcock, 1983).

As Barrett and McIntosh (1982) point out, Lasch is also setting himself against alternative forms of sexuality, and in his book he includes vituperative attacks on lesbian feminists for hating men as one of the symptoms of the culture of narcissism. Barrett and McIntosh argue that Lasch's argument throws out what was most radical about psychoanalysis, the assertion that human sexuality is not conditioned by biology but that we have to give an account of the development of sexual desire which connects it with culture. Other psychoanalytic critics of Lasch have also argued that it is possible to see narcissism as being a necessary, and healthy, aspect of experience. For Freud, all individuals go through a narcissistic period in infancy, and this leaves traces in 'normal' relationships later on. Kovel (1988) argues, for example, that narcissistic aspects of relationships lead to more cooperative experiences, and that they are then the positive basis for moral belief systems which challenge competitive individualism. Although such critics argue that there are positive aspects of narcissism, however, they are still not necessarily overjoyed by trends in contemporary culture. Here they contrast markedly with the analysis offered by the celebrants of postmodernity.

Postmodernity and cultural fragmentation

Lyotard (1979) claims in *The Postmodern Condition*, a report written for the Canadian government on the impact of new technology, that the overarching 'metanarratives' of modern Enlightenment culture have given way to the 'little stories' which constitute postmodernity. Instead of socialist and psychoanalytic attempts to understand individual and social oppression and to look to ways of gearing science to personal improvement and historical progress, we are subjected instead to a bewildering multiplicity of accounts which we travel around and play in without ever knowing which is best or finding a resting place. In place of truth, we have perpetual reflection on the impossibility of truth, and just as accounts of the social have lost their way in the postmodern condition, so has a sense of individual identity. The personal meanings of each citizen of the modern state have given way to fragmented experiences which cannot be interpreted to reveal the truth of the human condition. Humanism was the secularized translation of religious belief in the Enlightenment, but this now dissolves into hedonism or a feeling of resignation. We are offered 'intensity' of experience instead of the possibility of understanding what an experience might *mean*.

Some writers argue that there is a distinct break between modernity and postmodernity, and we could see this as mapping the break between the age of Enlightenment and the culture of Narcissism. Lyotard (1979) sometimes gives this impression, though he also tries to counter this with the argument that what we take to be the 'postmodern' as a heightened reflection on who and where we are is a *precondition* for the birth of modernity itself. Some writers helpfully emphasize the continuity with modernity, and trace the roots of the current state of culture to the beginning of nineteenth-century capitalism (Berman, 1982; Frosh, 1991). Some writers revel in the impossibility of telling one way or another what would be for the best, and they turn intellectual work itself into a game. Jean Baudrillard is the worst.

In Baudrillard's mirror

Baudrillard has been peddling notions of culture as wholly determined by the play of signs almost to breaking point for years, and arguing that it is now impossible to tell what is truth from what is fiction in a culture that is supersaturated with different kinds of media which pretend to provide 'information'. Baudrillard spent some time in the 1960s working with the ideas of the Situationists (Debord, 1967), and their notion that society had become a 'spectacle' which tamed and incorporated all forms of resistance to it, and 'recuperated' it as part of the play of signs that comprise capitalist culture. He also continues the tradition of McLuhan's media work (McLuhan and Fiore, 1967), which focused on the way that culture is fashioned by forms of mass communication. His work tends to be ignored by other French 'post-structuralist' or 'postmodern' writers, and it is actually much closer to the Frankfurt School tradition and that style of thought in North America than to trends in French philosophy (Levin, 1984; Kellner, 1989). The connection with Critical Theory is most explicit when he is developing accounts of objectification, of the turning of people into things.

Baudrillard's early work on objectification focused on the ways in which the consumption of commodities always also led the consumer to participate in the signifying system that constitutes that commodity. When we buy something, we become a certain kind of consumer, defined as a market fragment and symbolically tied to the object. We lose our 'own' identity, whatever that was, and we are drawn into the kinds of identities that ideal consumers are expected to display. In his sociology of consumer culture he argued that the purchase of a kitchen item, for example, is primarily the purchase of a part of a semiotic system and its meaning in that system. The semantic codes that determine the function of the object also come to define the person who stands in their kitchen using it. These consumer codes and networks of signs fabricate thousands of glittering surfaces in which we see ourselves and from which there is no escape to anything real behind them. This led Baudrillard to a concern with the symbolic sphere as consisting of layers of mirrors where what we take to be 'reality' is always already *simulated*. Culture thus becomes 'simulacral' to such an extent that the original object recedes into the distance to be totally eclipsed, so that a simulacrum is a copy for which no original exists. This culture locks us into place, and so, for Baudrillard, 'the liberal democratic consensus and the search for human rights and equality, are more dangerous to the symbolic order, more terrorist in practice, than the totalitarian regimes of the 1930s and 1940s' (Gane, 1995: 118).

Baudrillard developed an account of objectification in the powerful sign systems which comprise contemporary culture in order to go beyond Marxism, which seemed to him to appeal mistakenly to some 'real' human needs underneath those 'false' needs that are produced in an economic system (Kroker, 1985). His focus on the production of objects through processes of connotation (which function much the same way as Barthes' (1957) description of 'myth'), led him to a critique of appeals in Marxist analysis to the use value of an object; for what is 'use' but a part of the 'exchange value' of the object (Baudrillard, 1973)? The notion of 'use-value' presupposes a subject who is able to use and value an object, but now the subject has been completely dissolved in Baudrillard's account, and all that is left is the production of value through exchange independent of any subject. This also has consequences for psychoanalysis, which also too often thinks that it knows what people *really* need underneath what they are consciously aware of. Marxism and psychoanalysis, then, are for Baudrillard two systems of thought that exist as twins, and which are summarily dismissed: 'Parallel to the concepts of Necessity, Scarcity, and Need in the (vulgar or dialectical) materialist codes, the psychoanalytic concepts of Law, Prohibition, and Repression are also rooted in the objectification of Nature' (Baudrillard, 1973: 60).

Although Marxism is thoroughly dispensed with, however, Baudrillard still draws upon certain psychoanalytic themes to comprehend the place of the subject in the regime of signifiers that comprise contemporary postmodern 'hyperreality'. Psychoanalysis has to be modified, though, to focus upon the play of signs rather than pretending to discover hidden biological or psychic needs. For Baudrillard, then, it is the play of signs that constitutes the seductive effect, not another sexual force underneath the surface. Discussing the appeal of transvestism, for example, he argues that it is the play of signs, *'this transubstantiation of a sex into signs which is the secret of all seduction'* (Baudrillard, 1979: 135). Baudrillard (1983a) is also concerned with how things outside culture resist our attempts to understand and tame them, with what he calls the 'revenge of the crystal'. Here, objects take on a life of their own, and threaten to disrupt the organization of signifiers that once contained them. The experience of death, and the fear of death is what *produces* the unconscious as an attempt to refuse the reciprocity of life and death and to expend energy without getting paid back. The unconscious, then, is what resists exchange and the regimes of signifiers that make us weigh up the costs and benefits of our actions. This does not at all mean that this unconscious or any other resistance should be seen as the site of progressive change; however 'terrorist' consumer society is, the 'central characterization he presents is an active acceptance of the world, the acceptance of the world of catastrophe, catastrophe as naturally marvellous' (Gane, 1995: 121).

Reminders of death are all around in the activities of objects against conscious and rational control, particularly inanimate objects. Death, in this revival of pataphysics, is the revenge of the object, the revenge of 'the crystal'. For Baudrillard, *death*, the 'revenge of the crystal', also lies in the activities of those technologies of the mind that produce selves that might cope in the postmodern condition, and it lies hidden in the technologies that seem to promise self-understanding and a fuller life. For Baudrillard, such technologies are bound up with death, and psychoanalysis is itself seen as 'a production machine, not at all a desiring machine – a machine which is entirely terrorising and terrorist' (Baudrillard, 1983a: 26). He is a theorist who is thoroughly attuned to the worst developments in consumer culture, and he draws our attention to these changes partly through his own delighted exaggeration of them. He is someone who is able to digest and regurgitate bits of culture, mirroring the very phenomena of media and simulation he describes. He seems so useful in describing postmodern post-Enlightenment cultural phenomena because his theoretical descriptions of seduction, fetishism and narcissism correspond so closely to the way those notions *structure* the phenomena. Here, though, I treat him as a symptom of the phenomena, and we will find the things that Baudrillard says in the texts of the new age.

The new age movement is one of the contradictory responses to the postmodern mutation in culture, and it carries traces of that mutation at the same time as it challenges some of the more cynical aspects of it. New age practices celebrate the turn away from some of the excesses of modernity – individualism and industrialization – at the same time as they retrieve some human values from the postmodern world, values of community and understanding. Naturism, on the other hand, is a more stubborn response to modernity, and its attempt to escape looks back to the past. Naturism, which is no less contradictory than the new age movement, refuses the excesses of modernity and looks back to human values that have been lost. We could say that while naturism is on the cusp of the modern, looking into modernity and disliking what it sees, the new age movement is on the cusp of the postmodern, looking in and finding something positive as an alternative to what it disliked about modernity.

Narcissism and nature in the new age

We have not yet entered a postmodern condition of culture, even if there are narcissistic or postmodern sectors of society, and the possibility of social and personal enlightenment and progress is not over. However, something has changed in the last fifty years to our images of nature, and to the discourses that circulate, constitute and confirm what we imagine to lie 'outside' culture. This discourse looks very different, however, in the new age and naturist images of nature as they attract or repel psychoanalytic discourse.

New ages

The new age movement is a reflection of changes in images of nature, and it includes the holistic spiritual and natural health therapies which range from acupuncture to astrology, and from aromatherapy to astral projection. Postmodernity throws identity into crisis, and the new age movement is one response to that crisis which finds different ways of coping with the seductiveness of contemporary consumer culture, the fetishizing of bits of the body, and with narcissistic forms of self-identity. The new age movement can be seen as an attempt to fix meaning in a culture where meaning always seems to be slipping away.

New age networks attempt to get back to the real through close identification with cultures that seem closer to nature, but they do this by fixing upon a simulacrum for which no original seems to exist. One example is the vogue for American Indian culture in the new age world. There is a group in Poland, for example, which wears feathered headdresses and moccasins and lives in tepees. In this way the members are able to live in a simulacrum of the culture they romanticize, and they see the 'real' American Indian culture as less genuine than their own version which is replicating it. One of the members says of the fake 'real' Indians in America, 'They're plastic Indians – they speak English, they wear jeans and they don't know their own history. The truth is that the real Indians live in Bialystok' (Wiernikowska, 1992: 12). There is a fixing of the self upon a 'real' nature which is storied into existence, and an attempt to find identity in postmodern culture where everything feels as if it is fictional. The Bialystok Indians live out the postmodern condition and then try to resist it, finding fixed points of reference which can determine who they 'really' are, but at the same time ironizing that new identity.

Naturism

Naturists, on the other hand, think they know what is real and how to get back to real nature, and they do this by celebrating the naked body: it is simply, for some enthusiasts, 'about being comfortable without clothes' (Piper and British Naturism, 1992). Naturism developed at the turn of the century in Germany in a system of secret societies devoted to Aryan ideals, and these societies were then taken over by the Nazi movement before being banned in 1933 (Connolly, 1992). Clubs in the UK, such as 'Spielplatz' which was founded in 1937, sprang from this early naturist movement, and it linked up with the magazine *Health and Efficiency*, which 'was established in 1900 and has incorporated *Sunbathing Review* and *Vim*' (Editorial in each issue). Naturists like to walk around in places like Spielplatz, which they describe as 'virgin woodland' (Piper and British Naturism, 1992), but they try not to exoticize nature. Many naturists spend their holidays in caravans or chalets, and their literature reassures those going abroad that things are likely to be simple and familiar, even mundane. As one leaflet produced by the Central Council for British Naturism (CCBN) puts it, 'You will not be going to darkest Africa. Whatever you buy in your local shops will most likely be available where you go to, even if the brand names are different' (CCBN, Individual Holidays Abroad). It is difficult to imagine Baudrillard arguing that things might be the same for a customer underneath different brand names.

The ideals of the naturist movement in Germany were also tied to images of the periphery of Europe at the Mediterranean rim as a kind of place of original truth, and we are told that 'Naturists are people who prefer to swim and sunbathe and play without clothes – having respect for the human body which has its origins in Classical Greece, the source of our civilization' (Target, 1993: 10). Naturism was originally about being unclothed outside, but in contemporary naturism it is also something that can be practised *indoors* in private, as part of an attempt to escape the stress of public urban life (Knott, 1993). It has been adapted to meet changes in society, then, but it still does not absorb the popular psychotherapeutic notions that frame many other self-improvement movements in the West (Giddens, 1992). Recent publicity for naturism does talk about the unhealthy ways in which people are brought up to think that it is unusual to look 'at our own skin', and it speculates that this might say something about 'our attitude to ourselves' (Piper and British Naturism, 1992). This is the extent of their reflection on what it might mean to go naked. You just take off your clothes and stop worrying.

There is something curious about the way naturism seems to escape psychological and psychoanalytic discourses of mind and behaviour that penetrate so much of Western culture. There is, instead, an appeal to the spontaneity of being naked, almost as if an entanglement with thinking or interpreting would ruin it. For naturists there are threats, but these appear in the reactions of those in the clothed world that they see as perverts or puritans; as the caption for one picture in *Health and Efficiency* puts it, 'If you find this disgusting then you have a problem accepting humanity' (Target, 1993: 12).

Both naturism *and* the new age want to accept humanity and see humanity as tied to nature, and together they present useful polar opposites in an analysis of the way psychoanalytic discourse circulates and is adopted or rejected by different sub-cultures. Psychoanalytic categories of seduction, fetishism and narcissism structure the discourse of the new age movement, and the mutated Freudian forms that we find in Baudrillard's texts are useful to tap into this sub-culture as the cultural order lurches through what does sometimes feel like a postmodern schizophrenic nightmare. These categories are absent from naturism, however, and we can see, then, that images of nature do not *require* them. The categories are socially constructed, and they then help participants to reconstruct what they touch.

Seduction

Freud made an important conceptual double move into the realms of the unconscious and infantile sexuality, and this inaugurated psychoanalysis. At this moment he abandoned the view that real seduction always lies at the heart of pathogenic memories of childhood. Freud's (1896) assertion that children were actually 'seduced', as the passive recipients of sexual attention, was replaced with a theory of sexual *fantasy*, in which the child became the active source of desire and a magnet for the desires of others. The traumatic scene as an actual event was located in, and pushed into the individual child's unconscious, and the repression of the fantasy as it meets the outside world was now seen as the source of psychopathology. Such a Freudian double move was closely tied to images of children and their malevolence at the end of the nineteenth century, and psychoanalysis was founded on an image of unconscious fantasies in children and a repression of those images (Masson, 1984). In psychoanalysis proper, the activity of repression is located in the child. In the popular imagination, the repression is as much directed at the idea that there are such fantasies as at the effects of the fantasies themselves. We can see the discursive complex of seduction twisted in a Baudrillardian way away from modern psychoanalysis and at work in the new age.

NEW AGE ALLURE New age networks have followed through the idea that unconscious, preconscious or subconscious forces affect our awareness of the world and can be blocked in some way. In the new age networks, these unconscious energies are also located (and sometimes with explicit reference to Jungian ideas) in collective unconscious forces, and they are then extended beyond humankind to all forms of life or planetary being. The romanticization of the animal world is directed toward certain animals, and we can explore the way some of those images of animals function as representatives of nature. At the same time as the new age movement holds to the idea that there is something underneath, there is a concern, however, with the *interconnection* of experience and the idea that such interconnection can be evoked in fantasy through the play of signs. Like Baudrillard, then, the seduction is through the work of signs which evoke sensuality rather than the sensuality itself which is striking through to the surface.

In the new age movement, the magazine *Kindred Spirit: The guide to personal and planetary healing* gives news of 'An exhibition entitled The Healing Potential of Dolphins' which 'will celebrate the connection between humans and dolphins through the ages' (*Kindred Spirit*: 5). On the back cover of the magazine, there are advertisements promising sounds of whales and dolphins woven into the music of audiotapes. A tape for 'Whales and sounds of the sea' includes seductive messages: 'Ten high-quality 3-D recordings providing a unique ambience of lovely nature sounds with soothing subliminal suggestions (not audible consciously). These sounds envelop and revitalize you. . .' (*Kindred Spirit*, 10, 2). Another tape is called 'Way of the Dolphin', and the promise here is more sensual still: 'The alluring voice of Dolphins and Medwyn's sensitive music forge a joyous, tender and emotive union, reflecting back to the listener the great love and respect that is possible between our two species' (ibid.).

Celebration of the connection between humans and dolphins is also, at times, something that is politicized as a struggle to resist more traditional definitions of perversity. This issue came to the fore in the popular press in 1991 in the UK after one new age dolphin activist was targeted by a dolphinarium owner anxious to stop organized protests against the captivity of his dolphins. The activist was accused by the dolphinarium owner of carrying out lewd acts with one particular dolphin while swimming with him in the open sea. The detailed descriptions in the British tabloid press of the entangling of the dolphin's penis around the activist's leg were not really at issue in the court case, because the legal point the activist was being prosecuted over was that he had been carrying out these acts in a manner which would offend the public. Representatives of the public had been taken out to sea to watch these activities in the dolphinarium owner's boat. The activist was eventually acquitted, and resumed work as a gardener in Manchester.

There are strong connections between this dolphin-friendly strand of new age thinking and popular representations of dolphins as, variously, the wise old men of the sea carrying to the present the knowledge of past generations (as in, for example, the film *Cocoon*) and as the young frisky boys innocently and clearly seeing the way the things are now (as in, for example, the children's programme and film *Flipper*). The dolphin sexual abuse scare in this case was in the context of a moral panic in the press over child sexual abuse (Levidow, 1989), and the named dolphin, Freddy, was certainly infantilized in the reports. The lurid details of the activist's encounter with the dolphin and prurient interest in what unthinkable things might be going on underwater seemed to touch a fear that some last area of innocence was being despoiled.

It was the fact that the alleged obscene play with the dolphin could be *seen* that was at issue in the modern legal rules that were applied to protect Freddy. The connection between the visible and the obscene is made forcibly in Baudrillard's work. In pornography, for example, Baudrillard argues that:

> The end result of this degradation to a terroristic visibility of the body (and its 'desire') is that appearances lose all their secrecy. In a culture where appearances are desublimated, everything is materialised in its most objective form. Porno culture par excellence is simply one that everywhere and always endorses the function of the real.
>
> (Baudrillard, 1970: 150–151)

In the opposition between seduction and obscenity that Baudrillard subscribes to, the new age movements live in the realm of seduction (in their uses of music, colour and smell to evoke a connection with nature), while old brute realist moderns live in the realm of obscenity (in the practices of exposure and direct and complete visibility), and so they are all the more horrified by what is visible. It is the *fact* of visibility itself, rather than the specific representation that horrifies Baudrillard. While seduction is symbolic exchange for Baudrillard, the attempt to get beneath that exchange is an end to the erotic:

> The body is a symbolic veil, and is nothing but that; it is seduction that is to be found in this play of veils, where strictly speaking the body is abolished 'as such'. This is where seduction plays, and never where the veil is torn away in order to reveal a desire or truth.
>
> (Baudrillard, 1979: 150)

The danger of transparency and the threat of the real haunt Baudrillard's celebration of the postmodern, and the impossible flight from hyperreality into the actually existing unveiled body will end in madness. Metaphors of madness abound in postmodern writing, and in this case schizophrenia is seen as 'too great a proximity of everything' (Baudrillard, 1983b: 132). Technology invades and destroys the sea as a mysterious invisible place and animals living there, and the new age movement invests again these areas with a numinous quality. This is the romantic veiling work that the new age performs on dolphins. As things which were distant become close, the new age produces them again as new mysteries. The new age participates, then, in postmodern *fantasies* of nature rather than attempting to go straight back to the real, but it also tries to find in these dreams some *meaning*. The possibilities for *seduction*, for the sense of things desired being hidden and desired all the more for that, are under threat as the urban centres simultaneously spread and collapse: 'The loss of public space occurs contemporaneously with the loss of private space. The one is no longer a spectacle, the other no longer a secret' (ibid.: 130). The new age is one powerful response to this loss of public space during times of ecological crisis, and it is structured by the psychoanalytic notion of seduction which Baudrillard articulates.

NATURISM'S HEALTHY ATTRACTION   There is a quite different blank refusal to acknowledge that the innocent young might have desires or be desired, might seduce or be seduced, in naturism. There is an insistence that what they do is certainly not erotic simply because they have no clothes, and one follower argues in a BBC public access programme, for example, that 'the public confuse naturism with sex and exhibitionism ... these have nothing to do with naturism' (Piper and British Naturism, 1992). In the same programme, one of the novice naturists points out that 'women are more alluring partly clothed' (ibid.), reassuring the audience that to be entirely naked is not at all alluring. This novice also confesses that on his first visit to the indoor naturist centre he was worried about getting an erection, and there is repeated discussion of this in issues of *Health and Efficiency* as the kind of worry men in the 'clothed' world have about what would happen if they saw a naked body. The worry is located in the clothed world as an effect of a particular *form* of representation, not as representation as such. There is also a marked difference between the publicity for CCBN which includes carefully desexualized images of naked bodies including children, and *Health and Efficiency* where the photographs play with soft porn genres and posing by women naturists, but with no pictures of children. The surrounding text in the latter is contradictory, mixing genres. In one issue (*Health and Efficiency*, 1993, 94: 4), for example, there are teenage magazine problem-page queries (e.g., 'My friend says that having a Jacuzzi can stop you being a virgin, is this true?'), direct challenges to men who want to know how to chat up a girl on a naturist beach ('it might be a good idea to look at your whole attitude to women. We don't want to be "chatted up" '), and a cover-story on sexual signals ('You can tell if she wants you in the first 5 mins').

There are appeals to versions of 'normality' that will then ward off the possibility of seduction and perverse threats coming from the 'clothed' world and those outside proper family relationships:

Alas! One of the present disadvantages of an Official Naturist beach is the number of inadequate men who gather to watch from a safe distance. These are mainly 'normal' men with binoculars peeping at girls and women, and they are to be pitied for their personal problems. And sometimes there are homosexuals meeting friends. But this disadvantage is one shared by many public places, such as pubs and clubs.

(Target, 1993: 42)

In some of the naturist clubs, single men are not admitted, and members whose wives die may then be excluded (Connolly, 1992). Two connected images appear in the representations of outsiders looking in on the official naturist beach. One is that of 'watching at a safe distance', and the other is that of men 'peeping through binoculars'. Together these images produce a powerful rhetorical frame which sets up a contrast between the distance and mediated perception of the pervert with the closeness and direct transparent visibility of the naturist.

There are also differences between new age and naturist notions of fetishism, and again the new age looks forward into a world structured by Baudrillard's postmodern psychoanalytic discourse, while naturism looks back to a time before the modern, before psychoanalysis.

Fetishism

An erotic attention to a particular part of the body or specific category of object is, in psychoanalytic terms, derived from a refusal to acknowledge, an inability to see an absence. It is, for Freud (1927a), a disavowal of reality, the reality of the absence of the phallus, the signifier of power and subjecthood, where the infant's fantasy has expected it to be, and the consequent attempt to locate the phallus somewhere else. What has been refused at one point is marked at another. The repudiation of the loss of the object fails as this lost object returns in the form of a fetish. This understanding of sexual fetishism in the classical psychoanalytic tradition is transformed in Baudrillard's (1970) discussion of the role of signs in the production of desire, in the production of commodity fetishism, and – this is crucial for this analysis of the place of the new age in the popular imagination – this version of the theory of fetishism is brought closer to psychoanalytic discourse in contemporary common sense.

Baudrillard gives voice to popular notions of fetishism, now linked more directly with commodities and the commodification of identity and sexuality than in modern psychoanalysis, as a pathological obsession with adornment. In oppositional valorizations of perversion, such as the practice of 'homovestism' in which one knowingly and ironically dresses in the clothes of one's own sex (Barford, 1992), this permits an alternative and progressive use of dress. Discussing Nico, a 1960s New York underground icon who ended her life in North Manchester, for example, Baudrillard argues that she 'only seemed more beautiful because her femininity was purely an act. Something more than beauty, almost sublime emanated from her, a different seduction. The deception to be uncovered was that she was a false drag, a real woman playing at drag' (Baudrillard, 1979: 134). The issue here is not whether Baudrillard is correct or mistaken in his exaggeration of fetishism to cover all of our perceptions of signs in postmodern hyperreality, but how that extended notion of fetishism, a notion still underpinned in one way or another by desire, connects with the role of markers of identity in new age networks. For Baudrillard, anything will serve to rewrite the cultural order on the body; and it is this that takes the effect of beauty. The erotic is thus the reinscription of the erogenous in a homogeneous system of signs (gestures, movements, emblems, body heraldry) whose goal is closure and logical perfection – to be sufficient unto itself.

(Baudrillard, 1970: 94)

NEW AGE ZONES OF THE BODY   Let us turn to consider the meanings of adornment in the new age networks. The use of make-up as such is not a good example, in part because of the movement of personnel from aging burnt out New Left networks into new age practices (a movement that runs concurrently with the Left's flight into therapy), and this is a population that still carries with it a politically correct antagonism to cosmetics. Make-up reappears in other ways, in body painting in shamanism, for example, but a more excessive attention to bodily parts comes in the form of piercing. This practice has spread from the centre to the edges of the new age movement, from the fake American Indian tepee to the metropolitan high street. The insertion of pieces of metal marks the pierced parts of the body out for particular attention, and holds it there. These parts of the body may stand, in classic psychoanalytic vision, for the absent phallus, in the ear, tongue, eyelid or nipple, or lower lip (where the metal is called a labret). The parts of the body may be marked as the location of what is absent, in piercing of the inner labia or clitoral hood, or, in an increasingly popular practice in the UK, in the marking of the phallus itself, a fetishistic guarantee against absence. One London body piercer has 'an apadravya (vertical bar bell through the head of the penis); an ampallang (lateral version of the above); and a Prince Albert (a ring through the urethra and out under the glans) with balls on' (Forna, 1992: 9). This last appliance is so named, apparently, because Prince Albert (husband of Queen Victoria), not a noted new age devotee, wore a ring through his foreskin which he pulled down inside his trouser leg and hooked to a garter.

In fetishism then, there is disavowal of absence and a consequent valorization of a part that stands for that which is missing. The new age movement, while still being a largely white sub-culture, often fetishizes a new nature embodied in peoples of colour, ranging from American Indians to Alaskan Inuit. Body piercing not only guarantees a part of the body as a reference point, a mark of identity in a world of shifting signs, but it also connects the pierced body of the Western devotee with the pierced bodies of fetishized 'others' in cultures where the practice is a defining characteristic of membership. What is 'other' is fetishized, and is continually re-marked on the body in new age practices. While it sometimes looks like an attempt to retrieve what has been lost or to keep present what may disappear, it actually looks to something entirely new, something which will break from the modern and shift forward to fix on something more exotic, as if they have just been discovered at the end of modernity.

The anonymity of the post-industrial mega-city also provokes this kind of *fetishism*, an increasingly massive investment of libidinal energy in fetishistic processes as defence mechanisms to guarantee the integrity of the self: 'The metaphor of fetishism, wherever it appears, involves a fetishization of the conscious subject or of a human essence, a rationalist metaphysics' (Baudrillard, 1970: 89). While the new age often falls across the threshold of modernity into this Baudrillardian future and this kind of postmodern defence against a culture in crisis, naturism stubbornly refuses to step over the threshold even into the modern world and the ills it sees accumulating there.

NATURISM'S BITS OF THE BODY   Naturists are not, of course, so interested in playing with the fashion system, but they still have to negotiate the fetishistic activities of the clothed world, and their difficulties in doing this are expressed in their discussion of different kinds of bodily adornment. There is some suspicion and opposition in naturism to the adornment of the naked body, for this would threaten to draw attention to the body in the way that clothing does. There are reports of shaving of pubic hair, tattooing and body piercing at the Naturist Foundation near Orpington in Kent in the UK (Connolly, 1992), and *Health and Efficiency* has also discussed the function of shaving as reaching a closer approximation to the real body and freer enjoyment, and as an expression of 'individuality' (Williams, 1993). Nevertheless, the predominant wish in contemporary naturism is that they could escape from all forms of dressing up.

If, in fetishism, there is a disavowal of absence and a consequent valorization of the part that stands for that which is missing, in naturism there is a disavowal of the possibility that any part should be sexualized against the whole clean body. Here, the *refusal* of fetishism can be read as a kind of fetish for 'normality'. One naturist describes representations of the body in early issues of *Health and Efficiency* as 'anatomically incorrect' (Piper and British Naturism, 1992), for example, because they failed to include diversity of body shapes and sizes. Although there are not many fat bodies in the magazine, this comment is linked to a comment on the role of the clothed world in suppressing 'individuality'. There is also, in other naturist accounts, a resistance to the clothed world as a world which fetishizes the norm, and which locks participants into a signifying system which privileges certain kinds of body. As well as an acceptance of a diversity of bodies, though, there is an underlying concern with normality which is expressed in other ways. There is the argument that taking off one's clothes removes all social and class barriers, because these things are 'artificial'. One naturist claims that naturists are 'all on the same level', and naturism treats 'everybody as equal' with 'no difference between rich and poor' (ibid.). Naturism is seen here as the leveller, as if culture did not also construct our representations of the body. There is also the argument that naturists turn out, after all, to be 'normal'. One novice naturist describes going to an indoor club and his way of overcoming his initial embarrassment: 'It was perfectly normal to meet and speak to families in a normal way, as though they were dressed. It didn't occur to me that they weren't' (ibid.).

However, the refusal of fetishism is still only spoken about here in terms of items of clothing. As already noted, another novice naturist pointed out that 'women are more alluring partly clothed' (ibid.), and here it is the *part* that is the problem. The reluctance to adorn the body in mainstream natur- ism, or even to wear make-up, can be interpreted as a refusal of the possi- bility of any fetish and as a retreat to a normative system that disavows fetishism itself. After all, Baudrillard argues that fetishism is 'the sanctifi- cation of the system as such, of the commodity as system' (Baudrillard, 1970: 92). Naturism refuses fetishes, then, but it cannot escape the cultural processes of fetishization that surround it in the clothed world. Naturism refuses fetishism by looking back, and trying to evade modernity by finding places, in the unclothed body, where it thinks modernity could not reach.

Narcissism

The redirection of libidinal interest upon one's own self, the recathexis of the ego is likened by Freud (1914a) to that of a single-celled organism. It is like an amoeba sending out parts of itself, the pseudopodia, for the material in these limbs will always return and be absorbed again into the body of the creature. Narcissism, which revolves around a visual metaphor, of Narcissus gazing into the pool at his own image, is also, then, to do with the sucking inward of energy. The sense of self-absorption that one identifies in others as narcissism is bound up with a sense on the part of an observer that nothing, no interest, nor attention, nor investment is being sent out. The self is being invested as if it were an other. Libidinal energy is returning from the object to the ego, and there is, then, at this point, always, for the narcissist, a *mediated* relationship with the self. Non- mediated pleasure would be mere auto-eroticism. Narcissistic bodily prac- tices, then, require an other for whom the display is intended. For Baudrillard, this variety of mediation is built into contemporary subjec- tivity.

For postmodern subjects it is not enough to return to an infantile state, for notions of infancy are themselves mediated. Baudrillard (1986) looks to the possibilities of cloning as the future mode of reproduction. One of the consequences of people cloning themselves, and being clones of an other is that a process of mirroring replaces the tangle of Oedipal relation- ships:

> The digital Narcissus replaces the triangular Oedipus. The hypostasis of an arti- ficial double, the clone will henceforth be your guardian angel, the visible form of your unconscious and flesh of your flesh, literally and without metaphor. Your 'neighbor' will henceforth be this clone of an hallucinatory resemblance, consequently you will never be alone again and no longer have a secret.... Thus love is total. And so is self-seduction.
>
> (quoted in Kellner, 1989: 102)

Baudrillard's mutation of modern psychoanalytic notions of narcissism makes it into a kind of psychoanalytic discourse that new age movements inhabit and struggle with.

NEW AGE MEDIATED DESIRE   In the new age networks there is always a sense of mediation, either through energies flowing through chakras, ley lines and so forth, or through rituals in like-minded spiritual communities. The closest to immediate connection in these networks, self-trepanation, is actually quite far out on the fringe. But it is its very distance from the core of the new age movement that can help mark a point where the new age ends and more crude bodily practices begin. This distance makes self-trepanation an instructive example to compare with other new age talk. Self-trepanation serves as a limit point for us to mark the boundaries of the new age. More acceptable versions of trepanation in new age circles are to be found in such things as cranial osteopathy.

Modern self-trepanation was first advocated by a Dutchman, Dr Bart Huges, who developed a theory of 'brainbloodvolume' as the ratio of blood to matter in the brain, a ratio that could be increased by standing on one's head or restoring the cranium to the state it was in infancy by cutting a small disk of bone out of the skull with a drill. One of Huges' followers, Joseph Mellen, describes how he managed to drill a hole in his head on the third attempt with a trephine (a special trepanning tool) he found in a surgical store: 'There was an ominous-sounding schlurp and the sound of bubbling' (quoted in Sieveking, 1991: 43). A friend who assisted him, Amanda Feilding, used a flat-bottomed electric drill for her own operation; there was a power cut in the middle of it, but she was successful after about half-an-hour drilling. She has stood for the British parliament twice on a 'free trepanation on the National Health Service' ticket. She describes the feeling afterwards as 'an internal economy pleasantly floating above the poverty barrier' (Feilding, 1991: 44).

Feilding (1991) talks about a post-trepanation feeling of loss of ego, and interprets this as a heightened awareness. Self-trepanation promises a return to childhood, through the drilling of the hole, to become again the open-headed infant, but it actually still lies at the edge of the more psychoanalytically informed fantasies of new agers. This distance from psychoanalytic notions of narcissism is apparent if we consider the prognosis offered for narcissistic modes of being in the postmodern condition of hyperreality that Baudrillard offers. Baudrillard's extension of narcissism is of a piece with his exhorbitation of psychoanalytic categories, and in this case the simulacra of the self that multiply in the postmodern condition also spell the end of old modern psychoanalysis. For the postmodern subject the idealized infantile state is itself always already mediated.

Self-trepanation is a fairly local and limited, inward-looking we might say, expression of the new age on the cusp of the modern. New age networks also attempt to work through the narcissistic paradoxes on a wider

world stage where the postcolonial 'other' returns to fuse with the excolo-
nial centre, working through and with, for example, the idealization and
defence of 'indigenous peoples'. It is not a question of opening the head
to let brains out, but opening up to what is 'natural' through shamanist
ritual, world music or political activity around issues of development that
has become more important. By returning to something that is natural, the
new age finds something fixed in an hallucinatory, always mediated
relationship with nature. Narcissism is also reproduced through the
medium of the television and computer screen such that 'The group connected to the video is also only its own terminal. It records itself, self-
regulates itself and self-manages itself electronically. Self-ignition,
self-seduction' (Baudrillard, quoted in Kellner, 1989: 148).

NATURISM'S DIRECT LINE TO WHAT IT WANTS   While the narcissistic fantasies
of the clothed culture which is riddled with psychoanalytic senses of self
and other might be expected to infuse the way naturists talk about the
body and nature, naturist discourse is actually stubbornly set against this.
A CCBN leaflet reprints advice from a North American naturist pamphlet
'Dare to go bare', which contains this characterization of childhood:

> Don't worry about your children, they like us, were born nude and enjoy
> nothing better than to play in the nude with their friends. It isn't until they grow
> older that they learn about social attitudes and by then they will have learnt
> acceptance of the human body without the hangups developed by non-naturist
> children.
>
> (CCBN)

In this respect, then, naturism should be seen as a *contrary* position, and
in part as defined against psychoanalytic notions of infancy. Psychoanalytic discourse does not, for a start, see childhood play as 'innocent',
and the acceptance of the body in naturism promises an unmediated
return to nature. In so far as naturism participates in contemporary
psychoanalytic culture – whether that is in a culture of narcissism (Lasch,
1978) or a postmodern hyperreal ecstasy of communication (Baudrillard,
1983b) – it does so by *refusing* the category of narcissism.

The absence of psychoanalytic conceptions of a narcissistic relation
to the body in naturism also raises some issues about the circulation
of forms of self in discourse through Western culture. There are overarching differences between the naturists and new age people which
bear on the circulation of psychoanalytic discourse. There are differences
between North America and parts of continental Europe, on the one
hand, as sites where psychoanalysis has had a fairly long-standing and
deep-rooted implantation in the popular imagination, and the anti-
erotic hygienist social work climate in Britain on the other, where
blunt common sense tends to refuse talk about sensuality and repression.
The naturist texts explored in this chapter have been transplanted
and then home-grown in a fairly cold climate for psychoanalytic concepts.

There are also important class differences in the percolation of psycho-analytic ideas. It is often claimed that a psychodynamic vocabulary for self-understanding is one of the peculiar elaborated codes of the middle class (Gellner, 1985), and this is what psychotherapists look for when they are assessing whether someone is 'psychologically minded' enough to benefit from a talking cure (Coltart, 1988). The class character of psycho-analytic discourse may be significant when we are attempting to account for why naturism does not seem to have taken up psychodynamic notions as much as the new age networks. It does seem to be the case that the naturist movement, in the UK at least, is composed of working-class or lower middle-class men and women, while a glance at any glossy brochure will reveal that the new age movement is largely middle class and the speakers at the British annual 'Festival of Mind, Body and Spirit' include a fair sprinkling of knights and peers of the realm.

Psychoanalysis and postmodernity

The relationship between psychoanalysis and postmodernity have been explored in two main ways; either by using psychoanalysis as a modern Enlightenment system of thought to understand developments in this new postmodern culture which is breeding forms of narcissistic pathology, or through using postmodern ideas to rework psychoanalysis to make it compatible with the changed state of things. Those using psychoanalysis from the object relations tradition to understand postmodernity have included Young (1989), writing from a Kleinian standpoint, who sees it as being 'spoiling and spiteful', and Frosh (1989, 1991), who also uses Bion's writing and sees the shift to the postmodern as a change of stance toward culture rather than a change in culture itself. Good use has also been made of Fairbairn's quasi-Kleinian work to explore schizoid mechanisms and narcissistic fantasies in contemporary capitalism (Richards, 1984b), and of Winnicottian notions of mirroring and transitional zones (Finlay, 1989).

Something of the *dialectic* of enlightenment in the postmodern con-dition is maintained in Frosh's (1991) descriptions of contemporary culture as a time of fluidity and turbulence, and of difficult contradictions that should be seen as opening up opportunities as well as posing threats. The positive aspect is that there are always deeper meanings to be dis-covered, and Kleinian theory is seen as able to respond to the feeling of threat and incomprehension which modernity and then postmodernity produced because it theorizes the threat as being *inside* the self. The feel-ings of threat are the feelings of the destructiveness (death instinct, para-noid-schizoid position, envy) which can be overcome by making reparation. The postmodernists are dangerous because they encourage people to follow through to an extreme end-point the options which modernism opens up but which modernists always utilized carefully and critically, and they risk romanticizing psychosis as an escape from the social. Baudrillard represents the terminal point of this argument of course, and he is happy to celebrate all that the old enlightened moderns are so frightened of. Ostensibly, 'postmodern' forms of psychoanalysis scorn the possibility of changing things for the better, and, like Chasseguet-Smirgel, they tend to describe political activity as symptomatic of psychopathology.

The new age tries to escape modernity and find something of value in the postmodern psychoanalytic twists on narcissism, fetishism and seduction that Baudrillard describes so well, while naturism tries to avoid modernity and return to something pre-psychoanalytic. These are two quite different contradictory reactions to modern Enlightenment culture, and they each fail to tackle the contradictoriness of that culture, and the necessity for a dialectical engagement with it. The Frankfurt School tradition still holds to that agenda of dialectical engagement, with a focus now in the work of Axel Honneth (1994, 1995), successor to Habermas in the third generation of the School, and an emphasis on 'recognition' described by Hegel as the ground for identity and truth (Alexander and Lara, 1996). Honneth draws on object relations theory to link Hegel to psychoanalysis, a move that has also been made by some feminist writers (e.g., Benjamin, 1984, 1988).

While these links are being forged to maintain a critical progressive account of society and subjectivity against the postmodernists, similar links have been made for many years in French psychoanalysis. The psychoanalyst offering an account most congenial to the postmodern condition, and producing an account which emphasizes the role of narcissism as an inescapable aspect of human development, and who provides a conceptual point of contact between the German and French traditions of psychoanalytic social theory, particularly in his use of Hegel, is Jacques Lacan. This book takes neither psychoanalysis nor postmodernity as its starting point, but focuses on the forms of discourse and practice which weave these things into sites for contemporary subjectivity. Now, in the third part of the book, we will examine the way in which Lacanian subjectivity is woven into the fabric of modern (and postmodern) culture.

PART III:
POST-THEORIES: SUBJECTIVITY AND THE SOCIAL

> Europeans need easy explanations; they will always choose a simple lie over a contradictory truth
>
> Peter Høeg ([1992]1993: 300) *Miss Smilla's Feeling for Snow*

Psychoanalytic theory in the Lacanian and post-Lacanian tradition is marked by confusion and misunderstanding, for at least three reasons. First, partly because Lacan's (1977, 1979) reading of Freud is not, as he claims, a 'return to Freud', but a theoretical re-presentation of psychoanalysis which brings notions from structural linguistics and phenomenology to bear on Freud's early writings. The object relations version of psychoanalytic discourse discussed in Part I of this book took off from Freud's later writings, and the Frankfurt School version discussed in Part II was rooted more in the middle period of his work. There is already a paradox, which is typical of Lacanian theory, which is that this most avant-garde version of psychoanalysis picks up Freud's (1900) earliest accounts of the unconscious, and some post-Lacanians now see Freud as sliding into error after those first accounts (Laplanche, 1996). Secondly, confusion and misunderstanding has been exacerbated by the elliptical and elitist translations and explanations of Lacan in the English language in the early 1970s. A version of Lacanian discourse was imported then which was framed by the concerns of film, literary and cultural theorists, and the claim that it could be reduced to complicated juggling of signifiers and signifieds (Coward and Ellis, 1977; Lemaire, 1977). This not only served to obscure what was most Freudian about this version of psychoanalytic discourse, but it also seemed to revel in its status as a high theory which must necessarily be esoteric and removed from clinical practice. A paradox marks the reception of this version of Freudian theory, then, which is that Lacanian and post-Lacanian psychoanalysis, which is so difficult to comprehend in the English-speaking world, is actually the most globally widespread as a clinical practice, and – mostly organized through the Freudian Field – predominates in French, Portuguese and Spanish-speaking cultures (Roudinesco, 1990).

The third reason why Lacanian theory is marked by confusion and misunderstanding is that it is designed to disturb and unravel the idea that it is possible to have a certain knowledge of the self as an undivided centre or to construct a secure model of society or culture that individual selves could observe, map and move around in. Lacanian notions of subjectivity and the social see those two sides of the equation – subjectivity and the social, the inside and outside, the unconscious subject and language – as intertwined, as each constituting the other and making it seem as if each were separate things. It was always a mistake to see Lacan as a 'structuralist' or even as a 'post-structuralist', but Lacanian and post-Lacanian psychoanalytic discourse effectively functions now in the broader problematic of postmodern writing. The Lacanian mutation of psychoanalytic discourse that circulates in postmodern responses to the cultural-political crises of late capitalism feed certain kinds of fantasy spaces and subject positions. This psychoanalytic discourse draws upon and reproduces forms of social space and subjectivity which are uncertain, anxious and contradictory right to the heart.

The structure of human experience and the second nature which binds individuals to social structures are seen by Lacanian theorists as discursive properties which are also *material*. The language we must speak to enter the symbolic order which structures culture and defines what human nature we believe ourselves to possess also enters us, and it bewitches us at the very moment that it promises to provide direct access to realities and relationships. Language provides us with the means to articulate our desires, but it also simultaneously turns experience into something symbolically mediated and broken from that which it is supposed to express, that which vanishes into the unconscious as a fantasy space constituted at the very same moment. Chapter 7 describes how these discursive operations form the unconscious, and how Lacan's use of structural linguistics is a metaphor for this phenomenological splitting. We then turn to the varieties of postmodern space in virtual reality that provoke this phenomenological splitting, and to how new forms of 'cyberpsychology' constitute a Lacanian subject in certain discursive practices. These discursive practices which structure postmodern spaces are sites in contemporary culture where Lacanian mutations of psychoanalytic theory circulate and produce subject positions marked by distinct notions of memory and anxieties about reality.

Lacanian theory once held out the promise for some Marxists of developing a superior account of ideology, and of the ways in which subjects were 'interpellated' into positions in the symbolic (Althusser, 1970). The misrepresentation of the self as a sort of 'centre' which could operate independently of social context is, for Lacan, prepared by the first imaginary relationship with the mother driven by demand for food and warmth and sensual contact, and a recognition of oneself in a mirror-relationship with her which is really a 'misrecognition' of oneself as unitary. What appears to be the most direct and unproblematic perception and representation of oneself and others, then, turns out to be the most thoroughly mistaken. This Lacanian account is valuable in drawing attention to the way ideology operates through forms of *mediation*, but it has also led to the pessimistic conclusion for some writers that it is impossible to evade ideology by producing a better representation and so, perhaps, we could only hope for escape by moving outside representation altogether. In Chapter 8, we will see how this Lacanian narrative followed its course through the work of Julia Kristeva. There is always a counterpart to the illusion of self-sufficiency which is that it would be possible to express one's true demands in another place, and we will turn to the ways in which attempts to escape capitalism in Local Exchange Trading Schemes fail to find this other place, and the way they reproduce certain forms of subjectivity structured by the hopeless attempt to escape representation.

Psychoanalysis revolves around the attempt to turn theory into action, and radical analysts in the Frankfurt School tradition tried to link the self-reflective activity of the individual to social concerns in a praxis which would change culture at the same time as it transformed the modern self. The Lacanian tradition worries away at the possibility of *personal-political* change, and so, despite its scepticism about the Real it still tries to grasp how personal and political historical events have a material basis at the same time as being always mediated. Here we also return to one of the starting points for psychoanalytic theory, and the attempt to account for the way in which real events in childhood which were seductive and trau-matic might be represented and understood. In Chapter 9 we look at the way the Lacanian unconscious revolves around the possibility of truth and the core of lies that structure the subject. The fantasy space of the uncon-scious and the idea that one might find the truth there function as lures which often prevent rather than catalyse change. We explore this through a consideration of Jean Laplanche's (1989) theory of general seduction, Jean-François Lyotard's (1974) account of the libidinal band, and Slavoj Žižek's (1989) reading of Lacan on mechanisms of transference. Each writer draws attention to how Lacanian mechanisms operate in culture and as settings for the production of Lacanian forms of subjectivity. Differ-ent varieties of psychoanalytic discourse structure much psychotherapy as a technology of the self in private places and the hope that something might be caught and repaired or made anew, but postmodern cultural forms carry Lacanian psychoanalytic discourse through them in the public domain where we are recruited into subject positions which frustrate that task. Therapeutic discourse functions as a space in modern and post-modern culture where the subject is found and opened and unravelled and lost.

7
Symbolic Orders, Subjects and Cyberspace

Every historical rupture, every advent of a new master-signifier, changes retroactively the meaning of all tradition, restructures the narration of the past, makes it readable in another, new way ... in the symptom, the repressed content is returning from the future and not from the past

Slavoj Žižek (1989: 56) *The Sublime Object of Ideology*

Jacques Lacan trained as a psychiatrist in the 1920s and as a psychoanalyst in the 1930s. He was eventually expelled from the International Psychoanalytical Association in 1963 (with complaints against him directed at his practice of varying the length of psychoanalytic sessions, his declared hostility to American ego-psychology, and his authoritarian behaviour). He set up his own group, which he periodically closed down and revived until he died in 1981. The leadership of the Lacanian movement then passed to Jacques-Alain Miller, his son-in-law (Roudinesco, 1990). There are three key components to Lacan's work (J.-A. Miller, 1985): structural linguistics founded by Saussure (1974); the Subject as a philosophical category developed from a version of Hegel's (1807) phenomenology; and the 'mirror-phase' derived from empirical study of infants. That third element, which connects the Lacanian account of mirroring and misrecognition with mainstream psychoanalytic notions of child development and narcissism, will be discussed in Chapter 8. The first two elements – structuralism and phenomenology – reframe the way psychoanalytic discourse operates, and the kinds of space that are laid open for the subject who speaks within it. Together, they construct a dualist universe of epistemology and ontology (of knowledge and being) in which structural linguistics delimits the alienating system of signs in which we must speak and lose ourselves and phenomenology defines the activity of the subject seeking recognition from others as we try to use and break the system.

This chapter briefly reviews Lacan's use of structural linguistics and the theoretical paraphernalia of signifiers and signifieds that made it seem to many English-speaking followers in the 1970s and early 1980s as if this was simply a 'structuralist' psychoanalysis prescribed by the formula 'Freud + Saussure = Lacan' (e.g., Bird, 1982). Structuralism does help us to capture something of the nature of the symbolic order as the overarching system of signs which includes the language we learn to be recognized as human and which governs social identities in culturally specific versions of the reality principle. We then turn to Lacan's theory of the subject which picks up notions from Kojève's (1969) reading of Hegelian phenomenology, for it is this tradition that provided Lacan with a formula for desire as being the desire of an other (Dews, 1987; Macey, 1995). Phenomenology revolves around the attempt to capture the ways in which we try to comprehend the horizon of meaning that makes us who we are, and give an account of experience that is true to the internal world but also formed in relation to others. These two competing theoretical traditions provide the setting for Lacan's 'return to Freud', and for the retrieval of Freud's account of memory as *Nachträglichkeit*, or 'deferred action', in which present understanding makes the past come to be. Structuralism and phenomenology, and the Surrealism Lacan encountered in the 1930s, disturb representations of reality and the illusion that it would be possible to observe or touch reality directly. In Lacan's writing, the Real functions as an impossible place of certainty and rest in relation to others, somewhere we try to find secure reference points and find them lacking.

We then need to ask what kinds of settings would make Lacanian specifications for subjectivity make sense, and this is where the 'postmodern' character of Lacan's mutation of Freud becomes apparent even if Lacan himself was not at all a postmodernist. The idea that a postmodern age is upon us, and that all claims to truth, personal integrity, progress and rational understanding, are dissolving, has now set in play a series of celebrations and anxieties about the nature and evaporation of language and reality (as we saw in Chapter 6). In the process, some of the speculations about the relationship between technology and humanity in science fiction writing in the last half-century have entered the language and life-world of postmodern subjects (Bukatman, 1993; Broderick, 1995). The futures that science fiction texts open up throw new light on what we have become. New forms of experience and social relationships are created in science fiction, and these new forms offer distinctive vantage points, different arrays of subject positions from which to view the present. And, as the past is reinterpreted by the new 'master-signifiers' in these texts, what we take to be reality in technology and nature starts to break up. Often this reaches the point where it is unclear which reality is correct in the myriad of alternative realities that are described.

Virtual reality in science fiction, and then in electronically mediated postmodern space in the present-day, also offers to contemporary culture an arena for the representation and experience of something quite different from the type of modern psychology hitherto demanded by the 'real' world (Macauley and Gordo-López, 1995). The texts which flow through science fiction, and then through the discursive hardware of information technology and virtual reality are suffused with psychoanalytic theory. These texts – in novels, films, television and software – have been written and rewritten in a psychoanalytic culture, and those who speak them and live within them then become, to one degree or another, psychoanalytic

subjects. However, the forms of psychoanalytic discourse, and so also subjectivity, that are reproduced in these texts are as close as you can get to a
postmodern psychology, storying into being a new fluid and dispersed,
electronically circumscribed and software-dependent 'cyberpsychology'
(Gordo-López and Parker, forthcoming). Representations of virtual reality
and the self online evoke and reproduce forms of subjectivity that are
structured in line with the postmodern mutations of psychoanalysis that
circulate in Lacanian texts. We will explore these forms of subjectivity, and
anxieties about language, memory and reality in the second half of this
chapter. Let us turn first to Lacanian 'postmodern' mutations of psychoanalysis.

Lacan's linguistics

Language has always, of course, been crucial to psychoanalysis (Forrester, 1980). Traditional psychoanalysis sees the unconscious as being
'outside' and 'before' language, and the human capacity for creativity,
imagination and fantasy is what makes the use of language possible
(Freud, 1915c). This idea is sometimes expressed in the slogan that 'the
unconscious is the condition for language'. Lacan turns this claim on its
head, claiming that 'language' – understood in its broadest sense to
include all systems of signs, whether they be verbal or visual, behavioural or tactile – is necessary not only for communication but also for
the emergence of conscious subjectivity and an 'unconscious' other to
consciousness: 'the moment in which desire becomes human is also that
in which the child is born into language' (Lacan, 1977: 103). For Lacan,
then, the unconscious does not exist before language but is an *effect* of it
as much as consciousness is, and so we need to turn that traditional
Freudian slogan around to read 'language is the condition for the unconscious' (cf., Archard, 1984).

There is a further complication, which is that the unconscious is not,
according to Lacan, pushed 'outside' language when it is pushed away
from consciousness, but rather is bound up with the structure of language.
Lacan claims that '*the unconscious is structured like a language*' (1979: 20) or
that it is 'articulated like a discourse' (1977: 193), and this is because the
process of learning a language involves a double-move; the child enters
language and becomes able to enjoy the consciousness that it weaves for
it, and language enters the child to give that effect of consciousness but
also to carry into the child the incomprehensible, unspoken, latent meanings that flow through a culture. Language is split between what can and
cannot be said, and now the speaking child is split between what it is conscious of and what becomes thrown into 'another place', the unconscious.
Language, which belongs to the general population of 'others' in society,
conditions and so structures the unconscious, and so, even when now

fused with the idiosyncratic personal history of the child, 'the unconscious is the discourse of the Other' (ibid.).

References to specific theories of linguistics appear quite late on in Lacan's work, with the first references to Roman Jakobson and 'structural linguistics' in 1950 and to Ferdinand de Saussure a few years later (Macey, 1988). Saussure (1974: 16) argued that 'A science which studies the life of signs within society is conceivable; it would be part of social psychology and consequently of general psychology; I shall call it semiology'. This science of signs was to be realized in the period of high structuralism in France and then elsewhere in the 1950s and 1960s, with Saussure honoured as the founding father of an approach that spread through anthropology, philosophy and political theory (Pettit, 1975; Hawkes, 1977). Saussure, who actually used the term 'system' rather than 'structure', sets up four main distinctions – langue-parole, diachronic-synchronic, signifier-signified, paradigmatic-syntagmatic – as the basis of his new science, and we can see how each of these redefines psychoanalysis in the Lacanian take on structuralism.

Langue and parole

Saussure drew a distinction between the overall symbolic system, which he referred to as 'langue' (which translates as 'language'), and the manifestations of that system in the utterances of individual members of a language community, which he called 'parole' (or 'speech'). It is not possible to understand 'meanings' which inhere in a culture by looking at the idiosyncrasies of parole, for the meanings are given by the shared system of relationships which individuals then draw upon to make sense to one another. The task of structural linguistics, then, is to reconstruct langue. This led structural anthropologists such as Claude Lévi-Strauss (1958) to seize on Saussure's ideas and to take as their object of study the system of rules and relationships in a culture which function independently of individual intention, and which condition how an individual will give meaning to their behaviour.

Lacan was to see structural linguistics as a further twist in the 'decentering' of the human being; Copernicus had argued that the planets do not revolve around the earth, Darwin had knocked the human being off the pedestal into the rest of the animal kingdom, and Freud had shown that each individual consciousness was but a part of a mass of unconscious thought processes. Saussure's description of meaning as being a function of a language system of which we cannot be completely conscious was, for Lacan, then, of a piece with psychoanalysis. Saussure's linguistics, 'whose model is the combinatory operation', is something that is 'functioning spontaneously, of itself, in a presubjective way', and 'it is this linguistic structure that gives its status to the unconscious. It is this structure, in any case, that assures us that there is, beneath the term unconscious, something definable, accessible and objectifiable' (Lacan, 1979: 20–21).

This psychoanalysis, then, is also an alternative to humanism, and operates as part of the terrain of theoretical 'anti-humanism' in structuralist and post-structuralist thought (Homer, in press):

> Symbols in fact envelop the life of man [sic] in a network so total ... that they give the words that will make him faithful or renegade, the law of the acts that will follow him right to the very place where he is not yet and even beyond his death.
>
> (Lacan, 1977: 68)

Diachronic and synchronic

Traditional linguistics focused on the historical production of meanings, as a 'diachronic' study of the way a term changes over time. However, as Saussure pointed out, this does not really help us to understand what the term actually means to us in the present day. What we need to do, then, is to shift to a 'synchronic' study of language which attends to the way in which terms function as part of a complete, actually-existing system. This system then redefines how we will understand the 'past', and what sense we will make of the various different meanings that have been attached to a term up to now.

It could be argued that psychoanalysis has never been concerned with an accurate reconstruction of the past, and that the process of coming to an understanding of the meaning of past events involves fitting them into place, into the system of meanings that structure the patient's internal life-world. Freud did often try to trace meanings back to childhood, and to that extent his approach was diachronic rather than synchronic. The step that Lacan takes, though, is to insist that even such an ostensibly diachronic endeavour is predicated on the system of meanings that the patient has available to them as an adult. Meanings that are unavailable to the patient are not sealed away independent of present-day life, and although there will be a process of repression that needs to be tracked in order to understand why certain things are difficult to think, these things have significance because they are 'memories' which function for us in certain ways now, and which will then function differently as the analysis proceeds. Memory works through a process of *Nachträglichkeit* or 'deferred action', and so Lacan describes the process of analysis as follows:

> I identify myself in language, but only by losing myself in it like an object. What is realized in my history is not the past definite of what was, since it is no more, or even the present perfect of what has been in what I am, but the future anterior of what I shall have been for what I am in the process of becoming.
>
> (Lacan, 1977: 86)

Signifier and signified

For Saussure, the system ('langue' at any 'synchronic' moment) is made of signs, and each sign comprises a 'signifier', which is the sound image or inscription, and a 'signified', which is the concept attached to it. (Saussure is not concerned here with the referent, which is the thing in the world to which the concept corresponds.) Different people may have different, idiosyncratic, signifieds attached to the signifier, and so this makes a study of the overall network of terms (signifiers) even more important if the meaning (signified) of any particular term is to be understood. The relationship between the signifier and signified in a sign is, Saussure says, like the two sides of a sheet of paper, but he argues that this relationship is arbitrary. There is no reason why any particular sound image (the word you hear when I speak) should be connected to a concept (that which you think of when you hear me). Saussure argues that over the course of time, and he is referring to long historical periods here, the development of language can involve a change in the relationship between signifier and signified such that the signified (concept) can 'slide' under the signifiers to be attached to new signifiers (sounds). Such sliding will then, of course, also change the overall system of signs, and so the meaning of particular signs.

It is possible to make a connection here with Freud's (1915c) distinction between the conscious and the unconscious as comprising 'word presentations' and 'thing presentations' respectively. This mapping of concepts from structural linguistics onto psychoanalytic concepts serves to emphasize the way that concepts (Freud's 'thing presentations') are attached to inscriptions ('word presentations') as the two aspects of the signs which make up language. Unconscious meanings, then, are locked into language as a kind of underside to the network of conscious meanings; they are glued to the structure of language rather than being 'outside' it. Lacan takes this conceptual mapping further still to argue that the 'sliding' of signifieds under signifiers is a process that occurs continuously over the lifetime of a speaking subject, often with the effect of ambiguity and uncertainty of meaning for speakers and sometimes as a process of repression. However, Lacan argues that the unconscious also consists of signifiers rather than signifieds, and that repression occurs through signifiers falling 'under' the network of signifiers, as if to the level of signifieds. For Lacan, then, the signifier does not refer to a signified, but to *another signifier* (and this 'sideways' move across from signifier to signifier rather than to something more meaningful also makes his form of psychoanalysis more congenial to postmodernists). This means that our experience of subjectivity, through the many other signifiers attached to the signifier 'I', is continually shifting, and we are unable to find a stable resting place where we know what we mean when we refer to ourselves: 'the subject is always a fading thing that runs under the chain of signifiers' (Lacan, 1973: 194). A sense of 'self', then, is dependent on the organization of language, and the 'I' points to a concept which is not really there, and so, Lacan (1977: 89) argues, the 'ego' is 'formed of a verbal nucleus ... dependent on the signifier'.

Paradigmatic and syntagmatic

For Saussure, the terms in language can only be defined by way of their relationship to other terms. There are no real, definable, meanings without this differentiation, and so meaning is a function of the differences in the system: 'in language there are only differences without positive terms' (Saussure, 1974: 120). These differences are structured on two dimensions, along the 'paradigmatic' and 'syntagmatic' axes. The paradigmatic axis specifies the range of terms that can be substituted at any point in a grammatical sequence. For example, in the phrase 'the cat sat on the mat', the term 'cat' can be replaced with 'dog' or 'baby', 'sat' could be replaced with 'stood' or 'scratched', and 'mat' could be replaced with 'chair' or 'floor' among the many different terms available. The grammatical sense of a phrase would not be changed, but the meaning would. The syntagmatic axis organizes the different combinations which position terms in various relationships to each other. In a menu, for example, 'soup then main course then sweet' defines relationships within which a number of paradigmatic substitutions can be made, but the syntagmatic axis would still be specifying that there should be an order for eating the food.

This view of language reinforces the anti-humanism of the structuralist approach, for people do not produce meaning anew each time they speak. Rather, it is meaning that produces us such that we are written into place in the paradigmatic and syntagmatic axes that lay out how we might order our lives and what alternative things we might do at each point. As Lacan puts it, 'I am not a poet, but a poem. A poem that is being written, even if it looks like a subject' (Lacan, 1979: viii). The consequences of Saussure's distinction between the paradigmatic and syntagmatic axes of substitution and combination for Lacanian psychoanalysis are clearer if we look at the way they correspond to the account given by Jakobson.

Jakobson, metaphor and metonymy

Lacan draws on Jakobson's (1975) work on aphasias to connect Saussure with psychoanalysis. Jakobson's clinical description of the two dimensions of language is slightly different from Saussure's, but for Lacan's purposes they correspond well enough, with the paradigmatic dimension appearing in Jakobson's account as the 'axis of selection' and the syntagmatic dimension as the 'axis of combination'.

In the axis of selection, which we can think of as a vertical axis, we may make items of a similar type stand in for any particular item, and Jakobson was interested in the way one category of aphasics suffer from a 'similarity disorder' in which they seem unable to do this. These aphasics are unable to think of alternative items from this axis, and Jakobson demonstrates that their speech is closely tied to context as a consequence of this; he gives the example of a patient failing to comment on the name of an object (a pencil) in an examiner's hand (which would be to select a term for it) but instead continuing a description of it (by saying, for example, 'to write'). The speech of the patient is, then, 'merely reactive: he easily carries on conversation, but has difficulties in starting a dialogue' (Jakobson, 1975: 77). One crucial expression of this patient's difficulty is that they have lost the ability to use metaphor, for metaphor works along the axis of selection.

In the axis of combination, on the other hand, we are able to fit together terms in a sequence (and this will usually be a grammatical sequence) to bring about different effects. We can think of this axis as being a horizontal axis, and here items are connected with one another by relations of contiguity, for it is as if they are next to each other along that dimension. The second group of aphasics that Jakobson describes had lost the ability to put items together in a meaningful way, suffering what he termed a 'continuity disorder'. The style of speech for this group was 'telegraphic', and 'The less a word depends grammatically on the context, the stronger is its tenacity in the speech of aphasics with a contiguity disorder' (ibid.: 86). This makes it difficult, then, for such patients to understand the relationship between words that usually exist in combination, and they are grasped only as distinct, separate words (for example, 'thanks', 'giving', and 'Thanksgiving'). One crucial expression of their difficulty is that they have lost the ability to use metonymy, for metonymy works along the axis of combination.

Lacan then connects Jakobson's elaboration of these vertical and horizontal dimensions to Freud's (1900) account of dreaming. In dreams, two key aspects of the dream-work (aside from 'considerations of representability' and 'secondary revision') are 'condensation' and 'displacement'. Lacan argues that condensation, as the pressing together of different ideas in one image, is a process of metaphor. Metaphor condenses ideas that cannot be expressed in language, and the extra twist that Lacan now adds is to assert that repression is a metaphorical process in which a signifier has slid under other signifiers, 'that fixes in a symptom the signification inaccessible to the conscious subject in which the symptom may be resolved – a symptom being a metaphor in which flesh or function is taken as a signifying element' (Lacan, 1977: 166). As a counterpart to this, Lacan argues that displacement, as the substitution of one term for another, is accomplished by a process of metonymy. As the unconscious is formed, metonymy fixes on and then slides away from an experience of the first ideal love object as something 'next to' that which was desired, so that we are 'eternally stretching forth towards the *desire for something else* – of metonymy' (ibid.: 167). While repression and symptomatology are seen as forms of metaphor, then, desire is a form of metonymy: 'the symptom *is* a metaphor whether one likes it or not, as desire *is* a metonymy' (ibid.: 175). Structuralism provides a language for Lacan to 'return to Freud', then, and a sense of unconscious processes as rooted in the symbolic, but to understand how Lacan's subject emerges in relation to the unconscious as 'the discourse of the Other', we must turn to phenomenology.

Lacan's subject

The category of the 'subject' is not the same as the 'self' or the 'ego', and is not, in Lacanian psychoanalysis, a single discrete entity. Lacan does not describe what the subject *is*, then, but draws on a number of traditions to show aspects of its nature and the way it is expressed in language, memory and attempts to touch the real. Lacan develops an interpretation of the subject in Freud's account, and draws upon phenomenology as an alternative tradition, and also upon Surrealist notions.

Freud's subject

The following passage occurs in *The Interpretation of Dreams*:

> The dream thoughts to which we are led by interpretation cannot, from the nature of things, have any definite endings; they are bound to branch out in every direction into the intricate network of our world of thought. It is at some point where this meshwork is particularly close that the dream-wish grows up, like a mushroom out of a mycelium.
>
> (Freud, 1900: 672)

Freud argues that the tangle of associations cannot be traced through to arrive at a definitive interpretation, and even the place of the dreamer, as a kind of imaginary centre of the dream, is put into question. Freud (ibid.: 662) also argues that 'whatever interrupts the progress of analytic work is a resistance', but although something is resisting, Freud is not proposing that this something which does not understand and does not want to understand is a conscious or deliberate agent. For Lacan too, it would be a mistake to imagine that the unconscious contains a kind of homunculus with its own intentions. Rather, he is concerned with the way the 'subject' is something split between the language they must speak and the repressed unconscious meanings that evade them.

The splitting starts with the separation that occurs when the infant conceives of itself as something separate from the mother but as powerfully connected to, identified with that first love object. Even this first sense of oneself as something separate is set against a background of fragmentation and helplessness (as we will see when we look at the mirror-phase in Chapter 8). However, this splitting is compounded further by the entry into the symbolic order, and even the sense of subjectivity which runs through the mycelium of signifiers in the unconscious will fail to escape by finding shape in the insufficient signifier 'I': 'I think where I am not, therefore I am where I do not think. Words that render sensible to an ear properly attuned with what elusive ambiguity the ring of meaning flees from our grasp along the verbal thread' (Lacan, 1977: 166).

Lacan often takes pains not to talk about *what* might be repressed and split and trying to find voice as if it were a thing, and uses terms like 'being there' or 'want-to-be' to evoke something of the processual nature of what it is to 'be' a human being. At some points, though, the hope that a 'truth' of the subject may be expressed rings through, as in his striking reworking of Freud's (1933a: 112) description of the aims of psychoanalysis as 'Where id was, there ego shall be. It is the work of culture – not unlike the draining of the Zuider Zee'. The image of the draining of the Zuider Zee sends us along the wrong track, to the idea that the realm of the civilized ego should be extended to supplant the territory of the uncivilized id. Part of the problem here is the *Standard Edition* translation into English, which can be corrected to an extent by noting that 'id' translates *Es* as the German for 'it' and that 'ego' translates *Ich* as German for 'I'. Lacan (1977: 128) also points out that 'Freud did not say "*das Es*", nor "*das Ich*", as was his custom when designating the agencies', and claims that Freud in any case used these designators 'in order to maintain this fundamental distinction between the true subject of the unconscious and the ego as constituted in its nucleus by a series of alienating identifications' (ibid.). We are thus led to a correct translation, which would be 'Where it was, there I shall be', and Lacan then pushes this a step further to argue that the aim of psychoanalysis is not to replace 'it' with 'I', but to allow 'I' to emerge *from within* 'it'; 'I must come to the place where that was' (ibid.: 171).

Lacan was, then, adamantly opposed to the work of the US 'ego-psychologists' (e.g., Hartmann, 1939) who assumed that the goal of psychoanalysis was to strengthen the ego through a kind of identification with the healthy 'conflict-free' part of the analyst's ego. Lacan struggled to retrieve an account of the unconscious as something that touches and transforms every aspect of experience, and as a source of something closer to 'truth' than an ego designed to adapt to the reality principle of North American culture:

> In actual fact, this dimension of the unconscious that I am evoking *had been* forgotten, as Freud had quite clearly foreseen. The unconscious had closed itself up against his message thanks to those active practitioners of orthopaedics that the analysts of the second and third generation became, busying themselves by psychologizing analytic theory, in stitching up this gap.
>
> (Lacan, 1979: 23)

To keep the gap open, Lacan drew on phenomenology, and, to an extent, on his involvement with the Surrealists.

Phenomenology

Lacan was one of many French intellectuals who attended Alexandre Kojève's lectures on Hegel in Paris in the 1930s, and it is Kojève's (1969) version of the Hegelian dialectic of recognition and consciousness that underpins the Lacanian 'return' to Freud (Dews, 1987; Macey, 1995).

The Hegelian dialectic rests on an anthropological fairy-tale to describe

the origins of human consciousness and a reconstruction of the phenomenology of childhood as something that repeats that narrative in the
dawning awareness of each individual as they become aware of themselves and others. For Kojève, this is a never-ending, and rather more
brutal story than the one Hegel originally told (Riley, 1981). At the beginning of human history there is a battle for recognition, an attempt to gain
recognition from another in order to become conscious. Such recognition
is necessary for a human subjectivity to appear, and when we desire
another, it is their desire for us that we desire. The search for recognition
is a battle because the winner will be the one who is granted the position
of being subject of another's desire, while the other who gives that desire
will have been reduced to an object, to a means to an end. That other who
has lost the battle then, as Sartre (who also attended Kojève's lectures) puts
it, 'appears to me and he appears to himself as *non-essential*. He is the *Slave*
I am the *Master*; for him it is I who am essence' (Sartre, 1943: 237). This
Master–Slave relation is a *dialectic* because the Slave is not at all 'non-
essential', of course, for the Slave is absolutely essential to the Master's
position. As awareness of the Master's dependence on the Slave dawns on
each of them, so there is a reversal of positions; the Slave gains recognition
from the Master, and the Master who has been humbled into being a mere
provider of recognition becomes Slave.

It is possible to then read the relation with the first other in childhood
as a similar battle, but one a good deal more uncertain and unpleasant
than that described by the humanist Carl Rogers (1961), who was also
influenced by Hegel's account but saw the giving of recognition by the
parents as a necessary but benign and reciprocal process. Hegel (1807)
described the Master–Slave dialectic as arriving at a kind of synthesis in
which both parties would gain, but Kojève's presentation, which was
picked up by Lacan, saw thesis and antithesis as continuing to structure
desire in a kind of 'see-saw' from infancy to death:

> The subject's desire can only be confirmed in this relation through competition,
> through an absolute rivalry with the other, in view of the object towards which
> it is directed. And each time we get close, in a given subject, to this primitive
> alienation, the most radical aggression arises – the desire for the disappearance
> of the other in so far as he supports the subject's desire.
>
> (Lacan, 1988: 170)

We can imagine the developmental narrative the dialectic might trace.
The Master–Slave dialectic is replayed in the relation between infant and
(m)other, where the infant is an object and source of desire for the
(m)other, and so where the (m)other desires the infant's desire. The dialectic reverses when the infant becomes able to experience (the illusion of)
omnipotent control, and it becomes the recipient of the (m)other's desire,
of (what is imagined to be) undivided attention. The infant thus becomes
a *subject*, and the dialectic continually reverses back and forth in the
developing relationship between child and parent until the parent takes
the position of a child who is perhaps physically dependent on the

offspring (cf. Benjamin, 1988). Relationships between lovers can also be interpreted as a 'see-saw' of dependence and omnipotence, as the realization develops for each one in turn that the other is desirous of the desire of an other, and as the partners switch from positions of vulnerability to power in declarations of love and threats to reject, in demands for love and the fear of being rejected. Lacanian cultural analysis is then able to take this further by focusing on the 'gaze', and the experience of looking at an other (who is desired, but invested with the fantasies of desiring the viewer as subject) and being looked at (in which one is desired, but invested with fantasies which reduce one to an object) (e.g., Mulvey, 1975; Rose, 1986).

Lacan (1979) then uses this dialectic to set up distinctions between three conceptual levels. There is *need*, which is biologically-wired, instinctual, and which is satisfied by an object. There is *demand*, as a call to an other for recognition, in which the expression of needs will play a role in driving such a demand for desire. Such demands cannot be satisfied, for one never knows on what basis the demands are being met. The infant does not know, for example, if the food is provided with care or exasperation. And there is *desire*, which emerges in the gap between need and demand, where a demand is experienced even when the driving need has been subtracted. This desire is insatiable, and is metonymic in structure, as we are driven by the hopeless attempt to find the fantasized 'original' object, which never really existed as such, that which Lacan calls the 'objet-petit-a'. This interplay of need, demand and desire also provokes an impossible looping back to recreate the object in fantasy and to find the trauma that made it disappear, and here again we find the notion of the making of the past in Lacanian psychoanalysis: 'to reorder past contingencies by conferring on them the sense of necessities to come, such as they are constituted by the little freedom through which the subject makes them present' (Lacan, 1977: 48). The realization that this drive to make something real was impossible, and that the real itself was more and less than it seemed is one lesson Lacan learned from the Surrealists.

Surrealism

The Surrealists founded the journal *Littérature* in Paris in 1919, and the first issue included work by Philippe Soupault and André Breton on automatic writing:

> we did indeed observe that the mind, once freed of all critical pressures and school-bound habits, offered images and not logical propositions; and that if we adopted what the psychiatrist Pierre Janet called the practice of automatic writing, we produced texts in which we found a 'universe' as yet unexplored.
> (quoted in Roudinesco, 1990: 12)

Already, there was a deep interest in matters psychiatric and psycho-analytic in the Surrealist movement, and Freud's (1920) discussion of the death drive inspired Breton and others to investigate the links between sex, death and suicide. By the time of the 'Surrealist Manifesto' of 1924, Breton could define Surrealism as 'Pure psychic automatism, by which we propose to express the real functioning of thought, verbally, in writing, or by any other means. The dictation of thought, in the absence of any control exercised by reason and regardless of any aesthetic or moral preoccupations' (quoted in Macey, 1988: 51). Lacan was close to the Surrealists in the early 1930s, and contributed to their journals.

Lacan's closest links were with Salvador Dalí, and they discussed Dalí's 'paranoiac-critical method'. Dalí argued that paranoia was 'pseudo-hallucinatory' in that although it involved a delusional representation of reality, it was also underpinned by a systematic critical attempt to find sense. This paranoiac method is at work in his paintings (with 'Metamorphosis of Narcissus' being the most well-known example) in which, he explains,

> It is through a plainly paranoid process that it has been possible to obtain a double image, that is, the representation of an object that (without the slightest anatomical or figurative distortion) is simultaneously the representation of another object, similarly bereft of any deformation or abnormality that might reveal any arrangement.
>
> (quoted in Roudinesco, 1990: 110)

A theme that runs through Lacan's later work is that it is in the delusions of paranoia that the 'true subject' may be able to emerge, and such paranoia has its roots in narcissism, an experience of love and splitting.

Lacan made his mark with the Surrealists with his 1932 doctoral thesis on psychosis. The case discussed in the thesis was that of a thirty-eight-year-old railway clerk 'Aimée' who had tried to murder a well-known actress, was taken in for reports, released and then disappeared. Lacan was focusing on, and effectively celebrating, a favourite motif for the Surrealists in the 1930s, in which they looked for manifestations of irrational, natural truth, and attempted to uncover it in 'convulsive beauty', and this motif appears time and again in Lacan's later writing (Mitchell and Rose, 1982). Such 'convulsive beauty' was to be found in women who turned against society and murdered their employers. A series of cases hit the French newspapers at the time, and the theme of doubling of identity was an added thrill in the case of the Papin sisters: 'they fling themselves on the bodies of their victims, smashing in their faces, exposing their genitals, lacerating their thighs and buttocks, and daubing them with each other's blood. Then they wash up the instruments they used for their atrocious rites, clean themselves up and go to sleep in the same bed' (Lacan, quoted in Macey, 1988: 69).

Lacan argues that Aimée was the subject of a series of powerful women figures (the most important of which was her elder sister), and the construction of a powerful ego-ideal as a symbol of perfection led to fantasies of being like, and being controlled by, desired others. So, Lacan writes in 1932 in his doctoral thesis, 'Each of the persecutors is simply a new image, still trapped by narcissism, of the sister our patient turned into an ideal' (ibid.: 71). Lacan's diagnosis was 'self punishment paranoia', and he was later to develop the argument that splitting and doubling of the subject lies at the basis of all human experiences of self. When we desire an other's desire, we desire an other modelled on the image of our own selves (and we will see how this notion appears in Lacan's account of the mirror-phase in Chapter 8). Into the structuralist account of the organization of language and subjectivity and the phenomenological description of the dialectics of recognition and reconstruction of the past, then, Lacan stirs in Surrealist preoccupations with some true irrational and impossible reality under the surface that tries to break through in sensual, murderous and beautiful acts of defiance. Lacan's description of the Symbolic, the Subject and the Surreal resonated with avant-garde movements in the 1930s looking to base nature as a site of resistance, but we now find something close to Lacanian subjectivity fabricated in contemporary technology.

Cyberpunk subjectivity and postmodern space

Lacanian descriptions of subjectivity are sometimes seen as 'postmodern' (e.g., Finlay, 1989), but we need to locate the 'postmodern condition' and the new forms of subjectivity it provokes in material developments in the economy and technology. What truth there is in the cultural transformations that Lyotard (1979) identified lies in the economic restructuring of industry on the heels of a third post-war technological revolution in Europe and America, and in a period of 'late capitalism' (Jameson, 1984) rather than, as some 'post-Marxist' writers fervently wished, a new 'postcapitalism' (cf. Mandel, 1974). In fact, the original brief for Lyotard's study, the emergence of information technology, should still be the focus of writers wishing to locate postmodern fantasies in material conditions. The swelling of the service sector in the first world after the Second World War has been further gorged by the arrival of new technologies geared for the mass circulation of information as entertainment, including virtual reality. The spread of electronic mail in academic institutions and surreal simulations of conflict scenarios in military institutions are but two expressions of the emergence of new spaces that these economic changes have made possible. Computer science in late capitalism has now created the material conditions for subjects to move, interact and think in new varieties of space (Benedikt, 1991). Information technology has indeed given rise to an array of alternative realities that can be lived by human subjects away from the enclosed and increasingly restricted spaces in the cities of the industrialized world (Makulowich, 1993).

Cultural representations of postmodern space opened up by new technologies are widespread in science fiction, and a sizeable chunk of the population is able to experience virtual reality vicariously through film, television and novels. Any account of the appeal of such representations needs to attend to the mass circulation of psychoanalytic theory and to the preparation of subjects who will then be able to work in virtual reality.

Postmodern space is not, after all, newly born fully formed out of computer technology. As a variety of mental space, it is only able to receive subjects already schooled in the culture of machine life and alternative parallel realities. The inhabitants of this technological space are, in some senses, living in science fiction.

In science fiction we project fantasies into the future and are then caught in those fantasies both because they seem to confirm what has always been deeply true and hidden about human nature and destiny and because, we believe, we will eventually meet up with the fantasies when we arrive in the future. Science fiction rests on the rhetorical trick of anticipating the future as a range of possibilities, extensions of the present. It is temporal 'projective identification' (to return for a moment to Kleinian terminology) as scientific prophecy and the embodiment of structures of group identity in a realm which will embrace us as we must move forward in time. Science fiction is also a kind of religious belief in action, for it projects from the present into the future our subordination to a higher power, to the power of technology, and the possibility of our merging with a higher form of being, of a more intelligent civilization. The terrors of evil forces are still there too, and often far more demonic than those in the present. There is a tension between different varieties of science fiction narrative, and it is possible to see the uncertainty and lack of truth in science fiction speculation as playful, progressive and optimistic (Squire, 1991). The link between technology and subjectivity need not entail the domination of 'nature' nor operate as a sanction for war, and manifestos for 'cyborgs' have also, for example, been calls for a different socialist feminist way of thinking about the self (Haraway, 1991). Some of the most interesting symptomatic science fiction descriptions of technological subjectivity have come from the cyberpunk sub-genre. Here, the future is very close, and close enough for some writers to argue that it is a vicarious reality for a sector of contemporary high-tech junkies (Rushkoff, 1994).

Language

In William Gibson's cyberpunk novel *Neuromancer* the following characterization of cyberspace is provided by the voice-over introduction to one of the virtual reality programmes that Case, the main character, jacks into:

'Cyberspace. A consensual hallucination experienced daily by billions of legitimate operators, in every nation, by children being taught mathematical concepts. (...) A graphic representation of data abstracted from the banks of every computer in the human system. Unthinkable complexity. Lines of light ranged in the nonspace of the mind, clusters and constructions of data. Like city lights receding ...'

(Gibson, 1984: 67)

This symbolic space is already like the unconscious understood in psychoanalytic terms, and this language system invades the subject as an unconscious for them. In a later Gibson novel the main character jacks into an electronic dossier: 'It came on, again gradually, a flickering, non-linear flood of fact and sensory data, a kind of narrative conveyed in surreal jumpcuts and juxtapositions' (Gibson, 1986: 40).

Neal Stephenson's *Snow Crash* describes something similar in the 'Metaverse' as 'a fictional structure made out of code' (Stephenson, 1992: 197), and here 'people are pieces of software called avatars. They are the audiovisual bodies that people use to communicate with each other in the Metaverse' (ibid.: 33). Selves as software also appear in other accounts, such as Rudy Rucker's *Software*, where one of the characters has to come to terms with this symbolically mediated subjectivity:

> Cobb Anderson's brain had been dissected, but the software that made up his mind had been preserved. The idea of 'self' is, after all, just another idea, a symbol in the software. Cobb felt like *himself* as much as ever. And, as much as ever, Cobb wanted his self to continue to exist on hardware.
>
> (Rucker, 1982: 149)

In Jeff Noon's *Vurt*, the symbolic is a site of identity and sensuality and pain which penetrates and forms the subject, as Des and Scribble discover: ' "You have come for knowledge," the figure said. "There will be pleasure. Because knowledge is sexy. There will also be pain. Because knowledge is torture"...' (1993: 170). Language, in these accounts is no mere resource for the subject to speak, and there is a sense of the very language system that gives us a sense of self twisting around and sabotaging our attempt to make sense or understand ourselves.

Memory

In Gibson's writing there are also psychoanalytic notions of the past in relation to others, and in the ways in which significant others recreate a form of reality for the subject:

> The intimacy of the thing was hideous. He fought down waves of raw transference, bringing all his will to bear on crushing a feeling that was akin to love, the obsessive tenderness a watcher comes to feel for the subject of prolonged surveillance.
>
> (Gibson, 1986: 41)

Noon's future takes virtual reality as a technological form and uses that as a template to describe the way forms of self are destroyed and recreated at different levels of the symbolic through different coloured chemical feathers. Some feathers remake the past into something beautiful: 'Curious Yellow is the exact opposite. It makes the past into a nightmare, and then strands you there, with no hope of release' (Noon, 1993: 209).

Pat Cadigan's *Fools* revolves around Marva, a method actress who must trace the internal structure of a series of memories that now inhabit her and that she must perform as if they were real. Marva oscillates between different versions of truth and the past, and the novel lurches from one kind of subjectivity to another as different forms of memory are activated. Here, Marva realizes, 'The future was set long before I came into existence, it was only my past that changed' (Cadigan, 1992: 144). One of the persistent and troubling things about memory is its attempt to attach itself to something that really happened:

> Sometimes you eat a bad memory somewhere that gives you the being-used creeps. You find yourself taking a little daytrip to the scene of somebody else's crime all because you've got the memory of what happened and where. Like the memory knows somehow it's in the wrong head and it wants to get back to where it started.
>
> (Cadigan, 1992: 103–104)

Here is a memory as a process that will always bewitch and betray us. Rather than simply recalling events from the past, these representations inhabit us and frame what we know. Memory retroactively transforms who we imagine we were and leads into a future that then reshapes what was.

Reality

There is also a powerful anxiety about the real in cyberpunk writing. In *Neuromancer*, one of the characters has to be rebuilt as an effective agent in a Toulon psychiatric institution: 'Eating, excreting, and masturbating were the best he could manage. But the underlying structure of obsessions was there' (Gibson, 1984: 146). The real of the body is referred to as the 'meat', but even here there is an uncertainty about whether that real is only a delusion. Later in the novel, Case finds his girlfriend from the past, whom he knows is dead, and finds a 'place':

> It belonged, he knew – he remembered – as she pulled him down, to the meat, the flesh the cowboys mocked. It was a vast thing, beyond knowing, a sea of information coded in spiral and pheromone, infinite intricacy that only the body, its strong bland way, could ever read.
>
> (Gibson, 1984: 285)

Even here, though, it turns out Linda is a figure in the programme, a product of the symbolic, and only functions as an element of the real in so far as Case invests her with meaning as the real, as meat.

In some cyberpunk, the real is a kind of fantasized 'meat' which must be escaped:

> Real life seems so physical these days; so very *meaty*. And the one subject that transfixes you, more than any other? How can I get higher? How can I get out of this hole? How can I get to live like the Cat? In other words; let me get my hands on some KNOWLEDGE FEATHERS.
>
> (Noon, 1993: 117)

In Stephenson's (1992) description of the Metaverse, which 1930s Surrealists would have appreciated, reality is a place that lures but cannot be reached, and life in the Metaverse is as real for

> the liberal sprinkling of black-and-white people – persons who are accessing the Metaverse through cheap public terminals, and who are rendered in jerky,

grainy black and white. A lot of these are run-of-the-mill psycho fans, devoted to the fantasy of stabbing some particular actress to death.

(Noon, 1993: 38)

Rather than being a stable reference point, 'reality' in this science fiction sub-genre is as uncertain as any other anchor. Even when more extreme characterizations of the real – often as meat – appear in this writing, they are still quickly undercut and dissolve into software.

Cyberpunk writing pushes us to the edge of a new 'cyberpsychology', and there are clearly specifications for subjectivity in cyberpunk that are very close to what we find in Lacanian writing. It is as if this postmodern mutation of psychoanalytic discourse now threads its way through the technological spaces that are the material supports for the postmodern condition in sectors of contemporary culture. Cyberpunk has a mass audience, and so it also locks into fantasies of language, memory and reality that are already fairly widespread among people who may never have surfed the net. We can throw that audience net even wider, though, if we look at some of the science fiction representations of subjectivity in film, and so the next section of this chapter turns to an analysis of the 1990 film *Total Recall* (Verhoeven, 1990), which was inspired by a short story written twenty-five years earlier by Philip K. Dick. We will find in Dick's writing, and then in the film, some disturbing postmodern and Lacanian discursive complexes which hold an audience and produce for it a distinct range of subject positions.

Virtual recall

Philip K. Dick's stories and novels revolve around the paranoiac and postmodern questions 'What is real, and whose reality is it?' (Freedman, 1984). In *Martian Time-Slip* (1964), for example, which is set on Mars in 1994, different characters slip into schizophrenic confusions in which it is unclear whose delusion is structuring the delusions of the others. The account in this book, as with many of Dick's others, is deliberately and explicitly informed by the writings of the existentialist analyst Ludwig Binswanger, and Dick was to succumb to psychotic episodes and periods on heavy medication eventually himself. In *Ubik* (1969), the narrative revolves around the race to find the mysterious commodity that will arrest the reversal of time, but the main character does not know if he is being led by someone who is in cryogenic half death, or whether he has been killed already and is merely receiving orders from one who survived. *Ubik*, and Dick, has been linked to the postmodern predicament (Hebdige, 1986) in which reality is revealed to be fantasy, and fantasy is the only reality. Attempts to link *Ubik* more closely with a critique of commodification came to naught when French Marxist literary critics visited Dick in 1974 and he promptly reported them to the FBI (Sutin, 1989).

Dick's work did not sit easily with the technological optimism of the dominant ideology in the United States in the 1960s and 1970s, and it is understandable in hindsight that Asimov's science fiction vision of new worlds in space, in which robots would assist human beings, for example, should be more popular than Dick's uncertainty about whose vision this would serve. The transformation in cultural climate in twenty-five years, and the changing reception and readings of Dick's work, is symptomatic of a disillusionment with the notion of progress *and* the attempt to cover over that disillusionment to make it acceptable. What Dick saw as a psychotic nightmare in which reality dissolved is now, in the supposed postmodern condition, a celebrated uncertainty in which anxieties about what will happen to the real are more carefully managed and kept at bay. The entry into virtual reality requires this shift, for the subject must be able both to leave usual taken-for-granted reference points behind and to return to them when it is time to leave the terminal. There is always a certain level of anxiety which keeps the subject attached to an image of the real as a site from which they have flown as they move along the channels of cyberspace.

We can remember it for you wholesale

There are some differences between the short story 'We can remember it for you wholesale' (Dick, 1966a) and the film *Total Recall* (Verhoeven, 1990) which are symptomatic both of 1960s-style modernity and of the speed with which postmodern notions have been absorbed by the mass media. Anxieties about the nature of 'the real' which structure both the story and the book are turned in slightly different directions. For this reason it is instructive to compare Dick's short story, originally published in the pulp magazine *Science Fiction & Fantasy* in 1966, with the film version that hit a mass audience 1990.

In 'We can remember it for you wholesale' (Dick, 1966a), the main character, Douglas Quail, goes to 'Rekal Incorporated' to have an 'extra-factual memory implant' (ibid.: 208) which would substitute for a holiday on Mars, a craving which he could not afford. The implant would provide as real a memory as would an actual trip, but it is cheaper, and Quail opts for the 'secret agent' scenario, in which he would have been sent there on an assignment. In the course of implanting the memory, Rekal discover that Quail does actually already have such a memory, and, rather than risk provoking a 'psychotic interlude' (ibid.: 212) by grafting false memories over the real ones and setting up a confusion between the two, they send him home without the implant. Unfortunately, Interplan police, for whom Quail had really worked as an assassin on Mars, find out that the deep real memory of the mission has now surfaced. There is one solution, short of killing Quail, to stop his desire for Mars returning him to the memory, and that is to implant another memory which would be 'more vital than standard memories' (ibid.: 222), something that would address a deeper 'absolute, ultimate fantasy wish' and then fulfil that wish 'in vicarious surrogate retrospection' (ibid.: 223). Only by going back beyond the desire to go to Mars to another earlier desire would the desire to go to Mars (which would then recall the secret agent mission and expose Interplan again) be circumvented. A psychiatrist helps Quail arrive at a 'grotesque dream' (ibid.: 223) of childhood in which small alien life-forms are saved by Quail, and, in return, they promise not to invade Earth while Quail is alive. Quail's fantasy, then, is that by merely existing he keeps the rest of the world safe, and the psychiatrist explains to him that 'this is bedrock in your psyche; this is a life-long childhood fantasy' (ibid.: 224). Rekal start implanting this memory, to make it 'real', but discover, again, that Quail does actually already have such a memory ...

In some ways, this is standard *Twilight Zone* stuff, and what the victim remembers as their reality is now more powerful than those in power could ever have dreaded when they tried to suppress it. Reality itself dissolves and reforms around the one main character at the moment that authority tries to assert itself as part of reality. In this 1960s story, then, the denouement is more modern than postmodern. We discover what the truth of Quail's desire is, what truth it represents, what forces of ideological mystification benefited, and how they will lose when the truth is out. The confusion about the nature of memory and reality is anchored in the connection that the hero is able to make with a particular narrative (in this case, the narrative of deferred alien invasion).

Total Recall

The film *Total Recall* (Verhoeven, 1990) manages this confusion of identity and memory in a different way. Now, the main character, here called 'Quaid' (played by Arnold Schwarzenegger), who is haunted by the desire to go to Mars, is placed at Rekal corporation in a machine, the 'implant chair' (as opposed to the 'hygienic table' of the 1960s version), to insert the vacation-as-a-secret-agent memory package. In this version, part of Quaid's Mars fantasy revolves around a woman, and the eventual resolution of the narrative is where he is able to return to her as he knew her, when he was the secret agent.

The overall narrative of *Total Recall* helps us to forget the question for Quaid as to which memory is correct, but the hinge point between different realities raises and smooths over an anxiety about the past, the nature of the symbolic order and the place of the Real in characteristically postmodern terms. There is a scene roughly half-way through the film where Quaid has managed to travel to Mars to try to make sense of the confusion that events at Rekal have provoked, and to find out what the secret agent mission was. At this point in the narrative we have already seen Quaid leave Rekal after they discovered that the real memory is already in place exactly where they had intended to implant the false memory. A doctor from Rekal enters Quaid's hotel room and tells him that he, Quaid, is still in the implant chair at Rekal on Earth, and that he must recognize that so that he can be brought out into reality. Quaid's wife then enters the room and appeals to her husband to return.

Wife: I want you to come back to me.
Quaid: Bullshit!
Doctor: What's bullshit Mr Quaid? That you're having a paranoid episode triggered by acute neurochemical trauma, or that you're really an invincible secret agent from Mars who's the victim of an interplanetary conspiracy to make you think he's a lowly construction worker. Stop punishing yourself Doug. You're a fine upstanding man whose [sic] got a beautiful wife who loves you.
Wife: I do.
Doctor: Your whole life is ahead of you, but you've got to want to return to reality.
Quaid: Let's assume I do, then what?
Doctor: Swallow this.
        (He holds up a small red pill.)
Quaid: What is it?
Doctor: It's a symbol, of your desire to return to reality. Inside your dream you'll fall asleep.
Quaid: Alright, let's say you're telling the truth and it's all a dream, then I could pull this trigger and it won't matter.
Wife: Doug, don't.
Doctor: It won't make the slightest difference to me Doug, but the consequences to you would be devastating. In your mind I'll be dead, and with no one to guide you out you'll be stuck in permanent psychosis.

Now Quaid puts the pill in his mouth while he continues holding the gun to the doctor's head. He watches the doctor, and notices a bead of sweat trickle down his face. He spits out the pill, and kills the doctor and the wife. Now the film is on course again, reality is back on track, and we know Quaid is 'really' on Mars.

We can track the influence of Lacanian psychoanalytic discourse in this text by organizing the reading around discursive complexes. There is a concern with a new higher order of meaning that operates as a powerful enclosed symbolic system, with the past as something that is reconstructed, and with a reality that lies outside as something intangible but crucial to the way subjectivity is worked.

THE SYMBOLIC   Lacan's 'return to Freud' has language, organized in the symbolic order, constituting the unconscious at the very moment the infant starts to speak. The entry into the symbolic splits the child between conscious and unconscious, and the realm of the imaginary unified image produced in the mirror-stage is both confirmed and sabotaged by language as it opens up a variety of different subject positions.

In the extract from *Total Recall*, Quaid is invited to return to the symbolic order, but that 'return' is mediated through a 'symbol', the pill that the doctor offers. And the use of the symbol will not work alone, for it must be driven by desire, here a 'desire to return to reality'. Quaid must 'want to return to reality', and his desire is further provoked by the desire of another. In Lacanian terms, desire is always the desire of another, and in this case the 'beautiful wife' beckons from the symbolic order that structures the 'paranoid' fantasy Quaid is trapped in; she has already declared that she wants him to 'come back' to her, and she affirms that love, in a replication of words from the marriage vow, one of the anchoring points of heterosexual desire in the symbolic, when the doctor says she loves Quaid, with 'I do'. It is telling that the choice that Quaid must make is framed by continued existence *in the dream*. If he refuses to take the pill, he will remain in the dream. He will not immediately break out of the delusion that he is on Mars, 'the victim of an interplanetary conspiracy', if he swallows the pill, but will fall asleep in the dream. Dreaming is not directly counterposed to reality, then, but inhabited by it. It is as if Quaid's unconscious life is itself structured by the symbolic order, and he can enter the symbolic or indulge in a futile flight from it, in 'permanent psychosis', but not escape it with any form of rationality or self remaining intact.

The relationship between dreaming and 'reality' is reversed in Lacanian psychoanalysis. The dreamer finds in the dream the revelation of a truth, the truth of the subject that is perpetually obscured by the vagaries of the reality principle, which is now understood as a fake principle wholly dependent upon the symbolic order. The subject in relation to the symbolic in this theoretical framework is also close to some of the most paranoiac writing of Dick. In *The Game Players of Titan* (Dick, 1963), for example, it is only quite late in the book that it is revealed that the game the Bindmen play for cities and mates on Earth is but a mirror of the bigger game the vugs from Titan are playing to consolidate their invasion. The members of the Pretty Blue Fox team start by losing bits of California at the first most immediate level of this symbolic game matrix, but they then have to enter a more wide-ranging cosmic symbolic order, which structures the different perceptions of the Titanians and the Terrans, to play for the Earth. There is a progressive move, then, from one lower level to a higher level, and the latter structures the former.

DEFERRED ACTION   Just as the symbolic organizes the first relationship with the mother, and the mirroring that makes imaginary (mis)recognition of the self as single and undivided self possible, so it produces a version of 'history' for the subject. Psychoanalysis with a significant other is then conducted within a transferential relationship in which the subject's past is recreated as something that 'was to have been', something that is grasped at the moment it is formed as a reality for them.

What is at stake in Quaid's choice between which story to believe when he is confronted by the doctor from Rekal is what *position* he will take in relation to different narratives of the past. In one scenario, which the doctor lays out, the first trauma is the 'neurochemical' one which triggered the 'paranoid episode'. If Quaid does not recognize that he is 'a lowly construction worker' with 'a whole life' ahead of him, and shoots the doctor, this second trauma will be 'devastating'. What has been a 'paranoid episode' will become 'permanent psychosis'. The second trauma will then *reconstitute* the first trauma as the primary originary cause of Quaid's flight from reality, and even actions which take place in fantasy (which 'won't make the slightest difference' to the doctor) will trigger disaster. In the second scenario, which Quaid chooses, the second trauma, which is this scene in which reality is thrown into question when he shoots the doctor, confirms the first trauma, which is the buried memory of the assassination mission on Mars, as the efficient cause of the train of events. Quaid's action in each scenario thus *recreates* the past, and finds in that recreated past the *cause* of the present state of affairs.

The return of the repressed actual memory, activated by Quaid's desire to return to the scene, is in line with Lacan's (1977: 86) description of analysis as provoking the 'future anterior of what I shall have been for what I am in the process of becoming'. Even in the original story, this structure of deferred action plays itself out in Quail's visit to Rekal, 'which sooner or later had to happen' (Dick, 1966a: 206), but which then constitutes that which must happen again, and again, as a consequence of the visit. *Counter-Clock World* (Dick, 1967) is a more disturbing version of the same process, and those subject to the 'Hobart Phase', in which time is reversed and the life journey is from death back to birth, anxiously and persistently erase what they know and the traces of what they anticipate knowing along the way.

THE REAL   The Lacanian argument that the real 'is the opposite of the possible' (Lacan, 1973: 167) is structured into the film with the representation of some impossible and traumatic anchoring point around which conscious and unconscious fantasy revolves. The traumatic 'thing' is that which appears to resist symbolization, but which structures the symbolic order.

It is no easy matter for Quaid to return to 'reality', for what is fantasy and what is real is jumbled and indeterminate. Various anchor points are identified – 'neurochemical trauma', the 'beautiful wife' – for Quaid to define himself against. The most 'real' thing that could pull Quaid back, however, is itself only a senseless artefact constructed within the fantasy. The pill is 'a symbol' of a 'desire to return to reality', but it can only work as a function of the symbolic, not as something that lies completely outside it. Different forms of fantasy, all of which are structured by the symbolic order, invade the conscious and unconscious life of the subject. In this case, swallowing the pill will produce an effect 'inside the dream', but it too is structured by the very symbolic system to which the subject is being invited to return. What appears to be a hard bedrock reality, which is outside and resistant to language, is only, in this case, effective in so far as the subject invests it with meaning.

Although Quaid sees his wife and the doctor with his own eyes, he still finds it difficult to distinguish between what is real and what is illusory. It is symptomatic of the recuperation of postmodern themes within modern film that it is eventually *sight* that leads Quaid to the truth. He sees the doctor sweat, and concludes that if he is so afraid, then shooting him *will* make a 'difference'. Quaid makes a rush for the reality he takes to be true. Again, then, the film manages the anxieties about reality that postmodernism provokes. This representation of postmodern anxiety about the nature of reality is finally anchored by a fantasy of direct and unmediated observation of the real. Virtual reality, then, is held in check by real vision even in a science fiction text that threw notions of reality into question. This reality will work for the time being, but it will not provide the security that the subject searches for. The film fudges this uncertainty and comforts the audience, but if someone in the audience were tempted to turn to Dick to find out more after seeing the film, they would find that reality disturbed again.

In Dick's *Now Wait for Last Year*, for example, the Real becomes an impossible frightening traumatic thing outside the symbolic, but pressing into it, into the life-world of the subject:

> the impenetrability of even the smallest objects around her now seemed almost infinite; she sat rigidly, unable to move, incapable of thrusting her great body into any new relationship with the crushingly heavy objects that surrounded her and seemed to be pressing nearer and nearer. . . . The objects had lost their heritage of the familiar; by degrees they became cold, remote, and – hostile. Into the vacuum left by the decline in her relatedness to them the things surrounding her achieved their original isolation from the taming forces which normally emanated from the human mind; they became raw, abrupt, with jagged edges capable of cutting, gashing, inflicting fatal wounds.

> (Dick, 1966b: 73–74)

Representations of postmodern space and subjectivity

This exploration of the collective fantasies of postmodern space has focused mainly on the writings of North Americans who have absorbed psychoanalytic categories from their culture and reworked them, unwittingly or not, in accounts of emerging technologies of the mind and the futures those technologies hold open. Some North Americans, Western Europeans and Japanese do already live in this postmodern space, and elements of the comprador techno-intelligentsia of the Third World have been recruited into it. For much of the audience of *Total Recall*, however, this space exists only as a fantasy, and these science fiction writers were only anticipating something they were almost touching but not yet directly experiencing. Characters in Philip K. Dick's novels, for example, still use carbon paper when they write letters, and William Gibson used a manual typewriter to write his earliest cyberpunk novels, with his knowledge of word-processing, let alone email and the internet, gained second-hand from friends. The issue here, then, is not so much how far these forms of subjectivity are actually hosted by cyberspace – whether a quasi-Lacanian 'cyberpsychology' is constructed for the inhabitants of the net – as how this version of psychoanalytic discourse circulates in representations of cyberspace as a place we could escape to, and how this psychoanalytic discourse locks us into certain kinds of subject positions as we hope to escape mundane modern life. Lacanian postmodern fragmentation operates as a romantic alternative to capitalist society, and we will see how this plays itself out in the next chapter in attempts to develop new free communities of contract against economic exploitation and alienation.

8

Mirroring, Imagining and Escaping the Local Economy

> Where do correct ideas come from? Do they drop from the skies? No. Are they innate in the mind? No. They come from social practice, and from it alone. They come from three kinds of social practice, the struggle for production, the class struggle and scientific experiment.
>
> Mao TseTung ([1963]1971: 502) Where do correct ideas come from?
> *Selected readings from the works of Mao TseTung*

Psychoanalysis and politics have always been interlinked in some way, even when analysts and activists have done their best to keep them apart. Descriptions of psychodynamic processes often turn into prescriptions for what is normal, and so psychoanalysis has often been seen as a liability for those concerned with political change. Lacanian psychoanalysis became overtly interweaved with radical politics, however, in France in the 1960s. During the events of May 1968, for example, a manifesto supporting the student protests was signed by seventy psychoanalysts, and Lacanian analysts played an active role in the events. Already, in 1963, the Communist Party philosopher Louis Althusser had invited Lacan to bring his seminars to the École Normale, and in 1968 Lacan was told to leave because of the disruptive influence he was thought to be having on the students (Turkle, 1992). Althusser used Lacan's work to develop an account of the grip of ideology on subjects of the 'Ideological State Apparatuses', and this work impelled many Communist Party youth further to the left, mainly toward Maoism. Lacan and Mao were seen by some, such as Jacques-Alain Miller and those around the journal *Tel Quel*, as both having broken from orthodoxy, from old Freudianism and Marxism. Julia Kristeva, who developed an internal critique of psychoanalysis to radicalize its accounts of language and subjectivity, was one of those involved with *Tel Quel*. This chapter reviews the way Althusser and Kristeva tried to understand the formation of the individual subject, the way that subject was locked into ideology and the way it might resist.

The connections between Lacanian and Maoist currents ended badly, with some of the most prominent of the intellectual activists in the so-called *Nouvelle Philosophie* in the late 1970s utilizing the most reactionary aspects of Lacan's work, concluding, as Lacan himself had always insisted, that revolutionary hopes were always an expression of psychopathology:

> If the subject is irreducible to the signifier, is at the same time dependent on the signifier, there can be no subject beyond or outside language. The most that can

be hoped for is that, through analysis, the subject can be brought to a tragic acceptance of its own alienation, and of the ultimate inaccessibility of truth.

(Dews, 1980: 8)

There has been a two-way effect of this fateful linking of psychoanalysis and politics among French intellectuals through the 1980s; with political theorists using Lacan to justify their rapid shift to the far right, and the authoritarianism of Communist Party and Maoist politics feeding into groups in the Freudian Field:

> One should acknowledge openly what many a critique of the alleged 'totalitar-
> ian', 'Stalinist' nature of the Lacanian communities makes a big deal of by
> allusion: yes the 'spirit', the structuring principle, which expressed itself dis-
> tortedly in the Stalinist Party, found its proper form in the Lacanian community
> of analysts.

(Žižek, 1994: 171)

The attempt by some writers to make a link between psychoanalysis and the left and feminism in France, and disappointment at their abject failure, mark the trajectory of Althusser's and Kristeva's readings of Lacan. What they have left, though, are accounts of the way capitalism is structured around a symbolic order which calls its subjects into line and the way in which those who try to escape the capitalist order often reproduce the very same ideological structures. This is not to say that there are no elements of positive transformation in these escape attempts, and in the final section of this chapter I will show how these accounts operate as conceptual frameworks for understanding the predicament of those involved in Local Exchange Trading Systems (LETS) trying to find an alternative to the capitalist economic order. Lacan's and Kristeva's different descriptions of the relationship between the symbolic order structured in the modern world by capitalism provide powerful lenses through which we may view LETS because these kinds of descriptions are already present *in capitalist culture* as different overlapping discursive resources which those who want to challenge that culture must draw upon. But first, more on Lacan.

The mirror and the matrix

Lacanian writing on language revolves around a preoccupation with the way language of all kinds organized in the symbolic order not only produces need, demand and desire, and the individual's sense of themselves as a rational unitary subject, but also continually and necessarily *misrepresents* those things. That representation and misrepresentation, however, is not confined to language. There are processes of recognition and misrecognition of the self and others which occur in the imaginary, and which lay down a matrix for the symbolic 'I' to appear. The foundation for this matrix is, according to Lacan (1977), laid down in the mirror-phase. It is in the mirror-phase that the subject develops the rudiments of an 'ego', and it is then prepared for its immersion not only in language but also, according to Althusser, in *ideology*. A psychoanalytic understanding of the construction of human subjectivity in the mirror-phase is also, then, necessary for our understanding of how we become subject to images in the symbolic order, subject to ideology and the Law of the father through processes of 'interpellation'.

Observing the mirror-phase

In his account of the mirror-phase, which was first presented in 1936, Lacan sets out the third of the components of his theoretical system identified by Miller (J.-A. 1985), but this component (unlike structuralism and the theory of the subject discussed in Chapter 7) is supposed to rest on empirical observational evidence. There are three kinds of empirical data cited by Lacan. The first is work by Lorenz and Tinbergen on imprinting, on ethological studies which demonstrate the importance of the primary care-giver as first object for the new-born animal, and to this extent Lacan is following Freud in grounding his description of human experience in evolution. The second is the phenomenon of 'transitivism', discussed in the work of Bühler (1930), in which children of about eighteen months old mimic, reproduce and so seem to experience with the same intensity the emotions of others. Here are acts of intense identification which Lacan will see as a fundamental mechanism for the formation of the ego. The third kind of data concerns observations of children in front of mirrors, actual mirrors which are fascinating to the child. Lacan noticed that these mirror images hold a continual fascination for the child, and that there is a qualitative difference between this fascination and the novelty and then boredom which other primates show in front of a mirror. On this basis he formulated his description of the mirror-phase.

The pre-mirror-phase

The mirror-phase is such a dramatic turning-point for the human infant because of what it has experienced up until then. The processes identified in the 'pre-mirror-phase' correspond roughly to the level of the real in Lacanian theory, though that experience of the real is still, of course, always already mediated. Up until about six months old the infant experiences its body as fragmented, as a collection of uncoordinated parts and experiences, images and fantasies of those parts. There is little distinction between what is in the infant and what is outside, and little sense of what the relationship is between movements initiated by the motor system that affect the body, and movements brought about by the care-givers. There is no inside and no outside, and so the infant is, as Freud insisted, *helpless*. The human infant is marked, Lacan points out, by the 'prematurity' of its birth.

The infant is an *it*, for although it has a biological sex, it has no gender. It has had no opportunity to internalize an image of what it is as a distinct being and so no sense of sexual difference, of male and female varieties of social being. It is also, in Freud's words, 'polymorphously perverse', and the drives have aims but no fixed objects. Although there are objects of some kind, these are shifting fantasized bits of the body and frozen, eroticized movements and stimuli. There are many sources for the drives around the infant's body which will then, as it develops an awareness of inside and outside, become located at the margins, at the borders between inside and outside. That physical boundary between body-subject and what it is not will then be eroticized as a marker of sexual differentiation and of contact with others. The lack of boundary between inside and outside means that the infant *becomes* what it experiences and fantasizes, and the fragmented experiences it seizes upon become represented as part of, and wholly identified with the infant. The necessary, immediate and direct connection between the drive and an experience of bits of the body makes a solely biological conception of the instincts in human beings impossible. The 'drives' must be, as Freud argued, strange compound phenomena at the border of the physiological and the psychical.

For Lacan, there are three consequences of this direct connection between the drive and experience. The first is that there are specific experiences which become part of the fantasized, and later unconscious, drives. Lacan describes these as mental representations of castration, mutilation, dismemberment, dislocation, evisceration, devouring and bursting out of the body. We can note here links with violent images in Surrealist painting and also connections with destructive fantasies attributed to young infants by Melanie Klein – whose work Lacan promised to translate and might have done, had he not lost the manuscript (Macey, 1988). Secondly, there is a confusion between the real body of the infant and different fantasized experiences of it. The parts of the body can only be understood by way of their *difference* from other parts and so they become part of a rudimentary signifying system. The infant is unable to conceptualize what the experiences mean though, and they are not, then, 'full signs'. Instead, they are what Lacan calls 'letters', abstract disconnected signifiers of the body. These little letters only signify desire, and we should note here the way in which, even before language, even before the development of the ego, desire is necessarily mediated. The third consequence of the direct connection between drive and experience is that parts of the body which are identified as pleasurable or 'desirable' do not only include parts of the physical body (the organs or erogenous zones). The objects of desire held by the little letters include the eye, which Freud (1905a) had already included in his list of erotogenic zones, objects of the gaze and the voice of care-givers. These are turned into signifiers of desire, and so there will always be parts, and not necessarily 'fetishes' in a clinical sense, that remain sexually stimulating to the subject in later life.

The mirror-phase

The infant breaks out of this enclosed, incomprehensible universe of experience between six and eighteen months of age during the 'mirror-phase' and it then enters the level of the imaginary. It recognizes its image in a mirror as an image of itself, as an image of its body which will become the basis of its representation of self, the 'ego', and it does this through identifying with a *Gestalt* of its own body, as a 'whole form', but this form is only an image, an illusion which does not correspond to what it really is. The 'ego' that is built up out of this image 'represents' the subject to itself in a peculiar way, and Lacan is concerned with the way this representation is a *mis-representation*. The ego, then, is built up out of a mis-representation, a mis-recognition of itself. At the same time as the infant identifies with a *Gestalt* of its own body, it identifies with the mother. That is, it is able to make sense of (mis-recognize) the mother as a whole being (and not only as a collection of disconnected fantasized parts), as something like itself.

The infant, therefore, only experiences the mirror-phase as a relationship to others in which the mother is related to through an image, understood as if it were that mirror-image *Gestalt* of the infant's self. What is desired about the mother object, then, is that it is an idealized image of the 'self' which is 'projected' out. Desire is, therefore, among other things, about the fantasy of finding images of the self in others, others like one's self, and so *narcissism* is both a necessary stage in the production of self-identity and a lingering force in the production of later relationships. The mother reinforces the *Gestalt* through continuous care, and the disruption of this continuously present image releases the fantasies of fragmentation which have been pushed away by the formation of this relatively secure sense of self. There is a continual contrast now between the motor inco-ordination felt by the infant and the drives connected to signifiers of desire and the image it has of itself, which is the rudimentary 'ego'. The 'ego' is then reinforced by the images of the mother as an 'ideal ego', and this is not a completely formed agency; it is still in a fragile relationship with the mother and with the fantasized internal projections of itself onto the image of that mother as a projection screen.

A crucial part of the identification with the mother is with the desire for the desire of the other such that a symmetry and identity is set up between the experience of gazing (desiring) and being gazed at (being desired). When this becomes mapped onto gender relations as the infant enters the symbolic, the fantasies evoked by the gaze reproduce sexed subjectivity at an unconscious imaginary level. The 'mirror' image is also desired, for it is not only a flat reflecting sheet, and the mirror can be taken as a metaphor for the mother 'reflecting' back to the infant its own actions and giving a whole intentional sense to it (and this is the move Winnicott (1967) makes, for example, in his reading of Lacan's account of the mirror-phase). Out of the real, then, as a set of biological givens which have been experienced so far without any comprehension of their origin or meaning, is developed an imaginary sense of position from which to experience the real. This imaginary mediation is compounded by the entry into language, into the symbolic order in which there is mediation not only of self-identity but also of the identity of others.

For some writers, such as Althusser and Kristeva, this is an 'ideological' mediation. Kristeva focused on the relationship between the 'semiotic' space, as a form of signification before the imaginary, and the symbolic as organized by patriarchal structures. Althusser, whom we will look at first, was concerned with the way the symbolic called subjects into their proper places to maintain capitalism.

Ideology and interpellation

Althusser (1970) used Lacan's account to explain how ideology works. Ideology as a symbolic system fixes us but it makes us do the work our-selves, and to understand how that happens, we have to understand how the infant enters the symbolic.

The entry into language

While the mirror-phase gives us a sense of self in the imaginary, lays down a matrix for the development of the ego, we have to enter language in order to be able to refer to our-selves and conceptualize ourselves as sep-arate. This entry into the symbolic changes us radically, for as we enter the symbolic, the symbolic enters us. There are two aspects to this double-entry. First, as we enter the symbolic we obtain signifiers for the self, the most crucial being 'I'. When we learn to use the signifier 'I', the ego emerges as 'verbal nucleus' within the matrix of the 'ideal ego' formed in the mirror-phase. A consequence of this is that the subject becomes split between spoken discourse and an 'outside' of that discourse.

In spoken discourse the signifier 'I' is used to refer to a location, and this is acknowledged by other speakers who also operate on the assumption that their use of 'I' refers to a similar location for them, inside them. This 'I' also exists in a system of signifiers in relation to, and so constituting, a 'you'. The relationship between the infant and the mother, then, is trans-formed as the infant speaks from a position in language ('I') to a position in language (marked by the others as 'you') as well as from the position of 'ego' to the (fantasized) mother (and this is still a relationship to an other who is a particular mother). There is a paradox here, for the speech of the subject is the nearest it can come to expressing itself; while unconscious signifiers may never match the signifier 'I', they at least have a closer connection to it than does the subject to the ego, which is built out of a mis-recognition of itself as whole in the mirror-phase.

At the same time, there is a sense of being outside discourse, in which

the associations to the signifier 'I' are general to the culture, and are produced by the differences between the signs in the symbolic. The ability to
use signifiers in a language requires the acquisition of a network of signifiers, and these do not correspond to the experience of the infant. To learn
to speak, the infant must repress this 'underside' of language, and this
underside of language becomes the unconscious. There is, by the same
token, a continuing, albeit repressed, relationship here between the subject
and the rest of the language system, and this is the unconscious relationship between the (unconscious signifiers of the) subject who speaks and
others, a generalized other. This other, the symbolic, also contains a system
of categories for the specification of individual beings which legitimizes
the (mis)recognition of the 'ego' as repository of rational thought.

The second aspect of the double-entry into language is that the use of
language also allows us to deal with separation from mother, for the terms
in language become substituted for the mother. Freud (1920) describes his
grandson, Ernst, playing with a cotton-reel to replay and control the
absence of his mother, Sophie. When Ernst says *'fort!'* ('gone') and *'da!'*
('there') with the absence and presence of the cotton-reel on a string, he
not only masters his experience of loss, of Sophie his mother, but he also
replaces her with terms in language. Typically, the terms become 'I' (separate, sufficient) 'miss' (have an experience given meaning in language,
understood rationally by the ego) 'you' (an other different from me).

Subjection to ideology

Althusser's (1970) use of psychoanalysis to understand the grip of ideology focuses on the way the symbolic is organized and organizes us as subjects. Althusser's work represents the point at which structuralism, having
become influential as a system of explanation in many academic fields,
entered Marxism. It did seem to some Marxists then as if Lacanian theory
would be the key to unlock ideology (e.g., Jameson, 1977), though this
hope has now all but evaporated (Homer, 1996). The impact of this, for
Althusser (and then more so for post-Althusserian writers) is that
Marxism shifts away from economic determinism, conceived of as the
'base', to an attention to the power of culture, written off by some traditional Marxists as the 'superstructure'.

Althusser, who was in analysis with Lacan for a while, justified his use
of psychoanalysis, against the Communist Party orthodoxy, to provide an
understanding of ideology. Althusser (1964: 182) argued that 'Freud had
to think his discovery [of the unconscious] in imported concepts'; that is,
his work was affected by the dominant biological ideas of his time but the
development of structural linguistics could now rescue Freud. It was now
possible to produce a new science whose object is the unconscious, though
Althusser acknowledged that the term 'unconscious' carries unfortunate
biologistic and essentialist connotations and suggested that it should be
dropped when a better term is found. Althusser also defended the opacity

of Lacan's writing by arguing that Lacan was still struggling against dominant concepts, and so it was not possible for him to be too clear, for that would be at the cost of being absorbed into those concepts.

Ideology works through two dimensions of experience, the imaginary and the symbolic. The child lives 'in the mode of the imaginary fascination of the ego, being itself that other, any other, every other, all the others of primary narcissistic identification, never able to take up the objectifying distance of the third *vis-à-vis* the other or itself' (ibid.: 193). When it does take up the distance of the third, as the figure of power identifying with the law of the father, it is in the symbolic where it takes up positions given by language. That is, it can act as if, or as if one day, it will be the 'third term', in the structural position laid out in the nuclear family for the father. Both of these aspects are governed by the structure of the symbolic order which sets out a place for the child before it is born, which determines the rhythm of feeding and comfort and so the conditions for its separation from the mother, and which allocates primary care-giving roles on a class and gender basis through the structure of the family: 'Lacan demonstrates the effectiveness of the order, the Law that has been lying in wait for each infant born since before his birth, and seizes him before his first cry, assigning to him his place and role, and hence his fixed destination' (ibid.: 195).

As part of the symbolic, then, ideology is defined by Althusser as 'a structure of misrecognition' in which the subject misunderstands its place, and is formed at a position in society as a bearer of society:

> Freud has discovered for us that the real subject, the individual in his unique essence, has not the form of an ego, centred on the 'ego', on 'consciousness' or on 'existence' – whether this is the existence of the for-itself, of the body-proper or of 'behaviour' – that the human subject is de-centred, constituted by a structure which has no 'centre' either, except in the imaginary misrecognition of the 'ego', i.e. in the ideological formations in which it recognises itself.

> (Althusser, 1964: 201)

The key process in the power of this structure of misrecognition is 'interpellation', and Althusser uses Lacan here to show how ideology works through 'Ideological State Apparatuses' to understand *the reproduction of the conditions of production* (Althusser, 1970: 123). Althusser (ibid.: 162) argues that 'all ideology hails or interpellates concrete individuals as concrete subjects, by the functioning of the category of the subject'. This means that the notion of the 'individual' and our understanding of the term 'I' as well as our understanding of our proper name is ideological. The process of hailing, calling out, 'recruits' subjects in the manner of a policeman calling 'Hey, you there', and the recognition of themselves, which is often manifested in physical movements as these subjects which have been hailed turn to acknowledge and accept their place in the symbolic, reinforces the categories that are being used.

The model form for this production of individual subjects is a grand Subject with whom we identify. The Subject may be God or a leader, or an exemplary cultural icon, and there is 'the duplication of the Subject into subjects and of the Subject itself into a subject-Subject' (ibid.: 168). The structure of the ideology where each subject identifies with the Subject is as a kind of a mirror-structure in which each subject is guaranteed that their recognition of, for example, God the Subject, will lead to them being recognized:

> The duplicate mirror-structure of ideology ensures simultaneously: 1. the inter-pellation of 'individuals' as subjects; 2. their subjection to the Subject; 3. the mutual recognition of subjects and Subject, the subjects' recognition of each other, and finally the subject's recognition of himself; 4. the absolute guarantee that everything really is so, and that on condition that the subjects recognise what they are and behave accordingly, everything will be alright: Amen – 'So be it'.

> (Althusser, 1970: 168–169)

Subject to class

One of the main problems with Althusser's account is that he splits his account of the work of 'Ideological State Apparatuses' into two; there is a psychoanalytic account of the subject derived from Lacan, and then a fairly orthodox Marxist account of society as being equivalent to class divisions and class struggle. The family, for example, is seen as a site for the reproduction of the conditions of production, but there is no consideration of how the family reproduces patterns of gender and sexuality. Althusser recruits Lacan into a theory of the hold of capitalism on and in the subject, but has no account of patriarchy: 'although he used some Lacanian ideas in thinking about ideology and "the subject", Althusser remained completely unaffected by them in going about his usual theoretical business as a Marxist' (Barrett, 1993: 172). What we get from Althusser is an account of the symbolic order structured by 'Ideological State Apparatuses' (of the school and the family, for example) calling subjects into place, and an insistence that it would be impossible to think of a society without some kind of ideological cement. What we will find in Kristeva is an attempt to think through how other kinds of signification weave into the symbolic, and what kinds of resistance might be possible.

Semiotic space

Julia Kristeva arrived in Paris in 1965 from Bulgaria, and very quickly became an important part of the French intellectual scene, participating in the tortuous and impassioned debates over structuralism and post-structuralism and the relationship between language and subjectivity. Kristeva argued that the mirroring that constitutes the ego and prepares the infant for its immersion in the symbolic also takes place in a signifying system – the *semiotic* – that continues to pulse and weave its way through adult life. Kristeva was the only writer who took to its limits the engagement between psychoanalysis and semiotics . . . an engagement which had in many ways seemed to stall at the concepts of 'identification', 'interpellation' and 'the subject's position in language' which had been brought in, via Lacanian psychoanalysis, to buttress Althusser's theory of ideology and the state.

(Rose, 1993b: 42)

In her early work this engagement was through an identification with Maoism, which was expressed in a quasi-anthropological-cum-tourist account of feminism and 'a new humanity':

in China, a tradition – so long as one managed to free it from its hierarchical-bureaucratic-patriarchal burden – made it possible that (as from the *anatomical*) there would be no more *symbolic* difference between two metaphysical entities (men and women) – but rather a subtle differentiation on each side of the biological barrier, which itself would be recognized by a social law only to be contested again and again.

(Kristeva, 1974a: 198–199)

In her later work there is a three-fold shift which runs at three levels, with a rejection of the idea that it is possible to introduce politics directly into the unconscious, the abandonment of politics in favour of 'a highly individualistic conception of dissidence and worth', and an attention to the formation of sexual identity with the view that 'identity is necessary but only ever partial and therefore carries with it a dual risk – the wreck of all identity, a self-blinding allegiance to psychic norms' (Rose, 1993b: 47). Here we will review her account of the semiotic, abjection and othering before turning to the way in which her notion of the symbolic circulates in psychoanalytic discourse in attempts to return to the 'local economy'.

Symbolic, semiotic and the chora

For Kristeva, the infant's encounter with signification occurs in the mirror-phase and in the entry into the symbolic. As well as the imaginary level of recognition and mis-recognition in Lacan's account, however, the mirror-phase is already organized around a signifying system that Kristeva calls the *semiotic*. She defines the semiotic as 'pre-sign functioning, which is internal to language but also capable of autonomy, giving rise to other signifying systems' (Kristeva, 1974b: 40). The semiotic is produced in a space or 'receptacle' that Kristeva calls the *chora*, and this space is provided by the mother's body: 'The mother's body is therefore what mediates the symbolic law organizing social relations and becomes the ordering principle of the semiotic *chora*' (ibid.: 26). This chora functions as the first secure site for the subject to experience and participate in signification, and, before the narcissistic mirror-phase described by Lacan, it operates in later life as an imaginary site of perfect communication to which the fragmented speaking adult who is subjected to the law of the symbolic may wish to return.

This structure of signification is at once a developmental stage and an aspect of meaning-making that will be necessary for successful negotiation of language as an adult: 'The *chora* is a modality of significance in which the linguistic sign is not yet articulated as the absence of an object and as the distinction between real and symbolic' (ibid.: 26). However, there is a radical separation that occurs when the infant moves out of the chora and into language. When the infant does learn to speak, and thus enters the symbolic, it has to break from the space of the chora, and so language learning is 'an acute and dramatic confrontation between positing-separating-identifying and the motility of the semiotic *chora*' (ibid.: 47). Because the chora is structured by the mother's body, it is identified as a 'feminine' site of signification, and the symbolic sphere which revolves around men will be experienced as a 'masculine' site.

It would be tempting to read Kristeva's account as one which pits the semiotic against the symbolic, and which promises a way out of the overall system of signs that organize the social and which function ideologically to ratify and secure the positions of the powerful and powerless within it. It would also be tempting then to imagine that *women* might be able to return to the semiotic as a point of resistance to patriarchal symbolic order and the Law of the father. However, Kristeva is not proposing that the semiotic or the chora could operate independently of the symbolic, and the only hope for change lies through reconfiguring the way in which one operates in relation to the other:

> Kristeva's theory is one of the modalities of language and precisely does not pretend to be a simple isomorphic model of ontogenetic development. As such the *semiotic* is only intelligible through language, as slips of the tongue, rhythm, punning or prosody for example; the relation of the speaking subject to his or her pre-Oedipal structuration is not posited by Kristeva as one that could produce a 'natural' or 'autonomous' sexuality.
>
> (Pajaczkowska, 1981: 155)

In fact, Kristeva has harsh words for those who imagine that they could escape the Law of socially structured signification.

Rejection and abjection

Kristeva sees the entry into the symbolic as inevitable, and, like other psychoanalysts, sees the separation from the mother and humbling to the law of the father as painful but necessary: 'this transformation of semiotic motility serves to remove it from its autoerotic and maternal enclosure and, by introducing the signifier/signified break, allows it to produce signification' (Kristeva, 1974b: 48). The entry into the symbolic is the point at which the infant simultaneously learns to speak and 'discovers' castration; it is able to attain some power as a speaking subject recognized as a member of a language community but it also loses that power when its illusion of omnipotence is shattered. The infant's discovery that it is now powerless in a different kind of way is played out differently for men and women in a symbolic system which is organized around the power of men; with boys learning that rights to speak are dependent on their subordination to the symbolic, and girls learning that they must learn to speak as subordinates inside and outside the symbolic.

What infants and adults must learn, then, is that it is not possible to return to the semiotic space of the chora and that it is not possible to break the symbolic. On the one hand, the fantasy of return will be an abandonment of language: a recognition of castration is the condition of possibility for the symbolic field, and this operation

> constitutes signs and syntax: that is, language, as a *separation* from a presumed state of nature, of pleasure fused with nature so that the introduction of an articulated network of differences, which refers to objects henceforth and only in this way separated from a subject, may constitute *meaning*.
>
> (Kristeva, 1979: 23)

On the other hand, Kristeva argues that attempts by 'radical feminist currents', for example, to escape and construct a kind of 'countersociety', will just end up with something 'constituted as a sort of alter ego of the official society, in which all real or fantasized possibilities for *jouissance* [sexual and linguistic pleasure] take refuge' (ibid.: 27). Worse than this, the 'logic of counterpower' is eventually to lead to violence, and she cites the 'large numbers of women in terrorist groups' as evidence for this. The case of radical feminism which refuses a symbolic contract with men is one example, but Kristeva sees this logic of 'fetishistic counterpower' as applicable to all revolts against society which operate as if there were a secure place outside from which to launch an assault on the system:

> this is the inevitable product of what we have called a denial of the sociosymbolic contract and its counterinvestment as the only means of self-defense in the struggle to safeguard an identity. This paranoid-type mechanism is at the base of any political involvement.
>
> (Kristeva, 1979: 28)

Kristeva argues that when there are attempts to build an alternative to the symbolic, such a countersociety will be 'based on the expulsion of an excluded element, a scapegoat charged with the evil of which the community duly constituted can then purge itself' (ibid.: 27). This expulsion of what feels disgusting to the subject is then taken further by Kristeva (1980) in her account of abjection. The separation from the mother calls into being an array of symbolically represented objects, but it also involves the production of something *abject* as that which escapes the ordering of desire in the social world: 'it is something rejected from which one does not part, from which one does not protect oneself as from an object. Imaginary uncanniness and real threat, it beckons to us and ends up engulfing us' (ibid.: 4).

This abjection is a product of the first attempt to break away from the mother, and so it is manifest in culture in the figure of the 'monstrous-feminine' that underpins much horror-film imaginary:

What is common to all of these images of horror [in such films as *Alien*] is the voracious maw, the mysterious black hole which signifies female genitalia as a monstrous sign which threatens to give birth to an equally horrific offspring as well as threatening to incorporate everything in its path. This is the generative archaic mother, constructed within patriarchal ideology as the primeval 'black hole'. This, of course, is also the hole which is opened up by the absence of the penis; the horrifying sight of the mother's genitals – proof that castration can occur.

(Creed, 1987: 63)

The abject is something expelled, then, and that disgusting something can be a representation of something already 'outside' or something inside the self, even the self itself.

Others to ourselves

Kristeva's writing during the late 1980s, apart from the main clinical work on depression, has been on the way that which feels so different and 'strange' to us is a product of fantasies within ourselves. When we enter a symbolic community we have to make ourselves into a kind of subject which is self-identical and the 'same', but we also have to recognize others as simultaneously woven into our own identity and as 'different' from us. Psychoanalysis provides a way of thinking about sameness and difference: 'With the Freudian notion of the unconscious the involution of the strange in the psyche loses its pathological aspect and integrates within the assumed unity of human beings an *otherness* that is both bio-logical and symbolic and becomes an integral part of the *same*' (Kristeva, 1988: 181).

In *Strangers to Ourselves*, Kristeva explores the fantasies of otherness in the French symbolic, but draws some rather banal conclusions: 'By recog-nizing *our* uncanny strangeness we shall neither suffer from it nor enjoy it from the outside. The foreigner is within me, hence we are all foreign-ers. If I am a foreigner, there are no foreigners' (ibid.: 192). It should be pointed out that this generous liberal position has not stopped her from also calling on immigrant communities in France to be tolerant, and insist-ing that they should show some gratitude and respect for French culture. Again, we have to locate her rather disappointing rumination on other-ness in the context of her earlier accounts of the relationship between the symbolic and the semiotic. Not only is the relationship between the two one of balance and interweaving, but we also learn right back in the chora that we must subject ourselves to a signifying system to be a subject at all: 'the semiotic *chora* is no more than the place where the subject is both generated and negated, the place where his [sic] unity succumbs before the process of changes and stases that produce him' (Kristeva, 1974b: 28). Kristeva's subject, then, is continually offered the hope of something outside the symbolic but must learn that they can only find an alternative semiotic mode of signification *in* the symbolic. Now we are a long way from Mao: 'Ideas don't fall out of the sky. They arise from little things, everyday details, the body, love relationships, passion' (Kristeva, quoted in Hughes-Hallett, 1992: 26).

Kristeva's complicity with psychoanalysis

Kristeva has been accused of being one of the 'dutiful daughters' of psychoanalysis, following in the tracks of Freud and Lacan and cautiously reworking accounts of the symbolic and the semiotic to make them interweave and complement each other rather than looking to points of resistance (Grosz, 1990). Her later work on religion has been praised by the conservative US psychoanalyst Otto Kernberg, who notes, in his foreword to the English translation of *In the Beginning Was Love: Psychoanalysis and Faith* (Kristeva, 1985), that the 'underlying theme' is a 'Lacanian analyst's critical, yet appreciative, disengagement from her theoretical background, as she makes her way on the road toward the contemporary mainstream of French psychoanalytic thinking' (Kernberg, 1987: ix). There is a rather pathetic echo of this welcome by the 'mainstream' in an attempt by one follower to account for her shift from any radical political engagement, with the argument that 'this change in emphasis has resulted from her deepening personal commitment to analytic practice' (Lechte, 1990: 208). In place of 'a too-severe dethronement of the Father – of identity', now 'her work urges a striving for a certain equilibrium in the social and psychic experience of individuals – between language (symbolic) as meaning, and (potentially) poetic non-meaning (semiotic)' (ibid.: 208–209).

As Butler (1993: 165) points out, Kristeva 'alternately posits and denies the semiotic as an emancipatory ideal. Though she tells us that it is a dimension of language regularly repressed, she also concedes that it is a kind of language which can never be consistently maintained'. There is also a general question, which is, 'how do we know that the instinctual object of Kristeva's discourse is not a construction of the discourse itself?' (ibid.: 173). The answer should surely be that all the instinctual objects and mental processes that she and other psychoanalysts discuss are constructions in discourse. The argument in this book is that they now function as fairly enduring constructions which then play a part in constructing forms of subjectivity in other cultural phenomena, and then, in the process, they feel all the more true to those who speak psychoanalytic discourse.

In the next section we will see how notions from psychoanalytic discourse that Althusser and Kristeva articulate so cogently, themselves articulate two discursive frames which structure the ways some groups have mobilized against capitalism in recent years and tried to escape its grip.

Local exchange and debt

There is a scattered resistance to capitalism in a number of English-speaking countries (Australia, Canada, New Zealand, UK and the USA) which has developed from the early 1980s and which works on the premise that it is possible to construct an entirely different economic space which would be cooperative and communicative. This resistance is organized in LETS. The initials 'LETS' in the UK stand for 'Local Exchange Trading Systems' (Seyfang, 1994), but in Canada, where the idea first started in 1983, there is a more ambitious remit in the 'Local Employment and Trading System' (Dobson, 1993). In 1993 there were ten LETS systems in Canada and ten in the USA, eighty systems in New Zealand and two hundred in Australia, and two hundred in the UK, the largest, with four hundred members, being in Manchester (Seyfang, 1994). LETS operate through a double-entry book-keeping system in which goods or services rendered are recorded in imaginary units of currency as a credit for the giver and a debit for the receiver. The recording of face-to-face exchanges means that the system stays local and that an accumulation of resources is discouraged. A range of metaphors is used to explain how the system operates, and we will examine these below.

Seyfang (1994) points out that attempts to implement alternative forms of money go back to at least the seventeenth century. These experiments have often been driven by socialist principles and a hostility to capitalism. In the early nineteenth century Robert Owen, for example, introduced a system at the New Lanark mills in Scotland called 'Equitable Labour Notes'. Recently, that utopian socialist spirit has been augmented by a green agenda and a local community politics that is concerned with protecting resources. The LETS schemes are part of this new movement. That green socialist impetus is acknowledged in Canada, though there have also been attempts to distance LETS from an explicit political identification with any particular party (Dobson, 1993). In the UK it is argued that 'there is very little about LETS which makes it *inherently* compatible with any one political tradition' (Seyfang, 1994: 14), even if the Green Party has committed itself to LETS and there have been glowing accounts in some Left magazines (Brosnan, 1994; Gosling, 1994; Rowthorn, 1994). There have also been a spate of articles in the liberal-Left UK daily newspaper *The Guardian* (Jukes, 1994; Vidal, 1994; Gibbs, 1995).

The analysis in this chapter focuses on books, articles and leaflets which are either sympathetic to or actively promoting the development of LETS. The analysis is organized around two discursive complexes, the 'symbolic' and the 'sociosymbolic', and the way each complex constructs an other to itself in two further discursive complexes, the 'imaginary' and the 'semiotic'. As in previous chapters, the argument is not so much that we can use psychoanalytic theory to interpret or pathologize LETS (though this may indeed be one of the functions of the analysis), but that particular notions of the social and subjectivity that are gathered and crystallized in the writings of Althusser and Kristeva circulate in the wider culture and then their versions of psychoanalytic discourse play a part in structuring the way in which LETS are described and practised. In this case the analysis is also of the discursive field in which LETS operates, and is slightly more complicated because of the way each complex constructs an other which appears to map onto one of the other complexes, but does not do so exactly. There are two overlapping discursive frames, then, which structure the way in which an alternative order of cooperative exchange may be counterposed to the capitalist symbolic order. One discursive frame is of the kind Althusser discusses, and the other is of the kind Kristeva elaborates.

The first discursive frame consists of the discursive complex of the *symbolic*, which is almost Althusserian in aspect and which constitutes a discursive complex of the *imaginary* as other. This then lays open a discursive space for LETS to function against capitalism as a place of real values and innocent moral example. At the same time, there is a slightly different second discursive frame which consists of the discursive complex of the *sociosymbolic* (which inhabits the same discursive space as the Althusserian symbolic). This constitutes a slightly different discursive complex of the *semiotic*, which is quasi-Kristevan in character (and which inhabits almost the same discursive space as the Althusserian imaginary). This semiotic struggles against the sociosymbolic as a site of opposition which is held in place by notions of natural money and thoughtful moral refusal. The analysis, then, tries to capture the contradictoriness of LETS rhetoric, and the ways in which different representations in the two discursive frames of the economy and the local economy coexist within it. A variety of subject positions are constructed in this discursive field, and different political agendas and consequences are played out as competing notions of LETS as an alternative to capitalism are presented.

Symbolic and imaginary (discursive frame I)

The first discursive frame consists of two discursive complexes which together structure a particular kind of conceptual opposition between capitalism and a progressive alternative economic order. Here we find capitalism depicted by LETS texts as if it were the kind of symbolic order that Althusser described, and so the alternative LETS activists wish for is seen as an imaginary site. This opposition between representations of capitalism and LETS opens up certain kinds of subject positions but also constrains and pathologizes participants.

SYMBOLIC   The discursive complex of the symbolic is structured around the Althusserian model of the entire symbolic order of culture as organized around capitalism as the key motif, and with the social field being treated as if it were equivalent to class. This class system is a dangerous overarching mechanism full of power, and is challenged by the hope that 'local communities could wrest back some power from unaccountable banks, supermarkets, chancellors and the infernal, mysterious supranational economic system' (Vidal, 1994: 25). One of the initiators of LETS in the UK, for example, refers to the openness of the scheme and contrasts this with the 'hidden interest' in the national economy (in ibid.). LETS is then defined against this economic system, for 'LETS currency is not capitalist money' (Seyfang, 1994: 20), and the kinds of problems that are identified concern the lack of control that people have over the national system: 'national currency is mobile, and is easily exported from local economies by banks and firms with outside interests; if it is re-imported it is usually under external control' (ibid.: 1).

IMAGINARY The Althusserian symbolic constitutes the discursive complex of the imaginary as its other, as an infantile place which is bathed in the gaze of the adult. The position that LETS marks out in this relation to the symbolic is structured around the tropes of childhood and reflective communication with others which is uncontaminated by the adult world.

The childhood trope is expressed in the group of initials 'LETS' which are then attached to other words to evoke enthusiasm for the project with an address to the reader as if they were an infant, as in 'LETS get going!' (Manchester leaflet for pilot project, 1993), or 'LETS abolish money' (Gosling, 1994). First introductions to LETS in Canada are through a Monopoly-style boardgame called LETSPLAY (Dobson, 1993: 80). In the starter pack reproduced in Dobson's (ibid.: 184) overview of LETS, there is a page which asks you to 'Figure Out What You Can Do For Others', and the first 'individual starter suggestions' invite the reader to fill in the spaces which read 'I like to:' and 'I hate to:'. The infantile position that is staked out against the adult symbolic order is also expressed in many of the newspaper reviews of LETS, which pick up on the variety of affectionate local terms that members choose for their own currencies ('Bobbins' in Manchester, 'Pigs' in Scunthorpe, 'Acorns' in Totnes, and so on), and then string them together to make light of the activity of exchange, as if the exchange were a game: 'Take a few pigs along to the Pie in the Sky cafe and watch payment go bob-bob-bobbin' along' (Vidal, 1994); 'Twelve acorns for a hair cut' (Kellaway, 1993).

There is also, in this imaginary relation which is constructed as an alternative to the symbolic, a notion of direct and unmediated reflection between the members of a local scheme and unmediated exchange: 'what LETS actually does is create money *only* when something is exchanged, so the money supply exactly matches demand' (Seyfang, 1994: 18). The task, then, is to mirror something, rework it, and make it something better: 'by internalising fully the costs of production, efficiency will be improved with social and environmental benefits' (ibid.: 3), so 'changing the nature and social meaning of exchange' (ibid.: 27). While this first Althusserian discursive frame is important, a much more powerful conceptual structure is provided by Kristevan notions of the currencies of meaning and power.

Sociosymbolic and semiotic (discursive frame II)

The second discursive frame consists of two discursive complexes which together structure another particular kind of conceptual opposition between capitalism and a progressive alternative economic order. Now we find capitalism being depicted close to the ways that Kristeva elaborated, and the opposition to the dominant economic order now carries a slightly different set of subject positions for participants and slightly different risks when they speak about themselves and their hopes for something better than capitalism.

SOCIOSYMBOLIC   The discursive complex of the sociosymbolic is consti-tuted as an artificial and masculinized place which comprises all that must be abjected.

The issue here is not so much that the units of currency in the national and international economy are forms of money *per se*, but that the economy consists of 'selfish money' (Seyfang, 1994: 26). The task of LETS, then, is to challenge what happens when that selfish money turns all of the members of the community into selfish people: 'something like the LETSystem is the necessary key to *unlocking our addiction to commodity money*, and the destruction that follows upon that addiction' (Dobson, 1993: 78). One of the rhetorical forms which reproduces this picture of the sociosymbolic is to treat it as a place where there is the accumulation of resources, and so necessarily the accumulation and exercise of power over others: one of the advantages of LETS, then, is that the emphasis on the exchange function 'discourages the role of money as a *store of value*' (Seyfang, 1994: 18). Unlike the sociosymbolic order which accumulates units of currency, and so, it would seem, units of force, 'it is not possible for those with stores of LETS money to have power over others' (ibid.: 20).

If LETS are nourished as a semiotic alternative, as if they were in the chora as the space of the mother's body, then they are pitted against some-thing which is quintessentially masculine. Here the sociosymbolic is not so much 'capitalist' (as it is in the Althusserian first discursive frame) as a patriarchal order which is organized by the Law of the father: 'the "market" economy, where we still use hunter language', 'the competitive economy of the hunt, herding, trade and war', '*outer-directed*' (Dobson, 1993: 58). Like an addiction, the destructiveness of the sociosymbolic enters the subject, and must be rooted out and expelled:

> It should be noted that it took me about two years of theorizing and writing to purge (even imperfectly) monetary concepts from the vocabulary with which I now describe the LETSystem and its functions. Our indoctrination into the money system and its imperatives is terribly deep.
>
> (Dobson, 1993: 88)

SEMIOTIC   The discursive complex of the semiotic is created along the lines of Kristeva's account of a place as something that is secure, as if it were the chora created by the mother's body, closer to the feminine and to nature.

The notion of community in the semiotic is as a place which is secure, and which can be contained as a safe place against the threat of separation that the symbolic will force. The national recruitment leaflet for LETS in the UK, for example, claims that 'LETS brings back community spirit', and it then uses a metaphor that is employed time and again in the Canadian literature, which is that 'It helps plug the leaks in the local economy, keeps money in the locality'. A local leaflet repeats the message that 'cash leaks out of the local community' (Manchester leaflet for pilot project, 1993). The 'Community Circle' introductory booklet for the Canadian scheme starts with a description of 'Our Community Barrel And How It Leaks', and the problem is that 'Our communities now depend almost entirely on inputs from the national-international "World" economy, and on outputs that flow to that world economy', so the promise is that 'maybe someday we won't need many inputs from outside, or a pump' (in Dobson, 1993: 172–174). An article reproduced in the UK LETS recruitment leaflet makes it clear that such 'inputs' are to be avoided: 'Intertrade between systems does take place, but we are really in favour of using LETS to enhance local development'.

As would be expected, the community is identified with face-to-face contact, with the Manchester leaflet for a pilot project (1993), for example, repeatedly evoking the 'local community', and 'local people' as the organizers. The community is so important that even a sympathetic writer has made the scornful remark that 'unless you think communal identity is important there is no reason for LETS, except as a tax fiddle' (Rowthorn, 1994: 31). One of Seyfang's (1994: 54) interviewees says that 'there is a sense in which getting it on LETS seems like getting it for free . . . it's extras'. There is a notion in some accounts that a potential is being held back by the reigning system, and so 'The struggle is to create the structures to let co-operation come out' (Jukes, 1994: 4). LETS consists of 'convivial money' (Seyfang, 1994: 26). It is also seen as *'natural money'*, with the task being *'unlocking the restrictions that universal money-use* has placed upon the *natural money* we all possess in our learned and innate skills' (Dobson, 1993: 78). Because it is natural, it is also something 'real': 'LETS currency which is never scarce has only "trading value", and *represents* real value' (Seyfang, 1994: 19).

LETS is portrayed as something which is able to replace the alienating separation and misunderstanding that occurs in the sociosymbolic with open transparent communication. One aspect of this is that LETS is viewed as an autonomous signifying system; Seyfang (1994: 8) describes LETS as 'an information system'. Dobson (1993: 83) cites the belief that 'the necessary inter-personal communication, together with the economic advantages of dealing with one another instead of with value-alienating forces, are sufficient for both social and economic development'. Another related aspect is that relationships are built on the basis of trust: one local activist in the UK argues that LETS 'restores people's faith in each other, links them, helps them' (in Vidal, 1994: 25). This faith in others then secures the continued participation of members: 'LETS is based on principles of trust and community support, and it is generally assumed that

this will not be a problem; the resulting loss of social credibility being sanction enough' (Seyfang, 1994: 9). This is 'the internal economy of the hearth,
planting and gathering, in which the sustaining, sacral flow of the *gift* can
function day by day rather than as a rare *charity*' (Dobson, 1993: 59). 'LETS
is a system of freely created, decentralized, non-tangible, interest-free local
currency' (Seyfang, 1994: 5), and it is argued that what the record of
'payment' for a task amounts to is

> true credit – it is *trust*. The provider of goods and services *trusts* in the freely
> given commitment *and capacity* of all other members, *and of the community itself*,
> that they will and *can* perform services or value, or provide goods of value, so
> that he or she can receive value in return, later, from someone in the system.
>
> (Dobson, 1993: 140)

Although it is not always explicit, there is a powerful rhetorical device
used to champion LETS, which is that it is an economic system that is more
woman-friendly than capitalism. The first account in a series of articles
about LETS in a UK Left magazine *Red Pepper*, for example, was of an
Asian women's trading scheme using 'motis' (Hindi for 'pearls') as the
local currency, and the observation that LETS 'have a special value for
women' (Gosling, 1994: 28). One of the advocates of LETS in Canada
argues that the scheme is closer to the activity of women in hunter-
gatherer society, where 'the *gatherers* (mostly women and children) feed
most of the tribe most of the time with a natural harvest of roots, berries,
fruits, vegetables and small game', and this is still living on now, for 'the
co-operative economy of the hearth, planting and gathering, is *inner-
directed*' (Dobson, 1993: 59).

The discursive complex of the semiotic, then, operates in this discursive frame as a pattern in the accounts of the LETS activists which offers
a slightly different range of subject positions than that which is specified
by the discursive complex of the imaginary (in the first discursive frame).
This Kristevan discursive complex of the semiotic operates in relation to
the capitalist economic order represented and reproduced as a certain
kind of signifying system for the participants and organized around the
discursive complex of the sociosymbolic, while the Althusserian discursive complex of the imaginary operates in relation to capitalism organized as a conceptual space by the discursive complex of the symbolic.
These two overlapping discursive fields each help LETS participants to
understand their enemy and construct forms of organization that might
supplant it. However, each discursive field structures the agenda of LETS
such that the fantasy of escaping capitalism serves to obscure the way in
which that fantasy is itself part of capitalist ideology. Just as Althusser
and Kristeva worked with psychoanalytic discursive resources which
were, despite their radical pretensions, part of the common currency of
capitalist culture, so LETS draw on discursive resources which may end
up locking activists into the very system of rules and regulations they
want to undo.

Rules and regulations

The symbolic order described by Althusser makes us imagine that there is no escape, and that any attempt to speak against it will be caught in a specular relation with the symbolic that still reproduces the symbolic at that very moment that it defines itself in relation to it. Kristeva's account of the symbolic (captured in the analysis in this chapter through the term 'sociosymbolic') is as certain that we cannot step outside, but she still invites us to think that the semiotic is an alternative mode of signification, and that it should be possible to weave our way through language differently. In both accounts, the reigning structure of signification locks us into place and lures us into 'another place' that feels more secure but is still tied to the Law.

Might there be a way of thinking about this that finds a way of stepping back *without* imagining that we are simply stepping 'outside'? Althusser and Kristeva each feed into a version of psychoanalytic discourse that makes that difficult, but if we treat psychoanalytic discourse as woven into history rather than being a static regime of truth, we would then be able to link better with what is progressive about alternative forms of life and alternative forms of economic system.

A reader asked a UK daily newspaper recently 'What is the difference between a rule and a regulation? If none, why do people refer to "rules and regulations"?' Another replied:

> The apparent redundancy of 'rules and regulations' goes back to English law in the centuries following the Norman conquest, when the rulers spoke French and the ruled English. When it came to a matter of law, pairs of words – one known to French speakers and one to English – were used. Thus we have aid and abet, fair and equitable, let or hindrance. This class divide is also seen in the English words for meat. The name of the animal, tended or hunted by the ruled, is of an Anglo-Saxon root: thus cow, sheep, pig (or boar), and deer. Its meat, consumed by the rulers, is known by a word with a French root: thus beef, mutton, pork and venison.
>
> (*The Guardian*, 16 August 1995: 4)

The symbolic itself contains historical traces of domination, and it is when we locate ourselves as part of history that we can imagine something different. Similarly, when the discursive practice of LETS is located as part of a history of resistance, we are better able to appreciate what is progressive about it and what kind of alternative system it might prefigure.

To do that we have to make the kind of historical double-shift that Žižek (1989) accomplishes in his analysis of the symptom in Freud and the commodity in Marx. Žižek, a Slovenian Hegelian Lacanian viewing these issues simultaneously from the inside and outside of Western capitalism and psychoanalysis, helps us see why Althusser and Kristeva are right to inveigh against a simple appeal to things outside the symbolic and how LETS fall into the trap of making that appeal a central part of their practice. Althusser and Kristeva may simply seem to be spoilsports, doubting the possibility of breaking out of the symbolic, but they are also being true to Lacan, and perhaps to Freud. The point of dream analysis (as we saw in Chapter 7) is not to find the hidden core of the dream, and Freud (1900) talks about a 'mycelium' branching out without a centre. As Žižek (1989: 11) points out, the task is not to arrive at the latent meaning, rather it is to ask 'why have the latent dream-thoughts assumed such a form, why were they transposed into the form of a dream?', and then the same is the case for Marx:

> It is the same with commodities: the real problem is not to penetrate to the 'hidden kernel' of the commodity – the determination of its value by the quantity of the work contained in its production – but to explain why work assumed the form of the value of the commodity, why it can affirm its social character only in the commodity-form of its product.
>
> (ibid.)

Žižek argues that Marxism is very like psychoanalysis, then, in its attempt to show how things have come to be the way they are rather than trying to recover real things that lie hidden under the surface, as if they were repressed and lay in the unconscious waiting to be released or as if they existed as true values concealed by the machinations of the capitalist economy. More than that, psychoanalytic notions of repression as *producing* that which is repressed are rooted in a kind of economic system which is so alienating precisely because it lures us into the search for something else that we might connect with, something which is so patently missing from it: 'The "normal" state of capitalism is the permanent revolutionizing of its own conditions of existence; from the beginning capitalism "putrefies", it is branded by the crippling contradiction, discord, by an immanent want of balance' (Žižek, 1989: 52). Capitalism is built around a lack which it cannot fill, and its subjects feel that lack and try to find something to make them whole. LETS also tries to fill that lack and restore balance, and that is why it reproduces what it tries to escape. We might wonder, then, where this leaves Žižek and the task of trying to find truth in psychoanalysis as a psychotherapy. We turn to that matter next.

9

Real Things, Recovery and Therapy

Everything I'm doing is my own catharsis. . . . My work is a kind of self-portrait. The whole delving into erotica and dealing with my sexual fantasies was my own inner struggle with the way I was raised. . . . It's about my own inner struggle with repression.

Madonna, quoted in J. Pareles (1994: 2) *Alone again naturally*

Psychoanalysis structures social relations in Western society. Psychoanalytic theory threads its way through culture, setting up subject positions in a variety of alternative social movements and providing participants with discursive material from which they may fashion themselves and believe that what they have made is true. The popular image of psychoanalysis as a 'talking cure' is of it as a series of techniques for unravelling the language of patients and discovering what real things happened to cause their hysterical misery. Psychoanalytic practice, however, has been a little less certain about the relationship between language, truth and reality (e.g., Hobson, 1986; Lomas, 1987; Scott, 1996), and Freud was pessimistic from the start about the possibility of doing more than turning 'hysterical misery into ordinary unhappiness' (Freud, 1895b: 393).

The turn to discourse in French psychoanalysis has been all the more insistent that language cannot be peeled away to reveal something real and true, but there has been a peculiar double-movement in this tradition. On the one hand, there is a strong emphasis on misrecognition in the formation of personal identity and upon the 'impossibility' of the real, and a corresponding suspicion of those who claim to be able to find the actual referents for the things we feel to be underneath or outside discourse. This suspicion is reinforced by Lacan's use of structuralism. On the other hand, there is also a search for 'true speech' and this form of psychoanalysis holds open the possibility of the subject finding itself in the gaps in discourse, where it does not think. This hope of grasping and speaking a core of truth is theoretically driven by Lacan's use of phenomenology. Lacan's (1992a: 302) hostility to US ego-psychologists flows from the 'moral goal' in their practice which he saw as 'psychological normalization', but he did then still see the moral goal of his psychoanalysis as helping the patient to follow the line of their desire, for 'the only thing of which one can be guilty is of having given ground relative to one's desire' (Lacan, 1992b: 319). In Lacanian psychoanalysis the analyst does not respond to the demand for happiness from the patient, and so 'To have carried an analysis through to its end is no more or less than to have encountered that limit in which the problematic of desire is raised' (Lacan, 1992c: 300).

There are two issues that we need to consider in an assessment of the development of the Lacanian view of psychoanalytic practice and cultural images of the goals of psychotherapeutic work. The first is that this tradition has been elaborated and challenged, stretched almost to breaking point by a number of other writers. While the Lacanian psychoanalytic institutions organized through the Freudian Field and still led by Jacques-Alain Miller are sure they know where Lacan's work leads as a therapeutic practice, a number of dissident strands are less certain. These dissident strands have engaged with Lacanian psychoanalytic discourse and pressed certain distinctive folds into it. Some writers, such as Lyotard, have explicitly opposed Lacan and employed quite different theoretical traditions, including a Nietzschean account of the 'real' which was fashionable in France in the 1970s (cf. Deleuze and Guattari, 1977). Others, such as Laplanche, are working more cautiously within the Lacanian problematic and appeal to early Freud to provide an account of how things are made real for the subject in its first encounter with the social. And Lacanian cultural analysts, such as Žižek, are faithful and critical, arguing for the contradictoriness of Lacan's writing and working in the cracks to show how language forms the subject around a traumatic kernel of the real. Lyotard, Laplanche and Žižek have been influential as commentators on psychoanalysis and psychoanalytic culture, and they have also helped to elaborate some of the forms of talk and practice that constitute that culture.

The second issue is that if we are to understand how the Lacanian transformations of psychoanalysis are played out in culture, we need to take seriously the wider conditions of possibility for the formation of therapeutic practice. Modern culture, with its wellsprings in the Western Enlightenment of the eighteenth century, traces and advertises narratives of personal meaning, progress, and science. Modern philosophy understood itself to be the 'mirror of nature' (Rorty, 1980), and modern psychology developed the project of accurately mirroring and measuring behaviour. Psychoanalysis too is a thoroughly modern endeavour. It rests upon the belief that intense and painful self-reflection will yield self-knowledge, that this is a progressive endeavour, and that a rational, even scientific understanding of mental development will assist practitioners.

Now, the supposed mutation of the whole of culture into a 'postmodern condition' spells serious trouble for traditional psychoanalytic notions, for a thorough postmodernist will distrust metaphors of depth; there is no self or internal experience to be recovered from the patient's past, there is no path forward to be taken for self-understanding, and there is no narrative, scientific or otherwise, that could be privileged over any other. The postmodern condition is a world of surfaces and a perpetual present. The dangers that this holds for a therapeutic view of the self include a refusal to take claims about the past seriously (Burman, 1997). The argument that therapists can only implant 'memories' in patients when they look for things under the surface could be seen as one particularly pernicious expression of the postmodern spirit, though the zeal with which this argument is advanced and combated is also evidence that some modern notions of certainty and truth are still, fortunately, alive and well. Of course, the idea of a deep, 'primitive' self lying beneath the surface is not only a psychoanalytic notion. Psychoanalysis picks up and replays images of the self and others that developed through the Enlightenment, and it then turns these images in strange directions that we now feel to be natural, to be part of our everyday commonsense.

This chapter focuses on psychoanalytic notions that underpin therapeutic discourse, and explores the ways in which we can comprehend the work of therapeutic discourse in forming subjects by employing again the analytic methodological device of the 'discursive complex'. This account of therapeutic discourse focuses on content, but it will then be argued that we need to take a further step to look at the way *formal* aspects of communication in sectors of postmodern culture are also structured around psychoanalytic patterns of reasoning. To do that, though, we need to move well beyond Freud. Developments in psychoanalytic writing, including work by Lacan, Laplanche and Žižek, follow the postmodern shift of emphasis from the interior of the self to patterns of discourse, and it is not surprising, perhaps, that these developments have been seen first in the realm of French 'post-structuralist' theory which nurtured Lyotard's speculation that the 'grand narratives' of cultural and individual improvement were over and have given way to a multiplicity of 'little stories'. The grandiose diagnoses of a new 'postmodernity' conveniently overlook the fact that many people still find it helpful to think about the role of economic, social and personal history in their lives, but they do draw attention to some of the effects of the new discursive-technological forms that comprise late capitalism. This chapter is also concerned, then, with some of the effects of those new forms upon therapeutic discourse.

New technological forms augment the ways in which modern therapeutic concepts position those involved in the work of psychoanalytic self-understanding. This overview and analysis focuses on what is *given* to therapists and patients, and it will be argued that an account of creativity in psychotherapy has to include an understanding of the discursive and technological conditions and limits to that creativity. First though, we need to follow through some of the developments in Lacanian psychoanalytic discourse in the work of Lyotard, Laplanche and Žižek.

True lies

In each of these 'postmodern' strands of work psychoanalysis is unwittingly being unravelled from the inside; it is self-deconstructing as psychic processes become located in discourse rather than in the self-enclosed interior of individual minds. At the same time as psychoanalysis is being thrown into question though, new technological forms which provide the material infrastructure for the 'postmodern condition' also provide a setting for some new varieties of psychoanalytic theory, and new versions of therapeutic discourse.

Lyotard's libidinal band

Despite the progressive role of some radical Lacanian analysts in the events of May 1968 in Paris, the 'structuralist' and then 'post-structuralist' turn to discourse in French intellectual thought tended to lead to deep pessimism about the possibility for change among those participating in that turn. The turn to discourse was also, for many, a turn away from politics. Lacanian analysis, like other forms of psychoanalysis, insists that the world and the psyche are more complicated and resistant to change than revolutionaries would like to believe, and Lyotard's critical engagement with psychoanalysis in his book *Libidinal Economy* (1974) is all the more critical of those who would appeal to some human activity or experience that is not always already alienated. This text is also important because, like Baudrillard's work (discussed in Chapter 6) it prefigures discussions of the breakdown of the Enlightenment in Western culture, and it recruits some Lacanian characterizations of psychoanalysis to postmodernism. It is sometimes argued that Lyotard's (1979) work on the 'postmodern condition' is a 'new phase' in his writing that moves out of the 'dead end' of *Libidinal Economy* (e.g., Dews, 1987: 143), but the book does anticipate some of the ways in which hopes for liberation will be scorned and patterns of intensity on the surface of culture celebrated in his later work. Lyotard himself now rarely refers to the book, referring to it as his 'evil book, the book of evilness that everyone writing and thinking is tempted to do' (Lyotard, 1988: 13), but it is still an important text as voicing something symptomatic of the way the symbolic order is experienced now in some varieties of psychoanalytic discourse. Ideas in that text also feed into contemporary cultural images of language, subjectivity and 'therapeutic' self-work.

Dews (1987: 134) argues that the key difference between Lyotard and Lacan is over what consciousness does to our understanding of the world and of ourselves: 'To be conscious of an object is to be conscious – even if implicitly – of consciousness *of* that object. Hence a distance from the object is built into the very concept of consciousness'. As a consequence of this position, 'Lyotard returns to the Nietzschean – and Freudian – view that consciousness itself is already a form of exclusion and repression' (ibid.). If this is the case, then the role of reflection or understanding will necessarily be trapped in the same 'distance', in 'exclusion and repression'. The notion of the 'libidinal band' in Lyotard's account functions here as something which is close to the primary process that Freud describes but which is also intimately and necessarily bound into forms of thought *about* the primary process. The libidinal band produces an arrangement of libidinal forces or 'intensities' that cannot escape representation, and so the activity of reflecting upon desire is itself a particular organization, stretching and tightening of the libidinal band. We could think of the libidinal band as that which follows Lacan's symbolic order into the subject as the subject learns to speak and which then both incites and strangles the hope of escape.

In Lacanian theory, the term *'jouissance'* is used to refer to the kind of sexual pleasure that the subject enjoys as something which is simultaneously outside and inside language (Benvenuto and Kennedy, 1986). Lyotard pushes this link between the inside and outside of representation even further in *Libidinal Economy*, and then spells out the implications of this. First, as far as reflection on society is concerned, we must abandon the hope of stepping outside the symbolic order to comprehend what it may be doing to us:

> in the immense and vicious circuit of capitalist exchanges, whether of commodities or 'services', it appears that *all the modalities of jouissance* are possible and that none is ostracized. On these circuits, it is just as much a piece of the libidinal band which becomes clear in its ephemeral and anonymous polymorphism. Now, therefore, we must completely abandon critique.
>
> (Lyotard, 1974: 139–140)

Lyotard thus takes his distance from the Marxist and libertarian groups that he had once been a member of in the 1950s and 1960s, and resorts to some of the most pessimistic arguments in psychoanalysis to warn others away from the lure of radical politics: 'For what happens to whomever does not want to recognize that political economy is libidinal, is that he [sic] reproduces in other terms the same phantasy of an externalized region where desire would be sheltered' (ibid.: 107).

Secondly, as far as reflection on the self in psychoanalytic psychotherapy is concerned, Lyotard turns his fire on Lacanians who fall into the trap of thinking that there can still be a 'cure', and he portrays Lacanian theory as an endeavour which 'results from a simple reversal which assures the subject, split in two all the same, of a second-level unity, a meta-unity, which is not, of course, that of consciousness itself, but rather of language' (ibid.: 125). The operation of the libidinal band tied into language makes this linguistic 'meta-unity' completely impossible of course. Dews (1987: 138) points out that although Lyotard did still, at this time, seem to appeal in other essays to a 'pure libidinal economy' which would provide a source of resistance, 'he has already grasped that this is impossible: any action, any discourse, any aesthetic structure can serve as an equally good, or equally bad, conveyor of intensity'. If all that can be hoped for are different varieties of intensity of the libidinal band, then the symbolic has succeeded in saturating the core of the subject, washing and wasting any point of resistance to oppression or repression. Lyotard thus takes some aspects of the Lacanian exhorbitation of language to its logical extreme, and intensities of experience on the surface of language replace any hope of finding a subject of depth underneath. The symbolic, then, penetrates and saturates the subject through the libidinal band.

Laplanche's enigmatic signifiers

One of the paradoxes of the Lacanian turn to discourse is that while it drags psychoanalysis forward into the orbit of structuralist and post-structuralist theory, reframing Freud's account in the light of avant-garde accounts of language and textuality, it also returns to the earliest of Freud's writings to find a warrant for its re-reading and to challenge the orthodoxy of the IPA. This return is marked most dramatically in Laplanche's (1996: 8) argument that 'in 1900 the analytical method is already complete', and that it was from that point on that psychoanalysis degenerated: 'in the decade following 1900, psychoanalysis underwent a change which was important as it was disastrous, with the appearance of the reading codes whose names are *symbolism* and *typicality*' (ibid.). Symbolism is opposed by Laplanche because it promises a direct translation of the dream or speech of the patient into a narrative that is correct. Laplanche points out that it is only in later editions of Freud's (1900) *Interpretation of Dreams* that Freud proposes that there are certain symbols that can be interpreted in this way. The lure of direct translation using psychoanalytic theory as a kind of symbolic dreambook or textbook also cuts across the activity of free association and the activity of the patient tracing connections. The other reading code, which Laplanche calls 'typicality', is where the analyst imagines that certain kinds of dream, text or case can be unlocked using a certain code. 'The psychoanalytic method, in its originary moment, works not with keys but with screwdrivers. It dismantles locks rather than opening them. Only thus, by breaking and entering, does it attempt to get at the terrible and laughable treasure of unconscious signifiers' (Laplanche, 1996: 12). The key question for psychoanalysis, then, is *how* repression operates rather than *what* is being repressed, *how* we make ourselves rather than *what* we really are as 'true selves'.

Laplanche challenges some of the more dubious modern assumptions in Freudian theory, and helpfully uncouples psychoanalysis from approaches which claim to be able to dredge up a true self from the depths of the unconscious, the notion that the 'id' is 'something primordial and primal' (Laplanche, 1989: 28). It is, rather, he says, that it becomes 'a stranger who lives within us as a result of the very process which constitutes the psychic apparatus and repression' (ibid.: 28–29). In cultural representations of experience, including those that are structured by psychoanalytic discourse, there is an elision between that which feels to be most deeply buried and those things which we imagine to have happened first in our own personal experience or in the history of humankind. Laplanche insists that '"original" and "deepest" are not synonymous' (ibid.: 39). The mistaken search for real hidden experiences in much psychoanalysis leads Laplanche to ask 'Does the gesture of separation come before the result of separation? Or does it *establish* the element it separates off?' (ibid.: 29).

Laplanche was one of those in the Lacanian tradition responsible for recovering the Freudian notion of *Nachträglichkeit*, the way in which memory reconstructs itself around a traumatic event to make it traumatic (Laplanche and Pontalis, 1964), and he sums this position up when he says '*it always takes two traumas to make a trauma*, or two distinct events to produce repression' (Laplanche, 1989: 88). This still leaves psycho-analysis with the problem of how to account for actual traumatic events, and he argues that Freud's abandonment of the 'seduction theory' was due to his

> confusion between the contingency of so-called 'perverse' adult sexual behav-iour and the general nature of the seduction situation. Freud cast aside his 'neu-rotica', whereas perhaps he would have done better to go deeper into it, notably in the direction of fundamental and primal seduction.
>
> (Laplanche, 1992: 189)

Laplanche tries to go deeper and to account for the production of trauma by arguing that communications by the parent to the child produce a 'trauma' by virtue of certain sexualized discursive elements being incom-prehensible to the child. These communications, which are confusing, frightening and 'seductive' are what Laplanche calls 'enigmatic signi-fiers'.

An example he often gives is the message that is given by the mother when she offers her breast to the infant. The infant does not know what the fantasies of the mother are, but it knows that there are fantasies of some kind: 'what is perceived is that this gesture has something of another meaning, another meaning that is even unknown to the mother herself' (Laplanche, 1990a: 22). The parents making love, or abstaining from making love for that matter, also sends such enigmatic messages to the infant: 'the parents are not completely aware of what sexual pleasure means for them, of the sexual fantasy behind their own intercourse' (ibid.: 23). Parents kissing in the presence of the child would be another case (Laplanche, 1990b). The 'enigmatic messages' that are communicated to the child are unconscious partly because the infant is struggling to make sense of meanings that cannot be grasped by it consciously and partly because the adult is sending the messages unintentionally, 'uncon-sciously': 'the adult for his or her part "has" an unconscious, which is especially stirred up by the relation to the small child which he or she once was. These messages are most often non-verbal – acts of care, mimicry, gestures; but sometimes verbal too' (Laplanche, 1996: 11). He sums this up in the statement that 'The *enigma* is in itself a *seduction* and its mechanisms are unconscious' (Laplanche, 1989: 128).

Laplanche has pointed out that '*psychoanalysis invades the cultural*, not only as a form of thought or a doctrine, but as a *mode of being*' (ibid.: 12), and this attention to the cultural conditions which make psychoanalytic discourse and psychoanalytic subjectivity possible is also important to Žižek.

Žižek's Che vuoi

Psychoanalysis sometimes promises to find 'truth'. Žižek insists that when we delve deep into the unconscious we should understand how impossible this is. He gives the example of Freud's visit to the Škocjan caves in Slovenia where he encountered the anti-Semitic mayor of Vienna, Lueger. Not only are the caves a perfect metaphor for the unconscious, but the word 'Lueger' has neat associations with the German *Lüge*, a lie. Freud's encounter draws attention to the difference between those new age therapies which promise to find the true self and psychoanalysis: 'what we discover in the deepest kernel of our personality is a fundamental, constitutive, primordial *lie*, the *proton pseudos*, the phantasmic construction by means of which we endeavour to conceal the inconsistency of the symbolic order in which we dwell' (Žižek, 1996: 1). For Žižek, the unconscious and the symbolic order revolve around a 'traumatic kernel' of the real, and this fantasy of some horrific 'Thing' which feels so lost drives us to attack those who we imagine might have stolen it. Žižek's (1990) comments on the break-up of Yugoslavia, for example, stress the way in which the different communities all imagine that the others are responsible for the 'theft of enjoyment' and homes in on the fantasy that the others possess the mysterious 'Thing' which holds a nation together and which forms the core of national and personal identity.

Žižek claims that what Lacanian psychoanalysis forces us to recognize is that we will not find the truth inside ourselves, but find those lies that structure our existence around a traumatic kernel of the real, the traumatic kernel which structures the symbolic order. There are three aspects to this fantasy of truth. The first is that, unlike many others in the Lacanian tradition, Žižek is engaging in a kind of ideology critique, for he is concerned with unravelling the way in which the symbolic order operates. He gives the example of the Stalinist show trials in which the super-ego of the Party maintained 'reality' for the subject, and incited them to confess their unreal crimes because the only alternative was the loss of all reality. The confession here is a way of binding the subject into the Law, and while the Law controls the subject, the super-ego calls to the subject to participate, with enthusiasm:

> Law is the agency of prohibition which regulates the distribution of enjoyment on the basis of a common, shared renunciation (the 'symbolic castration'), whereas superego marks a point at which *permitted* enjoyment, freedom-to-enjoy, is reversed into *obligation* to enjoy – which, one must add, is the most effective way to block access to enjoyment.
>
> (Žižek, 1991: 237)

The second aspect is that if psychoanalysis 'frees' us from anything it is from our fear that our existence is dependent on others, for we then understand that we must let go of the hope of 'existing' as a substance or self:

in contrast to the notion that I can be absolutely certain only of the ideas in my own mind, whereas the existence of reality outside myself is already an inconclusive inference, psychoanalysis claims that reality outside myself definitely exists; the problem, rather, is that I *myself* do not exist.

(Žižek, 1994: 170)

Psychoanalysis is a space where we may speak and eventually do so without fear of the other.

This brings us to the third aspect of the fantasy of truth, which is where we are recruited into forms of ideology which demand that we respond to a call from the symbolic order. Here Žižek takes up Althusser's (1970) account of interpellation, or the 'hailing' of subjects (with the paradigmatic example of a policeman calling out 'Hey, you there!'), but he points out that there are two aspects to this hailing. As well as our protestations of innocence when we are summoned by the Law there is a feeling of deep incomprehensible guilt which is compounded by the feeling that it may be our very ignorance of the cause of the guilt that is our deepest crime:

> What we have here is the entire Lacanian structure of the subject split between innocence and abstract, indeterminate guilt, confronted with a non-transparent call emanating from the Other ('Hey, you there!'), a call where it is not clear to the subject what the Other actually wants from him ('Che vuoi?').

(Žižek, 1994: 60)

So, 'prior to ideological recognition we have an intermediate moment of obscene, impenetrable interpellation without identification', and so 'there is already an uncanny subject that *precedes* the gesture of subjectivization' (ibid.: 61).

For Žižek, this subject is a 'lack', something missing in the structure of the symbolic order that is represented by a signifier, something which the subject is desperate to read as something true about themselves, something traumatic in the symbolic order which they fashion themselves around. The key here is that question which the Other throws out to the subject, *Che vuoi*, which Žižek (1989: 111) translates as 'You're telling me that, but what do you want with it, what are you aiming at?' In this way 'The subject is always fastened, pinned, to a signifier which represents him for the other' (ibid.: 113), and so,

> the subject is automatically confronted with a certain '*Che vuoi?*', with a question of the Other. The Other is addressing him as if he himself [sic] possesses the answer to the question of why he has this mandate, but the question is, of course, unanswerable. The subject does not know why he is occupying this place in the symbolic network. His own answer to this '*Che vuoi?*' of the Other can only be the hysterical question 'Why am I what I'm supposed to be, why have I this mandate?'

(Žižek, 1994: 113)

We will trace the ways Lyotard's, Laplanche's and Žižek's reading and elaboration of Lacanian psychoanalytic discourse plays itself out in postmodern sectors of contemporary culture later, but first let us turn to therapeutic discourse as a *modern* phenomenon.

Modern therapeutic discourse

There is something quintessentially modern about psychoanalysis, and, like many modern movements, there is a tension between two opposing impulses. On the one hand, psychoanalysis is founded upon the idea that self-improvement and understanding comes from delving into the interior of the self and in coming to terms with fantasies which structure the past of the individual. The force of a psychoanalytic interpretation here may be to locate the problem in the subject, and those who suffer are then seen as really deep down wanting to suffer (Lomas, 1987). On the other hand, there is an attempt to understand rationally what is *really* the case, and this is the dynamic in Anglo-American object-relations accounts. The shift of attention in these accounts from the role of the father in prohibiting what the infant wants, to the role of the mother in furnishing the infant with an idea of what it may want has also entailed looking at how different varieties of mothering actually affect children (e.g., Stern, 1985; cf. Cushman, 1991).

The key slogan in a recent British Telecom advertising campaign was 'It's good to talk' (and, rather bizarrely, the slogan was also picked up and used by one of the loyalist candidates in local elections in the North of Ireland in 1995). The point of the BT campaign was to encourage people to use the telephone more, but there is another powerful moral message being conveyed to the audience here about the value of talking *per se*. To understand how that message works, how it could make sense to millions of people as a pun linking telecommunication and psychotherapy, we need to have some account of the discursive 'conditions of possibility' for this type of talk to appear. The benefits of dynamic therapy are often advertised by its subjects with an evangelizing zeal. Barbra Streisand talked about her psychoanalysis at a concert in London in April 1994:

> She said she had begun to appreciate herself 'flaws and all' as she aged. Introducing the song On a Clear Day, she said: 'It has taken me 2,700 hours on various couches and $300,000 to be able to sing this but it was worth every hour and every penny'.
>
> (*The Guardian*, 24 April: 24)

The issue here, however, is not simply how people might decide that psychoanalysis would be good for them because celebrities sell it so enthusiastically, but how culture carries psychotherapeutic discourse to people who may never actually meet a therapist. We need to be able to capture the way in which therapeutic notions run through and structure contemporary commonsense.

Discursive complexes with therapeutic content

We can do this by conceptualizing therapeutic discourse as organized by discursive complexes. Therapeutic discourse will be described here as composed of discursive complexes that are patterned, in the first instance, around Freudian concepts. Therapeutic discourse is organized around three discursive complexes – intellectualization, trauma and transference. This reading focuses on the *content* of therapeutic discourse, and some illustrative examples will be described of places where it appears.

INTELLECTUALIZATION Freud (1925b) makes a distinction between ideational elements and affect, and this distinction is then employed to describe the way in which the patient may render an account of their experience which is formally correct but not *felt*. Intellectualization in psychoanalysis is also discussed by Anna Freud (1936) in her work on defence mechanisms. There are a cluster of assumptions in the discursive complex of intellectualization about the relationship between talk and experience. It picks up on Freud's (1895a, 1900) early distinction between the realm of 'thing presentations' that comprise the unconscious, and the realm of 'word presentations' which fashion consciousness. Although Freud (1915c) argued that thing presentations in the unconscious were not the actual things in themselves completely free of interpretative work, the goal of psychoanalysis is still to reach in and to 'connect' with them. It is not good enough to remain at the level of word presentations, to simply talk about an event, even if that talk accurately represents what the problem is. There must be a combination of speech and emotional tone for there to be a genuine cathartic, insightful or healing experience.

The question of emotional tone is important in a classic juxtaposition in Western animal nature television programmes between the savagery of the picture and the smoothness of the commentary. A case in point is where the narrator speaks in hushed and soothing tones over a scene of lions stalking, killing and disembowelling wildebeest in the African savannah. Here it is the contrast between the deep brutality of life in the raw and the civilized process of coping and understanding that highlights what is depicted as a necessary and tragic aspect of nature and, by implication, human nature. This juxtaposition of savage nature and soothing narration structures the therapeutic encounter as the therapist and patient together uncover the most miserable pain and rage but render it into a discourse and emotional tone that is rational and respectful. This is not only a case of candy-coated talk being layered on unpleasant violent emotions that have been excavated during the course of the therapy. Rather, the issue here is that therapeutic discourse incites a certain kind of talk about what lies below the surface as something that will operate in relation to another kind of talk that comments upon it. The conventions of commentary in these wildlife programmes is so thoroughly anthropomorphized that it becomes difficult sometimes not to experience these animals as being *us* (Coward, 1985).

Forums for public talk about human experience in Western culture express exactly these types of notion about what is spoken and what is really felt deep down. Take the example of confessional television, in US shows like 'Oprah Winfrey' or 'Ricki Lake'. What is striking about the ways in which confessing subjects are mobilized and displayed in these programmes is how the talk *appears* to be open and direct but *actually* reproduces the idea that there are varieties of experience too deep to be conveyed to others. The closest that one gets to 'real communication', we are led to believe as viewers, is when the subject of the programme baring their soul breaks down and cries. When that happens, the programme host has succeeded in opening up the innermost secrets of the subject, but at that moment we also feel that we have abandoned language and are watching something being uncovered that cannot be communicated directly to us. Also symptomatic of this discursive complex of intellectualization that structures confessional televisual talk is the way subjects are brought in as representatives of different support groups ranging from mainstream Alcoholics Anonymous to (in one 1994 example on 'Donaghue') 'Women who get even with boyfriends who cheat on them'. These representatives can speak about what holds them together, but it is in the nature of this form of specific self-help that we imagine that the experience cannot be rendered into a common language. The shared distress lies under the surface as something that must be touched by those who have experienced the same sorts of problems if they are to be comforted, but it can only be understood at an intellectual level by those outside. One of the things we learn when we watch these programmes is that there must be a gap between what we think and what we feel.

TRAUMA The second discursive complex revolves around events that are at the heart of psychoanalysis, of course; the different ways of conceptualizing how real or imagined frights or shocks are carried through to the present, and represented in symptoms, form the history of the birth of psychoanalysis (cf. Freud and Breuer, 1893–1895; Freud, 1926). Trauma is seen in psychoanalytic writing as an excessive increase in stimulation that is too powerful to be dealt with by the subject, and which thus breaks, in some way, the protective mechanisms that normally allow the subject to cope with life. One of the effects of a 'breach' in the protective shield is that it is as if a 'foreign body' is contained in the psyche. As a discursive complex, the trauma functions as an anchoring point in an account of the way in which individuals experience the relationship between the past and the present, and construct elements of the past as the causes of present distress.

Another contemporary example will also serve to illustrate the ways in which the emergence of psychoanalytic preoccupations in Western culture are tied to images of child development. The Disney film, *The Lion King*, is structured by at least three psychoanalytic themes in the narrative. First of all, the predicament that the baby prince lion, Simba, finds himself in is freudianized Hamlet – his father is murdered by his uncle, who then takes the king's place (cf. Freud, 1942). Simba cannot challenge the uncle, for he feels that *he* was responsible for the death of his father. Secondly, in a further psychoanalytic twist, Simba has actually *seen* the uncle kill his father, but this 'forgotten' image only flashes back at a later point of trauma, when he is forced to fight the uncle. Thirdly, there is a therapeutic moment for Simba after he has gazed at the sky and lamented to his dead father: 'You said you would always be there for me, but you're not.' He is goaded by the mandrill shaman into breaking from the easy surface pleasures of life governed by the principle of '*Hakuna Matata*' (Swahili for 'no worries'), which involves denying the past, and accepting, instead, who he really is. The mandrill accomplishes this by the paradoxical rhetorical ploy of hitting Simba on the head with a stick and declaring, when challenged, 'What's the matter, it's in the past'. 'But it hurts', Simba says, and at that moment, when he turns to face the past that hurts, he is cured, cured of the present that hurts. Psychoanalytic and therapeutic notions are *embedded* in the film and in many other cultural narratives. This means that the solutions they advertise are actually relatively enduring constructions, and we have to look at how these constructions fix forms of subjectivity.

One can see the discursive complex of trauma at work in the ways in which the effects of frightening events in public disasters are represented. Now, soon after the first reports of a tragedy and the numbers of people who have been killed or injured appear in newspapers or on television, we can expect accounts of the arrival of trauma counsellors, or interviews with therapists or other professionals talking about the importance of therapeutic support for survivors. The term 'Post Traumatic Stress Disorder' is now available as part of everyday discourse to explain how survivors of such events *must* be experiencing them. It is interesting to note the ways in which traditions in therapy which are most hostile to psychoanalysis, from within the cognitive tradition, for example, have picked up on what is essentially a psychodynamic notion and medicalized it (e.g., Ryle, 1990). In this way we are invited to think that what *appears* to be a straightforward cognitive process is *actually* something which must be assumed to exist at a deeper and temporally distant level of the mind, and we thus forget the way images of stress and dissociation of the personality are historically constituted (Hacking, 1995). This component of therapeutic discourse invites, even incites us to discover at some buried and past location in our body and history a still potent cause for our present-day and conscious discontent.

TRANSFERENCE   In psychoanalytic clinical work the patient replays patterns of perception and experience from a significant other onto the figure of the psychoanalytic psychotherapist or psychoanalyst. Transference, for Freud, was first of all a problem (e.g., Freud, 1905b), but the idea that transference is a necessary component of the therapeutic relationship became central to psychoanalysis (Freud, 1912). These communications will often require decoding, interpreting so that their transferential meaning is 'revealed'. In return for the subject's speech, the analyst communicates a question to the patient, 'are you addressing this to your father?' for example, and so on. The structure of power in the analytic situation is such that the patient, may, eventually, assent to such a question. In therapeutic discourse outside the analytic situation, transference operates as a pattern of concepts which capture and advertise the ways in which every relationship is the remaking of old relationships, the way, as Freud put it, that every process of finding an object is in reality, psychic reality, the 'refinding' of an object.

It is possible to find a host of examples of psychoanalytic discourse in popular culture, and images of transference run through many of these. Some are quite explicit, as in the song 'Mother', by the British band 'The Police' in the 1970s, which leads to the tormented chorus 'Every girl I go out with turns into my mother in the end'. This representation of relationships is also in tune with present-day anxieties about the production of pain through prophecy, in which it feels as if separation does indeed establish the trauma. Some of the cultural elements of this are also haunting and uncanny in the way they evoke classic transferential pictures of repetition in relationships. The representations of trauma and transference here are of things that cannot be grasped at a solely intellectual level. Sinead O'Connor has a song on the album *The Lion and the Cobra*, for example, which starts with the memory of a question to another, 'I said would you be my lover', and finishes with the repeated anguished cry of 'It's just like you said it would be'. The issue here again is the emotional tone which is transmitted in that cry of despair at the recognition that the pattern of relationships can be foretold and it is the deepest ones that will be worst.

This experience that subjects of psychoanalytic culture have of themselves as carriers of patterns of relating is evident in the way people who call radio counselling programmes now *start* with an account of their childhood. They no longer have to be invited by the presenter to link their present-day problems to past relationships. The expectation on the part of the caller that they speak about their past is also apparent in the frustrated admonishments by the host of the legal problem programme on the UK Talk Radio network that they should only describe the present problem. The power of the discursive complex of transference can be seen in a recent series of US films about boundary-breaking. Examples include *Final Analysis* and *The Prince of Tides* in which there are representations of psychotherapy in which the taboo on therapists sleeping with their clients is broken. For this representation of therapeutic relationships to work, for audiences to be hooked by the idea that there is something exciting and dangerous going on, there must be some structured culturally potent notion of transference that is being tapped. As well as being tapped, it is also being reproduced, of course, when the narrative of the film confirms that the breaking of the boundary is, in some sense, equivalent to incest. What appears to be a simple romance narrative is seen actually to be about the deeper underlying patterns that sabotage romance. These films which are about therapy, then, also reproduce certain notions about relationships and memory which are locked into therapeutic discourse. This discourse structures a narrative which generalizes to all viewers about how we should understand our feelings toward significant others as repetitions of feelings toward first familial objects, as imbued with transference.

These brief descriptions of discursive complexes are designed to map something of the shape of therapeutic discourse, and the way in which the content of therapeutic discourse is characterized by themes of intellectualization, transference and trauma. These notions are reproduced across the terrain of popular culture. They are, at the same time, deeply rooted in a classical Freudian conception of the subject. They thus also illustrate the way in which psychoanalysis has invaded modern culture. The rhetorical trick that is often being played here in these cultural narratives is to confuse what lies most deeply buried with what has actually come first. Popular representations of psychoanalytic subjectivity treat these two things as synonymous, and this is evident in *The Lion King*, where we have a narrative about the fundamentals of human subjectivity projected back, as in other animal documentary programmes, into our distant evolutionary past. It is also evident in episodes of *Star Trek*, for example, where the narrative is projected into the twenty-fourth century when human beings, with the help of Betazoid counsellors who are born empaths, can come to terms with what is buried deepest because they were *always* there. But they were not always there, and now, with postmodern mutations in some sectors of modern culture, what they are here is also changing.

Postmodern discursive technologies of the self

Psychoanalysis both risks individualizing distress and disempowering those who suffer, *and* it searches for an explanation for how that distress might have arisen. It both locates the problem in the irrational depths *and* it attempts to comprehend rationally how that problem appears. In this respect psychoanalysis carries the most progressive as well as the most dubious elements of the Enlightenment through modern culture. The tension between these aspects of psychoanalysis is manifest in the way it has tried to come to terms with the prevalence of child sexual abuse (Glaser and Frosh, 1993; Scott, 1996). The more dubious aspects of Enlightenment and psychoanalytic misogyny have been felt particularly, of course, by women, and it is not surprising, perhaps, that the most radical questioning of psychoanalytic knowledge from inside has come from feminist writers. There has been a progressive shift in the writings of Cixous (1976) and Irigaray (1985), for example, from internal critique, to the deconstruction of psychoanalytic categories, and then to the reworking of subjectivity so that it is itself seen as a form of deconstruction (Moi, 1985). Subjectivity, in these Lacanian and post-Lacanian feminist psychoanalytic writings, is not organized around familial structures but is mobile, not fixed but fluid. These writers have been responsible for turning psychoanalysis into something that looks more postmodern than modern.

However, the appeal to unreason, play and the rhythms of the body in these feminist psychoanalytic writings is also still often an appeal to the essential characteristics of a subject, this time the female subject. We can note a paradox here in this appeal to a true self in a postmodern paradigm, and see this as another indication that a full postmodern revolution in culture has not, thankfully, run its full course. There is something of the wish-fulfilment that suffuses much postmodern writing, the idea that to speak differently will dissolve psychic and social structures. Things are changing fast in culture though, and the ways in which social structures bear upon the psyche are now mediated by transformations in forms of communication in late modernity. These transformations also entail some mutation of traditional psychoanalytic notions.

Discursive complexes as technological forms

Rather than focus on content, we will now turn to look at how *forms* of communication reproduce and transform psychoanalytic subjectivity. The three discursive complexes already described will be the starting point, but will now be explored in relation to the particular structures of experience provoked by new forms of technology, new discursive-technological structures.

In each case, we will be tracing the ways in which the notion in Freud's own modern account is transformed through Lacanian and then post-Lacanian 'postmodern' writing. The argument here is that therapeutic discourse is mutating, but that a simple shift of emphasis from individual meaning to discourse, from the individual to the social, or from truth to uncertainty, does not of itself dissolve psychoanalytic narratives. Each discursive-technological form described is, in some sense, a *reversal* of one of the therapeutic discursive complexes. More specifically, whereas the discursive complexes of intellectualization, transference and trauma carry a conceptual opposition between what is apparent and what we must imagine to be actually the case underneath, these new technological forms – libidinal band, enigmatic signifiers and *Che vuoi* – situate what is actually the case *in* what is apparent. To this extent psychoanalysis is unravelling itself, but only to a certain extent, for one is still faced with an opposition which divides what is apparent from what is 'really' the case, albeit with the latter embedded in the former. Let us turn to the three forms.

LIBIDINAL BAND   In Freudian psychoanalysis there is an opposition between consciousness, the realm of word presentations, and the unconscious, the realm of thing presentations. The process of 'cure' consists in the return from what is apparent, the realm of words and our attempt to defend ourselves by using words in strategies of intellectualization, to what is actual, the realm of things and real experience. In the therapeutic narrative, then, thing presentations will come to be privileged over the word presentations. The Lacanian movement, however, overturns this privilege by rooting the unconscious itself in language. The symbolic order becomes the source point for the unconscious in each individual, and the infant only becomes a speaking subject with an unconscious when it enters the symbolic order and is, at the same moment, entered by it (Lacan, 1977). What is actual, as the truth of the subject which is revealed in the subject's unconscious, is now seen as lying not underneath or outside language but as contained *in* it. Lyotard's (1974) notion of the libidinal band presses the symbolic order all the further into the subject, to the point where it is impossible to imagine that there could be any escape, and where it is impossible to imagine that reflection on what is happening will succeed in striking a distance from it.

Consider the following technological sites, and the ways in which they reproduce this Lyotardian transformation and emergence of the first discursive-technological complex, the libidinal band. Ambient music, as one example, is the manifestation of the symbolic as structured around and inciting the libidinal band in all spheres of life. Ambient music technology permits the libidinal band to invade and pervade all activity as an accompaniment. There is no escape from ambient music in many settings, and the rhythm and tone of the music played is often carefully and centrally designed and relayed to different locations (Lanza, 1995). The gap between intellectual work and emotional engagement is thus dissolved as ambient music carries the libidinal band into all the places where either side of the gap may be experienced. Ambient music permits the symbolic to organize intensities of experience for the subject.

Similarly, and staying with music technology to provide a second example, karaoke invites the subject to participate in already structured performances. The libidinal band here gives meaning to the subject; they must sing with the song, and the expression of the subject is tied to a system of rules which exceeds it. The karaoke machine enables the subject to participate, but against an already prepared soundtrack in which not only the musical narrative but also the speed of execution is out of the individual's control. Again, an intellectual and emotional response is structured, at the very same time, by something symbolic 'exterior' to the subject. Now it also structures the enjoyment of the subject as we sing with the libidinal band. As a third example we could take electronic mail ('email') which provides a system of communication which closely defines the parameters for what may be said and to whom. Email also defines how other things outside language may be expressed in a much more clearly defined way than in face-to-face conversation. The rules about insulting others in email discussion groups are part of a system of 'netiquette' known as 'flaming', and the series of smiley or frowning faces constructed out of colons, dashes and parentheses [e.g., :-)], produce a subjectivity that is wholly contained within the system (Makulowich, 1993). The symbolic space for intellectual reflection is now coterminous with emotion, and the rules which bind the symbolic order together structure both aspects of experience. It has been suggested that for this reason email may provide the environment for a perfectly realized Lacanian analysis (Gordo-López, 1995).

What these new technological forms share is the capacity to transform the relationship between thought and emotion, and between language and the unconscious, such that whatever we might intellectualize about is still conceptualized as lying within the parameters set by the symbolic order. When we speak against the background of ambient music or use karaoke or email, we may imagine that we are still really expressing ourselves, but the way we reflect on what we say is structured to the core by the organization of those symbolic media. That which we must connect with is no longer felt to be outside language but is, rather, strictly codified by it.

ENIGMATIC SIGNIFIERS   In much psychoanalytic writing, the trauma is seen as something that occurred at a specific point in time, and as something to which we must return. There is, then, an opposition between the past and the present in which the past is privileged as a site of action, and the present is seen as the scene of its effects. The Lacanian notion of *Nachträglichkeit*, or 'deferred action', emphasizes, against this, that it is a combination of events that *produce* a sense of the past as traumatic. Laplanche's (1989) notion of 'enigmatic signifiers' is useful to comprehend how we are positioned much of the time now in relation to knowledge, in relation to the symbolic order. In some cases, postmodern technology deliberately sets up puzzles and invites the subject to enter new symbolic universes to find the answer.

As a first example, the easy availability of small video puzzles, such as 'Game Boys', constructs a world of levels of meaning where the relationship between the levels is impossible and enigmatic and they provoke the subject to search for a way through. These worlds of meaning are structured around puzzles for which there are immediate but not lasting solutions. The machine sets a series of conundrums which provoke the player to move up various levels, but there is never an underlying meaning or answer to the set of questions that comprise the game. The player is seduced by a series of enigma that remain incomprehensible right to the end. The 'Walkman', as a second example, provides a private arena for the subject, but one which is still situated in wider symbolic space and which is located in relation to other subjects who do not know what is being listened to (Moebius and Michel-Annan, 1994). The Walkman, like other new technological forms, produces a new relationship between users, and in this case the wished-for isolation of the subject is paralleled by the mixture of exclusion and resentment performed by non-users nearby. That mixture of exclusion and resentment also structures questions on the part of those outside who are still listening to the percussive fallout of they know not what. Now it is the experience of the user that functions as an enigma to those outside, those positioned as curious and irritated, infantile and impotent.

A third example, telephone technology, now makes it possible to frame the question of 'who is calling' through the call back facility, in which the addressee can either see the number of the caller flashed up on an LCD display before they lift the phone or automatically dial a caller if the phone was not answered in time, or trace it if it was an abusive call. The call-back facility in the UK was withdrawn the day before its highly publicized initial launch, which we could also take as symptomatic of the importance of the enigma, its role reinscribed at the moment that it seemed possible to solve it. The telephone system offers the possibility of more information about who is addressing the subject, but the subject is still faced with a series of puzzles about who is calling and why. Each of these technological forms promise an answer to troubling questions, but they are structured in such a way as to accompany each answer with the sense that the trouble lies embedded and unattainable in the fabric of the system.

CHE VUOI The third discursive-technological form entails a transformation in the discursive complex of transference; of the relationship between the patient, who replays past patterns, and the psychoanalytic psychotherapist or psychoanalyst, who receives them. What is being privileged in this relational opposition between patient and analyst is the direction of communication. The patient sends the transference in the form of attributed characteristics and questions in their speech to the analyst. Whereas in traditional Freudian analysis these communications will be decoded and the patient asked whether they might be addressing some other significant figure when they are speaking to the analyst, the Lacanian tradition of psychoanalysis works quite differently.

For Lacanians, the transference relationship structures the communication between patient and analyst by producing signifiers which are the signifiers of previous demands that have been important in past relationships. Transference, then, is not so much an underlying emotional phenomenon as a discursive one, and the analyst must not respond from the 'imaginary' position that this repetition of signifiers places them in. By refusing to respond, they thus refuse the position of the imaginary other (as the representation of the actual mother) but take the position of the 'Other' (as the representation of the symbolic order which structures language and the unconscious). The Other is then the symbolic field from which the *Che vuoi* question comes, and so the patient is addressed in the psychoanalytic situation in such a way that their own symbolic position and desire is thrown into question. The Lacanian school, with Žižek as one of the most important writers on culture, transforms the orthodox Freudian account of the transference relationship, then, with the notion of the *Che vuoi*, the experience of being addressed which continually haunts the subject and structures their experience of themselves and others. The question *'Che vuoi?'* makes the subject respond to a question from the

Other, from the very symbolic order which defines who they should be. What is actually the case in the relationship is thus now located *in* the relationship itself, rather than outside it in the subject's past.

If we turn to contemporary forms of technology we can find arenas in which the subject is addressed in exactly this way. One example is in the spread of mobile phones, so that not only is the symbolic order present in every private space and in the most remote places, but it can transmit a call to the subject, inciting the subject to respond. The call is addressed, with mobile phones, to the specific individual at a particular site, and the subject is drawn into a system of communication in which the underlying question is assumed, if rarely spoken, to be the question 'why are you telling me this?' The key difference between mobile phones and old fixed telephones is that the question can now be thrown out to the subject in any and every location. Readers who have been in a train carriage when someone is using a mobile phone will recognize the angry *Che vuoi* addressed to that person by everyone else as the relays of the Other and as something quite palpable. The networks of individuals who are enrolled by this technology are thus far greater than those who actually own mobile telephones. A second example is that of interactive CD Roms, in which questions can be posed to the system, but in which there is a series of pre-defined routes to the knowledge, routes which are structured around the repeated question addressed to the system user 'what do you want?' The questions are structured beforehand, but come into play in response to the user's engagement with the technology, and are then relayed as if from a living person. This electronic space thus structures a transferential question which is repeatedly sent out to each individual subject to affectively charge and draw them into the symbolic system and to reflect upon what they want and who they are.

A third example is the development of technologies which permit a large number of individuals to be addressed personally through mail shots which contain the name of the addressee at various points in the letter. A technological transformation of the symbolic order permits it to call *each* subject, and to invite each subject to wonder *why*, why it has been called. Often this is the question which begins the communication, 'why you?', as an anticipation of the subject's response 'why me?' Again, what is actual is contained *in* the structure, rather than outside it in the individual's idiosyncratic desire. The person is no longer simply being encouraged to think of relationships as transferential repetitions from significant others they have known, and over which they have some distinct personal memory. Now, the symbolic system through which they conduct relationships is able to construct forms of personal address and hook them into regimes of memory over which they have no control. These new discursive forms produce and reproduce transference, anticipated in reverse by the system, as a quality of the technology itself. Psychoanalytic discourse then travels through forms of information technology, and the way it addresses subjects is also transformed by that technology.

Analytic contradictions and transformations

So far we have traced the way psychoanalytic discourse is mutating as it circulates through new technological forms of communication. We may now want to ask how it structures the way a person, as therapist or patient, participates in the therapeutic enterprise.

What does the prevalence of modern therapeutic discourse mean for practice? One consequence is that when we are considering the content of a therapeutic system we have to be attentive to the way notions of intellectualization, trauma and transference emerge as discursive forms. One of the virtues of psychoanalytic psychotherapy is that it does engage with these discursive structures of experience. While other varieties of psychotherapy overlook the transference relationship, try to avoid notions of trauma, and may fail to take due account of intellectualization when it operates as a defence, psychoanalytic approaches tackle these processes. While this is because such therapists genuinely believe that the psychoanalytic model of the mind that includes these processes is true rather than taking due account of the influence of cultural forms, the net consequence is still that the discursive complexes are taken seriously, and treated as topics in the therapy rather than left as unacknowledged and potentially destructive forces. One of the dangers of a psychoanalytic psychotherapeutic practice that fails to reflect on its culturally and historically specific character thought, is that it reproduces these complexes as enduring characteristics of people's lives when it treats them as necessary to human subjectivity and it insists upon the existence of particular, in principle retrievable, experiences as lying, in some mysterious way, 'outside' language (Burman, 1997). In sum, considered simply as the *contents* of therapeutic discourse, the discursive complexes of intellectualization, trauma and transference provide the therapist with valuable cultural resources which can then be turned to good advantage, even to the empowerment of the patient.

What might the postmodern transformation of therapeutic psychoanalytic discourse in new technologies, and the *formal* character of the discursive complexes as discursive-technological structures, mean for practice? One consequence is that we should locate the practice of psychotherapy as a structural force in a rapidly changing cultural context. This means that we must be attentive to the power of the therapist as a participant in the symbolic order, as part of the regime of truth that defines what subjectivity must be like. It means that one must be attentive to the way a question, 'why are you telling me this?' is always structured into the relationship between client and therapist, and cannot be avoided. And it means that we have to be able to comprehend the ways in which psychoanalytic discourse itself operates as an 'enigmatic signifier' in therapeutic discourse. There are increasingly widespread and potent postmodern technological arenas for the fabrication of subjectivity, and although these have not displaced the modern therapeutic enterprise of self-knowledge and amelioration of hysterical misery, they do complicate the task of the therapist.

The new discursive-technological forms which comprise a postmodern condition for some people some of the time will affect what they hope to gain from therapy and where they imagine the truth lies. The trouble here is that the subject does not know what the truth is; nobody knows; and the most ostensibly open therapeutic dialogue may conceal within it, by virtue of its structure as psychoanalytic discourse embedded in new technologies of the self, a position for the client that is disempowering. This highlights the way in which any system of therapeutic talk conveys an enigma to the subject, and positions the subject in a regime of truth. Then it may not be good to talk.

Psychoanalytic discourse: construction and deconstruction

Freudian images of the self are central to modern Western Enlightenment culture, and are interwoven with the structure of groups, our sense of individuality and the organization of language as a material force in human relationships. The structure of modern experience in capitalist culture is riddled through with descriptions and prescriptions provided by such writers as Bion, Winnicott and Klein, and these descriptions and prescriptions make us imagine that we know what human nature is, even when it is only 'second nature'. Psychoanalytic forms of language carry these accounts through culture, and they lay out subject positions from which we speak.

The beliefs we have about our-selves are fashioned as forms of ideology which do more than simply mislead us, then. They construct us, and are the media through which we speak to each other about ourselves, media we cannot escape. Critical writers – from Fromm and Marcuse to Reich and Habermas, and even to Lasch and Baudrillard – try to strike some distance from those ideological forms, and even when they are most pessimistic about the possibility of making something better they still help us to reflect on how psychoanalysis is both a resource and a topic, both the key and the lock. In this critical tradition, we suffer psychoanalysis until we can use it to step back and remake ourselves in social relationships that do not need it: 'psychoanalytic therapy is necessary only where it is not possible, and possible only where it is no longer necessary' (Žižek, 1994: 15).

Psychoanalytic practice here is a certain kind of action, and psychoanalytic discourse also frames the way we understand our actions in relationships and groups, and the way that action is fired by certain patterns of libido, certain lines of force which will permit or frustrate happiness. In an ideal dialectical synthesis of reason and desire, theory and experience, psychoanalytic discourse in critical work also holds open the promise of a praxis which will bring fulfilment and also lay the conditions for the fulfilment of others. Psychoanalytic discourse has always, even at its most pessimistic moments, lured people into the thought that it might increase individual happiness, and even the sum total of human happiness, but to accomplish that our action or praxis must also involve personal change. Whether it is Lacan, Althusser, Kristeva, Lyotard, Laplanche or Žižek, psychoanalytic discourse always finds its way back to truth, and finds that inside us.

This book has traced the various ways psychoanalytic processes are to be found in cultural phenomena, the way those processes saturate and support cultural phenomena and the way those phenomena reproduce and transform psychoanalytic processes. While psychoanalytic theory in the theories we have explored and the cultural phenomena we have examined has persistently and relentlessly tried to find its source in the self, we have been concerned to locate it as a function of discourse in Western culture, in psychoanalytic discourse.

References

Adler, A. (1930) *The Science of Living*. London: George Allen and Unwin.

Adorno, T.W. (1951) Freudian theory and the pattern of fascist propaganda. In A. Arato and E. Gebhardt (eds) (1978) *The Essential Frankfurt School Reader*. Oxford: Blackwell.

Adorno, T.W. (1973) *Philosophy of Modern Music*. London: Allen Lane.

Adorno, T.W. and Horkheimer, M. ([1944]1979) *Dialectic of Enlightenment*. London: Verso.

Adorno, T.W., Frenkel-Brunswik, E., Levinson, D. and Sanford, R. (1950) *The Authoritarian Personality*. New York: Harper and Row.

Alexander, J.C. and Lara, M.P. (1996) Honneth's new critical theory of recognition. *New Left Review*, 220: 126–136.

Alt, J. and Hearn, F. (1980) Symposium on narcissism: the Cortland conference on narcissism. *Telos*, 44: 49–58.

Althusser, L. ([1964]1971) Freud and Lacan. In *Lenin and Philosophy, and Other Essays*. London: New Left Books.

Althusser, L. ([1970]1971) Ideology and Ideological State Apparatuses (notes towards an investigation). In *Lenin and Philosophy, and Other Essays*. London: New Left Books.

Amendola, S. (1992) Animal mutilations: 'legitimate questions'. *Enigmas: Strange Phenomena Investigations*, August–September: 17–20.

Anon. (1992) Iron dong. *Casablanca*. Pilot Issue: 23.

Anthony, A. (1992) Wild at heart. *The Guardian Weekend*, 17 October.

Archard, D. (1984) *Consciousness and the Unconscious*. London: Hutchinson.

Armistead, N. (ed.) (1974) *Reconstructing Social Psychology*. Harmondsworth: Penguin.

Badcock, C. (1983) *Madness and Modernity: A Study in Social Psychoanalysis*. Oxford: Blackwell.

Bakan, D. ([1958]1990) *Sigmund Freud and the Jewish Mystical Tradition*. London: Free Association Books.

Ballard, J.G. (1995) Introduction. *Crash*. London: Vintage.

Banyard, G. (1992) Right to reply. *UFO Brigantia*, 52: 32–33.

Barbour, L. (1993) Consensual relationships. *AUT Woman*, 29: 2.

Barford, D. (1992) Pleasures and pains. *The Psychoanalysis Newsletter*, 9: 2–3.

Barrett, M. (1993) Althusser's Marx, Althusser's Lacan. In E.A. Kaplan and M. Sprinker (eds) *The Althusserian Legacy*. London: Verso.

Barrett, M. and McIntosh, M. (1982) Narcissism and the family: a critique of Lasch. *New Left Review*, 135: 35–48.

Barthes, R. ([1957]1973) *Mythologies*. London: Paladin.

Basterfield, K. (1991) Abused by aliens. *Fortean Times*, 58: 48–51.

Baudrillard, J. (1970) Fetishism and ideology: the semiological reduction. In J. Baudrillard (1981) *For a Critique of the Political Economy of the Sign*. St Louis: Telos Press.

Baudrillard, J. ([1973]1975) *The Mirror of Production*. St Louis: Telos Press.

Baudrillard, J. (1979) The ecliptic of sex. In P. Foss and J. Pefanis (eds) (1990) *Jean Baudrillard, Revenge of the Crystal: Selected Writings on the Modern Object and Its Destiny, 1968–1983*. London: Pluto Press.

Baudrillard, J. (1983a) Revenge of the crystal: an interview with Jean Baudrillard by Guy Bellavance. In P. Foss and J. Pefanis (eds) (1990) *Jean Baudrillard, Revenge of the Crystal: Selected Writings on the Modern Object and Its Destiny, 1968–1983*. London: Pluto Press.

Baudrillard, J. (1983b) The ecstasy of communication. In H. Foster (ed.) (1985) *Postmodern Culture*. London: Pluto Press.

Baudrillard, J. (1986) Clone boy. *Z/G*, 11: 12–13.

Baudrillard, J. (1988) *Selected Writings*. Cambridge: Polity Press.

Baumann, Z. (1989) *Modernity and the Holocaust*. Cambridge: Polity Press.

Bell, D. (1996) Primitive state of mind. *Psychoanalytic Psychotherapy*, 10 (1): 45–57.

Benedikt, M. (ed.) (1991) *Cyberspace: First Steps*. Cambridge, MA: MIT Press.

Benhabib, S. and Cornell, D. (eds) (1987) *Feminism as Critique*. Oxford: Polity Press.

Benjamin, J. (1977) The end of internalization: Adorno's social psychology. *Telos*, 32: 42–64.

Benjamin, J. (1984) Master and slave: the fantasy of erotic domination. In A. Snitow, C. Stansell and S. Thompson (eds) *Desire: The Politics of Sexuality*. London: Virago.

Benjamin, J. (1988) *The Bonds of Love*. New York: Pantheon.

Benjamin, W. (1936) The work of art in the age of mechanical reproduction. In W. Benjamin (1973) *Illuminations*. London: Fontana.

Benjamin, W. (1939) Theses on the philosophy of history. In W. Benjamin (1973) *Illuminations*. London: Fontana.

Bentley, M. (1937) The nature and uses of experiment in psychology. *American Journal of Psychology*, 50: 454–469.

Benvenuto, B. and Kennedy, R. (1986) *The Works of Jacques Lacan: An Introduction*. London: Free Association Books.

Berger, P. L. (1965) Towards a sociological understanding of psychoanalysis. *Social Research*, 32: 26–41.

Berman, M. ([1982]1983) *All That Is Solid Melts Into Air: The Experience of Modernity*. London: Verso.

Bettelheim, B. ([1976]1978) *The Uses of Enchantment: The Meaning and Importance of Fairy Tales*. Harmondsworth: Pelican.

Bettelheim, B. ([1983]1986) *Freud and Man's Soul*. Harmondsworth: Peregrine.

Bhaskar, R. (1989) *Reclaiming Reality: A Critical Introduction to Contemporary Philosophy*. London: Verso.

Billig, M. (1976) *Social Psychology and Intergroup Relations*. London: Academic Press.

Billig, M. (1979) *Fascists: A Social Psychological Study of the National Front*. London: Academic Press.

Billig, M. (1982) *Ideology and Social Psychology: Extremism, Moderation and Contradiction*. Oxford: Blackwell.

Billig, M. (in press) Freud and Dora: repressing an oppressed identity. *Theory Culture & Society*, 14(3): 29–55.

Bion, W. (1961) *Experiences in Groups, and Other Papers*. London: Tavistock Publications.

Bion, W. ([1962]1984) *Learning from Experience*. London: Karnac Books.

Bion, W. (1970) *Attention and Interpretation*. London: Heinemann.

Bird, J. (1982) Jacques Lacan – the French Freud? *Radical Philosophy*, 30: 7–14.

Black, M. (1992) *A Cause for Our Times: Oxfam the First 50 years*. Oxford: Oxfam.

Bléandonu, G. (1994) *Wilfred Bion: His Life and Works 1897–1979*. London: Free Association Books.

Bly, R. ([1990]1991) *Iron John: A Book About Men*. Shaftesbury, Dorset: Element Books.

Boadella, D. (1985) *Wilhelm Reich: The Evolution of His Work*. London: Arkana.

Boadella, D. (1988) Biosynthesis. In J. Rowan and W. Dryden (eds) *Innovative Therapy in Britain*, Buckingham: Open University Press.

Bocock, R. (1976) *Freud and Modern Society*. London: Van Nostrand Reinhold.

Boswell, J. (1994) *The Marriage of Likeness: Same-Sex Unions in Pre-Modern Europe*. London: HarperCollins.

Bowlby, J. (1944) Forty-four juvenile thieves: their characters and home lives. *International Journal of Psychoanalysis*, 25: 19–53 and 107–28.

Bowlby, J. (1973) *Attachment and Loss, Vol. II: Separation: Anxiety and Anger*. Harmondsworth: Penguin.

Brewer, M. (1979) Ingroup bias in the minimal intergroup situation: a cognitive motivational analysis. *Psychogical Bulletin*, 86: 307–334.

Brinton, M. ([1970]1975) *The Irrational in Politics*. London: Solidarity Pamphlet 35.

British Psychological Society (1988) *The Future of the Psychological Sciences: Horizons and Opportunities for British Psychology*. Leicester: British Psychological Society.

Broderick, D. (1995) *Reading by Starlight: Postmodern Science Fiction*. London: Routledge.

Brookesmith, P. (1995) Do aliens dream of jacob's sheep? *Fortean Times*, 83: 22–30.

Brookman, J. (1993) Sex, romance, and the single academic. *Times Higher Education Supplement* (Research Students Service Supplement), 1087: iii.

Brosnan, J. (1994) Manchester notes. *Red Pepper*, 6: 32–33.

Bruins, J.J. and Wilke, H.A.M. (1993) Upward power tendencies in a hierarchy: power distance theory versus bureaucratic rule. *European Journal of Social Psychology*, 23: 239–254.

Buck-Morss, S. (1977) *The Origin of Negative Dialectics: Theodor W. Adorno, Walter Benjamin, and the Frankfurt Institute.* Hassocks, Sussex: Harvester Press.

Bühler, C. (1930) *The First Year of Life.* New York: Day.

Bukatman, S. (1993) *Terminal Identity: The Virtual Subject in Post-Modern Science Fiction.* Durham, NC: Duke University Press.

Bulhan, H.A. (1981) Psychological research in Africa. *Race and Class*, 23 (1): 25–81.

Bullard, T. (1991) Interview with Eddie Bullard. *Fortean Times*, 60: 46–49.

Burman, E. (ed.) (1990) *Feminists and Psychological Practice.* London: Sage.

Burman, E. (1992) Developmental psychology and the postmodern child. In J. Doherty, E. Graham and M. Malek (eds) *Postmodernism and the Social Sciences.* London: Macmillan.

Burman, E. (1994) *Deconstructing Developmental Psychology.* London: Routledge.

Burman, E. (1995) Constructing and deconstructing childhood: images of children and charity appeals. In J. Haworth (ed.) *Psychological Research: Innovative Methods and Strategies.* London: Routledge.

Burman, E. (1997) False memories, true hopes and the angelic: revenge of the postmodern on therapy. *New Formations*, 30: 122–134.

Burman, E. and Parker, I. (eds) (1993) *Discourse Analytic Research: Repertoires and Readings of Texts in Action.* London: Routledge.

Burnell, P. (1991) *Charity, Politics and the Third World.* Hemel Hempstead: Harvester Wheatsheaf.

Burston, D. (1991) *The Legacy of Erich Fromm.* Cambridge, MA: Harvard University Press.

Butler, J. (1993) The body politics of Julia Kristeva. In K. Oliver (ed.) *Ethics, Politics and Difference in Julia Kristeva's Writing.* London: Routledge.

Cadigan, P. (1992) *Fools.* London: HarperCollins.

Carter, C. (1996) Believing in everything and nothing: the cult of the Xfiles. *Sightings: Investigating Alien Phenomena*, 1 (2): 38–45.

Carter, M. and Brule, T. (1992) Of mice and men. *Elle*, April.

Cathie, S. (1987) What does it mean to be a man? *Free Associations*, 8: 7–33.

Chaplin, J. and Haggart, C. (nd) *The Mass Psychology of Thatcherism.* London: West London Socialist Society.

Chasseguet-Smirgel, J. (1985a) *The Ego Ideal: A Psychoanalytic Essay on the Malady of the Ideal.* London: Free Association Books.

Chasseguet-Smirgel, J. (1985b) *Creativity and Perversion.* London: Free Association Books.

Chasseguet-Smirgel, J. and Grunberger, B. ([1976]1986) *Freud or Reich? Psychoanalysis and Illusion.* London: Free Association Books.

Chodorow, N.J. (1985) Beyond drive theory: object relations and the limits of radical individualism. *Theory and Society*, 14: 271–319.

Cixous, H. (1976) The laugh of the medusa. *Signs*, 1: 875–899.

Cocks, G. (1985) *Psychotherapy in the Third Reich: The Göring Institute.* Oxford: Oxford University Press.

Colman, A. (1991a) Psychological evidence in South African murder trials. *The Psychologist*, 4 (11): 482–486.

Colman, A. (1991b) Are there theories at the bottom of his jargon? *The Psychologist*, 4 (11): 494–495.

Coltart, N.E.C. (1988) The assessment of psychological-mindedness in the diagnostic interview. *British Journal of Psychiatry*, 153: 819–820.

Condor, S. (1989) 'Biting into the future': social change and the social identity of women. In S. Skevington and D. Baker (eds) *The Social Identity of Women.* London: Sage.

Connolly, C. (1992) Just come as you are. *The Independent on Sunday*, 16 August: 2–4.

Cornet, B. (1995) Telepathy, abduction, aliens and a scientist! *Encounters*, 1: 57–65.

Coward, R. (1985) *Female Desire*. London: Paladin.

Coward, R. and Ellis, J. (1977) *Language and Materialism: Developments in Semiology and the Theory of the Subject*. London: Routledge and Kegan Paul.

Creed, B. (1987) Horror and the monstrous-feminine: an imaginary abjection. *Screen*, 28 (1): 44–70.

Curt, B. (1994) *Textuality and Tectonics: Troubling Social and Psychological Science*. Buckingham: Open University Press.

Cushman, P. (1991) Ideology obscured: political uses of the self in Daniel Stern's infant. *American Psychologist*, 46 (3): 206–19.

Dalal, F. (1988) The racism of Jung. *Race and Class*, 29 (1): 1–22.

Däniken, E. von (1976) *Chariots of the Gods*. London: Pan.

Danziger, K. (1990) *Constructing the Subject: Historical Origins of Psychological Research*. Cambridge: Cambridge University Press.

Davies, B. and Harré, R. (1990) Positioning: the discursive production of selves. *Journal for the Theory of Social Behaviour*, 20 (1): 43–63.

Debord, G. ([1967]1977) *Society of the Spectacle*. Detroit: Black and Red.

Deleuze, G. and Guattari, F. (1977) *Anti-Oedipus: Capitalism and Schizophrenia*. New York: Viking Press.

Dews, P. (1980) The 'new philosophers' and the end of leftism. *Radical Philosophy*, 24: 2–11.

Dews, P. (1987) *Logics of Disintegration: Post-structuralist Thought and the Claims of Critical Theory*. London: Verso.

Dews, P. (1992) *Autonomy and Solidarity: Interviews with Jurgen Habermas* (2nd edn). London: Verso.

Dick, P.K. (1963) *The Game Players of Titan*. New York: Ace.

Dick, P.K. (1964) *Martian Time-Slip*. London: Victor Gollancz.

Dick, P.K. (1966a) We can remember it for you wholesale. In P.K. Dick (1991) *We Can Remember It For You Wholesale: Collected Stories of Philip K. Dick, Vol. 5*. London: HarperCollins.

Dick, P.K. ([1966b]1993) *Now Wait for Last Year*. New York: Vintage.

Dick, P.K. ([1967]1990) *Counter-Clock World*. London: HarperCollins.

Dick, P.K. ([1969]1973) *Ubik*. London: HarperCollins.

Dicks, H. (1960) Notes on the Russian national character. In E. Trist and H. Murray (eds) (1990) *The Social Engagement of Social Science: A Tavistock Anthology: Vol. 1, The Socio-Psychological Perspective*. London: Free Association Books.

Dobson, R.V.G. (1993) *Bringing the Economy Home From the Market*. Montréal: Black Rose Books.

Doi, T. (1990) The cultural assumptions of psychoanalysis. In J.W. Stigler, R.A. Schweder and G. Herdt (eds) *Cultural Psychology: Essays on Comparative Human Development*. Cambridge: Cambridge University Press.

Doise, W. (1978) *Groups and Individuals*. Cambridge: Cambridge University Press.

Donzelot, J. ([1977]1979) *The Policing of Families*. London: Hutchinson.

Dvorchak, R.J. and Holewa, L. (1991) *Milwauke Massacre: Jeffrey Dahmer and the Milwauke Murders*. London: Robert Hale.

Dyer, C. (1993) High court judge urges sex bar between lawyers and their clients. *The Guardian*, 20 December.

Easthope, A. (1984) Nineteen eighty-four. In C. Norris (ed.) *Inside the Myth: Orwell, Views from the Left*. London: Lawrence and Wishart.

Easthope, A. (1986) *What a Man's Gotta Do*. London: Paladin.

Edley, N. and Wetherell, M. (1995) *Men in Perspective: Practice, Power and Identity*. London: Prentice-Hall.

Einstein, A. (1933) Why war? In A. Richards (ed.) (1985) *Civilization, Society and Religion: Group Psychoholoogy, Civilization and its Discontents and Other Works, Pelican Freud Library Vol. 12*. Harmondsworth: Pelican.

Eiser, J.R. (1980) *Cognitive Social Psychology: A Guidebook to Theory and Research*. London: McGraw-Hill.

Elias, N. (1994) *The Civilizing Process*. Oxford: Blackwell.

Ellemers, N., Doosje, B., Van Knippenberg, A. and Wilke, H. (1992) Status protection in high status minority groups. *European Journal of Social Psychology*, 22: 123–140.

Elliott, A. and Frosh, S. (eds) (1995) *Psychoanalysis in Contexts: Paths Between Theory and Modern Culture*. London: Routledge.

Engels, F. ([1884]1972) *Origin of the Family, Private Property and the State*. New York: Pathfinder Press.

Estés, C.P. (1995) *Women Who Run With the Wolves: Contacting the Power of the Wild Woman*. London: Rider.

Evans, C. (1973) *Cults of Unreason*. London: Harrap.

Evans, G. (1993) Cognitive models of class structure and explanation of social outcomes. *European Journal of Social Psychology*, 23: 445–464.

Eysenck, H. J. and Wilson, G. C. (1973) *The Experimental Study of Freudian Theories*. London: Methuen.

Faludi, S. (1992) *Backlash: The Undeclared War Against Women*. London: Chatto and Windus.

Farr, R.M. and Moscovici, S. (eds) (1984) *Social Representations*. Cambridge: Cambridge University Press.

Fee, D. (1992) Masculinities, identity and the politics of essentialism: a social constructionist critique of the men's movement. *Feminism and Psychology*, 2: 171–176.

Feilding, A. (1991) Interview with Amanda Feilding. *Fortean Times*, 58: 44–45.

Finlay, M. (1989) Post-modernizing psychoanalysis/psychoanalysing post-modernity. *Free Associations*, 16: 43–80.

Finnigan, M. (1995) Sexual healing. *The Guardian*, 10 January.

Forna, M. (1992) The hole truth. *The Guardian*, 4 December: 9.

Forrester, J. (1980) *Language and the Origins of Psychoanalysis*. London: Macmillan.

Foucault, M. ([1966]1970) *The Order of Things*. London: Tavistock.

Foucault, M. ([1969]1986) *The Archaeology of Knowledge*. London: Tavistock.

Foucault, M. ([1976]1981) *The History of Sexuality, Vol. I: An Introduction*. Harmondsworth: Pelican.

Fox, N. (1995) Postmodern perspectives on care: the vigil and the gift. *Critical Social Policy*, 15 (2/3): 107–125.

Freedman, C. (1984) Towards a theory of paranoia: the science fiction of Philip K. Dick. *Science Fiction Studies*, 11: 15–24.

Freeman, J. ([1970]1983) *The Tyranny of Structurelessness*. London: Dark Star Press.

Freud, A. (1936) *The Ego and the Mechanisms of Defence*. London: The Hogarth Press.

Freud, S. (1895a) On the grounds for detaching a particular syndrome from neurosthenia under the description 'anxiety neurosis'. In A. Richards (ed.) (1979) *On Psychopathology, Pelican Freud Library Vol. 10*. Harmondsworth: Pelican.

Freud, S. (1895b) The psychotherapy of hysteria. In A. Richards (ed.) (1974) *Studies on Hysteria, Pelican Freud Library Vol. 3*. Harmondsworth: Pelican.

Freud, S. (1896) The aetiology of hysteria. In J. Strachey (ed.) (1962) *The Standard Edition of the Complete Psychological Works of Sigmund Freud, Vol. III*. London: The Institute of Psycho-Analysis and The Hogarth Press.

Freud, S. (1900) The interpretation of dreams. In A. Richards (ed.) *The Interpretation of Dreams, Pelican Freud Library Vol. 4*. Harmondsworth: Pelican.

Freud, S. (1905a) Three essays on the theory of sexuality. In A. Richards (ed.) (1977) *On Sexuality, Pelican Freud Library Vol. 7*. Harmondsworth: Pelican.

Freud, S. (1905b) Fragment of an analysis of a case of hysteria ('Dora'). In A. Richards (ed.) (1977) *Case Histories I: 'Dora' and 'Little Hans', Pelican Freud Library Vol. 8*. Harmondsworth: Pelican.

Freud, S. (1907) Obsessive actions and religious practices. In A. Richards (ed.) (1985) *The Origins of Religion, Pelican Freud Library Vol. 13*. Harmondsworth: Pelican.

Freud, S. (1909a) Analysis of a phobia in a five-year-old boy ('little Hans'). In A. Richards (ed.) (1977) *Case Histories I: 'Dora' and 'Little Hans', Pelican Freud Library Vol. 8*. Harmondsworth: Pelican.

Freud, S. (1909b) Family romances. In A. Richards (ed.) (1977) *On Sexuality, Pelican Freud Library Vol. 7*. Harmondsworth: Pelican.

Freud, S. (1910) A special type of choice of object made by men. In A. Richards (ed.) (1977) *On Sexuality, Pelican Freud Library Vol. 7*. Harmondsworth: Pelican.

Freud, S. (1911a) Psychoanalytic notes on an autobiographical account of a case of paranoia (dementia paranoides) (Schreber). In A. Richards (ed.) (1979) *Case Histories II: 'Rat Man', Schreber, 'Wolf Man', Female Homosexuality, Pelican Freud Library Vol. 9*. Harmondsworth: Pelican.

Freud, S. (1911b) Formulations on the two principles of mental functioning. In A. Richards (ed.) (1984) *On Metapsychology: The Theory of Psychoanalysis, Pelican Freud Library Vol. 11*. Harmondsworth: Pelican.

Freud, S. (1912) The dynamics of transference. In J. Strachey (ed.) (1958) *The Standard Edition of the Complete Psychological Works of Sigmund Freud, Vol. XII*. London: The Institute of Psycho-Analysis and The Hogarth Press.

Freud, S. (1912–1913) Totem and taboo: some points of agreement between the mental lives of savages and neurotics. In A. Richards (ed.) (1985) *The Origins of Religion, Pelican Freud Library Vol. 13*. Harmondsworth: Pelican.

Freud, S. (1914a) On narcissism. In A. Richards (ed.) (1984) *On Metapsychology: The Theory of Psychoanalysis, Pelican Freud Library Vol. 11*. Harmondsworth: Pelican.

Freud, S. (1914b) Remembering, repeating and working-through (further recommendations on the technique of psycho-analysis II). In J. Strachey (ed.) (1958) *The Standard Edition of the Complete Psychological Works of Sigmund Freud, Vol. XII*. London: The Institute of Psycho-Analysis and The Hogarth Press.

Freud, S. (1915a) Instincts and their vicissitudes. In A. Richards (ed.) (1984) *On Metapsychology: The Theory of Psychoanalysis, Pelican Freud Library Vol. 11*. Harmondsworth: Pelican.

Freud, S. (1915b) Thoughts for the times on war and death. In A. Richards (ed.) (1985) *Civilization, Society and Religion: Group Psychology, Civilization and its Discontents and Other Works, Pelican Freud Library Vol. 12*. Harmondsworth: Pelican.

Freud, S. (1915c) The unconscious. In A. Richards (ed.) (1984) *On Metapsychology: The Theory of Psychoanalysis, Pelican Freud Library Vol. 11*. Harmondsworth: Pelican.

Freud, S. (1920) Beyond the pleasure principle. In A. Richards (ed.) (1984) *On Metapsychology: The Theory of Psychoanalysis, Pelican Freud Library Vol. 11*. Harmondsworth: Pelican.

Freud, S. (1921) Group psychology and the analysis of the ego. In A. Richards (ed.) (1985) *Civilization, Society and Religion: Group Psychology, Civilization and its Discontents and Other Works, Pelican Freud Library Vol. 12*. Harmondsworth: Pelican.

Freud, S. (1923a) The infantile genital organization (an interpolation into the theory of sexuality). In A. Richards (ed.) (1977) *On Sexuality, Pelican Freud Library Vol. 7*. Harmondsworth: Pelican.

Freud, S. (1923b) *The Ego and the Id*. In A. Richards (ed.) (1984) *On Metapsychology: The Theory of Psychoanalysis, Pelican Freud Library Vol. 11*. Harmondsworth: Pelican.

Freud, S. (1924) The dissolution of the Oedipus complex. In A. Richards (ed.) (1977) *On Sexuality, Pelican Freud Library Vol. 7*. Harmondsworth: Pelican.

Freud, S. (1925a) A note upon the 'mystic writing-pad'. In A. Richards (ed.) (1984) *On Metapsychology: The Theory of Psychoanalysis, Pelican Freud Library Vol. 11*. Harmondsworth: Pelican.

Freud, S. (1925b) Negation. In A. Richards (ed.) (1984) *On Metapsychology: The Theory of Psychoanalysis, Pelican Freud Library Vol. 11*. Harmondsworth: Pelican.

Freud, S. (1926) Inhibitions, symptoms and anxiety. In A. Richards (ed.) (1979) *On Psychopathology, Pelican Freud Library Vol. 10*. Harmondsworth: Pelican.

Freud, S. (1927a) Fetishism. In A. Richards (ed.) (1977) *On Sexuality, Pelican Freud Library Vol. 7*. Harmondsworth: Pelican.

Freud, S. (1927b) The future of an illusion. In A. Richards (ed.) (1985) *Civilization, Society and Religion: Group Psychology, Civilization and its Discontents and Other Works, Pelican Freud Library Vol. 12*. Harmondsworth: Pelican.

Freud, S. (1930) Civilization and its discontents. In A. Richards (ed.) (1985) *Civilization,*

Society and Religion: Group Psychology, Civilization and its Discontents and Other Works, Pelican Freud Library Vol. 12. Harmondsworth: Pelican.

Freud, S. (1933a) New introductory lectures on psychoanalysis. In A. Richards (ed.) (1973) *New Introductory Lectures on Psychoanalysis, Pelican Freud Library Vol. 2.* Harmondsworth: Pelican.

Freud, S. (1933b) Why war? In A. Richards (ed.) (1985) *Civilization, Society and Religion: Group Psychology, Civilization and its Discontents and Other Works, Pelican Freud Library Vol. 12.* Harmondsworth: Pelican.

Freud, S. (1940a) An outline of psychoanalysis. In A. Richards (ed.) (1986) *Historical and Expository Works on Psychoanalysis, Pelican Freud Library Vol. 15.* Harmondsworth: Pelican.

Freud, S. (1940b) Splitting of the ego in the process of defence. In A. Richards (ed.) (1984) *On Metapsychology: The Theory of Psychoanalysis, Pelican Freud Library Vol. 11.* Harmondsworth: Pelican.

Freud, S. (1942) Psychopathic characters on the stage. In A. Richards (ed.) (1985) *Art and Literature, Pelican Freud Library Vol. 14.* Harmondsworth: Pelican.

Freud, S. (1953–1974) *The Standard Edition of the Complete Psychological Works of Sigmund Freud* (24 Vols) London: Hogarth Press.

Freud, S. (1950) Project for a scientific psychology. In J. Strachey (ed.) (1966) *The Standard Edition of the Complete Psychological Works of Sigmund Freud, Vol. I.* London: The Institute of Psycho-Analysis and The Hogarth Press.

Freud, S. and Breuer, J. (1893–1895) Studies on Hysteria. In A. Richards (ed.) (1974) *Studies on Hysteria, Pelican Freud Library Vol. 3.* Harmondsworth: Pelican.

Fromm, E. (1932) The method and function of an analytic social psychology: notes on psychoanalysis and historical materialism. In A. Arato and E. Gebhardt (eds) (1978) *The Essential Frankfurt School Reader.* Oxford: Blackwell.

Fromm, E. ([1942]1960) *The Fear of Freedom.* London: Routledge and Kegan Paul.

Fromm, E. ([1956]1963) *The Sane Society.* London: Routledge and Kegan Paul.

Fromm, E. (1962) *Beyond the Chains of Illusion: My Encounter with Marx and Freud.* London: Abacus.

Fromm, E. (1967) *Psychoanalysis and Religion.* New York: Bantam Books.

Fromm, E. (1974) *The Anatomy of Human Destructiveness.* London: Cape.

Frosh, S. (1987) *The Politics of Psychoanalysis: An Introduction to Freudian and Post-Freudian Theory.* London: Macmillan.

Frosh, S. (1989) Melting into air: psychoanalysis and social experience. *Free Associations*, 16: 7–30.

Frosh, S. (1991) *Identity Crisis: Modernity, Psychoanalysis and the Self.* London: Macmillan.

Fukuyama, F. (1992) *The End of History and the Last Man.* Harmondsworth: Penguin.

Gane, M. (1995) Radical theory: Baudrillard and vulnerability. *Theory, Culture and Society*, 12: 109–123.

Gauld, A.O. and Shotter, J. (1977) *Human Action and its Psychological Investigation.* London: Routledge and Kegan Paul.

Gay, P. (1988) *Freud: A Life For Our Time.* New York: W. W. Norton and Co.

Gellner, E. (1985) *The Psychoanalytic Movement, or The Coming of Unreason.* London: Paladin.

Gergen, K.J. (1989) Social Psychology and the Wrong Revolution. *European Journal of Social Psychology*, 19: 463–484.

Gergen, K.J. (1991) *The Saturated Self: Dilemmas of Identity in Contemporary Life.* New York: Basic Books.

Gibbs, G. (1995) Growing from tiny acorns. *The Guardian*, 25 April: 13.

Gibson, W. ([1984]1993) *Neuromancer.* London: HarperCollins.

Gibson, W. ([1986]1993) *Count Zero.* London: HarperCollins.

Giddens, A. (1992) *The Transformation of Intimacy: Sexuality, Love and Eroticism in Modern Society.* Cambridge: Polity Press.

Gilligan, C. (1982) *In a Different Voice: Psychological Theory and Women's Development.* Harvard: Cambridge, MA: Harvard University Press.

Gilman, S. L. (1993) *Freud, Race, and Gender.* New York: Princeton University Press.

Gittins, D. (1993) *The Family in Question: Changing Households and Familiar Ideologies* (2nd edn). Basingstoke: Macmillan.

Glaser, D. and Frosh, S. (1993) *Child Sexual Abuse* (2nd edn). London: Macmillan.

Goffman, E. (1959) *The Presentation of Self in Everyday Life*. New York: A. Knopf.

Gordo-López, A.J. (1995) Boundary objects and the psycho-techno-complex: psychology, resistance and regulation. Unpublished PhD thesis, University of Manchester.

Gordo-López, A.J. and Parker, I. (eds) (forthcoming) *Cyberpsychology*.

Gosling, P. (1994) Lets abolish money. *Red Pepper*, 6: 28–29.

Greenberg, J. and Mitchell, S. (1983) *Object Relations in Psychoanalytic Theory*. Cambridge, MA: Harvard University Press.

Grinberg, L. (1985) Bion's contribution to the understanding of the individual and the group. In M. Pines (ed.) *Bion and Group Psychotherapy*. London: Routledge.

Grinberg, L., Sor, D. and Bianchedi, E.T. De (1975) *Introduction to the Work of Bion: Groups, Knowledge, Thought, Transformations, Psychoanalytic Practice*. London: Maresfield Library.

Groddeck, G. ([1923]1950) *Book of the It*. New York: Basic Books.

Gronemeyer, M. (1992) Helping. In W. Sachs (ed.) *The Development Dictionary: A Guide to Knowledge as Power*. London: Zed Books.

Grosskurth, P. (1986) *Melanie Klein*. London: Hodder and Stoughton.

Grosz, E. (1990) *Jacques Lacan: A Feminist Introduction*. London: Routledge.

Grünbaum, A. (1984) *The Foundations of Psychoanalysis: A Philosophical Investigation*. Berkeley, CA: University of California Press.

Gwyther, M. (1993) Doctors in disgrace. *The Observer*, 11 October.

Habermas, J. (1969) The movement in Germany: a critical analysis. In J. Habermas (1971) *Toward a Rational Society*. London: Heinemann.

Habermas, J. (1970) On systematically distorted communication. *Inquiry*, 13: 205–218.

Habermas, J. (1971) *Knowledge and Human Interests*. London: Heinemann.

Habermas, J. (1982) The entwinement of myth and enlightenment: re-reading *Dialectic of Enlightenment*. *New German Critique*, 26: 13–30.

Habermas, J. (1985) A philosophico-political profile. *New Left Review*, 151: 75–105.

Hacking, I. (1995) *Rewriting the Soul: Multiple Personality and the Science of Memory*. Princeton, NJ: Princeton University Press.

Haeberlin, H.K. (1980) The theoretical foundations of Wundt's folk psychology. In R.W. Rieber (ed.) *Wilhelm Wundt and the Making of Scientific Psychology*. New York: Plenum Press.

Halliwell, L. (1980) *Halliwell's Teleguide*. London: Paladin.

Haraway, D. (1991) *Simians, Cyborgs and Women*. London: Free Association Books.

Harper, D.J. (1996) Accounting for poverty: from attribution to discourse. *Journal of Community and Applied Social Psychology*, 6: 249–265.

Harré, R. (1979) *Social Being: A Theory for Social Psychology*. Oxford: Blackwell.

Harré, R. (1983) *Personal Being: A Theory for Individual Psychology*. Oxford: Blackwell.

Harré, R. (ed.) (1986) *The Social Construction of Emotion*. Oxford: Blackwell.

Harré, R. and Secord, P.F. (1972) *The Explanation of Social Behaviour*. Oxford: Blackwell.

Harris, B. and Brock, A. (1991) Otto Fenichel and the left opposition in psychoanalysis. *Journal of the History of the Behavioral Sciences*, 27: 157–164.

Harris, B. and Brock, A. (1992) Freudian psychopolitics: the rivalry of Wilhelm Reich and Otto Fenichel, 1930–1935. *Bulletin of the History of Medicine*, 66: 578–612.

Hartmann, H. ([1939]1958) *Ego Psychology and the Problem of Adaptation*. New York: International Universities Press.

Harvey, D. (1989) *The Condition of Postmodernity: An Enquiry into the Origins of Cultural Change*. Oxford: Blackwell.

Hawkes, T. (1977) *Structuralism and Semiotics*. London: Methuen.

Hayter, T. (1971) *Aid as Imperialism*. Harmondsworth: Pelican.

Hebdige, D. (1986) A Report on the western front: postmodernism and the politics of style. *Block*, 12: 4–26.

Heelas, P. and Lock, A. (eds) (1981) *Indigenous Psychologies: The Anthropology of the Self*. London: Academic Press.

Hegel, G.W.F. ([1807]1971) *The Philosophy of Mind*. Oxford: Oxford University Press.

Heimann, P. (1950) On countertransference. *International Journal of Psycho-Analysis*, 31: 81–84.

Hewstone, M., Jaspars, J. and Lalljee, M. (1982) Social representations, social attribution and social identity: the intergroup images of 'public' and 'comprehensive' schoolboys. *European Journal of Social Psychology*, 12: 241–271.

Hewstone, M., Johnston, L. and Aird, P. (1992) Cognitive models of stereotype change: (2) perceptions of homogeneous and heterogeneous groups. *European Journal of Social Psychology*, 12: 235–250.

Hinchcliffe, M. (1992) Releasing Wildness. *Asylum*, 6 (2): 33.

Hinshelwood, R.D. (1983) Projective identification and Marx's concept of man. *International Review of Psycho-Analysis*, 10: 221–226.

Hinshelwood, R.D. (1985) Projective identification, alienation and society. *Group Analysis*, 3: 241–254.

Hinshelwood, R.D. (1996) Convergences with psychoanalysis. In I. Parker and R. Spears (eds) *Psychology and Society: Radical Theory and Practice*. London: Pluto Press.

Hirst, P. and Woolley, P. (1982) *Social Relations and Human Attributes*. London: Tavistock Publications.

Hobart, M. (ed.) (1993) *An Anthropological Critique of Development: The Growth of Ignorance*. London: Routledge.

Hobson, R. (1986) *Forms of Feeling: The Heart of Psychotherapy*. London: Tavistock.

Høeg, P. ([1992]1993) *Miss Smilla's Feeling for Snow*. London: Flamingo.

Hollway, W. (1989) *Subjectivity and Method in Psychology: Gender, Meaning and Science*. London: Sage.

Homer, S. (1996) Psychoanalysis, representation, politics: on the (im)possibility of a psychoanalytic theory of ideology? *The Letter: Lacanian Perspectives on Psychoanalysis*, Summer: 97–109.

Homer, S. (in press) The terrain of theoretical anti-humanism. *Free Associations*, 43.

Honneth, A. (1994) The social dynamics of disrespect. *Constellations*, 1 (2): 255–269.

Honneth, A. (1995) *The Struggle for Recognition: The Moral Grammar of Social Conflicts*. Cambridge: Polity Press.

Höpfl, H. (1996) Authority and the pursuit of order in organizational performance. *Studies in Cultures, Organizations and Societies*, 2: 67–78.

Horder, J. (1991) Huggers on the warpath. *The Guardian*, 31 August.

Horney, K. (1967) *Feminine Psychology*. New York: W.W. Norton & Co.

Hough, P. and Randles, J. (1992) *Looking for the Aliens: A Psychological, Scientific and Imaginative Investigation*. London: Blandford.

Howarth, I. (1988) Chartered psychologists: what can we claim for them? *The Psychologist*, 1 (3): 96–98.

Howarth, I. (1989) Open letter to British Psychological Society academic members.

Howitt, D. and Owusu-Bempah, J. (1994) *The Racism of Psychology: Time for Change*. Hemel Hempstead: Harvester Wheatsheaf.

Hughes-Hallett, L. (1992) Egghead out of her shell. *Independent on Sunday*, 9 Feburary: 26.

Hurme, H. (1995) Wild man or golden bird: cultural readings of masculinity. *Culture and Psychology*, 1: 477–486.

Ingleby, D. (1985) Professionals and socializers: the 'psy-complex'. *Research in Law, Deviance and Control*, 7: 79–109.

Irigaray, L. (1985) *This Sex Which Is Not One*. New York: Cornell University Press.

Isbister, J.N. (1985) *Freud: An Introduction to His Life and Work*. Cambridge: Polity Press.

Israel, J. and Tajfel, H. (eds) (1972) *The Context of Social Psychology, A Critical Assessment*. London: Academic Press.

Jackson, R. (1981) *Fantasy: The Literature of Subversion*. London: Methuen.

Jacoby, R. (1977) *Social Amnesia: A Critique of Conformist Psychology from Adler to Laing*. Hassocks, Sussex: Harvester Press.

Jacoby, R. (1983) *The Repression of Psychoanalysis*. New York: Basic Books.

Jakobson, R. (1975) Two aspects of language and two types of aphasic disturbances. In R. Jakobson and M. Halle (1975) *Fundamentals of Language*. The Hague: Mouton.

Jameson, F. (1977) Imaginary and symbolic in Lacan: Marxism, psychoanalytic criticism, and the problem of the subject. *Yale French Studies*, 55/56: 338–395.

Jameson, F. (1984) Postmodernism, or the cultural logic of late capitalism. *New Left Review*, 146: 53–92.

Jaques, E. (1951) *The Changing Culture of a Factory*. London: Routledge and Kegan Paul.

Jaques, E. (1953) On the dynamics of social structure: a contribution to the psycho–analytic study of social phenomena deriving from the views of Melanie Klein. In E. Trist and H. Murray (eds) (1990) *The Social Engagement of Social Science: A Tavistock Anthology: Vol. 1, The Socio-Psychological Perspective*. London: Free Association Books.

Jay, M. (1973) *The Dialectical Imagination: A History of the Frankfurt School and the Institute of Social Research*. London: Heinemann.

Jiménez-Domínguez, B. (1996) Participant action research. In I. Parker and R. Spears (eds) *Psychology and Society: Radical Theory and Practice*. London: Pluto Press.

Jovanović, G. (1995) Reading and living images of masculinity: comments on Parker's 'wild men'. *Culture and Psychology*, 1: 487–496.

Jukes, N. (1994) Nick Jukes started a local exchange trading scheme. *The Guardian*, 7 October: 4.

Jung, C.G. ([1959]1987) *Flying Saucers: A Modern Myth of Things Seen in the Sky*. London: Ark.

Jung, C.G. (1983) *Jung: Selected Writings*. London: Fontana Press.

Jung, C.G. (1989) *Aspects of the Masculine*. London: Routledge.

Kakar, S. (1985) Psycho-analysis and non-Western cultures. *International Review of Psycho-Analysis*, 12: 441–448.

Keat, R. (1981) *The Politics of Social Theory: Habermas, Freud and the Critique of Positivism*. Oxford: Blackwell.

Keat, R. (1986) The human body in social theory: Reich, Foucault and the repressive hypothesis. *Radical Philosophy*, 42: 24–32.

Kellaway, L. (1993) Twelve acorns for a hair cut. *Financial Times*, 30 November: 20.

Kellner, D. (1989) *Jean Baudrillard: From Marxism to Postmodernism and Beyond*. Cambridge: Polity Press.

Kernberg, O. (1975) *Borderline Conditions and Pathological Narcissism*. New York: Jason Aronson.

Kernberg, O. (1985) Foreword to J. Chasseguet-Smirgel, *Creativity and Perversion*. London: Free Association Books.

Kernberg, O. (1987) Foreword to J. Kristeva, *In the Beginning Was Love: Psychoanalysis and Faith*. New York: Columbia University Press.

Kerrigan, W. (1993) Students and lechers I. *The Observer Magazine*, 3 October: 22–23.

Kershaw, A. (1991) How new man became new lad. *The Independent on Sunday*, 14 April.

Kirsch, B. (1993) To PC or not to PC. *The Lecturer*, December: 15.

Klapman, J.W. (1948) *Group Psychotherapy: Theory and Practice*. London: William Heinemann Medical Books Ltd.

Klein, D.B. (1985) *Jewish Origins of the Psychoanalytic Movement*. Chicago: University of Chicago Press.

Klein, M. (1928) Early stages of the Oedipus conflict. In J. Mitchell (ed.) (1986) *The Selected Melanie Klein*. Harmondsworth: Peregrine.

Klein, M. (1930) The importance of symbol formation in the development of the ego. In J. Mitchell (ed.) (1986) *The Selected Melanie Klein*. Harmondsworth: Peregrine.

Klein, M. (1935) A Contribution to the psychogenesis of manic-depressive states. In J. Mitchell (ed.) (1986) *The Selected Melanie Klein*. Harmondsworth: Peregrine.

Klein, M. (1946) Notes on some schizoid mechanisms. In J. Mitchell (ed.) (1986) *The Selected Melanie Klein*. Harmondsworth: Peregrine.

Klein, M. (1955) The psycho-analytic play technique: its history and significance. In J. Mitchell (ed.) (1986) *The Selected Melanie Klein*. Harmondsworth: Peregrine.

Klein, M. (1956) A study of envy and gratitude. In J. Mitchell (ed.) (1986) *The Selected Melanie Klein*. Harmondsworth: Peregrine.

Knight, C. (1974) *Sex and the Class Struggle: Selected Works of Wilhelm Reich*. London: Chartist.

Knott, C. (1993) No car but plenty of drive. *Health and Efficiency*, 94 (4): 24–25.

Kojève, A. (1969) *Introduction to the Reading of Hegel: Lectures on the Phenomenology of Spirit*. New York: Basic Books.

Kovel, J. (1983) *Against the State of Nuclear Terror*. London: Pan.

Kovel, J. (1988) *The Radical Spirit: Essays on Psychoanalysis and Society*. London: Free Association Books.

Kozulin, A. (1994) *Psychology in Utopia: Toward a Social History of Soviet Psychology*. Cambridge, MA: MIT Press.

Kreeger, L. (1975) *The Large Group: Dynamics and Therapy*. London: Maresfield.

Kristeva, J. ([1974a]1986) *About Chinese Women*. London: Marion Boyars.

Kristeva, J. ([1974b]1984) *Revolution in Poetic Language*. New York: Columbia University Press.

Kristeva, J. ([1979]1981) Women's time. *Signs: Journal of Women in Culture and Society*, 7 (1): 13–35.

Kristeva, J. ([1980]1982) *Powers of Horror: An Essay on Abjection*. New York: Columbia University Press.

Kristeva, J. ([1985]1987) *In the Beginning Was Love: Psychoanalysis and Faith*. New York: Columbia University Press.

Kristeva, J. ([1988]1991) *Strangers to Ourselves*. Hemel Hempstead: Harvester Wheatsheaf.

Kroker, A. (1985) Baudrillard's Marx. *Theory Culture and Society*, 2 (3): 69–83.

Kuhn, T.S. (1970) *The Structure of Scientific Revolutions* (2nd edn). Chicago: Chicago University Press.

Kvale, S. (ed.) (1992) *Psychology and Postmodernism*. London: Sage.

Lacan, J. (1973) Of structure as an inmixing of an otherness prerequisite to any subject whatsoever. In R. Macksey and E. Donato (eds) *The Structuralist Controversy: The Languages of Criticism and the Sciences of Man*. Baltimore, MD: Johns Hopkins University Press.

Lacan, J. (1977) *Écrits: A Selection*. London: Tavistock.

Lacan, J. (1979) *The Four Fundamental Concepts of Psychoanalysis*. Harmondsworth: Penguin.

Lacan, J. (1988) The see-saw of desire. In J.-A. Miller (ed.) *The Seminar of Jacques Lacan, Book I: Freud's Papers on Technique 1953–54*. Cambridge: Cambridge University Press.

Lacan, J. (1992a) The moral goals of psychoanalysis. In J.-A. Miller (ed.) *The Seminar of Jacques Lacan, Book VII: The Ethics of Psychoanalysis*. London: Routledge.

Lacan, J. (1992b) The paradoxes of ethics *or* Have you acted in conformity with your desire? In J.-A. Miller (ed.) *The Seminar of Jacques Lacan, Book VII: The Ethics of Psychoanalysis*. London: Routledge.

Lacan, J. (1992c) The demand for happiness and the promise of analysis. In J.-A. Miller (ed.) *The Seminar of Jacques Lacan, Book VII: The Ethics of Psychoanalysis*. London: Routledge.

Langer, M. (1989) *From Vienna to Managua: Journey of a Psychoanalyst*. London: Free Association Books.

Lanza, J. (1995) *Elevator Music: A Surreal History of Muzak Easy Listening and Other Moodsong*. London: Quartet.

Laplanche, J. (1989) *New Foundations for Psychoanalysis*. Oxford: Blackwell.

Laplanche, J. (1990a) The Kent seminar. In J. Fletcher and M. Stanton (eds) (1992) *Jean Laplanche: Seduction, Translation and the Drives*. London: Institute of Contemporary Arts.

Laplanche J. (1990b) The Freud Museum seminar. In J. Fletcher and M. Stanton (eds) (1992) *Jean Laplanche: Seduction, Translation and the Drives*. London: Institute of Contemporary Arts.

Laplanche, J. (1992) The drive and its object-source: its fate in the transference. In J. Fletcher and M. Stanton (eds) *Jean Laplanche: Seduction, Translation and the Drives*. London: Institute of Contemporary Arts.

Laplanche, J. (1996) Psychoanalysis as anti-hermeneutics. *Radical Philosophy*, 79: 7–12.

Laplanche, J. and Pontalis, J.-B. ([1964]1986) Fantasy and the origins of sexuality. In V. Burgin, J. Donald and C. Kaplan (eds) *Formations of Fantasy*. London: Methuen.

Laqueur, T. (1990) *Making Sex: Body and Gender from the Greeks to Freud*. Cambridge, MA: Harvard University Press.

Lasch, C. (1978) *The Culture of Narcissism: American Life in an Age of Diminishing Expectations*. New York: W.W. Norton & Co.

Lasch, C. (1981) The Freudian left and cultural revolution. *New Left Review*, 129: 23–34.

Le Bon, G. (1896) *The Crowd: A Study of the Popular Mind*. London: Ernest Benn Ltd.

Lechte, J. (1990) *Julia Kristeva*. London: Routledge.

Lemaire, A. (1977) *Jacques Lacan*. London: Routledge and Kegan Paul.

Letourneau, M. (1992) The most famous encounter in France. *International UFO Library Magazine*, 1 (3): 24–25 and 76.

Levidow, L. (1989) Witches and seducers: moral panics for our time. In B. Richards (ed.) *Crises of the Self: Further Essays on Psychoanalysis and Politics*. London: Free Association Books.

Levidow, L. (1995) Castrating the other: the paranoid rationality of the Gulf War. *Psychoculture*, 1 (1): 9–16.

Lévi-Strauss, C. ([1958]1972) *Structural Anthropology*. Harmondsworth: Penguin.

Levin, C. (1984) Baudrillard, critical theory and psychoanalysis. *Canadian Journal of Political and Social Theory/Revue canadienne de théorie politique et sociale*, 8 (1/2): 35–52.

Lewin, K. (1946) Action research and minority problems. *Journal of Social Issues*, 2: 34–46.

Lichfield, J. (1991) The new all-American man. *The Independent on Sunday*, 2 June.

Lichtman, R. (1990) Psychoanalysis: critique of Habermas's prototype of critical social science. *New Ideas In Psychology*, 8 (3): 357–374.

Lomas, P. (1987) *The Limits of Interpretation: What's Wrong with Psychoanalysis?* Harmondsworth: Pelican.

Lorenz, K. (1966) *On Aggression*. London: Methuen.

Lorenzer, A. ([1970]1976) Symbols and stereotypes. In P. Connerton (ed.) *Critical Sociology: Selected Readings*. Harmondsworth: Penguin.

Lukács, G. ([1923]1971) *History and Class Consciousness*. Cambridge, MA: MIT Press.

Lyotard, J.-F. ([1974]1993) *Libidinal Economy*. London: The Athlone Press.

Lyotard, J.-F. ([1979]1984) *The Postmodern Condition: A Report on Knowledge*. Manchester: Manchester University Press.

Lyotard, J.-F. (1988) *Peregrinations*. New York: Columbia University Press.

Macauley, W.R. and Gordo-López, A. (1995) From cognitive psychologies to mythologies: advancing cyborg textualities for a narrative of resistance. In C.H. Gray, H.J. Figueroa-Sarriera and S. Mentor (eds) *The Cyborg Handbook*. London: Routledge.

McDougall, W. ([1908]1948) *An Introduction to Social Psychology*. London: Methuen.

McDougall, W. ([1920]1927) *The Group Mind*. New York: G.P. Putnam and Sons.

McLuhan, M. and Fiore, Q. (1967) *The Medium is the Massage: An Inventory of Effects*. Harmondsworth: Penguin.

Macey, D. (1988) *Lacan in Contexts*. London: Verso.

Macey, D. (1995) On the subject of Lacan. In A. Elliott and S. Frosh (eds) *Psychoanalysis in Contexts: Paths between Theory and Modern Culture*. London: Routledge.

Maguire, M. (1995) *Men, Women, Passion and Power: Gender Issues in Psychotherapy*. London: Routledge.

Makulowich, J. S. (1993) Awesome sites. *World Wide Web Newsletter*, 1: 13 and 20.

Malinowski, B. ([1927]1960) *Sex and Repression in Savage Society*. London: Routledge and Kegan Paul.

Mandel, E. (1974) *Late Capitalism*. London: New Left Books.

Mao Tse Tung ([1963]1971) Where do correct ideas come from? *Selected Readings from the Works of Mao Tse Tung*. Peking: Foreign Languages Press.

Marcuse, H. ([1955]1974) *Eros and Civilization: A Philosophical Inquiry into Freud*. Boston, MA: Beacon Press.

Marcuse, H. (1972) *One Dimensional Man*. London: Abacus.

Marsh, P., Rosser, E. and Harré, R. (1974) *The Rules of Disorder*. London: Routledge and Kegan Paul.

Martin, H. and Flanagan, J. (1993) The undesirable side of academic affairs. *The Independent on Sunday*, 23 May: 8.

Marx, K. (1844) A Contribution to the critique of Hegel's philosophy of right. Introduction. In (1975) *Marx, Early Writings*. Harmondsworth: Penguin.

Marx, K. (1845) Concerning Feuerbach. In (1975) *Marx, Early Writings*. Harmondsworth: Penguin.

Marx, K. and Engels, F. ([1848]1965) *Manifesto of the Communist Party*. Peking: Foreign Languages Press.

Masson, J.M. ([1984]1985) *The Assault on Truth: Freud's Suppression of the Seduction Theory*. Harmondsworth: Penguin.

Masson, J. ([1988]1990) *Against Therapy*. London: Fontana.

Mead, G.H. (1934) *Mind, Self and Society: From the Standpoint of a Social Behaviorist*. Chicago, IL: Chicago University Press.

Meissner, W.W. (1990) The role of transitional conceptualization in religious thought. In J.H. Smith and S.A. Handelman (eds) *Psychoanalysis and Religion*. Baltimore, MD: Johns Hopkins University Press.

Menzies-Lyth, I. (1959) The functioning of social systems as a defence against anxiety: a report on a study of the nursing service of a general hospital. In I. Menzies-Lyth (1988) *Containing Anxiety in Institutions Vol. I*. London: Free Association Books.

Miller, A. (1985) *Thou Shalt Not Be Aware: Society's Betrayal of the Child*. London: Pluto Press.

Miller, J.-A. (1985) The mainstream of Lacan's thought. Paper presented at the Cambridge Psychoanalytical Study Group conference on Transmission and Psychoanalysis, Trinity College, Cambridge.

Miller, L., Rustin, M., Rustin, M. and Shuttleworth, J. (eds) (1989) *Closely Observed Infants*. London: Duckworth.

Millett, K. (1975) *Sexual Politics*. London: Virago.

Milne, T. (ed.) (1991) *The Time Out Film Guide* (2nd edn). Harmondsworth: Penguin.

Mitchell, J. (1974) *Psychoanalysis and Feminism*. Harmondsworth: Pelican.

Mitchell, J. (1986) Introduction. In *The Selected Melanie Klein*. Harmondsworth: Peregrine.

Mitchell, J. and Rose, J. (eds) (1982) *Feminine Sexuality: Jacques Lacan and the École Freudienne*. London: Macmillan.

Moebius, H. and Michel-Annan, B. (1994) Colouring the grey everyday: the psychology of the walkman. *Free Associations*, 32: 570–576.

Moi, T. (1985) *Sexual/Textual Politics: Feminist Literary Theory*. London: Methuen.

Moore, S. (1988) Getting a bit of the other: the pimps of postmodernism. In R. Chapman and J. Rutherford (eds) *Male Order: Unwrapping Masculinity*. London: Lawrence and Wishart.

Moscovici, S. (1972) Society and theory in social psychology. In J. Israel and H. Tajfel (eds) *The Context of Social Psychology: A Critical Assessment*. London: Academic Press.

Moscovici, S. (1976) *La psychanalyse: son image et son public* (2nd edn). Paris: Presses Universitaires de France.

Moscovici, S. (1986) *The Age of the Crowd*. Cambridge: Cambridge University Press.

Mowbray, R. (1995) *The Case Against Psychotherapy Registration: A Conservation Issue for the Human Potential Movement*. London: Transmarginal Press.

Mulvey, L. (1975) Visual pleasure and narrative cinema. *Screen*, 16 (3): 6–18.

Nietzsche, F. (1977) *A Nietzsche Reader*. Harmondsworth, Penguin.

Noon, J. (1993) *Vurt*. Littleborough: Ringpull Press.

O'Connor, N. and Ryan, J. (1993) *Wild Desires and Mistaken Identities: Lesbians and Psychoanalysis*. London: Virago.

O'Hagen, S. (1991) The re-invented man. *Arena*, May/June: 22–23.

Ollman, B. (1972) Introduction. In L. Baxandall (ed.), *Sex-Pol: Essays, 1929–1934*. New York: Vintage Books.

Ostrander, S. and Schroeder, L. ([1970]1973) *PSI: Psychic Discoveries behind the Iron Curtain*. London: Abacus.

Oxaal, I. (1988) The Jewish origins of psychoanalysis reconsidered. In E. Timms and N. Segal (eds) *Freud in Exile: Psychoanalysis and its Vicissitudes*. New Haven, CT: Yale University Press.

Packard, V. ([1957]1958) *The Hidden Persuaders*. New York: Cardinal.

Pajaczkowska, C. (1981) Introduction to Kristeva. *m/f*, 5/6: 149–157.

Paludi, M.A. and Barickman, R.B. (1993) *Academic and Workplace Sexual Harassment*, New York: SUNY Press.

Pareles, J. (1994) Alone again naturally. *The Guardian*, 1 November: 2.

Parker, I. (1989) *The Crisis in Modern Social Psychology, and How To End It*. London: Routledge.

Parker, I. (1992) *Discourse Dynamics: Critical Analysis for Social and Individual Psychology*. London: Routledge.

Parker, I. (1995) Discursive complexes in material culture. In J. Haworth (ed.) *Psychological Research: Innovative Methods and Strategies*. London: Routledge.

Parker, I. (1997) Discourse analysis and psychoanalysis. *British Journal of Social Psychology*, 36.

Parker, I. and Shotter, J. (eds) (1990) *Deconstructing Social Psychology*. London: Routledge.

Parker, I., Georgaca, E., Harper, D., McLaughlin, T. and Stowell-Smith, M. (1995) *Deconstructing Psychopathology*. London: Sage.

Pettit, P. (1975) *The Concept of Structuralism: A Critical Analysis*. Berkeley, CA: University of California Press.

Phillips, A. (1988) *Winnicott*. London: Fontana.

Philp, H.L. ([1956]1974) *Freud and Religious Belief*. Westport, CT: Greenwood Press.

Pines, M. (ed.) (1985) *Bion and Group Psychotherapy*. London: Routledge and Kegan Paul.

Piper, S. and British Naturism (1992) *Full Frontal* (BBC2 Television Community Access Programme). Northampton and London: British Naturism and British Broadcasting Corporation.

Plant, S. (1993) *The Most Radical Gesture: The Situationist International in a Postmodern Age*. London: Routledge.

Poster, M. (1978) *Critical Theory of the Family*. London: Pluto Press.

Pribram, K. and Gill, M. (1976) *Freud's Project Reassessed*. London: Hutchinson.

Prynn, J. (1996) 'Hands off' rule for car instructors. *The Times*, 11 April.

Radley, A. and Kennedy, M. (1992) Reflections upon charitable giving: a comparison of individuals from business, 'manual' and professional backgrounds. *Journal of Community and Applied Social Psychology*, 2: 113–129.

Randles, J. (1992a) J.R. comments. . . . *Northern UFO News*, 158: 2–3.

Randles, J. (1992b) Magpie speaks out. *Northern UFO News*, 157: 11–12.

Ratner, C. (1971) Totalitarianism and individualism in psychology. *Telos*, 7: 50–72.

Reich, W. (1929) Dialectical materialism and psychoanalysis. In L. Baxandall (ed.) (1972) *Sex-Pol: Essays, 1929–1934*. New York: Vintage Books.

Reich, W. (1932a) The imposition of sexual morality. In L. Baxandall (ed.) (1972) *Sex-Pol: Essays, 1929–1934*. New York: Vintage Books.

Reich, W. (1932b) Politicizing the sexual problem of youth. In L. Baxandall (ed.) (1972) *Sex-Pol: Essays, 1929–1934*. New York: Vintage Books.

Reich, W. (1934a) What is class conciousness? In L. Baxandall (ed.) (1972) *Sex-Pol: Essays, 1929–1934*. New York: Vintage Books.

Reich, W. ([1934b]1971) *What is Class Consciousness?* London: Socialist Reproduction.

Reich, W. ([1942]1968). *The Function of the Orgasm: Sex-Economic Problems of Biological Energy*. London: Panther.

Reich, W. ([1946]1975) *The Mass Psychology of Fascism*. Harmondsworth: Pelican.

Reich, W. ([1951]nd) *The Orgone Accumulator: Its Medical and Scientific Use*. London: Rising Free.

Reicher, S. (1982) The determination of collective behaviour. In H. Tajfel (ed.) *Social Identity and Intergroup Relations*. Cambridge: Cambridge University Press.

Reicher, S. (1991) Politics of crowd psychology. *The Psychologist*, 4 (11): 487–491.

Ribera, A. (1992) Abductions in Spain: a certain pattern. *International UFO Library Magazine*, 1 (3): 19 and 44.

Richards, B. (1984a) Civil defence and psychic defence. *Free Associations*, Pilot Issue: 85–97.

Richards, B. (1984b) Schizoid states and the market. In B. Richards (ed.) *Capitalism and Infancy: Essays on Psychoanalysis and Politics*. London: Free Association Books.

Richards, B. (1985) The politics of the self. *Free Associations*, 3: 43–64.

Richards, B. (1986) Military mobilizations of the unconscious. *Free Associations*, 7: 11–26.

Richards, B. (1989) *Images of Freud: Cultural Responses to Psychoanalysis*. London: Dent.

Richards, B. (1994) The cultural predicaments of psychoanalysis. *Free Associations*, 32: 549–569.

Rickert, J. (1986) The Fromm–Marcuse debate revisited. *Theory and Society*, 15: 351–400.

Rieff, P. (1973) *The Triumph of the Therapeutic*. Harmondsworth: Penguin.

Riley, D. (1983) *War in the Nursery: Theories of the Child and Mother*. London: Virago.

Riley, P. (1981) Introduction to the reading of Alexandre Kojève. *Political Theory*, 9 (1): 5–48.

Roberts, A. (1992) Editorial. *UFO Brigantia*, 52: 3–5

Rogers, C.R. (1961) *On Becoming a Person*. Boston, MA: Houghton Mifflin.

Roiser, M. and Willig, C. (1996) Marxism, the Frankfurt School, and working-class psychology. In I. Parker and R. Spears (eds) *Psychology and Society: Radical Theory and Practice*. London: Pluto Press.

Rorty, R. (1980) *Philosophy and the Mirror of Nature*. Oxford: Blackwell.

Rose, J. (1986) *Sexuality in the Field of Vision*. London: Verso.

Rose, J. (1993a) *Why War?: Psychoanalysis, Politics, and the Return to Melanie Klein*. Oxford: Blackwell.

Rose, J. (1993b) Julia Kristeva – take two. In K. Oliver (ed.) *Ethics, Politics and Difference in Julia Kristeva's Writing*. London: Routledge.

Rose, N. (1985) *The Psychological Complex: Psychology, Politics and Society in England, 1869–1939*. London: Routledge and Kegan Paul.

Rosemont, F. (1978) *André Breton and the First Principles of Surrealism*. London: Pluto Press.

Roudinesco, E. (1990) *Jacques Lacan and Co.: A History of Psychoanalysis in France, 1925–1985*. London: Free Association Books.

Rowan, J. (1987) *The Horned God: Feminism and Men as Wounding and Healing*. London: Routledge and Kegan Paul.

Rowthorn, B. (1994) Does money make the world go round (interview). *Red Pepper*, 6: 30–31.

Rucker, R. ([1982]1985) *Software*. London: ROC.

Rushkoff, D. (1994) *Cyberia: Life in the Trenches of Hyperspace*. London: Flamingo.

Russell, J. (1993) *Out of Bounds, Sexual Exploitation in Counselling and Therapy*. London: Sage.

Rustin, M. (1991) *The Good Society and the Inner World: Psychoanalysis, Politics and Culture*. London: Verso.

Rutter, P. (1992) *Sex in the Forbidden Zone*. London: Mandala.

Ryan, M. (1982) *Marxism and Deconstruction: A Critical Articulation*. Baltimore, MD: Johns Hopkins University Press.

Ryle, A. (1990) *Cognitive-Analytic Therapy: Active Participation in Change*. Chichester: Wiley.

Samuels, A. (1985) *Jung and the Post-Jungians*. London: Routledge and Kegan Paul.

Samuels, A. (1993) *The Political Psyche*. London: Routledge.

Sartre, J.-P. ([1943]1969) *Being and Nothingness: An Essay on Phenomenological Ontology*. London: Methuen.

Saussure, F. de (1974) *Course in General Linguistics*. London: Fontana.

Schachter, S. and Singer, J. (1962) Cognitive, social, and physiological determinants of emotional state. *Psychological Review*, 69 (5): 379–399.

Schatzman, M. (1973) *Soul Murder: Persecution in the Family*. London: Allen Lane.

Schnabel, J. ([1994]1995) *Dark White: Aliens, Abductions, and the UFO Obsession*. Harmondsworth: Penguin.

Scott, A. (1996) *Real Events Revisited: Fantasy, Memory and Psychoanalysis*. London: Virago.

Secord, P.F. (1991) Deconstructing social psychology? Why? How? *Contemporary Psychology*, 38: 33–34.

Segal, H. (1987) Review of 'Against the State of Nuclear Terror'. *Free Associations*, 9: 137–142.

Segal, H. (1995) From Hiroshima to the Gulf War and after: a psychoanalytic perspective. In A. Elliott and S. Frosh (eds) *Psychoanalysis in Contexts: Paths between Theory and Modern Culture*. London: Routledge.

Sekoff, J. (1989) Amnesia, romance and the mind-doctor film. In B. Richards (ed.) *Crises of the Self: Further Essays on Psychoanalysis and Politics*. London: Free Association Books.

Seyfang, G.J. (1994) The Local Exchange Trading System: Political Economy and Social Audit. MSc thesis, University of East Anglia, Norwich.

Sharaf, M. ([1983]1984) *Fury on Earth: A Biography of Wilhelm Reich*. London: Hutchinson.

Shaw, W. (1994) *Spying in Guru Land: Inside Britain's Cults*. London: Fourth Estate.

Shotter, J. (1975) *Images of Man in Psychological Research*. London: Methuen.

Shotter, J. (1984) *Accountability and Selfhood*. Oxford: Blackwell.

Sieveking, P. (1991) Holes in the head. *Fortean Times*, 58: 42–43.

Simon, B. (1993) On the asymmetry in the cognitive construal of ingroup and outgroup: a model of egocentric social categorization. *European Journal of Social Psychology*, 23: 131–148.

Smith, J. (1993) Students and lechers II. *The Observer Magazine*, 3 October: 22–23.

Squire, C. (1991) Science fictions. *Feminism and Psychology*, 1 (2): 181–199.

Stanton, M. (1990) Psychoanalysis in British universities, the Kent case. *Free Associations*, 19: 104–113.

Stephenson, N. ([1992]1993) *Snow Crash*. London: ROC.

Stern, D.N. (1985) *The Interpersonal World of the Infant: A View from Psychoanalysis and Developmental Psychology*. New York: Basic Books.

Stevens, A. (1986) The archetypes of war. In I. Fenton (ed.) *The Psychology of Nuclear Conflict*. London: Coventure.

Stevens, W. C. (1992) All 'grays' are not reticulans: reticulan extraterrestrials misjudged. *International UFO Library Magazine*, 1 (3): 16–17 and 42.

Stigler, J.W., Schweder, R.A. and Herdt, G. (eds) (1990) *Cultural Psychology: Essays on Comparative Human Development*. Cambridge: Cambridge University Press.

Stockholder, F. (1987) Mirrors and narcissism. *Theory, Culture and Society*, 4: 107–123.

Strachey, J. (1966) Editor's introduction. In J. Strachey (ed.) (1966) *The Standard Edition of the Complete Psychological Works of Sigmund Freud, Vol. I*. London: The Institute of Psycho-Analysis and The Hogarth Press.

Strieber, W. ([1987]1988) *Communion, A True Story: Encounters with the Unknown*. London: Arrow Books.

Sulloway, F. J. ([1979]1980) *Freud, Biologist of the Mind: Beyond the Psychoanalytic Legend*. London: Fontana.

Sutin, L. ([1989]1991) *Divine Invasions: A Life of Philip K. Dick*. London: Paladin.

Szasz, T. (1979) Sigmund Freud: the Jewish avenger. In T. Szasz, *The Myth of Psychotherapy: Mental Healing as Religion, Rhetoric, and Repression*. Oxford: Oxford University Press.

Tajfel, H. (1970) Experiments in intergroup discrimination. *Scientific American*, 223: 96–102.

Tajfel, H. (1972) Some developments in European social psychology. *European Journal of Social Psychology*, 2: 307–323.

Tajfel, H. (1979) Individuals and groups in social psychology. *British Journal of Social and Clinical Psychology*, 18: 183–191.

Tajfel, H., Billig, M., Bundy, R. and Flament, C. (1971) Social categorisation and intergroup behaviour. *European Journal of Social Psychology*, 1: 149–175.

Tan, S.-L. and Moghaddam, F.M. (1995) Reflexive positioning and culture. *Journal for the Theory of Social Behaviour*, 25 (4): 387–400.

Target, G. (1993) As nature intended. *Health and Efficiency*, 94 (4): 10–13.

Tatham, P. (1991) *The Making of Maleness: Men, Women and the Flight of Daedalus*. London: Karnac.

Timms, E. and Segal, N. (eds) (1988) *Freud in Exile: Psychoanalysis and its Vicissitudes*. London: The Hogarth Press.

Toussaint-Samat, M. (1992) *A History of Food*. Oxford: Blackwell.

Trist, E. and Murray, H. (eds) (1990) *The Social Engagement of Social Science: A Tavistock Anthology: Vol. 1, The Socio-Psychological Perspective*. London: Free Association Books.

Trotsky, L. (1933) What is national socialism? In L. Trotsky, *The Struggle Against Fascism in Germany*. Harmondsworth: Pelican.

Trotter, W. (1919) *Instincts of the Herd in Peace and War* (2nd edn). London: Ernest Benn.

Turkle, S. (1992) *Psychoanalytic Politics: Jacques Lacan and Freud's French Revolution* (2nd edn). London: Free Association Books.

Turner, J.C. (1975) Social comparison and social identity: some prospects for intergroup behaviour. *European Journal of Social Psychology*, 5: 5–34.

Turner, J.C., Hogg, M.A., Oakes, P.J., Reicher, S.D. and Wetherell. M. (1987) *Rediscovering the Social Group*. Oxford: Blackwell.

Vaillant, G.E. (1971) Theoretical hierarchy of adaptive ego mechanisms: a 30-year follow-up of 30 men selected for psychological health. *Archives of General Psychiatry*, 24: 107–118.

Vallee, J. (1979) *Messengers of Deception: UFO Contacts and Cults*. Berkeley, CA: And/Or Press.

Vallee, J. (1988]1990) *Dimensions: A Casebook of Alien Contact*. London: Sphere Books.

Van Ginneken, J. (1984) The killing of the father: the background of Freud's group psychology. *Political Psychology*, 5 (3): 391–414.

Varela, C.R. (1995) Ethogenic theory and psychoanalysis: the unconscious as a social construction and a failed explanatory concept. *Journal for the Theory of Social Behaviour*, 25 (4): 363–385.

Verhoeven, P. (1990) *Total Recall*. New York: Tristar Films.

Vidal, J. (1994) Take a few pigs along to the Pie in the Sky cafe and watch payment go bob-bob-bobbin along. *The Guardian*, 12 March: 25.

Vincent-Buffault, A. (1991) *The History of Tears: Sensibility and Sentimentality in France*. London: Macmillan.

Wangh, M. (1972) Some unconscious factors in the psychogenesis of recent student uprisings. *Psychoanalytic Quarterly*, 41: 207–223.

Ward, H. (1996) Myers-Briggs and the concern with techniques. In K. Leech (ed.) *Myers-Briggs: Some Critical Reflections*. Manchester: Blackfriars Publications.

Wehr, C. (1988) *Jung and Feminism: Liberating Archetypes*. London: Routledge and Kegan Paul.

Westphal, M. (1990) Paranoia and piety: reflections on the Schreber case. In J.H. Smith and S.A. Handelman (eds) *Psychoanalysis and Religion*. Baltimore, MD: Johns Hopkins University Press.

Wetherell, M. and Edley, N. (1997) Gender practices: steps in the analysis of men and masculinities. In K. Henwood, C. Griffin and A. Phoenix (eds) *Standpoints and Differences: Essays in the Practice of Feminist Psychology*. London: Sage.

Whyte, L.L. ([1960]1962) *The Unconscious before Freud*. London: Tavistock.

Wiernikowska, M. (1992) Tipis and totem poles. *Gazeta Wyborcza*. Reprinted in *The Guardian*, 24 November: 12.

Wilder, D. (1981) Perceiving persons as a group: categorization and intergroup relations. In D.L. Hamilton (ed.) *Cognitive Processes in Stereotyping and Intergroup Behavior*. Hillsdale, NJ: Erlbaum.

Williams, J. (1993) Smooth dudes and shaven ravers. *Health and Efficiency* (supplement), 94 (4): 8–13.

Winnicott, D.W. (1947) Hate in the countertransference. In D.W. Winnicott (1958) *Collected Papers: Through Paediatrics to Psycho-Analysis*. London: Tavistock.

Winnicott, D.W. (1953) Transitional objects and transitional phenomena. In D.W. Winnicott (1974) *Playing and Reality*. Harmondsworth: Penguin.

Winnicott, D.W. (1957) *The Child and the Family: First Relationships*. London: Tavistock.

Winnicott, D.W. (1965) *The Family and Individual Development*. London: Tavistock.

Winnicott, D.W. (1967) Mirror-role of mother and family in child development. In D.W. Winnicott (1974) *Playing and Reality*. Harmondsworth: Penguin.

Winnicott, D.W. (1969) The use of an object and relating through identifications. In D.W. Winnicott (1974) *Playing and Reality*. Harmondsworth: Penguin.

Wolfenstein, E.V. (1990) Group phantasies and 'the individual': a critical analysis of psychoanalytic group psychology. *Free Associations*, 20: 150–180.

Wolfenstein, E.V. (1993) *Psychoanalytic-Marxism: Groundwork*. London: Free Association Books.

Young, R.M. (1989) Post-modernism and the subject: pessimism of the will. *Free Associations*, 16: 81–96.

Young, R.M. (1994) *Mental Space*. London: Process Press.

Zajonc, R.B. (1989) Styles of explanation in social psychology. *European Journal of Social Psychology*, 19: 345–368.

Zipes, J. (1992) Spreading myths about fairy tales: a critical commentary on Robert Bly's Iron John. *New German Critique*, 55: 3–19.

Žižek, S. (1989) *The Sublime Object of Ideology*. London: Verso.

Žižek, S. (1990) Eastern Europe's republics of Gilead. *New Left Review*, 183: 50–62.

Žižek, S. (1991) *For They Know Not What They Do: Enjoyment as a Political Factor*. London: Verso.

Žižek, S. (1994) *The Metastases of Enjoyment: Six Essays on Woman and Causality*. London: Verso.

Žižek, S. (1996) *The Indivisible Remainder: An Essay on Schelling and Related Matters*. London: Verso.

Index